Bank Restructuring and Resolution

Bank Restructuring and Resolution

Edited by

David S. Hoelscher

First published 2006 by
PALGRAVE MACMILLAN
Houndmills, Basingstoke, Hampshire RG21 6XS and
175 Fifth Avenue, New York, N.Y. 10010
Companies and representatives throughout the world

PALGRAVE MACMILLAN is the global academic imprint of the
Palgrave Macmillan division of St Martin's Press LLC and of
Palgrave Macmillan Ltd.
Macmillan® is a registered trademark in the United States,
United Kingdom and other countries. Palgrave is a registered
trademark in the European Union and other countries.

ISBN-13: 978–0–230–01900–3 hardback
ISBN-10: 0–230–01900–5 hardback

This book is printed on paper suitable for recycling and
made from fully managed and sustained forest sources.

A catalogue record for this book is available from the British Library.

A catalogue record for this book is available from the Library of Congress.

10   9   8   7   6   5   4   3   2   1
15   14   13   12   11   10   09   08   07   06

Printed and bound in Great Britain by
Antony Rowe Ltd, Chippenham and Eastbourne

Contents

III. Options for Asset Management

IV. Country Experiences

List of Tables

List of Figures

List of Boxes

List of Abbreviations

ABS	Asset-backed securities
AMC	Asset management company
AMD	Additional market discipline
AMU	Asset Management Unit
BCC	Bank Consolidation Company
BDNI	PT Bank Dagang Nasional Indonesia
BI	Bank Indonesia
BIS	Bank for International Settlements
BITI	Bank of Investment and Technological Innovation
BNB	Bulgarian National Bank
BNI	Bank Negara Indonesia
BOK	Bank of Korea
BOL	Bank of Lithuania
BOP	Bailout pressure
BR day	Bank restructuring day
BRSA	Banking Regulation and Supervision Agency
BTO	Been taken over
CAB	Central Asian Bank
CAMC	Centralized Asset Management Corporation
CAR	Capital adequacy ratio
CBA	Currency board arrangement
CBT	Central Bank of Turkey
CD	Certificate of deposit
CEO	Chief Executive Officer
COD	Collection Department
CPI	Consumer price index
DBCP	Deutsche Bank Capital Partners
ERP	Early retirement program
EU	European Union
FAS	U.S. Financial Accounting Standards
FDIC	Federal Deposit Insurance Corporation
FDICIA	FDIC Improvement Act
FLC	Forward-looking criteria
FOBAPROA	Fondo Bancario de Protección al Ahorro
FRA	Thai Financial Sector Restructuring Agency
FRN	Floating rate notes
FSC	Financial Supervisory Commission
FSS	Financial Supervisory Service
FX	Foreign exchange
GAAP	U.S. Generally Accepted Accounting Principles

GBII	IMF/WB Global Bank Insolvency Initiative
GDP	Gross domestic product
HSBC	Hong Kong and Shanghai Banking Corporation
IAS	International Accounting Standards
IBRA	Indonesian Bank Restructuring Agency
IFRS	International Financial Reporting Standards
IMF	International Monetary Fund
ISO	International Organization for Standardization
ITCs	Investment trust companies
JVs	Joint ventures
KAMCO	Korea Asset Management Corporation
KBA	Korea Board of Audit
KDB	Korea Development Bank
KDIC	Korea Deposit Insurance Corporation
KEB	Korean Exchange Bank
KFB	Korea First Bank
LOI	Letter of intent
LOLR	Lender of last resort
LTL	Lithuanian litai
MARA	Mongolian Asset Realization Agency
MHC	Moral hazard cost
MOF	Ministry of finance
MOFE	Ministry of finance and economy
MOU	Memorandum of understanding
MPB	Ministry of planning and budget
NPA Fund	Nonperforming Asset Management Fund
NPL	Nonperforming loan
NPV	Net present value
OECD	Organization for Economic Cooperation and Development
P&A	Purchase and assumption
PCA	Prompt corrective action
PD	Payment delay time
PFOC	Public Funds Oversight Commission
PV	Present value
RB	Reconstruction Bank
RTC	Resolution Trust Corporation
SB	Savings Bank
SDIF	Savings Deposit Insurance Fund
SKr	Swedish kronor
SSB	State Savings Bank
TBTF	Too big to fail
TDB	Trade and Development Bank
TL	Turkish lira
Tog	Mongolian togrogs
W	Korean won

Acknowledgments

This book would not have been possible without the contribution of many people, both within the Monetary and Financial Systems Department (MFD) and in other departments of the International Monetary Fund. The guidance and supervision of the department's activities by the Director of MFD, Mr. Stephan Ingves, was critical to ensuring the highest quality of the final product. Special thanks are also due to Carl-Johan Lindgren, Deputy Director responsible for the division during 1998–2003 and to Jonathan Fiechter, current Deputy Director of MFD, for their support and assistance to the division as it dealt with numerous crises across the world. The editor also acknowledges each author's contribution to this volume. Early drafts of these papers have been presented at staff seminars and, therefore, have received extensive commentary and reviews by a large number of Fund staff. Moreover, the individual chapters have benefited from the comments of reviewers too numerous to mention here. Rather, the contributions are recognized in the individual chapters of the book. We would like to pay special thanks to Ms. Sandra Otero de Solares for her excellent editorial work and her efficient assistance in organizing the book. Finally, the editor would like to acknowledge the work done by Sean Culhane in the IMF's External Relations Department in advising and arranging for publication of this volume.

Foreword

The International Monetary Fund occupies a unique position among international financial institutions because of its universal membership. This vantage point allows Fund staff to view developments in the economic and financial systems of all of its 184 members. In recent years, the Fund's role in financial sector surveillance has expanded significantly, with the traditional analysis of macroeconomic developments being complemented with analyses of the role of the financial sector (both banking and nonbanking institutions) in achieving and maintaining economic stability.

In the face of systemic financial crises, the Fund's role is to assist national authorities develop and implement comprehensive economic policies. For individual countries, systemic crises are rare. However, given the broad nature of the Fund's membership, Fund staff is frequently assisting one or more countries each year in addressing financial crises. What is a rare occurrence for the authorities of one country can be a common experience for Fund staff specializing in managing systemic crises. For that reason, the Fund established, in 2000, the Systemic Issues Division, a division within the Monetary and Financial Systems Department. Division staff have specialized knowledge of techniques for managing systemic crises. They recognize both the broad principles that can lead to an efficient resolution of systemic crises and, at the same time, can recognize how to mold those principles to meet the specialized and specific needs of individual countries. They are experienced at tailoring their policy advice to the circumstances of individual countries, avoiding "off-the-counter" or "cookie cutter" approaches to crisis resolution.

An additional mandate of the Systemic Issues Division is the dissemination of information and lessons learned. This book forms a part of the ongoing efforts of the Fund to explain the standards and principles that guide its work in crisis management. The chapters in this volume concentrate on bank restructuring and bank resolution. Chapters cover both theoretical approaches and practical lessons learned from the implementation of these approaches. Many of the contributions in this book have appeared as internal papers, used to share experiences among Fund colleagues. This collection is aimed at sharing staff experiences with a broader range of readers. In the long run, we hope that these efforts result in a robust discussion of principles and techniques and that national authorities find these efforts helpful.

Ulrich Baumgartner
Acting Director
Monetary and Financial Systems Department
IMF

Preface

David S. Hoelscher

Banks fail, and bank failures can cause distress among creditors, losses for both owners and creditors, and, in the extreme, can threaten financial stability. Losses from bank failures must be distributed. The impact of that distribution on economic activity will depend, in part, on the conditions of the bank and, in part, on the role of the bank in the economy. If the bank is not deeply insolvent or if it plays a limited role in financial intermediation, the impact of the bank's failure is likely to be minimal. If the bank is deeply insolvent and plays an important role in financial intermediation, or the failure occurs during a period of financial uncertainty where contagion is a danger, the impact of the failure may be larger.

Well defined tools are available for addressing the failure of an individual bank. The narrow solution is the immediate closing of the bank and initiation of liquidation proceedings. Staff is laid off, insured depositors paid out, and other depositors and creditors receive a portion of the liquidation proceeds. Alternative measures, that may be less disruptive, include merger and sale of all or part of the bank's assets and liabilities. In this latter case, the bank may be closed as an institution but the profitable banking business is transferred to other sound institutions.

Resolution of a systemically important bank or resolution of a bank in the midst of a systemic crisis poses particularly difficult problems. Banking systems can be chronically weak, reflecting entrenched unsafe and unsound banking practices or structural weaknesses in the institutional framework. These conditions can persist for a considerable period until a systemic crisis is triggered by sudden loss of creditor confidence. Such loss of confidence may be triggered by a variety of economic or political developments, beginning a difficult and often chaotic period. The steps for managing systemic crises involve more than bank resolution issues but a complex set of policy decisions aimed at containing the crisis, resolving failed banks, rehabilitating weak banks and resolving assets of failed banks. Hoelscher and Ingves discuss this broad framework for systemic crisis resolution in Chapter 1.

Once the authorities turn to bank resolution and bank rehabilitation, strategies are designed on a case-by-case basis. Faced with a bank failure, authorities must select the appropriate technique for the resolution of a failed bank. Seelig (Chapter 3) surveys the alternatives, discusses the pros and the cons of the most common approaches to bank resolution, and provides some guidance on determining when an approach is appropriate. A systemic crisis poses particular difficulties for the authorities. A number of resolution techniques may not be available to the authorities or may be inefficient and relatively costly. They must first contain the crisis and then turn to bank-by-bank resolution. Several chapters describe the limitations that arise imposed when a country enters a systemic crisis and how the strategy followed will be influenced by the conditions of the bank or banks, the financial position of the shareholders, and the medium-term prospects of the bank's core client group. (See, for example, Andrews and Josefsson in Chapter 5.)

The first step in developing a bank restructuring strategy is the diagnosis of the financial condition of individual banks. The size and distribution of bank losses must be identified. As supervisory data may be outdated and not reflect the full economic impact of the crisis, supervisors may attempt to update available information based on uniform valuation criteria. The supervisors will also examine information on banks' ownership structures (public or private, foreign or domestic, concentrated or dispersed) to help determine the scope for upfront support from existing or potential new private owners. Alternatively, scope may exist for the use of international auditors (Andrews and Josefsson identify the pros and cons of such assistance in Chapter 5).

One of the most difficult decisions to make must be made quickly—which resolution strategy is most appropriate. An immediate decision is what to save—the bank as an institution or to unwind the bank and save the profitable business. Intervention has both costs and benefits and the policy decision is how to balance both. The question is whether the bank is sound and viable over the medium term or whether only a subset of its assets (and key clients) can reasonably be expected to perform. Frydl and Quintyn in Chapter 2 provide a theoretical framework for assessing the relative sizes of such costs and benefits as a guide to policymakers. The policy choice must include issues of burden sharing, market signals for other banks, and concerns about contagion of banking distress to other, sound banks are among the factors that influence the choice of techniques. Andrews and Josefsson (Chapter 5) complement this theoretical framework with a discussion of the principles and guidelines that have been used in practice.

Rapid determination must be made concerning the shareholders' willingness and ability to resolve the bank's underlying weaknesses. Assessment of such willingness can be facilitated by requiring presentation of business plans showing a bank's medium-term viability. A bank can be considered viable if (i) it can remain profitable and earn a competitive return over the medium term; and (ii) the shareholders are committed and able to support it. Supervisors may require that banks produce forward-looking business plans using common economic assumptions and that include time bound, measurable targets for monitoring purposes (see Hoelscher and Ingves, Chapter 1). While such plans may be relatively easy to develop, they must contain quarterly qualitative targets that permit the supervisors to measure progress and continually evaluate the bank's medium-term viability.

The tools used by supervisors must be clearly outlined in the legal structure. As described by Leckow in Chapter 7, the legal and regulatory framework for bank intervention and bank resolution determines the framework within which the authorities may act. While modification and reform of this legal framework is frequently undertaken before the crisis, modification during a crisis is substantially more difficult. Typically, this legal framework should give supervisors the authority to differentiate between banks that are (i) viable and meeting their legal capital adequacy ratio and other regulatory requirements; and (ii) viable but undercapitalized. In the latter classification, an additional assessment will be needed to determine whether the existing shareholders can recapitalize their bank within an acceptable period or if the use of public funding should be considered. Shareholders of undercapitalized banks must agree to a monitored recapitalization and restructuring plan with time bound targets. Failure to meet the targets would be cause for intervention and resolution of the bank. The plan should also include sufficient restrictions on bank operations as to establish incentives for shareholders to over perform in their restructuring.

Private sector solutions are often the most efficient and cost effective approach. In these solutions, the shareholders retain responsibility to recapitalize and restructure their bank. Under some circumstances, however, particularly in the midst of a systemic crisis, shareholders may be unable to recapitalize fully their bank immediately but they are fit and proper and the bank is deemed viable. Experience has shown that, under some circumstances, banks may be allowed to remain in the system under strict conditions. The bank's recapitalization could be phased in, with tight monitoring and requirements, including the suspension of dividend distributions until the required level of capital has been restored.

Experience has also shown that public sector support may be an effective complement to the restructuring efforts. Public sector support for the resolution process may be warranted to limit the costs to the real economy of too large a number of banking failures. Public sector assistance can use a variety of techniques. One option is to assist in joint public–private recapitalization programs. These programs can give the shareholders time to mobilize needed funds but also introduce distortions in the market. As described by Josefsson (Chapter 14), these programs can be designed to ensure that the appropriate incentive structure is established to avoid misuse. The public sector can also assist in the financing of the recapitalization program but care must be taken. Andrews (Chapter 4), discusses the techniques of issuing government banks to finance recapitalization but points out that some options will actually leave the banks facing serious risks.

Asset management and resolution is a critical part of the bank restructuring process. For banks that have been intervened and are in the process of resolution, proper management of the bank's assets is a critical and complex process. Successful management of the assets can be an important element in maintaining a functioning financial sector with proper incentives for continued financial intermediation. Broadly, there are two options for asset management. Existing banks can undertake loan restructuring and loan workouts or problem assets may be removed from the bank and transferred to an asset management company (AMC). Song (Chapter 8) outlines some of the techniques for loan restructuring and the prudential treatment of such loans. He surveys country practices in classification and provisioning of restructured loans and proposes "good" practices. Alternatively, the authorities may decide to remove the assets from the bank and transfer them to a separate AMC. Ingves, Seelig, and He (Chapter 9) discuss the role of AMCs in bank restructuring and specifies several policy lessons learned from international experience.

As described above, implementation of bank restructuring can be chaotic and difficult, with restructuring practices being adopted to local conditions. For this reason, country experiences are as important as descriptions of best practices being complemented by descriptions of case studies. In this context, examples of bank restructuring experiences are provided for Korea (Kang, Chapter 10 and He, Chapter 14), transition countries (Enoch, Gulde, and Hardy, Chapter 11), and Indonesia (Enoch, Chapter 12).

Notes on Contributors

Michael Andrews Head of consultancy, A. Michael Andrews and Associates.

Charles Enoch Deputy Director of IMF's Monetary and Financial Systems Department.

Edward J. Frydl Senior Economist of the Financial Systems Surveillance Division II, Monetary and Financial Systems Department, IMF.

Anne-Marie Gulde Advisor of IMF's African Department.

Daniel Hardy Deputy Division Chief of the Financial Surveillance Policy Division, Monetary and Financial Systems Department, IMF.

Dong He Division Head, External Department, Hong Kong Monetary Authority.

David S. Hoelscher Assistant Director of the Monetary and Financial Systems Department, IMF.

Stefan Ingves Governor of the Riksbank, Sweden.

Mats Josefsson Advisor of the IMF's Monetary and Financial Systems Department.

Chungwon Kang Was a visiting scholar (banking) at the IMF (2003).

George G. Kaufman Professor, School of Business, Loyola University, Chicago, Il.

Ross B. Leckow Assistant General Council, IMF.

Marc Quintyn Advisor and Technical Assistance Area Chief, Monetary and Financial Systems Department, IMF.

Steven A. Seelig Advisor of the IMF's Monetary and Financial Systems Department.

Inwon Song Senior Financial Sector Expert, Financial Supervision and Regulation Division, Monetary and Financial Systems Department, IMF.

Part I

Overview of Crisis Resolution and Bank Restructuring Policies

1
The Resolution of Systemic Banking System Crises

David S. Hoelscher and Stefan Ingves

> "For every complex problem, there is a solution which is simple, neat, and wrong."
>
> H. L. Mencken

I. Introduction

Banking crises can be chaotic and confusing events. Although pressures can build for a long time, crises emerge suddenly, triggered by unrelated events or sudden changes in private sector perceptions of financial sector soundness or macroeconomic policies. The authorities' goal is to reestablish macroeconomic stability and financial intermediation using a combination of macroeconomic and microeconomic tools. Immediate action may contain the situation but delays are common. The authorities may be slow to react or unprepared for the emerging crisis, hoping that macroeconomic instability is temporary and the banks' emerging weaknesses are manageable.

In this environment, financial difficulties become intertwined with political and social problems. Delays in action can generate uncertainty about the state of the financial system, rumors, and growing panic. This uncertainty brings out political rivalries and may lead to social chaos. The social and political deterioration, in turn, affects economic decision-making.

Crisis management under these conditions becomes both difficult and complex. Deciding on policy options is often made more difficult by an unclear picture of the true financial conditions of banks and by limitations in the legal and institutional framework. Political instability can add an additional layer of confusion and can limit the range of resolution options.

The Fund is often in the unenviable position of being required to act under conditions of extreme uncertainty and time pressure. The Fund is typically called in only once the crisis has erupted and conditions are rapidly deteriorating. Fund programs (including their bank restructuring component) have to be developed and implemented quickly. The premium is on rapid containment and effective implementation of a broad strategy. Staff involved in crisis management need to combine deep country-specific knowledge and an understanding of the lessons from past crises. Effective teams, therefore, are composed of local authorities, international experts, and, where useful, private sector financial consultants.

Crisis management can be organized into three broad stages. The initial priority is to contain the banking crisis. Once achieved, the authorities must turn to two additional components of a crisis management strategy: restructuring the banking system and managing assets from intervened and closed banks.

- Deposit runs must be contained before the authorities can turn to structural reforms. Measures should be taken to restore private sector confidence in the financial system.
- Restructuring the banking system involves the complex tasks of diagnosing the conditions of the banking system to distinguish viable from unviable banks; steps should aim at strengthening viable banks and resolving unviable ones.
- Asset management requires the choice of the appropriate institutional framework for asset resolution (public or private) and the introduction of incentives to reestablish sound relations between banks and borrowers.

This simplified framework is just that: simple and stylized. While providing a framework for organizing action, the complex economic, political, and social environment must be taken into consideration. Predetermined strategies—even ones that worked well in other cases—do not always work. As practitioners, we must be aware of the strengths and weaknesses of our tool kit, and select the mix of policy instruments that is appropriate and germane to the specific country circumstances.

This chapter has three objectives. First, the chapter will define systemic crises and describe the tools frequently used to contain and resolve the crisis. Second, the chapter will describe the pitfalls frequently encountered in applying those tools. It will be argued that crisis management tools can be extremely powerful and effective but they also carry risks that, if not considered in the strategic design, can distort the resolution process and jeopardize the final results. Finally, the chapter will outline some of the lessons learned concerning crisis prevention and resolution.

II. Managing systemic banking crises

A systemic crisis is identified by its threat to the stability of the banking system. Systemic crises are sufficiently severe to affect adversely the payments system and, in consequence, the real economy through reductions in credit flows, or the destruction of asset values. A typical feature of a systemic crisis is the difficulty in distinguishing between solvent and insolvent banks. Accordingly, creditors, including depositors, run from all banks and/or from the currency, threatening the stability of the entire banking system. The run is fuelled by fears that the means of payment will be unobtainable at any price, and in a fractional reserve banking system this leads to a scramble for high-powered money and a withdrawal of external credit lines.

Treatment of a systemic banking crisis contrasts in important ways with the treatment of individual bank failures in stable periods. Policies considered appropriate in stable periods may aggravate uncertainties in a systemic crisis, worsening private sector confidence and slowing recovery. In stable periods, for example, deposits have only limited protection, emergency liquidity assistance is given under very restricted conditions, and insolvent banks are resolved. In a systemic crisis, however, policies aim at (i) protecting the payment system; (ii) limiting the loss of depositor confidence; (iii) developing and implementing a strategy to restore solvency to the banking system; and (iv) preventing further macroeconomic deterioration.

A variety of tools have been used to achieve these objectives. These tools include emergency liquidity support, mechanisms for strengthening creditor confidence and bank strengthening and resolution techniques. While they have proven to be effective under some conditions, they are also subject to limitations. Understanding the conditions under which these tools can be used is critical to the effective management of systemic crises. In the following sections, the uses and limitations of these tools are discussed.

Crisis containment

The immediate priority of the authorities must be to contain the banking crisis. Adequate structural policies cannot be implemented in the face of depositor panic, macroeconomic deterioration, or an imminent threat of interruption in essential financial services. Experience points to the importance of emergency liquidity support and the potential for using blanket guarantees as part of the policies to address these problems. When these tools are ineffective, the authorities may be forced to turn to more intrusive, administrative measures.

Containment measures buy time but are not by themselves a solution. To have a lasting result, containment measures must be combined with strong macroeconomic adjustment policies and comprehensive bank restructuring strategies. Containment measures alone cannot restore market confidence when the macroeconomic situation continues to deteriorate, and the political and social situation is unsettled.

Emergency liquidity assistance

Emergency liquidity support is an essential element of crisis containment. In the early stages of a financial collapse, depositors are running from all banks in the system. As described above, the inability to distinguish good from bad banks, together with the fear that bank liquidity will disappear, cause even good banks to fail. Failure to ensure liquidity to banks will only accelerate the deterioration and collapse of the banking system.

An example of the importance of providing adequate liquidity was seen during the Turkish banking crisis. Sparked by a political dispute, depositors began withdrawing funds from the banking system in February 2001. Concern about domestic inflation and exchange rate stability led the Turkish central bank to withhold emergency liquidity support. Rather than stabilizing the situation, deposit withdrawals accelerated, lending to the collapse of the payment system and threats of deposit freezes. Once the central bank re-opened the emergency window (combined with appropriate open market policies to absorb the excess liquidity) depositor confidence stabilized and the Turkish government turned to the medium-term task of bank restructuring.

The experience during the Asian crisis also points to the importance of emergency support in the early phases of a banking crisis. The central banks in all four East Asian countries (Indonesia, Korea, Malaysia, and Thailand) provided liquidity to allow the withdrawal of deposits. Most central banks combined liquidity support with significant efforts at sterilization. Such efforts were largely successful in Korea and Thailand but less so in Indonesia, where protracted political and macroeconomic uncertainties resulted in continued deposit withdrawals and only limited opportunities for sterilization operations.[1]

Notwithstanding the importance of providing liquidity support, the instrument carries serious risks.

- The increase in monetary aggregates resulting from the use of emergency liquidity support can put pressures on both prices and the exchange rate.
- Banks that eventually become insolvent may be the most frequent users of central bank liquidity support, exposing the central bank to significant losses.
- The usual terms of emergency lending, such as penalty rates, short maturity, and acceptable collateral, may need to be relaxed during a systemic crisis to accommodate the implementation of a bank restructuring strategy. However, such action reduces the safeguards of the central bank and may introduce moral hazard if the new terms discourage banks from seeking alternative sources of liquidity.
- Liquidity support to weak banks is prone to abuse, and might in particular be relied upon to increase the bank's assets instead of reducing its depositor liabilities. In Indonesia, for instance, a Parliamentary inquiry commission concluded that during the 1997–98 crisis a large proportion of emergency support had been used to cover overhead expenses.

- Dollarized economies may not have the luxury of emergency liquidity support. Liquidity support results in a reduction of net international reserves that may not be replenished through open market operations.

The liquidity support mechanism must be designed in a way that takes these risks into account.

- The monetary authorities must sterilize monetary pressures. Macro-economic policies should be adjusted to prevent any prolonged "overshooting" of domestic interest rates. In Indonesia, the inability to implement such macroeconomic policies worsened the environment for crisis management. In contrast, in Argentina the central bank introduced central bank bills in 2002 following the crisis outbreak, successfully absorbing excess liquidity and preventing an inflationary surge.
- Liquidity triggers should be introduced to reduce the likelihood that liquidity assistance is provided to insolvent banks. As liquidity assistance increases as a percent of bank capital, increasingly severe supervisory measures should be triggered. Banks are first subject to special on-site inspections, followed by placement of supervisors on the boards of directors. At a point determined by law, liquidity triggers can permit supervisory intervention in the bank, thus overcoming other deficiencies in the bankruptcy regime.
- Enhanced supervision of banks receiving emergency support is necessary to reduce moral hazard and ensure that central bank liquidity is used as intended. Attention needs to be paid to corporate governance in these banks, particularly if problems are the result of poor banking rather than pure contagion.
- Central banks in highly dollarized economies have established (i) higher liquidity requirements than customary in non-dollarized economies and (ii) contingent loans from international banks.

Blanket guarantees

Blanket guarantees have proven useful in ending banking panics. Faced with accelerating deposit runs, many countries have found blanket guarantees effective in restoring private sector confidence in the financial system. Four Asian countries—Indonesia, Korea, Malaysia, and Thailand—relied on this instrument in the late 1990s, as did Turkey in its more recent banking crisis. A blanket guarantee gave the authorities time to diagnose fully the condition of the banking system, find agreement on the appropriate strategy, and then intervene and resolve unviable banks without risks of contagion.

But restoration of confidence comes at a cost, which has varied considerably among countries. When credible and effective, the immediate costs of blanket guarantees are minimal as, once the runs stop, the guarantee is not called. However, a guarantee also commits the authorities to restoring the solvency of the banking system. The costs of that guarantee depend on a number of factors. Key determinants are (i) the state of the financial system (its capital shortfall), and (ii) the effectiveness of the authorities' overall banking strategy. Recent analysis on Indonesia, for instance, suggests that failure to move quickly to halt the deterioration in the banking system, rather than the blanket guarantee, allowed resolution costs to soar. Half of the crisis costs in Turkey were due to the need to restructure the large public banks—an obligation of the government even in the absence of a blanket guarantee. Finally, countries that have been unsuccessful in the recovery of assets taken over as part of the resolution process have faced significantly higher crisis costs. Asset recovery is a powerful tool for reducing crisis costs, as seen in Sweden. Delays or inefficiencies create lost opportunities for addressing the limitations in other resolution tools.

While concern about the costs of guarantees is valid, the difficulty policymakers face is evaluating the counterfactual. The authorities must weigh the costs arising from the potential failure of a higher number of banks in the absence of a guarantee against the cost of resolving individual banks under a blanket guarantee. The case of Indonesia is telling. In January 1998, the exchange rate depreciated by almost 300 percent, half the deposit base was withdrawn, and Bank Indonesia had almost run out of currency notes. Announcement of the blanket guarantee on January 15, 1998 halted the

Table 1.1.   Fiscal Costs of Selected Banking Crises
(In percent of GDP)

	Crisis Period	Gross Outlay	Recovery	Net Cost	Assets[a]
Chile	1981–1983	52.7	19.2	33.5	47.0
Ecuador	1998–2001	21.7	0.0	21.7	41.3
Finland	1991–1993	12.8	1.5	11.2	109.4
Indonesia	1997–present	56.8	4.6	52.3	68.1
Korea	1997–present	31.2	8.0	23.1	72.4
Malaysia	1997–2001	7.2	3.2	4.0	130.6
Mexico	1994–1995	...	...	19.3	40.0
Norway	1987–1989	2.5	...	...	91.9
Russia	1998	...	...	0.0	24.9
Sweden	1991	4.4	4.4	0.0	102.4
Thailand	1997–present	43.8	9.0	34.8	117.1
Turkey	2000–present	31.8	1.3	30.5	71.0
United States	1984–1991	3.7	1.6	2.1	51.4
Venezuela	1994–1995	15.0	2.5	12.4	28.3

Source: Hoelscher and Quintyn, 2003.

[a] Assets of deposit money banks in the year before the first crisis year.

outflows and gave the authorities time to reassess the causes of the meltdown and identify a strategy. It is unclear what would have happened had the blanket guarantee not been announced. One possible outcome would have been an even greater collapse of the financial system and even greater political and social chaos.

When deciding on the appropriateness of a blanket guarantee, the following factors should be considered:

- A blanket guarantee must be credible. The private sector must believe that the government is in a position to honor the guarantee. The government debt position needs to be sustainable and the fiscal accounts relatively strong.
- The blanket guarantee must provide only the minimum protection needed, as excessive coverage only increases moral hazard. The coverage of blanket guarantees should be designed to meet the needs and conditions of the country. However, generally, groups that are not covered include shareholders, subordinated debt holders, connected depositors, and depositors in offshore subsidiaries. External interbank creditors may be included if they are an important source of instability.[2]
- The worse the financial conditions of the banking system, the higher will be the cost of the blanket guarantee. The authorities will have to recognize that the blanket guarantee would have to be accompanied with sufficient fiscal effort to ensure that the medium-term costs of meeting the guarantee can be incorporated in the fiscal accounts.
- The authorities must have adequate legal powers and the tools and the determination to restructure banks and move quickly to restore the system's solvency.
- A credible guarantee in highly dollarized economies would require some combination of low expected costs of restructuring the banking system, and sufficient international reserves to back the guarantee.
- The authorities must have adequate controls to prevent misuse of the blanket guarantee. Fraud can increase the cost of a guarantee through a host of possibilities, including the creation of fake deposits, misuse of lending to related parties, and uncontrolled transfer of offshore deposits (if uncovered).

Both emergency liquidity support and blanket guarantees have proven to be controversial. Concerns about the cost implications of both have led to suggestions that such instruments not be used in crisis management. The alternative proposed is to impose haircuts on the creditors of insolvent banks in the hope that confidence will eventually return and the deposit runs stabilize.[3] Were runs to continue in otherwise solvent banks, reflecting a generalized loss of confidence, this policy option would allow depositors to continue withdrawing funds until a number of these banks would become illiquid and be closed. This strategy aims at leaving only solid banks in the banking system and limits the resolution costs to the government.

There are serious limitations to this alternative resolution approach. First, as stated above, systemic banking crises are different from bank failures because of the difficulties in distinguishing between viable and nonviable banks.[4] As a result, depositors flee from all banks in the system.[5] Allowing all banks facing runs to fail implies accepting unnecessary and irreversible damage to some healthy sections of the financial system. Second, the economic and social costs of this alternative have not been evaluated. While the counterfactual arguments are difficult to quantify, eliminating an excessively large segment of the financial sector will result in significant disruptions in the distribution of financial services that will hurt the real sector and thus compromise the economic recovery. Third, government authorities have been reluctant to try such an alternative because of the political and social implications.

Imposing nominal losses (haircuts) on creditors during systemic crises is particularly disruptive to the financial system. Imposition of reductions in deposit balances is more costly to the depositor and more intrusive than modifying contract terms. Restoration of confidence, therefore, becomes more problematic. Moreover, depositors with residual balances in the bank may immediately withdraw remaining balances in the bank to prevent further confiscation, thus aggravating the banking crisis. The political costs of deposit haircuts are often seen as prohibitive. For these reasons, this policy has been used in only a few, extreme cases—Argentina (1989), Estonia (1992), Japan (1946), and the United States (1933).[6] Two of the cases (Japan and the United States) occurred when deposit insurance systems were not in place and the more recent cases (Estonia and Argentina) were part of a fundamental restructuring of not just the banking system but the entire economic framework for the country. For example, Argentina imposed depositor haircuts in 1989 following a prolonged period of hyperinflation and both a political and social collapse. The stabilization package reversed decades of populist macroeconomic policies, stabilizing prices and the exchange rate, revamping relations between the national and regional governments, and restructuring public sector finances. Under these circumstances, the negative impact of deposit haircuts may have been overshadowed by a positive impact arising from the wide ranging structural reforms.

Administrative measures

Plans for stabilizing systemic crises can go awry. The country may not meet the necessary conditions for efficient use of the stabilization tools, mentioned above. Macroeconomic developments can slip, worsening the crisis and preventing stabilization of private sector expectations. High levels of dollarization can so limit the effectiveness of traditional resolution tools that they are not viable options. Political or social developments can impede prompt crisis resolution.

Under such conditions, administrative measures may be the only alternative available to contain the generalized collapse of the financial system. These measures change the contractual terms of bank deposits, and can be referred to collectively as "deposit freezes." In designing these measures, three basic options are available: restrictions on deposit withdrawals, an extension of deposit maturities, and securitization of deposits. Such measures have been used sparingly in recent times. However, Argentina, Ecuador, and Uruguay have all relied on some form of this containment tool.

Administrative measures have serious limitations and should be used with caution. Such measures are disruptive to the payment system and to economic activity. Moreover, depositors will react negatively to all administrative measures. The measures, therefore, should be viewed as a final, desperate measure to stop a run on banks if all other measures fail. They should also be designed to mitigate as far as possible their negative impacts.

- All deposit freezes are disruptive to the economy as they limit access to the means of payments. When properly designed, securitization is the least disruptive in this sense, as deposits are converted into negotiable instruments that can be redeemed for liquidity in case of need, albeit at a discount.[7] More generally, administrative measures should always allow for a small amount of funds to be withdrawn to facilitate financial transactions.
- Deposit restrictions tend to lose effectiveness quickly as market participants learn ways of circumventing them. Country experiences suggest that restrictions used to substitute for necessary policy adjustments to address the fundamental causes of crises could not provide a lasting protection. Thus, if restrictions are imposed, they should be in place for limited time-periods and be used to buy the authorities time to work out a permanent solution.
- Political and social pressures have resulted in exemptions and the abuse of exemptions. Any exception to the general policy concerning deposit restrictions should be limited in order to avoid circumvention and loss of credibility.
- Unwinding deposit restrictions can be problematic. While a premature removal of deposit restrictions exposes the banking system to the risk of a new run, an excessively drawn out process can harm confidence in the banking system, increase uncertainties, and delay reintermediation.

In principle, any limitation on deposits should be applied uniformly across all banks. Asymmetric treatment can put extra financial burdens on those banks treated unfavorably, deteriorating their financial position and making them a drag on the recovery of financial intermediation. Asymmetric treatment of banks has been implemented in some cases. In Uruguay, for example, foreign banks were exempt from the deposit freeze imposed in 2002, on grounds that deposits were invested in high-quality, dollar-denominated securities that were easy to liquidate to meet deposit demand. Exceptions to the principle of uniformity of treatment, however, should be limited to exceptional circumstances, where the asymmetry is not perceived as arbitrary, the financial recovery is not jeopardized, and the motives are communicated in a transparent way to the public.

Bank restructuring

The main objective of the restructuring strategy is to restore individual banks and the system to profitability and solvency. The strategy should identify measures to strengthen viable banks, improve the operating environment for all banks, and resolve unviable banks. Bank restructuring is a multi-year process, often requiring the establishment or revision of laws and institutions; the development of strategies to liquidate, merge, sell, or recapitalize banks; and the restructuring and recovery of bank assets, operations, and procedures.

The bank restructuring strategy begins with a diagnosis of the financial condition of individual banks. The size and distribution of bank losses must be identified. As supervisory data may be outdated and not reflect the full economic impact of the crisis, supervisors may attempt to update available information based on uniform valuation criteria. The supervisors will also examine information on banks' ownership structures (public or private, foreign or domestic, concentrated or dispersed) to help determine the scope for upfront support from existing or potential new private owners.

Diagnosis of banking sector conditions in a crisis is typically hampered by data limitations. A frequently used measure of solvency is the risk-weighted Basel capital adequacy ratio (CAR). However, when data limitations delay the evaluation of banks' capital levels, supervisors may need to rely on other sources of information to determine bank viability. A bank is viable if (i) it can remain profitable and earn a competitive return over the medium term; and (ii) the shareholders are committed and able to support it. Supervisors may require banks to produce forward-looking business plans based on common assumptions with time bound, measurable targets for monitoring purposes.

Once the diagnosis is complete for each institution, the supervisors classify banks and develop appropriate resolution strategies. Typically, three categories are used: (i) viable and meeting their legal CAR and other regulatory requirements; (ii) unviable; and (iii) viable but undercapitalized. In the latter classification, an additional assessment will be needed to determine whether the existing shareholders can recapitalize their bank within an acceptable period or if the use of public funding should be considered. Once classified, the authorities must go through the arduous process of monitoring the restructuring process for viable banks.

Banks determined to be nonviable and insolvent must be removed from the system. Depositor protection will facilitate this clean up, as banks can be closed without fears of contagion. Countries in the Asian crisis as well as Turkey moved aggressively in removing failed banks, once the blanket guarantee was in place.[8]

Restructuring strategies for viable banks in a systemic crisis can be broadly divided into private sector solutions and public sector assisted solutions.

- Private sector solutions. Shareholders should always have the responsibility to recapitalize and restructure their bank. If the shareholders are unable to recapitalize fully their bank immediately but they are fit and proper and the bank is deemed viable, consideration could be given to allowing solvent but undercapitalized banks to remain in the system under strict conditions.[9] The bank's recapitalization could be phased in, with tight monitoring and requirements, including the suspension of dividend distributions until the required level of capital has been restored. If the original shareholders are unable to recapitalize, other private owners should be sought.
- Public sector-assisted solutions. Failure of private sector solutions and bank insolvency does not necessarily result in bank liquidation. Circumstances can exist where public sector action may be warranted to limit the costs to the real economy of too large a number of banking failures. Public sector assistance can use a variety of techniques: (i) joint recapitalization schemes; (ii) resolution through purchase-and-assumption (P&A) transactions or other sales methods, when public funds are used to back transferred liabilities or guarantee asset values; and (iii) nationalization (with a view to future reprivatization).

This restructuring phase is fraught with difficulties and potential setbacks. The efficiency with which the authorities implement these steps will determine both the overall cost of the bank restructuring efforts and the extent to which a vibrant and efficient banking system emerges from the crisis. However, experience points to a number of implementation problems.

- *Delays.* Failure to move expeditiously in restructuring will only allow the financial condition of the banks to deteriorate further and increase resolution costs. Banks rarely, if ever, grow out of serious financial difficulties.
- *Excessive forbearance.* Crisis resolution should not aim at protecting all banks. Viable banks should be closely monitored and nonviable banks should be removed from the system. The judgment on the viability of a bank is difficult but must be made based on the best information available.
- *Loss-sharing of shareholders.* In all cases, shareholders must be responsible for the accumulated losses of their banks. Otherwise, shareholders have the wrong incentives in managing their bank.

- *Comprehensive treatment of banks.* The resolution of banks must address all their outstanding problems. Partial resolution (while "praying for redemption") rarely works. The supervisors must be convinced of the inherent strength of the banks that remain in the banking system.
- *Inappropriate resolution tools.* Supervisors have a range of resolution tools such as liquidation, sale as a whole or in parts (including through P&A transactions), and nationalization. Authorities must ensure that the market conditions are appropriate for the tools used. For example, reliance on P&A transactions in an environment of shallow private markets can distort the resolution process.
- *Lack of political support.* Bank resolution necessarily implies redistribution of resources within the economy. Shareholders are expected to be first in line to absorb losses up to the full amount of their stake, but any additional losses might need to be absorbed by other stakeholders, such as holders of subordinated debt, depositors, other creditors, and the government (ultimately, the taxpayers). Differences within the government on how this burden will be shared can be exploited resulting in higher fiscal costs and a less efficient banking system.
- *Poor communications.* Lack of an appropriate communications strategy can limit the effectiveness of a resolution strategy. Private sector support is an important factor in implementing bank restructuring. Stability of private expectations gives a period of peace and calm; understanding of the government's objectives can generate important support.

Limitations in the legal system have been a key reason for suboptimal results in bank restructuring. Even when the banking strategy is comprehensive and fully agreed, weaknesses in the legal system have hampered bank resolution efforts. Such weaknesses have resulted in (i) incentives to postpone adequate treatment of failing banks; (ii) higher costs for bank resolution; and (iii) weaknesses in the banking system. Limiting legal factors include:

- *Inability to write down shareholder capital.* Bank supervisors should have legal powers to write off shareholders' equity to facilitate bank resolution.
- *Limited legal authority to facilitate bank sales.* Many supervisory authorities face restrictions on the sales or transfer of bank assets of failed banks. In some jurisdictions, shareholders continue to have legal rights even after bank failure, thus preventing the authorities from taking cost-reducing resolution actions.
- *Weak mandate of supervisory, deposit insurance, or resolution agencies to restructure banks.* Bank resolution entities should have a clear organizational framework, be adequately capitalized, and have a board composed by reputable professionals.

- *Ineffective procedures to implement P&A transactions.* In practice, banking legislations should give supervisors the necessary legal authority to transfer to a third institution a portion of "privileged" liabilities from a failed institution along with its good assets. This is meant to contain the risk of legal challenges from the remaining creditors.
- *Insufficient knowledge of judges on banking matters.* In some jurisdictions, judges have limited knowledge of banking matters, which has impeded the resolution of banks or the legal prosecution of the former managers and directors of failed banks.
- *Lack of legal protection to staff and board members of agencies responsible for bank restructuring.* Lack of legal protection from litigation for bona fide actions taken in the exercise of their duties impairs banking resolution efforts.

Asset management and corporate debt restructuring

Asset management and corporate debt restructuring are the final component of crisis management. Corporate and financial sector restructuring are inextricably intertwined, being two sides of the same issue. A key aspect of this process is the orderly transfer of ownership and management of weak assets. Strengthening this process may include both legal and institutional reforms. For this reason, resolution of the banking system issues is ideally carried out in conjunction with resolution of corporate sector issues.

The objective in establishing an asset management company (AMC) is to remove the nonperforming loans (NPLs) from the books of the banks, allowing banks to return to their normal business, and maximize the recovery value. Asset management is complex and one of the important benefits of establishing an AMC is the managerial. Managing nonperforming assets is different from managing a lending institution. Techniques for managing assets may include restructuring of loan terms, disposition through auctions or other sales methods (which transfers management decision to the purchaser), conversion into equity stakes, and liquidations through court or administrative procedures.

There are a number of institutional options for managing impaired assets (Figure 1.1). Banks can manage them directly, or sell them to a specialized AMC, either privately or publicly owned. Specialized institutions are necessary when managing NPLs interferes with the daily running of the bank or when specialized skills are needed. While each institutional setup has advantages and disadvantages, experience suggests that, in general, privately owned asset management companies can respond quickly and efficiently while government-owned centralized AMCs (CAMCs) may be relatively more efficient when the size of the problem is large, special powers for asset resolution are needed or the required skills are scarce.[10]

Institutional Arrangement

		Decentralized	Centralized
Mandate	Narrow	Private AMCs Private resolution trusts	Rapid resolution vehicles (US, RTC, Thai FRA)
	Broad	Bank workout units Private resolution trusts	Broad mandate CAMCs (Danaharta, KAMCO)

Figure 1.1.   Options for Asset Management

Empirical assessments of the effectiveness of AMCs have suggested that the most successful ones have had narrow mandates.[11] AMCs can have either narrow or expanded mandates—the former take over and liquidate assets from closed institutions; the latter purchase assets from going concerns with a view to expediting corporate restructuring. AMCs have had only limited success in corporate restructuring. Political pressures, limitations of market discipline, and conflicting objectives have hampered the expanded role of CAMCs. Moreover, expanded-mandate CAMCs have been used to recapitalize financial institutions by buying nonperforming assets at above market value. This recapitalization option is less transparent than more direct methods, converts the AMC into a loss-making operation to be covered by additional fiscal expenses, and provides the government with less leverage in the recapitalized institutions.[12]

An important issue in determining the effectiveness and impact of AMCs is asset pricing. As long as the ownership of the bank and the AMC is the same, NPLs can be transferred relatively rapidly as the transfer of assets is only an internal transaction. When ownership is different, pricing often becomes difficult. If an independent AMC is set up to purchase assets from going concerns, NPLs should be purchased at a price as close to a fair market value as possible. While it is difficult to price nonperforming assets (especially in the midst of financial crises), an approximation of their value, based on estimated recovery, cash flow projection, and appraisal of collateral, should be used for the purpose of the transfer.

In spite of considerable work on establishing and managing AMCs, success in resolving NPLs has been limited. AMCs have taken a significant portion of the failed assets arising from the Asian crisis of 1998. Similarly, an AMC was established in Turkey. Six years after the outbreak of the Asian crisis, progress has been made in resolving NPLs in both Malaysia (57 percent of assets resolved) and Korea (47 percent). Less striking progress has been made in Indonesia and China (a little over 30 percent in both cases).[13] In Turkey, the sale of assets of liquidated banks was significantly delayed and the process has just begun.

This slow pace reflects a number of common problems that arise with respect to asset disposition.

- *Weak market demand.* Market demand for distressed assets may be weak, depending on the depth of the local market, openness to foreign investors, and the type of assets. Local investors may lack resources for sizeable asset purchases in the midst of a crisis, particularly if the aggregate size of NPLs is large compared to the economy. Political sensitivities and legal restrictions to foreign ownership of assets may reduce market demand.
- *Weak property rights.* With unclear property rights and an inability of courts to enforce collateral, banks have little incentive to purchase NPLs or restructure existing NPLs. In effect, the bank restructuring process designed to date assumes that a well functioning legal and institutional framework for property rights already exists. If that is not the case, it is likely that NPLs will not only remain but also grow.[14]
- *Unrealistic expectations about the recovery rate.* The authorities may have unrealistic expectations about the market price of assets put up for sale. This may lead auctions to be cancelled. The low recovery rate may aggravate fears of legal action, making it important to provide staff and board directors of the AMC with legal protection.

III. The way forward

Given the chaotic nature of banking crises and the numerous sources of missteps and implementation problems, what is the best way forward? It is tempting to say that each crisis should be approached as a new case, avoiding a "cookie cutter approach" to resolution and seeking to identify the peculiarities of each country's legal, institutional, and cultural characteristics. However, broad guiding lessons can be identified for crisis prevention and crisis resolution.

The first best approach is to prevent or to minimize banking crises. The better we are at preventing crisis, the less necessary will resolution become. Experience also points to best practices or general principles for crisis resolution.

Prevention

Contrary to a common saying, "the best offense is a good defense." Efforts to prevent crises pay off handsomely in lowering the incidence of crises and lowering the costs when crises emerge. The supervisory and regulatory framework must be sufficiently robust to ensure rapid identification of banking weaknesses and implementation of corrective actions.

Prevention of systemic crises requires a broad based effort, aimed at establishing appropriate macroeconomic and microeconomic policies. Macroeconomic policies that aim at stable price levels and strong economic growth will support a strong banking system. Microeconomic policies should target a variety of internal factors to strengthen financial intermediation, including an appropriate operating environment, and internal governance of financial systems.[15] These factors should be supported by strong supervision and bank resolution framework.

Supervisory practices are an essential component of the framework for preventing banking crises. In reviewing international experiences of supervisory actions, the following framework has proven important for early warning and prevention of crises:

- Bank resolution framework. The authorities need sufficiently clear powers to implement their desired strategy.
- An independent bank supervisor with discretionary powers to act at an early stage. In a number of jurisdictions, as a result of legal limitations or political interference, bank supervisors have no independence to impose remedial actions to weak banks at an early stage. Furthermore, sometimes they must follow very rigid steps before intervening a bank, including a mandatory requirement for requesting weak banks to submit rehabilitation plans, which in some cases may simply delay bank resolution actions.
- Supervision on a consolidated basis. In some cases, financial groups have used unregulated affiliates (including offshore banks) to evade supervision and hide their true financial condition.
- Careful monitoring of loans to related parties. Due to political interference or weak supervisory capacity to enforce credit limit to insiders, a number of banks have failed as a result of large exposures to insolvent related parties.
- Strong legal protection for bank supervisors. The risk of legal retaliation from former bank shareholders also postpones the adoption of early bank resolution measures by banking supervisors.
- An additional factor in preventing crises is adequate planning. Good supervision will identify problems when they are still manageable. The earlier difficulties are detected, the more options are available. However, the authorities must move quickly to address small problems before they become big problems. Rapid and efficient action can limit subsequent costs and economic disruption. An equally important part of crisis prevention is planning for crises. Supervision cannot prevent banking failures. The authorities should be prepared, with clear options for addressing emerging and worsening crisis cases.
- Proper rules and practice runs during stable times pays. Countries find it useful to have considered the appropriate range of options concerning

the management of systemic crises before the crises emerge. While not able to predict the exact course of a crisis, identification of the key decisions that must be made, the sources of information and identifying who is responsible can speed development of an appropriate policy response.

Resolution

Supervision alone cannot resolve all crises once they have begun. Once a crisis breaks out, what are the policy principles that will limit the extent of the crisis and reduce the eventual costs?

- Strong political support. Crisis management and resolution implies a redistribution of wealth within the society. Political leadership is essential if this process is to be seen as fair. Moreover, public disagreements or expressions of doubt among prominent government participants can undermine confidence in the containment and restructuring process.
- Prompt recognition and resolution of banking distress lowers the cost of resolution. The sooner the problems come to light, the greater will be the options available to the authorities to tackle them. The faster the authorities get control of failed institutions, the lower will be the resolution costs and the faster the reestablishment of financial stability.
- Banks should be allowed to fail. Bank failure can be a positive force for banking system stability. The presumption should not be that all banks must be protected. In any decision to use public money to support a bank, the benefits of keeping a bank open must be judged explicitly against the costs to the public sector and to the banking system of maintaining a weak bank.
- Bank resolution should follow a principle of equity and fair treatment. Restructuring policies should be applied to all banks on a uniform basis. Existing shareholders should be the first to either inject additional capital or lose their investment.
- Bank restructuring must be comprehensive or financial difficulties will persist and, with time, grow. The resolution options chosen should not only resolve current banking problems, but also address the medium-term structural problems found in the legal and institutional framework. Any nationalized bank should be run by a third party with an established reputation and experience in bank management, or by new managers and board members that are fit and proper and isolated from political interference.
- Economic authorities must maintain close coordination. While a clear legal and operational division of labor is necessary to facilitate bank resolution, it is critical that a fluid mechanism to coordinate and

communicate actions is put in place. Furthermore, strong leadership is vital to shepherd the restructuring process and avoid influence from third parties.

- Restructuring of the banking system will be easier if depositors and other creditors are protected. When faced with a systemic crisis, experience suggests that, where feasible and when the costs can be covered by fiscal resources, a blanket guarantee can ease creditor fears and facilitate the closure of weak banks.
- Legal action must be taken against those responsible for banking failure. The prosecution of managers and directors responsible for wrongdoing in banks is the best recipe to impose market discipline. In cases when legal action has been taken, remaining actors in the market understand that the authorities are determined to have a sound and safe banking system. In the absence of such resolve, similar accidents will be repeated in the future.
- Asset resolution is an essential complement to bank restructuring. An early and active involvement in impaired asset management prevents credit discipline from eroding. A variety of institutional arrangements and techniques are available. They should be chosen in order to achieve the desired trade-off between rapid resolution and recovering the value of the impaired assets.
- Exit from guarantees. Any guarantees introduced as part of the restructuring strategy will have to be phased out as soon as possible without jeopardizing financial stability. Fears of renewed financial deterioration may lead to the tendency to postpone such a phase out. However, the longer guarantees are in place, the greater are the moral hazard implications. Successful guarantees have been phased out in progressive stages where each stage is seen by markets as a nonevent.

IV. The role of the fund

During the period 1980–2006, virtually every country in the world has undergone some form of financial crisis.[16] However, only a few countries have suffered multiple crises. Fortunately, at the country level, banking crises are low frequency events. As a result, the local knowledge of managing banking crises is often lost, as staff involved with the intensive period of crisis containment and post-crisis reconstruction retire or move to other responsibilities.

The Monetary and Financial Systems Department in the IMF is charged, in part, with assisting countries facing such crises. Following the Asian crisis, the Fund recognized the importance of assembling teams of professionals with experience in managing systemic banking crises. In response, the department established a dedicated division, staffed with experts who have helped resolve some of the most devastating banking crises. Experts in the division have been involved in every systemic crisis since the mid-1990s and have assisted countries address a myriad of banking difficulties. This staff provides a source of knowledge and experience concerning best practices and experiences in other countries and stands ready to assist members' countries within days of being called. Constant practice builds a knowledge base that is hard to maintain at the national level.

An important part of our work is the drawing of lessons and the identification of preferred practices. The department has published a series of papers drawing broad lessons from the crises since the mid-1990s. In addition, we are finalizing a series of detailed Ex Post Analyses that review the development of specific crises and a step-by-step review of the advice provided, the success in implementation of that advice, and the results. We hope that such work will strengthen our understanding of the forces unleashed in banking crises and the appropriateness of different combinations of containment and resolution tools.

V. Conclusions

Banking crises are chaotic events. Uncertainties and fears make identification of the problems and design of the solutions difficult. Moreover, economic difficulties become intertwined with political and social problems. Uncertainties about the conditions of the economy bring out political rivalries and may lead to social chaos. The social and political deterioration, in turn, affects economic decision-making.

Crisis management under these conditions is complex. As H. L. Mencken stated, as quoted at the beginning of this chapter, you can always find answers to complex problems that are "simple, neat, and wrong." The solutions tried during the last two decades have been innovative. Their effectiveness, however, has been mixed. To blame the instruments is too simple. A complex mix of economic, political, and social factors all affect how and when these instruments can be best used.

Crisis containment must be a priority in the initial stages of crisis management. Emergency liquidity support and blanket guarantees have proven to be powerful tools to achieve this containment. However, they must be used appropriately and there are conditions under which the tools are not credible or when they increase sharply the cost of the crisis. The authorities must be in a position to carefully evaluate the appropriateness and risks of these tools.

Bank restructuring is a bank-by-bank activity. It involves bank diagnosis and the design of appropriate bank-specific resolution strategies. There is no presumption that all banks must survive the resolution phase. Successful restructuring requires sound banks and strong shareholders, able to ensure the profitable management of their bank over the medium term.

The bank restructuring phase is fraught with difficulties and potential setbacks. Experience suggests that the biggest threats to successful restructuring of the banking system include failure to complete the restructuring, excessive forbearance, failure to ensure loss sharing of shareholders, inconsistent treatment of banks, and lack of political support for the process.

Given the difficulties and uncertainties of crisis management, prevention should be of significant concern to the authorities. A number of measures can strengthen the supervisory framework and the authorities' ability to prevent crises. Among these measures are creation of an independent banking supervisor with discretionary powers to act at an early stage, consolidated supervision of financial sector groups, careful monitoring of loans to related parties, and strong legal protection for bank supervisors.

Once prevention fails, bank resolution should be as efficient as possible. Bank resolution strategies should be comprehensive and complete. Moreover, the faster the recognition and resolution of banking distress, the more efficient and less costly will be the resolution. For that reason, strong political support is necessary to ensure the full implementation of the strategies designed. Particular efforts should be made to ensure that the legal system is adequate for the strategy adopted.

Notes

1. Lindgren and others (1999), p. 18.
2. This is because deposits are typically moved offshore in the first place for tax and regulatory evasion.
3. Haircuts are defined as nominal reductions in the deposit; net present value (NPV) reductions through maturity extensions or interest rate reductions are not termed a "haircut."
4. Under normal times, failed banks should be resolved and depositors protected only up to the maximum in the deposit insurance system. Imposing losses under such circumstances will not cause contagion as other depositors in the system will know the condition of their banks.
5. In the Argentina case, for example, deposit withdrawals were suffered by all banks in the system, including the strong international banks.
6. Baer and Klingebiel (1995). They also studied Malaysia (1986) where insolvencies emerged in financial cooperatives. Cooperatives represented about 3 percent of total deposit-taking institutions. Depositors in insolvent cooperatives received 50 percent in cash and the remaining 50 percent in securities. While representing an NPV reduction, nominal haircuts were not imposed.
7. This, however, can have adverse redistributional effects if the neediest depositors are forced to liquidate the securities at a discount, while the most affluent ones can afford to hold the bonds to maturity.
8. For example, Korea removed licenses of 19 banks; Indonesia removed the licenses of over 90 banks, Thailand closed 58 finance companies and intervened 5 banks; and Turkey removed licenses from 22 banks.
9. Undercapitalized banks are banks operating below the legal minimum CAR. Insolvency is often defined as operating with a CAR of zero or less. In some

countries with prompt corrective action regimes, the law may oblige supervisors to intervene a bank when its CAR falls below a certain threshold (between 2–4 percent in some countries).
10. Ingves, Seelig, and He (2004).
11. Klingebiel (2000) and Woo (2000).
12. Lindgren and others (1999).
13. Fung and others (2004).
14. Sheng (2003).
15. Lindgren, Garcia, and Saal (1996).
16. Lindgren and others (1996), and Hoelscher, "Issues in Bank Resolution," IMF Regional Conference on Bank Resolution, Honduras, 2004.

Bibliography

Baer, Herbert, and Daniela Klingebiel, 1995, "Systemic Risk When Depositors Bear Losses: Five Case Studies," in George Kaufman (ed.) *Research in Financial Services: Private and Public Policy*, Vol. 7 (Stanford, Conn: JAI Press), pp 195–302.

Fung, Ben, Jason George, Stefan Hohl, and Guonan Ma, February 2004, *Public Asset Management Companies in East Asia: A Comparative Study*, Occasional Paper No. 3, Bank of International Settlements.

Hoelscher, David, and Marc Quintyn, 2003, *Managing Systemic Banking Crises* (Washington: International Monetary Fund).

Hoggarth, Glenn, and Jack Reidhill, 2003, "Resolution of Banking Crises: A Review," *Financial Stability Review*, December, pp. 109–23.

Ingves, Stefan, Steven Seelig, and Dong He, 2004 "Issues in the Establishment of Asset Management Companies," Policy Discussion Paper 04/03 (Washington: International Monetary Fund).

Kane, Edward J., and Daniela Klingebiel, 2004, "Alternatives to Blanket Guarantees for Containing a Systemic Crisis," *Journal of Financial Stability* (forthcoming).

Klingebiel, Daniela, 2000, "The Use of Asset Management Companies in the Resolution of Banking Crises: Cross-Country Experience," World Bank Policy Research Paper No. 2284 (Washington: International Monetary Fund).

Lindgren, Carl-Johan, Gillian Garcia, and Matthew Saal, 1996, *Bank Soundness and Macroeconomic Policy* (Washington: International Monetary Fund).

Lindgren, Carl-Johan, Tomas Baliño, Charles Enoch, Anne-Marie Gulde, Marc Quintyn, and Leslie Teo, 1999, *Financial Sector Crisis and Restructuring: Lessons from Asia* (Washington: International Monetary Fund).

Sheng, Andrew, 2003, "Reflections on Financial Sector Restructuring," World Bank/ IMF/SEACEN Regional Seminar.

Woo, David, 2000, "Two Approaches to resolving Nonperforming Assets during Financial Crises," IMF Working Paper 00/33, Washington: International Monetary Fund.

2
The Benefits and Costs of Intervening in Banking Crises

Edward J. Frydl and Marc Quintyn[1]

I. Introduction

Official intervention to contain the dimensions of a banking system crisis and to resolve failed banks has become a common feature of the international financial system in recent years. Intervention refers to actions that authorities can take to stabilize and restructure a banking system in crisis. It is distinguished from prevention, which covers more forward-looking activities such as improving regulation and supervision, strengthening monitoring and incentives, and enhancing information transparency.

Typically, a systemic banking crisis has two principal dimensions that require intervention: first, a liquidity crisis that threatens widespread depositor panic; second, a degree of systemic distress represented by large losses in asset values that have generated widespread insolvency of banks and capital deficiencies. Decisions regarding the liquidity crisis must be taken under pressure in an environment of high uncertainty. After deposits are stabilized, decisions regarding the resolution of failed banks can be taken in a less volatile environment.

This chapter examines the reasons for intervention in banking crises from a public policy perspective and elaborates the benefits and costs of intervention. Section II presents an overview of the issues. Section III details the types of actions that can be taken to intervene under different circumstances and sets the stage for defining the fiscal accounting of intervention. Section IV examines the methodological issues of measurement related to intervention. Section V presents a conceptual framework for characterizing a banking crisis and examines how it will evolve with or without official intervention. Section VI provides a general cost-benefit framework for the full economic benefits and costs of intervening, including fiscal costs. Section VII describes estimation procedures for quantifying the accounting concepts developed in section VI. Section VIII applies the framework developed earlier to the case of Sweden. Specific measures of benefits and costs are constructed based on the institutional features of the Swedish economy and the availability of data.

II. Benefits and costs of intervening in banking crises: an overview

The prevalence of banking crises around the world over the past two decades has prompted governments to innovate approaches for dealing with the problems. This chapter is an attempt to conceptualize those intervention decisions in a framework that allows an assessment of their benefits and costs.[2] The technique of cost-benefit analysis provides a relatively simplified quantification of optimal decision rules. Whether such a technique is fruitful depends on whether the fundamental decision process is an economic choice. In that regard, the application of cost-benefit analysis to intervention in banking crises seems useful. Such intervention does not depend on a fundamental political choice, such as war or peace, whose implications cannot be easily reduced to economic quantities. The choice between letting a banking crisis run its course and using public funds to intervene in various fashions is essentially an economic investment decision, well-suited to cost-benefit analysis.

An additional factor affecting the utility of cost-benefit analysis is whether the relevant economic benefits and costs can be readily quantified. This problem is especially acute for estimating potential economic effects beforehand in applying decision rules. Difficulty in quantifying economic factors is a general problem of cost-benefit analysis, but the issue is of much practical importance in the decision on intervening in banking crises. The benefits of stopping the spread of a banking crisis typically involve avoiding a systemic breakdown. Since experience with systemic breakdowns is very limited, estimations of the benefits will entail speculative assessments that can be questioned. Also, costs associated with the future moral hazard provoked by intervention actions reflect subjective probabilities of risk taking and are hard to quantify. Nevertheless, the formalization of the decision-making process into a cost-benefit framework imposes consistency and focuses attention on whether hard-to-quantify factors will actually have a deciding effect on the decision if they are in any realistic range of values.

The nature of a crisis

The logic of cost-benefit analysis is straightforward: the government will maximize the net benefit, appropriately discounted, of its actions. Formally,

Net benefits = Benefits (Intervention actions) – Costs (Intervention actions), where the amount of both benefits and costs depends on the kinds and degrees of intervention actions taken.

The first necessary step in giving this formal rule content is to define the features of a crisis. Characterizing a crisis will specify the nature of the benefits and costs involved and the kinds of intervention actions that can be taken. A crisis represents a pathological condition of the banking system. In one dimension, the crisis state entails a greater degree of the kind of distress that may affect a banking system without posing a critical problem. Distress consists of accumulated losses that have generated capital deficiencies (relative to regulatory requirements) and insolvencies. The problem of distress is more severe if the accumulated losses are accompanied by chronic unprofitability rather than being the consequence of a one-time loss of asset value. Limited distress, affecting single institutions or narrow classes of banks, may prompt official actions, but on a small scale that does not require the commitment of extraordinary resources.

As distress grows, it becomes at some point systemic in scope and produces a qualitatively distinct feature characteristic of the crisis state—the threat of a banking panic. Panic concerns the liquidity state of the system. Liquidity problems, like distress caused by asset losses, can develop by varying degrees short of a systemic problem. In the mildest form of a liquidity problem, an individual institution may have to pay a premium but can still maintain deposit levels. In a more severe problem, a bank starts to lose deposits but is able to replace these with funds from the interbank market. If the interbank market dries up, the bank may seek lender-of-last-resort (LOLR) assistance.

An individual bank may find itself with a liquidity problem for reasons that are independent of its distress level. In principle, a systemic liquidity problem could emerge for a relatively distress-free system, for example, if a contagious depositor panic feeds off the failure of the banking system in a neighboring country with structurally similar economy. While such a scenario exists as a logical possibility, it seems to be an extremely rare historical occurrence. The emergence of a systemic liquidity problem in a banking crisis is typically the consequence of deepening and widening distress. Therefore, the prototype of a banking crisis examined in this chapter is characterized by two essential elements: a high degree of systemic distress and the imminent prospect of panic.

Intervening in a crisis

These characteristics of a banking crisis define the broad outlines of intervention actions. Intervention will occur in a two-step process. The threat of panic is the immediate problem and the government must first decide whether it is worthwhile to pay the costs to avert it. This step will entail some form of liquidity support, typically the guarantee of bank deposits by the government. If the guarantee successfully averts the spread of panic, the government is then exposed to costs arising from the distorted incentives produced by deep and widespread distress. These costs will include the potential fiscal costs of the deposit guarantee on banks that continue to fail and the economic costs of distorted bank behavior, including credit crunch effects and financial market uncertainties.

The government makes a choice about how aggressively to intervene according to the criterion of maximizing benefits, chiefly economic in nature, less costs, both fiscal and economic. It is possible that, following this criterion, the government will choose not to intervene. This outcome is more likely the greater is the initial damage to the banking system. A very large initial shock has two consequences. First, it leaves little value in the banking system to be defended from further loss. Second, it exposes the government to a relatively large payment on any guarantee of deposits to avert a panic because many banks will already be put in a position of deep insolvency. Both of these factors work against the government providing liquidity support and toward allowing a panic to run its course. In other words, if there is relatively little to be saved from averting a panic, the government may prefer to let depositors rather than taxpayers bear the cost of the crisis.

Another factor is the size of the banking system relative to the economy. If bank loans are not a large source of credit to the enterprise sector, the collapse of the banking system will have a less disruptive effect on investment and employment. In this case, the government will be less likely to stem a panic since the economic benefits of that intervention are relatively small. Even in this case, however, banking system collapse will disrupt the payment system. The economic costs of that disruption can be large. The case of Russia, for example, suggests that the collapse of a relatively small banking system can have serious economic costs through payments disruption. The reversion of large transactions to barter arrangements in the wake of the Russian banking system collapse greatly impeded economic efficiency and government tax collections.

If the government does intervene to avert panic, it must then determine how aggressively it will act to resolve distress within the banking system. The existence of distress produces distorted incentives that generate new economic losses and further banking system distress. The government can choose to eliminate distress and the economic costs that it produces. Actions to resolve banking system distress will involve closing or restructuring failed and weakened banks. In some cases, restorations can be carried out by private restructuring, but these efforts may involve some kinds of official assistance. In other cases, the direct use of government funds through payment under deposit guarantees or public recapitalization will be needed.

In general, the government's decision will balance the economic and fiscal costs of using public sector resources against the benefits of forestalling further economic deterioration through prompt action. In a case where the premium attached to the use of public sector resources is large, for example, because of a high current or prospective government debt burden, the government may pursue a very deliberative and slow intervention strategy in order to economize on the outlay of public monies, even at the expense of higher economic costs. An aggressive resolution strategy, on the other hand, will limit deterioration costs by cutting short the intervention period but may require a greater use of public funds by relying more on nationalization or liquidation of banks with payments to depositors and less on private recapitalization and merger, which are time-intensive resolution options.

Nature of benefits

The benefits of official intervention in a banking crisis can be organized into broad classes that reflect benefits of intervention both to stabilize the banking system and avert a panic and to restore the banking system to a healthy state, free from distress-related distortions. These benefits, which can also be interpreted as the avoided costs of failing to act, can be characterized as:

(1) *Maintain the integrity of the credit mechanism.* A dysfunctional banking system is subject to many kinds of distorted behavior that disrupt normal credit relationships. Different banks may simultaneously take uneconomic risks; restrict credit to viable borrowers; force acceleration of loans and, thereby, disrupt productive activities; force liquidation of assets, depressing prices below fundamental valuations; and so forth.

(2) *Maintain the integrity of the payments system.* The collapse of a banking system will disrupt the payments system in ways that will go beyond interruption to the clearing and settlement mechanism. Bank deposits will be destroyed and economic participants will be forced to hold the medium of exchange in the form of currency. The absence of bank deposits will inefficiently restrict transactions to currency and barter.

(3) *Maintain general financial stability.* The general financial uncertainty produced by a banking crisis increases the country's risk premium, which raises borrowing costs to all classes of borrowers, depresses asset prices, and spreads contagion effects to balance sheets outside the banking system.

(4) *Maintain economic stability.* The negative financial consequences of a banking crisis—a credit crunch, high borrowing costs, weak asset prices, liquidity squeezes—breed losses in wealth and recessionary contractions of output.

(5) *Promote an efficiently structured banking system.* A final benefit of intervention in a banking crisis is the opportunity it provides for a microeconomic reorganization of the banking system through an efficiently managed exit of unprofitable institutions.

Nature of costs

The costs of intervening in a banking crisis fall into two broad classes: fiscal costs and economic costs. Fiscal costs reflect actions that generate an actual outlay of public funds. Economic costs reflect the distortionary consequences of intervention actions on the incentives facing economic participants.

Fiscal costs

Fiscal costs can be organized according to the type of intervention activity they finance.

(1) **Liquidity support.** In the early stages of a banking crisis, official liquidity support may take the form of LOLR assistance from the central bank. This kind of lending is normally short-term and highly secured but, as conditions worsen for individual banks, it may have to be converted into longer-term official exposure. Also, as the crisis deepens and the threat of panic sets in, the authorities will have to move beyond LOLR liquidity support to blanket deposit guarantees. Both the conversion of short-term LOLR assistance to longer term lending and payments made under official deposit guarantees will generate explicit fiscal costs for liquidity support.

(2) **Recapitalization.** The second broad function of intervention is the recapitalization of distressed or failed banks. This activity can generate fiscal costs through the direct government takeover of failed banks or the use of public funds to rehabilitate impaired assets—say, through their purchase and segregation in an asset management company (AMC)—in order to facilitate private recapitalizations.

(3) **Other costs.** Operating expenses, tax subsidies, and the costs of searching for private counterparties to restructure distressed banks will also generate budgetary costs.

Economic costs

The economic costs of intervention arise as increased moral hazard. This moral hazard reflects a higher propensity for participants who benefit directly or indirectly from intervention to engage in risky or uneconomic actions that increase the chance of future economic costs. Moral hazard can be further divided into short-term and long-term.

(1) **Short-term moral hazard.** Once the decision is made to provide liquidity support and stabilize the system against panic, the distortions resulting from existing distress generate further economic costs until that distress is eliminated. The speed with which resolution is effected is the chief determinant of these costs. A slow resolution strategy (which may be less costly in other dimensions), therefore, entails high short-term moral hazard costs.

(2) **Long-term moral hazard.** Long-term moral hazard refers to whatever economic costs, if any, may be generated by an increased incentive for risk taking in the post-crisis future. In post-crisis conditions, the banking

system will have been restored to health and does not suffer distorted incentives from continuing distress. The tendency toward increased risk taking in the long run arises from the government's revealed preference to intervene in a crisis situation. For some market participants, this willingness to intervene will reduce the risk perceived in some future states and will, therefore, encourage risk taking.

III. Intervention actions

Government intervention in cases of widespread insolvency of banks should be designed appropriately to achieve the following three economic objectives:[3] (a) restore the viability of the financial system as soon as possible so that it can mobilize and allocate funds. (This requires having in place a core banking system to preserve the integrity of the payments system, capture financial savings and ensure essential credit flows to the economy.); (b) provide an appropriate incentive structure throughout the restructuring process to ensure effectiveness and minimize moral hazard for all parties involved; and (c) minimize the cost to the government by managing the process efficiently and ensuring an appropriate burden-sharing.

This section gives an overview of the types of government interventions that have typically been undertaken in systemic banking crises in recent decades. It sets the stage for the next section which discusses the fiscal accounting for government intervention. The section discusses the interventions more or less chronologically, i.e., liquidity support, deposit guarantee, recapitalization and impaired asset management.

Liquidity support

Typically, liquidity support from the central bank to troubled financial institutions starts long before the systemic nature of a banking crisis has been recognized. When a bank, or several banks, start experiencing withdrawals from depositors and creditors (both domestic and foreign), and they cannot borrow directly, or only at high rates, from the interbank market, the central bank becomes their "last resort." Very often this is the first clear sign of distress in a bank.

To address the problem, central banks may in the initial stages be more prepared to ensure funding for the distressed bank(s) by channeling interbank funds to them. This approach would not commit the central bank's own resources and emphasizes the reliance on markets to solve the problem. This approach, however, might be unsuccessful because other banks could become unwilling to lend to troubled institutions, once the latter are known to be in such a state. In that case, recourse to the central bank is the only alternative for the troubled bank.

In principle, central banks should only support illiquid but still solvent banks. However, during the early stages of an unfolding crisis, it is often very difficult to distinguish illiquidity from insolvency. Very often, it turns out that banks resorting to the central bank for liquidity support have been insolvent for a while, without this being known. In theory, central bank loans should always be fully collateralized to avoid losses for the central bank. This is even more the case when a bank is suspected to be in a state of distress, even though in such a situation it may become increasingly difficult to identify good collateral. When a state of distress is discovered in a borrowing bank, the bank should be inspected and monitored closely and further borrowing from the central bank (under an emergency facility) should be subject to specific conditions, decided upon in consultation with the supervisors. Such conditions are needed to avoid the central bank lending to a "lost case" and, thus, incurring more and more losses.

Depending on the origin and type of the unfolding crisis, a central bank may be forced to provide support other than under its traditional mechanisms, such as overdraft loans to support the payments system, broad discounting of eligible paper, reduction of required reserves or foreign exchange loans to banks (Dziobek, 1998). To keep the system afloat, the central bank may also be forced to reschedule short-term loans into medium- or long-term obligations.

Deposit insurance and blanket guarantee

Once the true nature of the crisis has been identified and bank insolvency has been revealed as widespread, other instruments are needed to stabilize the system. Quite often, countries have established limited deposit insurance funds, but experience has proven that, when faced with a systemic crisis, limited deposit insurance schemes become inadequate to restore confidence. On the contrary, as was clearly indicated in the Indonesian case, they may aggravate the crisis.

What is needed in such cases is the announcement of full protection for depositors and (most) creditors. Such a blanket guarantee aims to stabilize the banks' funding and prevent, or stop, bank runs. As such, it is mainly a confidence booster. In addition, announcing a blanket guarantee buys the government time while the restructuring work is being organized and carried out. A blanket guarantee entails a firm commitment by the government to depositors and most creditors of financial institutions that their claims will be honored.[4]

By announcing a blanket guarantee the government acquires a very sizeable contingent liability against assets of uncertain value. These assets are very often insufficient to pay for the contingent liability that the government may be called to honor. Finally, a blanket guarantee is only able to stabilize the banking system's domestic funding. Other measures—some of them already listed above under liquidity support—may be needed to stop a flight from the currency, if that is also an issue.

Bank resolution

Once some initial stabilization of the banking system has been achieved through a combination of liquidity support, announcing the blanket guarantee and, perhaps, the closing of some nonviable financial institutions (to stop the drain on government resources), governments need to devise a bank-restructuring plan. While private sector involvement should be sought from the start—in particular if the private banking sector is significant—the nature of the crisis itself may make government intervention a necessity.

Government intervention broadly takes three forms: closure and liquidation of nonviable banks and recapitalization through capital injections or through rehabilitating the assets. Both recapitalization approaches can be used separately, depending on the particular condition a bank is in, but more often they are combined when rehabilitating an insolvent bank. Because the cost involved in closure and liquidation boils down to paying out the depositors and other creditors under the blanket guarantee, as discussed above, this intervention will not be further discussed here.

Recapitalization: capital injections

A discussion of intervention techniques with a view to determining their impact on the budget needs to discuss two aspects: the **resolution techniques** used by the government to arrive at a least cost solution (from the government's point of view) and the **financial instruments** used to recapitalize the banks.

A stylized presentation of resolution techniques—assuming there is a blanket guarantee—broadly yields the following options:[5] the failing bank can be nationalized, or the government can resolve the bank through a purchase and assumption operation or the use of a bridge bank. Each of these options involves varying degrees of capital injections by the government and the choice of the option should be based on the least cost principle. Typically in a systemic crisis, all three techniques will be used (in addition to closures), depending on the condition of the failing commercial bank.

Nationalization of a failing bank means that the government becomes the (main) owner of the insolvent bank and recapitalizes it. The use of the term here is different from the more traditional nationalization that refers to a situation wherein the government takes over a solvent bank. In a systemic crisis, the government's aim is usually to own the bank temporarily and to seek to privatize it at an early date.

A *purchase and assumption operation* (P&A) typically involves the purchase by a solvent bank of the good assets of a failing bank, including its customers' base and goodwill, as well as part or all of the liabilities.[6] In a government-supported P&A operation, the government typically will pay the purchasing bank the difference between the value of assets and liabilities. Often the bad assets are liquidated or transferred to an AMC.

A variation of a P&A involves the use of a temporary financial institution, *a bridge bank*, to receive the good assets of one or several failed institutions. A bridge bank is a type of P&A where the government (or the restructuring agency) itself temporarily acts as the acquirer until the time that the institution is ready for a sale. The bridge bank may be allowed to undertake all or only some banking business such as providing new credit and rolling over existing credit. Bad assets are liquidated or transferred to an AMC. If it is expected that the bridge bank will be sold quickly to a solvent bank, the government may opt not to inject any capital in the bridge bank, which makes the bridge bank arrangement potentially a cheap arrangement for the government.

Among the above options, the initial fiscal impact is highest under a nationalization. The government needs to recapitalize the bank, at least up to the minimum capital/asset requirement, and preferably even higher. A P&A requires typically less capital from the government, while a bridge bank arrangement can be run without capital injection. Of course, if the bad assets in all cases are not written off, but transferred to an AMC, other costs for the government are involved. The other side of the coin is that the government receives dividends from the nationalized banks and, later on if the nationalization is seen as temporary, the proceeds from privatizing the rehabilitated bank.

A variety of **financial instruments** can be used to recapitalize banks (Enoch and others, 1999). Providing Tier 1 and Tier 2 capital can be done through capital instruments (different types of shares, bonds) and at least two means of payments. The choice of instrument has an impact on the type of control the government will be able to exert in the bank taken over and the type of payment has an impact on the budget. *Payments in cash or through bonds* are common practices, depending on the instrument used.

Recapitalization: rehabilitating the assets

Recapitalization can also be done through purchasing and rehabilitating bank assets and facilitating debt workouts to assist banks. Rehabilitation of bank assets is a key aspect of bank restructuring. There are many variations for managing and disposing of impaired assets that not only have an impact on the recapitalization of the troubled banks, but on the entire restructuring process. Key decisions concern the speed of disposition of the impaired assets and the use of a centralized versus decentralized management framework.

Regarding the latter choice, some countries facing a systemic banking crisis have decided to leave the rehabilitation of assets to the markets, by forcing or encouraging through certain incentives, banks to establish their own AMCs. In this case, the government is not, or only marginally, involved in the process and does not use this policy as a recapitalization method. The cost to the government is limited to the incentives—if any—given to the banks to establish their own AMCs.

Quite often in a deep and widespread systemic crisis, in particular when a large number of public banks is among the troubled banks, the government may opt for the use of public, and most often, centralized AMCs. The use of this approach to rehabilitate assets goes hand in hand with techniques to recapitalize the troubled banks. Typically, the AMC will buy impaired assets from troubled banks in exchange for bonds or cash. The bonds could either be issued by the government directly or by the AMC, in which case they usually are government-guaranteed (Enoch and others, 1999). A critical factor in this operation, which has a bearing on the cost to the government, is proper valuation of the impaired assets. If assets sold to the AMC are overvalued, such an operation leads to a backdoor recapitalization.

Given the critical nature of the impaired asset rehabilitation process for the entire restructuring process, the approach chosen may have very different outcomes in terms of cost and benefits. The longer the asset rehabilitation process takes, the likelier it is that asset values depreciate further, ultimately resulting in situations were they cannot be sold any more.[7] The most important potential benefit to the government, and the restructuring process, resulting from the use of a public AMC is that the government gets more leverage over the troubled bank since it can impose conditions linked to its purchases of assets (and the concomitant recapitalization). The most significant disadvantage of a public AMC is that the assets tend to be parked in the AMC and continue to lose value, increasing the fiscal cost to the government.

Other intervention tools

Governments may resort to some other intervention tools to expedite the restructuring process and enhance its efficiency. Such tools are used in conjunction with other tools, described above. While some of these tools have no impact on the fiscal cost to be borne by the government, their advantage is often that they limit the need to activate the blanket guarantee if the weaker bank(s) would fail in the absence of the operation.

Mergers can be assisted or unassisted. In the unassisted merger, a weaker partner is merged with a stronger one and the involvement of the authorities is limited to bringing the parties together and overseeing the merger process. An assisted merger involves some type of financial assistance to the acquirer (or tax incentives) by the government. As such, there is a fiscal cost involved, similar to the one involved in recapitalizations, but at a smaller scale. The benefit of mergers (both types) is in avoiding potential failures of the weaker partner(s) involved in the deal and, therefore, potentially limiting the resort to the blanket deposit guarantee. However, if mergers are not implemented properly, and the resulting new institution turns out to be weak, more costs might be involved in the future.

Transfers of deposits. To assist troubled banks, the authorities may decide to transfer government deposits from sound banks to troubled banks. In principle, such an operation should be neutral in fiscal terms, unless the troubled bank offers a lower interest rate on those deposits, or, even worse, the weaker bank fails at a later stage.

Tax incentives are sometimes given temporarily to weaker banks or to acquiring banks (either under P&As, bridge banks or mergers) to facilitate the operation and the return to profitability. They result in forgone revenue for the government.

Forbearance. To assist troubled but viable banks in the rehabilitation process, authorities may give these banks time to meet new loan loss provisioning rules or new capital adequacy requirements. There is an ongoing debate about benefits and drawbacks of forbearance. The benefits attached to such policies—as long as they are conducted transparently—are that they allow the banks to operate temporarily under less stringent conditions and therefore allow a continuous flow of credit to the economy. In addition, forbearance may avoid bank failures and, thus, indirectly reduce the cost that would otherwise fall on the deposit insurance scheme. However, some studies point out that forbearance results in higher long-run resolution costs. The FDIC (1998) states, referring to the 1980s experience with the savings and loan industry, that forbearance without proper oversight can create the opportunity for further deterioration of financial institutions and result in increased resolution costs as operating costs accumulate, thus leading to higher intervention costs in the medium and long run.

State guarantees are often attached to specific operations of troubled banks to facilitate their "return to normal" and to avoid interruptions in the flows of credit to the economy. For instance in the Asian crisis countries, governments provided guarantees on credit to the export sector or to the small and medium-sized enterprise sector. While no direct fiscal cost is attached to such operations, these guarantees create a contingent liability to the government.

IV. Methodological issues of quantifying benefits and costs

The decision to intervene in a systemic banking crisis is taken because the government hopes that through its interventions the benefits listed in Section II will outweigh the costs resulting from the unfolding crisis and the ensuing restructuring. However, the measurement of several of these costs and benefits is an almost impossible task, making it in the end very difficult to state clearly by how much the benefits have outweighed the costs. Two relevant questions in this regard include: (a) what can governments *ex ante* reasonably know about costs and benefits when deciding to intervene? And (b) to what extent can *ex post* observations from other experiences be used to evaluate the decision to intervene?

Ex ante versus ex post issues

When taking the decision to intervene in a banking system hit by a crisis, it is very hard for the government to form a reasonable ex ante estimate of the benefits and the costs. The nature of the identification process of costs and benefits is very different. At the onset of the crisis, the **gross costs** are a given factor (deposits are being withdrawn and assets are losing value). However, their amounts are unknown (and still growing). During the crisis, governments can try to minimize the **net cost** by using the most appropriate intervention techniques (the difference between gross and net can be considered a measurable benefit from the intervention). Some of these costs are quantifiable as they enter the fiscal accounts. Other costs are harder to quantify (disruption of the payments system and of credit flows, loss of confidence in the banking system, deteriorating macroeconomic conditions), as discussed in Sections VI and VII. Benefits of intervention are of a different nature. Some are of an immediate nature, while others will only become apparent in the medium and long run. Immediate benefits of the intervention are very often of a counterfactual nature: preventing the system from deteriorating further, i.e., keep credit flows going, keep the payment system going, restore depositor confidence. Medium- and long-term benefits are mainly the emergence of a more efficient banking system.

Establishing ex ante estimates of costs and benefits is rendered difficult by the following factors:

- Experience has proven that it takes time for the government to recognize that there is a crisis and that this crisis is of a systemic nature.
- Once the systemic nature is recognized, it takes time to make an inventory of the problems, while at the same time the situation is most likely still deteriorating.
- The initial estimate of the size of the problem will, in the course of the restructuring process change (sometimes dramatically) as a result of factors that are under the government's control, but more importantly by factors that are not under the government's control.

Under the government's control are:

- The speed at which initial measures are taken (blanket guarantee, liquidation of nonviable banks).
- The speed at which a restructuring strategy is worked out.
- The types of resolution procedures use (recapitalization, impaired asset management).
- The measures taken to address the crisis in the corporate sector.

Factors that are not, or only marginally, under the government's control include:

- The impact of the macroeconomic environment. Will it further deteriorate or stabilize?
- The size of the corporate sector crisis. This factor, taken together with the first one, will determine if restructuring will go through cycles, i.e., that following any initial clean-up period, more nonperforming loans will show up on the books of the banks, further increasing the cost of the crisis.
- The market's reaction to the government's measures (blanket guarantee, bank liquidations).
- The market's willingness to participate in the restructuring process, i.e., the willingness of the private sector to assist in the recapitalization process and willingness of the foreign sector to participate. Availability of capital in the private domestic and foreign economy will determine to what extent the government may have to provide incentives to attract these sources of capital. This will also add to the cost for the government.

Taken together, these factors make it very difficult to get a reliable ex ante idea of costs and benefits from intervening in a systemic crisis. To underline this point, Table 2.1 provides a comparison for selected countries between the fiscal costs estimated at the beginning of the crisis and the most recent estimate. Such a comparison clearly indicates the shaky nature of any ex ante estimates. It should be noted that this comparison only covers measurable fiscal costs. Other costs and benefits are even harder to forecast and compare.

In the same vein, it is difficult to base the decision to intervene or not on any specific ex post observation. There is a general belief and understanding that government intervention in a systemic crisis in the end yields more benefits than costs, but the specific nature thereof varies greatly from country to country.

The very factors that were listed above appear in different intensities in crisis countries and, therefore, lead to different costs to the government. Table 2.1 also compares across countries the estimated fiscal cost of some major banking crises in the 1980s and 1990s and clearly points out how difficult it is to infer any reasonable estimate from previous crises.

Furthermore, benefits and costs will also depend on the type of intervention. For example, interventions can be proactive or not, broad-based versus specific, aggressive or deliberate, and can rely heavily on nationalization or not. In most of these scenarios, the decisive factor is the difference in cost needed to achieve the same nature of benefits.

Table 2.1.   Comparisons of Initial and Final Fiscal Costs of Bank Restructuring

Country	Initial Estimate	Latest Estimate (Chronologically)
Indonesia (1997–99)	29 (11/98)[a]	45 (authort.)[b]
		42 (2/99)[c]
		51 (mid-99)[d]
		45–80 (9/99)[e]
Korea (1997–99)	17.5 (11/98)[a]	15 (authort.)[b]
		10 (2/99)[c]
		13 (mid-99)[d]
		15–40 (9/99)[e]
Mexico (1994–97)	8.4 (1996)[f]	14
		12–15 (10/96)[e]
		21.3 (1999)[f]
Malaysia (1997–99)	18 (11/98)[a]	12 (authort.)[b]
		11 (2/99)[c]
		5 (3/99)[d]
Sweden (1991–93)	4.7 (1994)[a]	1.2 (1997)[h]
		4–5
Thailand (1997–99)	32 (11/98)[a]	25 (end-98)[d]
		26 (2/99)[c]
		35–45 (9/99)[e]
Chile (1981–85)		19–41
Finland (1991–93)	14.7 (1994)[g]	8–10
Colombia (1982–87)		5–6
United States (1980–92)	0.07 (1984)[i]	2.4 (1992)[i]

Note: Estimates refer to gross fiscal costs as a percentage of GDP.

a IMF Staff estimates of November 30, 1998, World Economic Outlook.
b Authorities' estimates for the gross cost of financial sector restructuring. Occasional Paper No. 188.
c Merrill Lynch, "Asia-Pacific Banks: Progress and Issues in Restructuring," February 23, 1999.
d "Financial Sector Crisis and Restructuring: Lessons from Asia," Occasional Paper No. 188, 1999.
e GAO "Actions Taken to reform Financial Sectors in Asian Emerging Markets," September 1999.
f Fernando Montes-Negret, World Bank, Second WB/IMF Financial Sector Liaison Committee Seminar, January 11, 2000.
g Bulletin of Bank of Finland, August 1994.
h In Sweden the majority of bank support has been recovered in proceeds through the sales of Nordbanken/Gota Bank, Securum and Retriva. As estimated by Ingves and Lind (1997), SKr 48 billion or 73.8 percent of original support were recovered. Note: since almost all support has been recovered, this may not be the best example to illustrate that costs are being underestimated at the onset of the crisis. Instead, we have included as a case of underestimation the U.S. thrift crisis.
i Congressional Budget Office, "Resolving the Thrift Crisis," April 1993.

Proactive interventions (interventions before a real crisis breaks) seem to have been rare so far. However, if intervention is planned when the first signs of distress are discovered, the cost of intervention could be reduced significantly, while the intervention strategy could yield the same benefits as when the intervention takes place in a full-blown crisis. Lower costs would come from lower fiscal costs (less liquidity support, no resort to blanket guarantee, lower recapitalization because erosion of the capital base is interrupted earlier in the process) and lower costs associated with no (or smaller) disruption of the payments system and of credit flows.

Broad-based interventions are often more costly than *specific ones*, but may reap more benefits because they aim at more thoroughly cleaning the banking system, allowing a more efficient system to operate after the crisis. Specific interventions may lead to situations where inefficient or loss-making institutions can continue to operate in the system, leading to new problems at a later stage. *Aggressive or quick* strategies may be more costly in the short term, but again, they may lead to reaping the benefits of the intervention more quickly because a well-operating core banking system may be put in place more quickly than in the case of an intervention that allows banks time to restructure. Finally, depending on the size and nature of the crisis, widespread *nationalizations* early in the crisis could be beneficial in that they help stop runs and, therefore, lead to a faster restoration of confidence in the system. However, the ultimate cost of interventions that rely heavily on nationalization depends on how well these nationalized institutions are managed and sold, once intervened.

Budgetary accounting

This subsection discusses issues in budgetary accounting for the intervention techniques, building on Section III. Depending on their nature, some costs are fiscal, others are quasi-fiscal. Table 2.2 presents an overview of their nature and the way they should be accounted.

Liquidity support is typically provided by the central bank. This, and the fact that it comes early in the unfolding crisis, often leads to situations wherein the quasi-fiscal costs attached to the support are not taken into account in the final calculation of the cost of the restructuring. It is only when this liquidity support is actually recognized by the government as part of the restructuring bill that it draws attention as a fiscal item. Sometimes the government issues bonds to compensate the central bank for its support (Indonesia, Thailand), or the support is converted into equity or subordinated debt.

The budgetary implications of central bank instruments used to support banks differ, depending on the type of instrument used (Dziobek and Pazarbasioglu, 1997). Normal central bank lending (i.e., at market conditions) has no fiscal impact in principle. However, if lending takes place at below market rates or if the central bank applies broader than normal principles of discounting, there will be an impact on central bank income, and profit remittances to the government budget will be smaller. In the same vein, if other measures are taken, such as a reduction of reserve requirements to assist commercial banks, profit remittances will be lower through the impact on central bank income. In the worst case, such measures might lead to central

Table 2.2. Government Intervention Techniques and Their Fiscal Implications

Intervention Technique	Fiscal Cost	Fiscal Revenue	Fiscal Treatment
Liquidity support			
Lender of last resort (different types)	As long as cost stays with the central bank (CB), it is a quasi-fiscal cost. As explained in text, most types of LOLR that do not meet market criteria result in CB lower income, thus lower profit remittances to the budget		Lower profit remittances are forgone revenue. If central bank lending is converted into government bonds: interest payments annually and repayment of bonds at maturity.
Deposit insurance			
Limited deposit insurance	N/A in systemic crisis		Depends on arrangement. If privately funded, no fiscal contribution. Government contribution can be in cash or bonds.
Blanket guarantee	Is a contingent liability initially. When called upon, will be direct fiscal cost (when financed from budget) or quasi-fiscal cost (when financed through the CB). Ultimately always budget.		Depends on arrangement. Cash, directly from the budget or bonds. If bonds are used, interest payments enter annual budget, repayments of bonds at maturity.
Recapitalization through capital injections			
Capital Injections (nationalization, bridge bank, P&A) bonds versus shares	Cash outlays from budget For bonds: interest and amortization	Dividends Proceeds from (re)privatization at a later stage	Cash payments: directly from budget. Bonds: see above. Dividends: nontax revenue.

Recapitalization through rehabilitation of assets

Rehabilitation of bank assets through private AMCs	If incentives are given to establish private AMC, this is a cost, depending on the type of incentive. If bonds are issued: interest and amortization costs	None	Depends on type of incentive (most often forgone revenue or subsidy). Bonds and interests: see above.
Rehabilitation of bank assets through public AMCs		Sales of impaired assets	Sales of impaired assets: capital revenue for government.
Other techniques			
Merger (assisted and unassisted)	Assisted merger may involve tax advantages.	May avoid resort to blanket guarantee if weaker institution had failed.	Forgone revenue in case of tax advantages.
Transfer of government deposits	If new bank offers lower interest rates, there is forgone revenue for the government.	Same	Forgone revenue in some cases
Tax incentives			Forgone tax revenue
Forbearance		May avoid resort to blanket guarantee if weaker institution had failed. Or lower recapitalization costs for government.	
State guarantee	Is contingent liability		
Operational costs (operation of institutions such as BRA, AMC, asset valuation, experts)			Current government expenditures (operations and maintenance).
Others costs (macrocost from credit crunch, greater interest spreads)			

bank losses. If central banks provide foreign currency loans to commercial banks, central bank international reserves fall and so will the bank's income from capital.

Very often, faced with a systemic crisis, governments and central banks have no time to organize themselves properly to tackle the crisis. In such cases—as was seen in the Asian crisis—central bank liquidity is the main source of funds to the system in the initial stages. In Indonesia and Thailand, formal arrangements were worked out later, whereby the government compensated the central bank for any losses it had incurred while providing liquidity support to the system. As such, the issuance of government bonds to the central bank replaces the quasi-fiscal cost by an explicit fiscal cost. When central bank lending is converted into equity or subordinated debt, central bank income also falls and so do profit remittances to the budget.

Blanket guarantees. It is possible that blanket guarantees, mainly being confidence boosters, are not called upon. In other words, it is possible that the mere announcement of such guarantees suffices to stop bank runs and restore confidence in the banking system. However, if called upon, the affected banks' assets will most likely not be sufficient to pay for the contingent liability that the government may need to honor. So, the fiscal implications of the blanket guarantee may be significant. The guarantee can either be financed directly from the budget or through the central bank. In the latter case, the central bank would give a long-term loan to the agency in charge of the restructuring, and the government would guarantee this loan and pay the interest and amortization through the budget. While the direct fiscal cost of giving a blanket guarantee might be considerable, this cost might in the end be lower than the potential economic and social cost of a complete collapse of the banking system.[8]

Recapitalization. Capital injections and rehabilitation through purchases of impaired assets. The fiscal impact of straight capital injections depends on the methods and means of payment used. If government bonds are used, the fiscal accounts will reflect interest payments and, later on upon maturity, amortization. If payment in cash is used, the ways the recapitalization enters the fiscal accounts depends on the origin of the cash. Japan, for instance, has issued government bonds to fund the cash injections; Malaysia has used the proceeds from the sale of impaired assets as cash injection; Thailand converted LOLR support into equity in intervened banks; in Chile, the central bank issued central bank bills to replace nonperforming assets in the banks' balance sheets; and in still other countries, the government borrowed from the central bank.

The net fiscal cost of recapitalization will most likely be lower because, in the case of equity holding by the government, the payment of dividends to the government provides a flow of income. However, this flow comes later in the process when banks start to become profitable again. In addition, privatization of the nationalized banks will reduce the net cost of the operation significantly, and may even yield a profit to the government.

Government support through the **purchase of impaired assets** mainly takes place through the issuance of government bonds, or government-guaranteed bonds to replace the nonperforming assets in the books of the banks. Impaired assets can either be bought at book value or at market value. When buying impaired assets at book value, the operation amounts to a back-door recapitalization of the problem bank. Buying at market prices gives an incentive to the problem bank to continue the recovery efforts of its assets and to the AMC to sell the acquired assets at a better price, thus realizing a profit. The net cost/benefit of the operation depends in the end on the government's ability to sell the impaired assets (through the AMC).

In some countries (Chile, for example) assistance to banks took place through the issuance of central bank bills (long-term paper) in exchange for nonperforming loans. The impact on the budget of such operations comes through a fall in the asset quality and in the earnings of the central bank, leading to lower profit remittances to the government.

State guarantees on bank credits, like deposit guarantees represent a contingent liability for the budget. **Tax incentives** represent forgone revenue for the government. **Forbearance**, finally, should have no direct fiscal impact, but could have a medium- or long-term impact in the form of higher resolution costs later. Such costs of a prolonged or recurring crisis would be accounted for under one of the categories listed here.

Other costs that need to be taken into account and that have an impact on the budget include the salaries of experts hired to assist the government in addressing the crisis, the hiring of accounting firms to audit the troubled banks and to value bank assets, the hiring of experts (firms) to manage impaired assets and to prepare banks for sale. If central banks are involved in the restructuring process, their administrative costs will increase, since they will need experts to handle parts of the process.

V. The evolution of a banking crisis

This section develops an analysis of the nature of a banking crisis and how it will evolve with and without intervention actions. This analysis builds a conceptual basis for the formulation and estimation of the benefits and costs of intervening.

Shock and distress

Banking system distress can be characterized by varying degrees of severity. Systemic distress is not a simple concept but has several interrelated features, the most important of which are the extent of asset value loss, the extent of insolvency, and the risk of a liquidity panic. A stylized version of the structure and evolution of banking system distress that integrates these features and sheds some light on intervention strategy is presented in Figure 2.1.

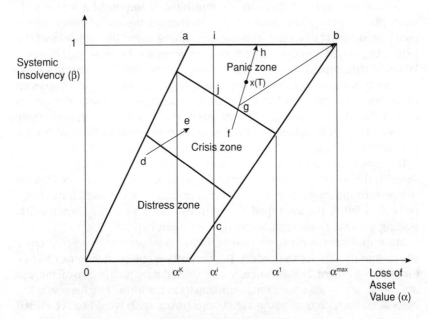

Figure 2.1. Structure and Evolution of a Banking Crisis

The axes represent two key characteristics of banking system distress, loss of asset value and the degree of systemic insolvency. The fall in assets, α, is measured by the ratio decline in the value of preshock assets

$$(1) \quad \alpha = 1 - A/A(0),$$

where A is the current book value of banking system assets and A(0) is the preshock level, valued at point 0. The maximum loss reached when all system assets must be liquidated is

$$(2) \quad \alpha^{max} = 1 - A(\mathbf{b})/A(0),$$

where A(**b**) is the liquidation value.

The degree of systemic insolvency, β, is measured by the share of the booked value of banking system assets held by insolvent banks

$$(3) \quad \beta = A_I/A,$$

where A_I is the volume of assets held by insolvent institutions.

A loss in asset value of a given size can be associated with varying degrees of systemic insolvency, depending on how that loss is distributed across the banking system. The line **0a** represents the maximum degree of insolvency for each level of loss in aggregate banking system assets. Similarly, the line $\alpha^K b$ represents the minimum degree of systemic insolvency corresponding to any loss of asset value. When the asset loss exceeds α^K, the aggregate precrisis capital of the banking system, some institutions must be insolvent. Minimum levels of systemic insolvency increase with asset loss along the line $\alpha^K b$, until the maximum degree of asset loss, α^{max}, is reached. The area $0ab\alpha^K$, then, gives the set of feasible outcomes (α, β) that characterize conditions of banking system distress.[9]

Starting from a given point in the feasible set, systemic distress will increase along any path that moves upward and to the right. As systemic distress increases, it is reasonable to think that liquidity problems among banks will become generally more widespread. At some point, the combination of banking system distress and emergent liquidity problems becomes so pervasive that the system reaches a state characterized by the prospect of qualitatively different behavior that can be categorized as a crisis rather than just general distress. A crisis, then, represents an advanced state of systemic distress combined with the prospect of systemic illiquidity.

When all banks in the system are insolvent, represented by outcomes on the line **ab**, risk-neutral depositors will have an incentive to panic. In that case, each depositor will realize that every bank lacks sufficient funds to meet all of its potential deposit withdrawals. Since banks meet deposit withdrawals on a first-come-first-serve basis, each depositor has an incentive to withdraw funds immediately, creating panic.

Risk-averse depositors, however, can panic even when $\beta < 1$. Some banks may not be insolvent but asset losses may be so great that depositors view the risk of systemic insolvency as unacceptably high. At any given level of systemic insolvency, higher levels of asset loss will raise the risk of additional insolvencies. Therefore, if depositors are risk-averse, there will be a larger set of points (α, β) that will induce panic than those lying on line **ab**. This set is labeled "Panic zone" in Figure 2.1. In this zone, every bank in the system can experience a run regardless of its capital condition, unless there is some guarantee on deposit values.

The beginning of an episode of banking system distress can be viewed as drawing an initial point (α, β) from the feasible set, which represents the initial shock. This initial shock may arise in two broad ways. First, there may be relatively abrupt changes in economic or financial conditions that negatively impact bank asset values, such as the onset of recession or a collapse in real estate values. This type of shock emerges from an actual change in the state of the world.[10] Second, there may be a relatively sudden realization of changes in the condition of the banking system that have built up gradually over time. Typically, this kind of shock represents an accounting event, such as the discovery of hidden fraud or of "evergreening," throwing good money after bad by propping up nonperforming loans through new credits. Also, a change in accounting rules that causes previously hidden shortfalls, such as losses on a securities portfolio or accumulated losses on subsidized lending to state-owned enterprises, to be marked to market or otherwise shown more transparently in the accounting information set can be the trigger for a crisis.

The initial shock that generates systemic distress will affect banks differently. How the banking system will evolve depends on the specific conditions created by the initial shock. Of particular importance is how asset losses are distributed across banks. The distribution of initial losses will determine the capital conditions of banks in the system. The capital condition of banks, in turn, will have a large effect on their liquidity condition and their risk behavior. These conditions together will affect the evolution of the system in the absence of official intervention. A detailed discussion of how conditions of distress generate distortions in bank behavior is presented in Appendix 2.I.

Factors causing increased distress

A distressed banking system is in a pathological condition. Banks that are knocked out of a healthy condition of capital adequacy and normal liquidity (classified as Class 1 banks in Appendix 2.I) by an initial shock face distorted incentives that lead to further expected deterioration in the state of the banking system unless the authorities intervene to resolve the problem. This further deterioration arises for several reasons:

(1) *Distortions that produce inefficient lending.* Banking system distress can produce inefficiencies in bank lending. These inefficiencies can be manifested in two broad ways: through excessive risk-taking, which will threaten to worsen bank asset losses, or through a "credit crunch," which will aggravate the economic costs of the crisis for business borrowers and further weaken bank loan quality.

   (a) *Risk taking.* Low net worth and insolvent banks have an incentive to "gamble for resurrection," that is, to take risky positions with low probabilities of large payoffs but negative expected returns, in order to try to recover from insolvency before being forced into closure. The illiquid condition of these banks will, of course, limit the extent of risk-taking in which they can engage, but will not prevent it. This risk-taking will manifest itself in many different ways, e.g., through taking off-balance sheet positions, mismatching maturities and currencies, or extending risky loans. It is likely that risk-taking banks will direct new loans to borrowers who were excluded in precrisis conditions, because they will offer the largest (but riskiest) potential payoffs, rather than to less risky borrowers that have been shut out by risk-averse banks after the initial shock, even if the latter offer a positive expected return.

(b)   Credit rationing. Relatively strong banks that have experienced some asset loss but are not near insolvency will become risk-averse. If they have slipped below regulatory minimum capital ratios, they will be reluctant to add to risk assets, even as they obtain inflows of funds, until they have rebuilt their capital ratios. In this regard, even if they are receiving inflows of funds as the counterparts to illiquid banks that are experiencing deposit withdrawals, they will not necessarily provide sufficient demand for assets or extend sufficient new loans to offset the negative effects of asset sales and loan liquidations by illiquid banks. If the initial shock is severe and pervasive enough that there are no Class 1 banks, no liquid institutions will be inclined to extend credit to borrowers who were squeezed by risk-averse banks. A consequence of this restriction of the supply of credit is that some previously creditworthy borrowers will be rationed out of the market—a credit crunch. So, a banking crisis can exhibit both credit crunch conditions and excessive risk taking simultaneously.

(2)   **Illiquidity.** Low net worth and insolvent banks will experience liquidity pressures that drive them to sell assets and liquidate loans, resulting in depressed asset prices and economic activity.

(3)   **Rise in risk premium.** A banking crisis can produce a loss of confidence among investors in the ability of the country to conduct a suitable macroeconomic policy. This loss of confidence, together with a general uncertainty about the full dimensions of the crisis that will exist until it is more clearly resolved, will work to raise the country risk premium. This increase in the risk premium is likely to be embedded in the borrowing costs for all classes of borrowers—banks, businesses, and government—not just in bank loans but in international and other domestic financial markets as well. Furthermore, this rise in the risk premium can spread credit crunch behavior even to healthy banks.

A credit crunch provoked by a banking crisis, then, develops along two dimensions. First, it is driven by the interaction of capital deficiency, distorted incentives and illiquidity. Second, even healthy banks may ration credit if the increased risk premium drives interest rate levels up to so high a level that the risk concerns of adverse selection—only impetuous or untrustworthy borrowers are willing to pay the prevailing rates—dominate the higher returns.

(4)   **Contagion.** The increases in uncertainty and risk premiums, the assets sales by illiquid banks, and the credit rationing by risk-averse and other banks associated with a banking crisis can disrupt the liquidity of financial markets, weaken the economy, and spread a broader contagion affecting other financial institutions. Public debt markets and the cost of issuing

domestic public debt may be adversely affected. Failures may result among other highly leveraged institutions, and derivatives transactions can extend the losses more broadly through the financial sector.

For these reasons, banking system distress will be expected to worsen after the initial shock if no intervention actions are taken to mitigate the problem. For example, in Figure 2.1, if point **d** represents the condition of the banking system after the initial shock, the system will experience over time an expected deterioration along the path **de** in the absence of intervention actions. Of course, all participants—the authorities, banks, customers, depositors—will have only uncertain expectations about the magnitude and direction of the path **de** and about how fast conditions will deteriorate.[11]

States of the system

Keeping that point in mind, we can make certain useful distinctions about different states of banking system distress. All of the initial starting points (α, β) that will eventually deteriorate into the panic zone if no intervention steps are taken are labeled "Crisis zone" in Figure 2.1. Starting from an initial point, **f**, in the crisis zone, the banking system would deteriorate without intervention along the expected path **fh**. The evolution of the system would not reach point **h**, however. At point **g** where it crosses into the panic zone, the system would shift to path **gb**, characterized by very rapid deterioration because of panic withdrawals of deposits and culminating in total liquidation of the banking system.

All other initial points that do not deteriorate into the panic zone are labeled "Distress zone."[12] Starting from point **d** in the distress zone, the system will, without intervention, cross into the crisis zone and reach the end point **e**. It will not deteriorate further, however, because the factors driving the deterioration will have burned out. For example, although risk-taking banks initially tend to go deeper into insolvency, they will eventually become bankrupt and be liquidated, ending their capacity to do further damage. Low levels of asset loss and insolvency, then, may produce conditions of distress that generate further deterioration, but not to levels sufficient to provoke systemic disintegration. Crisis distress and noncrisis distress evolve in much the same way, but crisis distress reaches a state advanced enough to trigger panic.

Depositor behavior and attendant bank liquidity problems differ in degree among the three zones and will be managed in different ways. In the distress zone, liquidity problems are most likely to be sporadic and limited to name problems for individual institutions. They can usually be managed through the normal functioning of an interbank market or through the extension of LOLR credit to individual banks in need.

In the crisis zone, liquidity problems are likely to be more extensive and may affect entire classes of banking institutions that are viewed as being especially impacted by the nature of the initial crisis shocks. Depositors will exhibit widespread "flight to quality" behavior and severe tiering may occur in the interbank market, with the classes of banks having problems being shut out from access to funds. These conditions will require interventions that go beyond ordinary LOLR actions. The central bank may have to inject general liquidity into the market and may have to organize "lifeboat"-style concerted lending to compensate for the seizing up in the interbank market.

Deposit guarantees to stop panic

Liquidity conditions in the panic zone are qualitatively worse. In the crisis zone, even though conditions are characterized by a pervasive flight to quality, funds still remain in the banking system and there is no damage to the payments system. Not so in the panic zone, where depositors are withdrawing funds from all banks, threatening an implosion of the stock of deposits and a collapse of the payments system.[13] These conditions cannot be easily managed by LOLR interventions. Central banks are generally heavily constrained from making direct loans to insolvent banks and insolvencies are widespread in the panic zone. While general liquidity support through massive open market operations (if the central bank has such capability) can mitigate the monetary contraction arising from depositor panic, it cannot readily restore confidence in the banking system and stanch the outflow of deposits and the resulting losses from forced asset liquidations and payments system disruption. The authorities are most likely in this situation to resort to granting emergency universal deposit guarantees to stabilize deposits.[14] Such guarantees are typically temporary but the conditions under which they will be removed are left unspecified at the time that they are granted.

In the context of Figure 2.1, a universal deposit guarantee means that the banking system will not shift onto path **gb** as it passes into the panic zone but will, rather, follow along the path **fh**. In other words, the guarantee neutralizes the system against the effects of passing into the panic zone.

Such neutralization comes at a cost, however. Guarantees enhance the level of moral hazard in the system. Low net worth and insolvent banks that have an incentive to take on more uneconomic risk will be less constrained by liquidity problems and will take on risk faster. The system will move more rapidly along the path **fh** once guarantees have been issued.[15] This development represents a problem of short-term moral hazard. It creates an incentive for the authorities to take quick action to resolve the crisis and prevent deterioration. On balance, deposit guarantees buy time for the authorities to take appropriate and value-conserving interventions to deal with the damage to the banking system by forestalling the threat of complete meltdown in a panic. However, deposit guarantees will tend to accelerate the actual rate of deterioration in the banking system by worsening the problem of short-term moral hazard before interventions are undertaken to relieve distress.

Another aspect of risk related to granting deposit guarantees can arise. The authorities may have information regarding the initial shock that allows them to form an expectation of α, the size of the asset loss, before they have information on β, the degree of systemic insolvency, or other conditions of banks in the system. Take the expected loss of asset value to be α^i in Figure 2.1. If $\alpha^k < \alpha^i < \alpha^l$, there is a probability, but not a certainty, that an asset loss of that size will lead to panic.[16] The authorities must decide on incomplete information whether to grant a guarantee. Suppose they do and conditions turn out to place the system in the distress zone at α^i. This action would increase the short-term and long-term moral hazard of dealing with the system's distress. On the other hand, not granting the guarantee could result in panic.

Resolving distress

After dealing with the threat of an incipient panic, the authorities must resolve the conditions of distress that generate short-term moral hazard, that is, they must take steps to stop the system's deterioration along path **fh**. This deterioration stems from (1) credit crunch effects arising from risk aversion created by capital deficiencies and general uncertainty; (2) the risk taking of insolvent and low net worth banks; and (3) the economic burden of a higher risk premium, which is itself generated by systemic insolvency and capital inadequacy.

A direct approach to overcoming credit crunch effects is to quickly restore the capital position of risk-averse banks. Encouragement for recapitalization through directions and incentives to retain earnings and issue new equity is one option. Temporary relaxation of capital requirements is another route, but this could have further negative effects on the country's risk premium and thereby produce additional self-defeating credit crunch effects. Finally, the authorities may use monetary or fiscal policy to try to offset the economic consequences of the credit crunch.

Shutting down the risk taking of insolvent and low net worth banks will require action to put the institutions under some form of conservatorship that will be charged with protecting asset values. The capacity for this kind of intervention will typically not exist and will have to be developed, which will be costly. The more quickly this step can be taken, however, the sooner deterioration can be slowed.

Restoration of a normal risk premium will usually depend on resolution of systemic distress. Achieving this outcome will involve a sequence of actions. The following steps make up a prototypical sequence. First, the bank restructuring authorities must pay a monitoring cost to determine which institutions have a positive franchise value. Those without a positive franchise value will be liquidated, which will generate costs for paying out on guaranteed deposits in excess of liquidated assets. Then, the authorities will seek to arrange private restructurings or mergers for banks with positive franchise values. This stage may entail search costs, as well as tax incentives or other implicit or explicit subsidies, such as temporary relaxation of various banking regulations. The impaired assets of such banks will often be transferred to a public AMC, which will also require a payout. Last, banks with positive franchise value that cannot be privately recapitalized or merged will be recapitalized with public funds with the aim of future reprivatization. In the long run, the authorities may realize cost offsets through recoveries on impaired assets or profits on reprivatizations.

Long-term consequences

There are also long-run consequences of intervention actions that will have their effect beyond the time horizon in which the bank crisis is resolved. Two types of these consequences are worth noting: long-term moral hazard and the efficient structure of the banking system.

(1) ***Long-term moral hazard.*** Interventions that contain some element of subsidy, notably granting deposit guarantees, will change the future direction of bank risk taking even after the episode of crisis is concluded and the emergency guarantees are removed. Under limited liability, bank equity holders, who typically control the decision on bank asset risk profiles in normal times, have an incentive to take on more risk than depositors prefer. Depositors can limit this risk taking by incorporating a risk premium into the return on deposits, if they have information on the risks that banks are assuming. However, if the government is willing to provide guarantees on deposits in certain states of the world, such as during a banking crisis, depositors will require a somewhat lower risk premium, since any risks that banks assume that result in those states being realized will not harm depositors.

Emergency guarantees, in contrast to a permanent system of universal deposit insurance, provide protection only in some states of the world when there is a state of systemic crisis. Therefore, an individual bank will still face the prospect of a rising risk premium on its deposits if it increases its idiosyncratic risk. This condition creates an incentive for different banks to take on risk in ways that are positively correlated, since such action increases the conditional probability that if a bad outcome occurs for an individual bank, it will be perceived by the government as part of a systemic problem. Granting emergency universal guarantees creates an incentive for the banking system to take on higher risk in the form of risks that are positively correlated across banks—for example, all banks increasing their lending to the real estate sector. Positively correlated risk taking, however, increases the risk of another systemic crisis, since it eliminates diversification benefits in the total banking system portfolio in the case of a negative exogenous shock. In this sense, granting emergency universal guarantees creates a perverse moral hazard incentive.

(2) *Efficient structure.* Intervention to stabilize the banking system in a crisis and conduct orderly resolution of problem banks can have the additional benefit of producing an efficiently restructured banking system at lower cost than will a disorderly liquidation. Both liquidation through panic and a more orderly resolution will remove badly mismanaged and truly insolvent banks and replace them, in the long run, with investments in new banks that have an efficient structure. However, a disorderly liquidation will require a more expensive investment to restore an efficient banking system structure, since it will also eliminate all well-managed banks with a positive franchise value. Orderly resolution procedures allow restructuring plans for these institutions and, hence, keep them intact.

VI. Accounting the economic benefits and costs of intervention

An accounting of the general economic costs and benefits of intervening in a banking crisis can be developed in terms of the conceptual framework discussed in Section V. Benefits and costs first must be allocated across time; future benefits and costs will be discounted to a present value. We make a distinction between the short run and the long run, demarcating the separation by T_E, the anticipated end date for the crisis when resolution actions are completed. There are, then, three time periods to consider: the immediate present ($t = T_0$), the short run ($T_0 < t \leq T_E$), and the long run ($t > T_E$).

Assume that the anticipation that T_E is the end of the crisis is realized. This assumption imposes a consistency that is often elusive in practice between ex ante plans, which are relevant to cost-benefit calculation, and ex post outcomes, which are the accounting data. The discussion will not deal with the complications that arise from revising intervention strategies.

Let $x(T)$ be a point on line **fh** in Figure 2.1 that represents the state of maximum distress reached during the resolution period. This state depends on the choice of $T (= T_E - T_0)$, the horizon of the resolution plan.[17] The authorities will choose T to maximize the net economic benefits of the resolution of the crisis. This choice involves a balancing of factors. The greater is T, the longer is the time available for negative influences, such as short-term moral hazard, to weaken the economy. On the other hand, shortening T will push the intervention strategy toward greater reliance on costlier techniques, such as liquidation, and away from time-intensive but less fiscally costly options, such as private recapitalization or merger. It will be most convenient to think of $x(T)$ as lying between **g** and **h** on **fh**, so that crossing into the panic zone could not be reasonably avoided. (Interpreting the immediate present to be the period before any resolution actions can be taken, the transition of the system from point **f** to point **g** will occur immediately.) The authorities, then, face a choice between an intervention strategy that includes granting a guarantee or not intervening.

Benefits of a deposit guarantee

The economic benefits of intervening can be defined in terms of economic costs that are avoided from letting a crisis run its course. These benefits can be divided into those arising from granting the deposit guarantee and those stemming from resolution actions. The benefits of granting the guarantee are the avoided costs of panic. We take these costs to be given by the condition of moving from point **g** to point **b** in Figure 2.1. The costs of panic are valued at point **b** and at $t = T_0$, because no intervention actions apart from a deposit guarantee can forestall these costs once point **g** is reached and because they proceed rapidly. These benefits are summarized in Table 2.3.

Avoiding liquidation of assets

The costs of panic can be classified into those caused by liquidation of bank assets and those arising from the disruption to the payments system. Liquidated bank assets are of two relevant types: marketable assets and nonmarketable assets, notably loans.

Marketable assets

Marketable assets—securities, commodities, real estate, etc.—are liquidated under duress at "fire-sale" prices. These depressed prices reflect the banking system's lost capacity to generate effective demand for the assets. The loss to the banking system is the difference in the bank value of marketable assets (their market value before liquidation) and the liquidation value of the assets (their market value at fire-sale prices). Other holders of these assets will suffer the induced market price decline on their holdings as well.

The wealth loss arising from fire sales is not permanent. In the long run, with the banking system reconstituted and its capacity to generate effective demand restored, asset prices will return to the preliquidation levels determined by long-term fundamentals. The avoided loss from fire-sale liquidation of marketable assets held by the banking system can be expressed as the difference between the undiscounted value of the immediate avoided loss and the discounted future value of the reversal of the loss:

$$(1 - \delta(t > T_E))N(M(\mathbf{g}) - M(\mathbf{b})), \ N > 1$$

where $M(\mathbf{g})$ is the value of banking system marketable assets at the crossover point **g** before the fire sale and $M(\mathbf{b})$ is the liquidation value. The total wealth loss is a multiple, N, of the banking system's loss.

Table 2.3. Economic Benefits of Intervening in a Banking Crisis

	Immediate ($t = T_0$)	Short run ($T_0 < t \leq T_E$)	Long run ($t > T_E$)
Benefits			
Deposit guarantee			
(1) Avoided liquidation of banking system assets			
(a) marketable assets	$N(M(g) - M(b))$		$\delta(t > T_E)N(M(g) - M(b))$
(b) nonmarketable assets	$A_C(g) - A_C(b)$	$\delta(T_0 < t < R_E)\lambda[(A_C(g) - A_C(b)) - (L(g) - L(b))]$	
(2) Avoided disruption to payments system	$[\mu(D(g) - A(b)) + vA(b)]$		$\delta(t > T_E)[\mu(D(g) - A(b)) + vA(b)]$
Resolution actions			
(1) Profit on asset disposition			$\delta(t > T_E)A_A(\rho(g))$
(2) Profit on reprivatization			$\delta(t > T_E)A_E(\rho(g))$
(3) Efficient restructuring			$(\gamma\delta(t > T_E)(A(0) - A_L(0))$

Nonmarketable assets

Costs related to the liquidation of nonmarketable loans can be more extensive. The analog to fire-sale liquidation of marketable assets is acceleration of the loan, which may lead to possible foreclosure and borrower bankruptcy. In any case, this step will result in the liquidation of underlying collateral, which will disrupt the economic activity that the loan finances. For example, bank loans may be collateralized by the capital equipment of the projects that they finance. At times this capital equipment is highly customized to the production processes of the borrowing firm and will not have an appreciable resale value.

Even when the liquidation value of the underlying collateral covers the value of the loan to the bank, the borrower will still suffer some loss of equity from the forced liquidation of the investment project. The losses in borrowing company equity value and in bank loan value that occur are permanent losses of a stream of future income. Moreover, other resources, especially labor, used in the liquidated projects may also have specific qualities that make their prompt reemployment difficult. So the forced liquidation of loans may generate a recessionary rise in unemployment that represents an additional, although temporary, economic cost.

The total benefits of the deposit guarantee arising from the avoided liquidation of bank assets are given by the sum of the permanent wealth loss and the recessionary effect of the forced liquidation of loans. The permanent wealth loss is equal to the liquidation loss on assets of companies in the business sector, given by $A_C(\mathbf{g}) - A_C(\mathbf{b})$, where A_C represents the asset values in the business sector, which are the underlying collateral on bank loans. These liquidation losses are spread among equity holders of the business sector, equity holders of the banking sector, and bank depositors, depending on, among other things, the degrees of leverage in the business and banking sectors.

The recessionary loss is assumed to be proportional to the wealth loss in the business sector. Since this amount equals the total wealth loss minus the liquidation loss on bank loans, the recessionary loss equals

$$\delta(T_0 < t < R_E)\lambda[(A_C(\mathbf{g}) - A_C(\mathbf{b})) - (L(\mathbf{g}) - L(\mathbf{b}))], \qquad \lambda > 0$$

where $L(\mathbf{g})$ and $L(\mathbf{b})$ are the values of banking system loans at the crossover point $\mathbf{g}$, and the liquidation point, $\mathbf{b}$, respectively, with 8 representing a proportionality factor that incorporates recessionary effects. The expression $\delta(T_0 < t \leq R_E)$, represents discounting terms applied to the costs at various times during the intervention period (see Table 2.3). These effects are discounted since they arise temporarily over the short run, although over a horizon, $R(= R_E - T_0)$, that may differ from T, the horizon of the resolution plan. The loss from forced liquidation of assets is valued from $\mathbf{g}$, the point of crossover into the panic zone. The deterioration from **f** to **g** is assumed to be unavoidable and is treated as occurring in the immediate period.

Avoiding disruption to the payments system

A separate benefit of granting a deposit guarantee is avoiding disruption to the payments system. This benefit is an independent factor from the avoided wealth loss arising from the forced liquidation of assets. The destruction of deposits that occurs in a panic is costly over and above the wealth loss because it destroys the medium of exchange as well. In addition, the flight to currency during the panic will also reduce the transactional efficiency of the medium of exchange, which is assumed to be, per unit of currency, a less damaging disruption than the destruction of deposits. The costs associated with these disruptions can be formalized as being roughly proportional to the deposit loss and the deposit shift:

$$\mu(D(\mathbf{g}) - A(\mathbf{b})) + \text{<}A(\mathbf{b}), \qquad \mu > \mu > 0$$

where $(D(\mathbf{g}) - A(\mathbf{b}))$ is the deposit loss from asset liquidation and $A(\mathbf{b})$ is the amount of deposits converted to currency, equal to the liquidation value of assets. Banks can only pay out the liquidation value of their assets against deposits valued at the beginning of the panic. Systemic costs may be limited by the extent of state-owned bank deposits, which may be more stable because of an implicit official guarantee.

Like the costs from marketable asset liquidation, the costs from disruption of the payments system are not permanent and will be reversed when the banking system is reconstituted in the long run. The net economic cost, then, of payments system disruption is:

$$(1 - \delta(t > T_E))(\mu(D(\mathbf{g}) - A(\mathbf{b})) + \mu A(\mathbf{b})).$$

Long-term benefits from efficient restructuring

In the absence of intervention, all banks are driven to insolvency and forced into liquidation. In the long run, the banking system will be reconstituted. Assume that it is reconstituted at its precrisis capacity. Similarly, after intervention is completed, the banking system will be reconstituted at precrisis capacity. However, the costs differ in the two cases.

Assume that the organizational set-up costs for *de novo* banks in the reconstituted system are proportional to the precrisis level of assets (the measure of capacity) held by banks liquidated during the crisis.[18] Without intervention, all banks wind up liquidated and set-up costs are proportional to systemic precrisis assets, $A(\mathbf{0})$. Under intervention, however, only the class of insolvent banks without a positive franchise value, designated C_L, is liquidated. Set-up costs in this case are proportional to the precrisis assets of that smaller set of liquidated banks, $A_L(0)$. The benefits of efficient restructuring, then, are given by:

$$(\delta(t > T_E)(A(0) - A_L(0))).$$

Fiscal-related costs

Deposit guarantee

The short-term economic costs of a deposit guarantee depend on the fiscal costs that are actually generated. These fiscal costs, in turn, depend on resolution actions that determine which banks are actually closed under orderly liquidation procedures that require a payment to depositors on the guarantee. All intervened banks that are liquidated are in C_L, representing the set of insolvent banks without a positive franchise value. The present value of the economic cost of the payment on the guarantee is given by

$$\theta\delta(T_0 < t \leq T_E)\underset{C_L}{\Sigma}(D(\mathbf{g}) - A[\mathbf{g}, \mathbf{x}(T)]), \qquad \theta > 0$$

where $D(\mathbf{g})$ is deposit value at the beginning of intervention and $A[\mathbf{g}, \mathbf{x}(T)]$ is realized values on assets between points $\mathbf{g}$ and $\mathbf{x}(T)$ for banks in C_L. The parameter θ represents the economic cost to the government of distributing losses from depositors to taxpayers. Its role is discussed in more detail later.

Resolution actions

Resolution actions generate fiscal and fiscal-related costs and moral hazard costs. Some economic costs associated with resolution actions must be accounted at their full fiscal cost, because they would not have occurred if intervention had not been undertaken. Basically, these items represent kinds of operating costs, of which two are particularly important—monitoring and search costs.

Monitoring costs

The resolution authorities must pay a monitoring cost to determine which insolvent banks have a positive franchise value. These costs, mC_I, are expended immediately and are fixed per institution at m, so that total monitoring costs depend only on the number of banks in C_I. Monitoring information allows the authorities to separate the banks into those that have a positive franchise value (C_{I+}) and those that do not (C_L). Banks in C_L are liquidated in an orderly manner and funds are paid out to depositors under the guarantee.

Search costs

For low net worth banks and insolvent banks with a positive franchise value—$C_4 + C_{5+}$, according to the categories established in Appendix 2.I—the

Table 2.4. Table 2.4. Economic Costs of Intervening in a Banking Crisis

	Intermediate (t = T_0)	Short Run ($T_0 < t \leq T_E$)	Long Run (t > T_E)
Costs			
Deposit guarantee			
(1) Fiscal-related		$\theta\delta(T_0 < t \leq T_E) \sum_{C_{L-}} (D(\mathbf{g}) - A[\mathbf{g}, x(T)])$	
(2) Long-term moral hazard			$\delta(t > T_E) \int_T^\infty [y(r_1, \omega(p_1), t) - y(r_0, \omega(p_0), t)]dt$
Resolution actions			
(1) Fiscal-related			
(a) monitoring costs	mC_1		
(b) search costs			
(c) support for private restructuring		$\delta(T_0 < t \leq T_E)(\Psi(\mathbf{g}) \sum_{C_P} A[\mathbf{g}, x(T)] + \theta \sum_{C_P \cap C_{I+}} (D(\mathbf{g}) - A[\mathbf{g}, x(T)]))$	
(d) temporary public recapitalization		$\delta(T_0 < t \leq T_E) \sum_{C_N} A(0) - A[\mathbf{g}, x(T)])$	
(2) Short-term moral hazard		$\delta(T_0 < t \leq T_E) \int_0^T \int_{f(z)=0} Y'(Z)dZ\, dt$	

authorities will search for private investors who will recapitalize or merge with the banks. Total costs associated with these searches, $s(\sigma, C_4 + C_{5+}, T)$ arise over the short run. They depend positively on each of the following: (1) σ, a government decision parameter that represents the total search cost per bank per time period, a measure of the intensity of the search effort; $C_4 + C_{5+}$, the total number of banks that are private restructuring candidates; and T, the time horizon of the resolution strategy.

The search will reveal a subset of $C_4 + C_{5+}$ for which private restructuring— recapitalization or merger—will occur. Let C_P represent this subset. The remainder of these intervened banks, C_G, will be recapitalized by the government to be reprivatized after the crisis has been resolved. Assume that the fraction of banks that is recapitalized by the government, n, depends on the value of the country risk premium, ρ, at the start of intervention; on search intensity, σ; and on T:

$$(4)\ C_G = n(\rho(\mathbf{g}), \sigma, T)\ (C_4 + C_{5+}).$$

C_G rises with $\rho(\mathbf{g})$; the higher is $\rho(\mathbf{g})$, the more reluctant are private investors to commit to a restructuring for a given set of incentives. C_G, of course, falls when more funds are expended on searching and when a longer time is taken for searching.

Support for private restructuring
To facilitate the private restructuring of banks in C_P, the government may have to segregate some assets. This action will generally generate further fiscal costs. For example, the government can purchase these assets at a "fair" value to be placed in an AMC for future disposition. Let $\Psi(\mathbf{g})$ represent the share of assets in C_P transferred to the government over the intervention period. For simplicity, assume that the government sets the criteria for Ψ on the basis of conditions at the beginning of intervention. The higher the level of the risk premium, the greater the amount of impaired assets with uncertain value that will have to be "cleaned up" before private capital will commit to restructuring. The present value of the cost of these asset transfers is

$$\delta(T_0 < t \le T_E)\Psi(\mathbf{g}) \sum_{Cp} A[\mathbf{g}, \mathbf{x}(T)].$$

Since the government enters into a bilateral negotiation with the banks about the terms of the transfer, the government can set the price at which it purchases the assets. If asset prices depend on the value of the risk premium, the government, then, has two options.

First, it can value the assets at the expected restored normal risk premium at the conclusion of the crisis, which is equivalent to the precrisis risk premium, $\rho(0)$. This valuation will appear beneficial to the private sector, which values assets at $\rho(\mathbf{g})$, the crisis risk premium, which is higher than $\rho(0)$.

This difference in valuations arises because the government is certain at the start of its intervention that it will take actions to resolve the banking crisis, while the private sector is not. In this case, the price at which the government purchases assets generates no expected long-term economic profits and will, therefore, induce relatively high short-term private sector involvement in restructuring. The government will expect to realize an accounting profit in the long run that covers the time value of money and a capital charge, so that the appropriately discounted expected value of assets disposed in the long run will equal the discounted expected value of assets transferred in the short run. The government will prefer this option if it has a strong priority to put restructured banks into private hands quickly in order to avoid the complications of operating them.

Alternatively, the government can set a price that incorporates the risk premium $\rho(g)$, which will allow the government to acquire assets at the prevailing market values and to maximize its expected economic profit on their disposition. Of course, the government can price assets somewhere in between these two values.

We assume that the government will purchase assets at prevailing market values to generate an expected economic profit and will accept the reduction in the amount of proposals for private restructurings that this action produces. The government will need a margin of expected profit to provide incentives for asset managers to get the best value. The expected profit on asset disposition is indicated in Table 2.3 by $\Pi_A(\rho(g))$.

For privately recapitalized banks that are technically insolvent, the government must provide additional funds to cover the hole between the value of assets and the value of guaranteed deposits. The economic cost of that payment is

$$\theta\delta(T_0 < t \le T_E) \sum_{C_P \cap C_{I+}} (D(g) - A[g, x(T)]),$$

where C_{I+} is the subset of C_{5+} that consists of technically insolvent banks. Note that the fiscal cost of covering the hole in asset value is multiplied by the distributional parameter θ. In the absence of private recapitalization of insolvent banks, the banks would be liquidated and the government would pay this amount of funds out under the deposit guarantee.

Temporary public recapitalization
Banks in C_G will be recapitalized by the government for future reprivatization. Assume that banks are recapitalized to a level, $A(0)$, that would sustain precrisis assets in compliance with capital standards. Discounted public outlays for recapitalization during the intervention period are

$$\delta(T_0 < t \le T_E) \sum_{C_G} (A(0) - A[g, x(T)]).$$

As with the case of asset transfers, the government can expect to receive an economic profit, indicated in Table 2.3 as $\pi_E(\rho(\mathbf{g}))$, that depends on the value of the crisis risk premium, which determines the value of assets. In the long run, with ρ at precrisis levels, government-owned banks will realize capital gains on assets and a rise in equity values that can be captured by reprivatization.

Fiscal cost versus economic cost

The economic cost of the deposit guarantee is different from the fiscal cost. The loss represented by the payments on deposit guarantees has already occurred before any payments are made and must be borne by some group, either depositors or taxpayers through the government. If the government were indifferent between these two groups, there would be no economic cost to the payout on the guarantee. But the government is not indifferent. The economic cost to the government, then, is given by the term θ. This term is positive since payouts, which effectively transfer the burden to taxpayers, are assumed to be more costly than losses borne by depositors because the government gives priority to the protection of taxpayer interests.[19] Governments grant depositor guarantees, therefore, not because they value depositor gains more highly than taxpayer gains, but in order to avoid the economic costs of depositor panic.

A similar premium does not apply to other disbursements of government money in interventions. Monitoring and search costs are not realized if the government does not take intervention actions. Public funds used to purchase and segregate impaired assets or to recapitalize banks represent new investment choices. The net return (or loss) on the face value of these investments is an accurate measure of the economic benefit (or cost).

Short-term moral hazard

Another kind of cost associated with crisis intervention has already been alluded to and can be characterized as short-term moral hazard. Essentially, it represents the deterioration in income that results from the persistence of banking system distress. Even if banking system distress does not increase, economic costs will increase from the initial level of distress as time passes until resolution is completed. So this cost must be aggregated over both time and conditions in the banking system. This moral hazard cost (MHC) is given by

$$\delta(T_0 < t \le T_E) \int_{T_0}^{T_E} \int_{f(z)=0} Y'(\mathbf{Z})d\mathbf{Z}dt,$$

where $\mathbf{Z} = (\alpha, \beta, \rho(\alpha, \beta))$ is a vector of the factors arising from the conditions of distress in the banking system that generate economic costs: as in Figure 2.1, α is the aggregate loss in banking system asset value; $\beta = (\beta_1, \ldots \beta_n)$ is a vector of the distress conditions in the banking system, with each β_i equal to the share of banking system assets held by banks in distress class i;[20] and $\rho(\alpha, \beta)$ is the risk premium induced by banking system distress.

The relation $f(Z) = 0$ implicitly defines the path of evolution of banking system conditions through the crisis and its resolution. Starting from point **g** in Figure 2.1, conditions will deteriorate to a point of maximum distress, $x(T)$, and then follow some path back to normality, represented by point **0**, when the banking system is reconstituted at the end of the resolution period. The authorities can minimize this cost, and search costs as well, by being very aggressive in their intervention strategy and setting T close at a low value. But that choice will maximize liquidations of banks and payouts to depositors, which may not be the efficient choice.

Long-term moral hazard

As discussed earlier, granting a guarantee can change incentives for future actions on the part of banks and depositors. More precisely, the degree of future risk taking that banks undertake depends on their expectation of government intervention in future crises. If the outcome of the government's decision whether to grant the guarantee or not is expected, no new moral hazard effects are generated. If the outcome is unexpected, future risk taking changes. In either case, the government will have to take account of what future risk taking will be in light of its decision.

The natural assumption is that market participants expect the authorities to issue a guarantee to forestall a panic; this action has typically been the actual choice of governments that have found their banking systems in extreme jeopardy. The discussion in this chapter, however, has used the case of no intervention as the baseline for discussing benefits and costs. By making no intervention the baseline expectation, the chapter will refer to the moral hazard costs of intervention rather than the moral hazard benefits of no intervention.

The essential element of long-term moral hazard is this: emergency deposit guarantees shift banks toward increased risk taking because the guarantees protect depositors in certain conditions, namely, a systemic crisis, and thereby lessen any discipline depositors may exert on bank decisions. It is unclear, however, whether this shift toward increased risk taking will have an economic cost.

To see this point, consider a simple comparison. Assume that the baseline case of no deposit guarantees is associated with a particular future path of economic growth. This outcome would occur if the availability of banking finance is actually a binding constraint on the development of some economic assets. Assume also that the shift to increased risk taking produced by the moral hazard of granting a deposit guarantee is manifested as recurrent episodes of temporary shortfalls from baseline growth—recessions caused by recurrent banking crises. The greater the degree of moral hazard, the greater is the frequency of these recurrent crises.

If the growth path that incorporates the moral hazard effects is no higher than the baseline path, then the riskier path clearly has a lower present value in terms of current income and moral hazard is costly. If, however, the higher risk assets that banks finance under moral hazard also generate a higher expected return, then the present value outcome of the change in future growth paths is unclear. In light of this ignorance, the government can reasonably take the expected value of the economic cost of long-term moral hazard to be zero and can neglect it as a factor in its decision regarding the granting of a deposit guarantee.

Formally, the cost (benefit) of long-term moral hazard can be represented as

$$\delta(t > T_E) \int_T^\infty [y(r_1, \omega(p_1), t) - y(r_0, \omega(p_0), t)] dt,$$

which is the discounted value of the difference in the growth paths with (subscript 1) and without (subscript 0) the deposit guarantee. The path of y depends on time; on r, the growth rate of potential output; and on ω, a process that generates recurrent crisis episodes of shortfall from the potential output growth path. The process ω, depends on p, the probability of a banking crisis, with a higher probability producing more frequent and, possibly, larger crises. The moral hazard of granting a deposit guarantee implies that $p_1 > p_0$. But if $r_1 > r_0$, the value of the moral hazard term may be a positive net benefit.

When will $r_1 > r_0$? If the banking system in its precrisis risk-normal[21] condition was truly risk-neutral, it financed assets in priority of their expected returns only, regardless of their riskiness. In order to take on more risk, then, in light of the moral hazard of the deposit guarantee, the banking system in the future would have to adopt a risk-taking bias. To achieve this state, the banking system would have to switch into some lower yield but higher risk assets, which would actually reduce the potential growth path that it finances.

If, however, the banking system in its precrisis risk-normal condition was risk-averse, it could shift into riskier assets that also produce a higher yield, since not all high yield assets would have already been incorporated into the baseline growth path. As a consequence, r_1 could exceed r_0 and the net economic effect of moral hazard would be uncertain. It is not unreasonable to think that some degree of risk aversion, rather than strict risk neutrality, characterizes the risk-normal condition of the banking system. If so, the government would be justified in ignoring long-term moral hazard effects, since it could not form a clear expectation of the direction of these effects in terms of economic costs.

The government's decision process

The government's problem in intervening in a banking crisis is to maximize net benefits by choosing values of the policy variables that it controls. A crisis is defined so that intervention requires issuing a deposit guarantee followed by actions to resolve distress among capital-deficient and insolvent banks. Not intervening entails not issuing a deposit guarantee and allowing a panic to run its course.

The infrequency of proactive resolution

The alternative of taking actions to resolve distressed banks without issuing a deposit guarantee represents a strategy of proactive intervention under noncrisis conditions. Since such a proactive strategy would reduce economic losses and forestall distress from growing, possibly to the point of even threatening panic, it is somewhat puzzling why many countries have been reluctant to intervene against banking problems short of a crisis. The framework suggests two possible explanations: limited short-term moral hazard costs and myopic government.

Limited short-term moral hazard costs

The government may perceive short-term moral hazard costs as not rising indefinitely. Failing to intervene proactively will allow moral hazard costs to run up to their maximum but will save on fiscal costs. If the ex ante probability of panic is very low—making the expected benefits of avoiding panic negligible—and θ is very high, the net benefits of intervening can be negative and less than the costs of not intervening to resolve distress. Only when distress has reached a point at which the expected benefits of panic avoidance become significant is the government willing to grant a guarantee. Granting the guarantee works to increase the moral hazard costs of delaying resolution, so the government then has a greater incentive to eliminate distress. Therefore, if moral hazard costs do not rise indefinitely with time, a government may not be motivated to take resolution actions to eliminate distress until conditions have deteriorated substantially.

A government behaves in this fashion when it is surprised by moral hazard costs of inaction that turn out to be higher than it had first suspected. This outcome can result when it is hard to know the maximum level of moral hazard costs with precision. On the other hand, some governments could be expected to overestimate the maximum level of moral hazard costs, leading them to take prompt actions to relieve distress. The nature of the actions that governments take to relieve high levels of distress, however, may differ qualitatively from those undertaken at low levels of distress. Specifically, at low levels of distress, governments may have more options to induce rehabilitative actions through "quiet" interventions, such as moral suasion, supervisory pressure, tax breaks, etc. These actions may result in weak banks rebuilding capital or becoming acquisition targets of stronger banks. The government's intervention may be hard for outsiders to observe and the resolution of distress will look like unassisted private actions. At high levels of distress, government intervention actions are more constrained and require overt commitments of public funds that are easy to observe. So, the apparent asymmetry in government behavior that produces the noticed infrequency of proactive intervention is rooted in an asymmetry in observation.

Myopic government

Another potential explanation of why, in the absence of crisis, the perceived net benefit of resolution actions is not positive may rest on myopia in the government's perspective. This outcome could arise if the government—or, at least, that part of the government that must commit resources to the resolution of banking distress—is myopic in the sense that it seeks to avoid only those costs that appear as fiscal costs on its own account, not as economic costs in the general economy. A myopic government would ignore the prospective costs of banking distress, including potential losses in deposit values. However, when distress is great enough to produce a threshold probability of panic, the government will issue a blanket deposit guarantee to stabilize the situation. Under the guarantee, the government internalizes the costs of potential deposit loss and is motivated to act to eliminate the distress that produces those costs. In sum, the government may have little incentive in a precrisis situation to combat banking distress until, in a crisis, the deposit guarantee is switched on, generating a direct financial exposure.

Why would a myopic government ever issue a deposit guarantee? Although the economic costs of forced asset liquidation in a panic are qualitatively similar to those arising from bank runs in a noncrisis situation, one feature of a panic is qualitatively different: the disruption to the payments system. So long as a significant portion of the banking system remains viable, the payments system can function. When the level of systemic distress is high enough, however, all banks, regardless of financial condition, are subject to runs and the payments system collapses. This collapse can impose unique costs on the government, for example, by disrupting the efficient collection of taxes, that distress short of panic does not generate. As a consequence, the government will issue a guarantee only in crisis when the threat of panic is sufficiently high. This step internalizes for the government the prospective costs of banking distress and motivates it to take resolution actions.

Policy choices

While limited moral hazard costs or myopia may explain the infrequency of proactive resolution actions, this chapter presents a normative decision rule under which the government rationally considers the economic costs to the entire society when calculating the net benefits of banking sector intervention. In the decision-making framework of this chapter, the government controls three kinds of policy variables:

(1)   *The criteria on which it is willing to purchase impaired assets from banks that are candidates for private restructuring.* These criteria include the kinds

of assets that the government is willing to purchase—say, impaired assets as indicated by some degree of supervisory classification—and the price at which it will purchase. The broader the range of assets that the government is willing to purchase and the higher the purchase price, the more willing will investors be to undertake private restructurings of banks.[22]

(2) *The intensity of the search effort for private investors who will carry out private restructurings.* This effort consists of making inquiries in different markets about potential investor interest in mergers or restructurings. More funds expended on searching are likely to produce a higher volume of private restructurings, thereby saving on other public funds used for recapitalization.

(3) *The length of the resolution effort.* The principal policy choice for the government is the length of the intervention effort, T. This can be viewed as the decision to pursue either an aggressive or a deliberate resolution strategy. An aggressive strategy—a short length—will economize on short-term moral hazard costs but will reduce the efficiency of the search for private investors, leading to a relatively high level of bank liquidations and payouts on deposit guarantees. A more deliberate strategy has converse effects. The government will choose a value of T that minimizes the total of fiscal-related and economic costs.[23]

A "quick and dirty" method

A short-cut procedure for assessing the benefits and costs of actions to deal with a banking crisis can be developed along the lines of the framework presented above. This approach focuses on a general relation between an aggregate measure of the severity of the banking crisis and some measure of the overall macroeconomic costs that are avoided through intervention actions.

As noted earlier, resolution costs, as they appear in the fiscal accounts of the government, are not typically an accurate representation of the underlying economic costs of intervening in a banking crisis. A "rational" government, which would seek to minimize total economic costs, would recognize losses that had already occurred. A deposit guarantee transfers these losses from depositors to taxpayers but does not increase their size.[24]

The economic cost of redistribution under a deposit guarantee will be some proportion, θ, of the face value of the fiscal costs of the guarantee. This proportion will depend on a complex of factors, including the tax burden on taxpayers, the debt-servicing burden on the government, the share of guaranteed deposits held by individuals, etc. However, it is reasonable to assume that, other things equal, the government will place a premium on the use of public funds in order to protect taxpayer interests. As a consequence, we assume $\theta > 0$.

A first approximation of additional economic costs is to add to fiscal costs an estimate of the economic growth shortfall that arises from the distressed condition of the banking system—essentially, short-term moral hazard costs. These costs, as a fraction of GDP, grow with delay in taking intervention actions and, therefore, depend on the length of the intervention period, T:[25]

$$(5)\ MHC = kTY,$$

where Y is the level of GDP at the start of the crisis and k is the annual economic shortfall represented as a fraction of GDP.

Total costs of intervening in a banking crisis (C), then, are the sum of the economic burden generated by fiscal costs and short-term moral hazard costs:

$$(6)\ C = \theta FC + MHC.$$

A simple specification of the benefits of intervening is given by the expected avoided costs of a banking panic, represented by the probability of panic at the start of the crisis multiplied by an overall measure of panic costs. The avoided costs of panic are a measure of a counterfactual outcome and are, therefore, unobservable except in the case where panic is actually allowed to happen. Such cases are sporadic and it is even arguable that there are no clear examples at all of a full-scale panic allowed to run its course without some kind of intervention, at least in recent history.

A simple rough estimate of panic costs can be made by extrapolating to the whole banking system the experience of asset loss for individual banks that suffered runs.[26] An estimate of the panic loss as a percentage of assets, represented by α, an observed loss in asset value for individual banks experiencing forced liquidations, which we set at .33. Expected panic costs, C^P, then, are given by .33A, where A is the value of banking system assets, measured by loans to businesses at the start of the crisis.

The net benefits of intervention are:

$$(7)\ NB = pC^P - \theta FC - kTY.$$

Drawing on an estimate of the average economic costs of delaying resolution action based on a cross-section of banking crises,[27] we set k = .007. Ex ante fiscal costs are measured by their realized outcome taken at face value ($\theta = 1$).

To make this simple rule-of-thumb formula applicable to our case study, we insert variable values that correspond to the Swedish banking crisis. We date the Swedish crisis at 1991-Q1 to 1993-Q4; so T = 2.25. The value of A is given by the 1991-Q3 amount of banking system loans to business, Swedish kronor (SKr) 484 billion. This estimate underestimates the base of banking system assets subject to liquidation in a panic since it ignores the fire-sale liquidation of marketable assets. Fiscal costs are taken as the undiscounted sum of funds expended over the crisis period, SKr 64 billion, which exaggerates net fiscal costs by ignoring discounting and not taking account of offsets, such as gains from reprivatization. Base year (1991) GDP, Y, is SKr 1447 billion. At these values net benefits are given by

$$(8) \quad NB = .33 \times p \times 484 - 64 - .007 \times 2.25 \times 1447 = 160p - 87.$$

This calculation (which should be viewed as a high-end estimate of the break-even probability of panic) implies that the net benefits of intervention in the Swedish case were positive if $p > .54$, or if the odds of panic were roughly even.

VII. Quantification of economic benefits and costs

The next step in making the cost-benefit framework operational is to specify constructive procedures that produce reasonable estimates of the analytical concepts of benefits and costs using readily available data. These procedures are detailed in Appendix 2.II.

Benefits of intervention

Avoided costs of liquidation of marketable assets

Under panic conditions, the banking system is forced to dump its holdings of marketable assets. Assume that this fire sale immediately depresses asset prices to a new equilibrium.

Figure 2.2 illustrates the case. Forced liquidation by banks during a panic depresses the demand curve for marketable assets from **DD** to **D'D'**. Demand for marketable assets falls by $Q_0 - Q_1 = M(\mathbf{g})$, the level of the banking system's holdings at the start of the crisis. This decline depresses the equilibrium price level immediately to P_1 so that asset holders experience a wealth loss equal to $(P_0 - P_1)Q_0$. Since the percentage change in quantity demanded is fixed at the banking system's share of the market, the percentage change in asset prices and the wealth loss can be calculated if the price elasticity of demand is known.

Avoided costs of liquidation of nonmarketable assets

The economic cost of the liquidation of nonmarketable assets reflects the disruption of productive economic activities caused by banks canceling or accelerating loans and forcing the liquidation of underlying collateral. This disruption can result in a permanent loss of wealth from abandoned projects together with the temporary recessionary cost generated by displacing workers. The wealth loss unfolds from destruction of asset values in the company sector. This loss, $A_C(\mathbf{g}) - A_C(\mathbf{b})$, where A_C represents assets in the

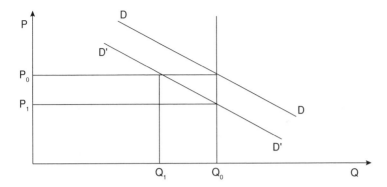

Figure 2.2.   Fire Sale of Marketable Assets by Banks

company sector, will be distributed among company equity holders and company debt holders, whom we take to be banks. The losses borne by banks are, in turn, distributed among bank equity holders and bank debtors, especially depositors.

The disruption of the combination of specific capital, knowledge and skills in the liquidated investments represents a permanent loss of wealth. Businesses must liquidate an amount sufficient to cover their bank loans: $L(\mathbf{g}) = (1-\Lambda)X(\mathbf{g})$, where Λ is the liquidation loss rate and $X(\mathbf{g})$ is the book value of the amount of liquidated assets. The loss in asset value, then, is given by

$$(9)\ A_C(\mathbf{g}) - A_C(\mathbf{b}) = L(\mathbf{g})/(1-\Lambda) - L(\mathbf{g}) = \Lambda L(\mathbf{g})/(1-\Lambda).$$

To get the liquidation losses on bank loans, first assume as a simplification that company sector borrowing from banks is subordinate to all debt owed to nonbanks and that the latter is included in company sector capital. Furthermore, note that for firms that cannot cover their loan values

$$(10)\ L(\mathbf{b}) = A_C(\mathbf{b}) = (1-\Lambda)A_C(\mathbf{g}).$$

In other words, the liquidation value on bank loans, $L(\mathbf{b})$, is just the liquidation value on the underlying collateral, $A_C(\mathbf{b})$, which is less than the book value of the loan. If it is possible to calculate this loss separately for each firm on the basis of individual balance sheet data, the total losses to banks on their loans will be given by the summation of losses across individual businesses, designated by the subscript i:

$$(11)\ L(\mathbf{g}) - L(\mathbf{b}) = \Sigma \text{Max}[0, L_i(\mathbf{g}) - (1-\Lambda)A_{C,\,i}(\mathbf{g})] = \Sigma \text{Max}[0, (k_i + \Lambda - 1)\,A_{C,\,i}(\mathbf{g})],$$

where $k_i = L_i(g)/AC_{,i}(g)$ is the (bank) debt/asset leverage ratio for a business. Firms for which the leverage ratio and the liquidation loss rate exceed unity ($ki+\Lambda>1$) will be liquidated into bankruptcy and will generate losses on their bank loans.

In addition to these permanent losses of asset value, there will be a temporary recessionary loss because workers displaced from liquidated investment projects will typically not be immediately reemployed. Assume that the economic loss from this recession is proportional to the loss in business sector capital, a measure of the size of the negative shock from banking sector panic that hits the business sector. This recessionary loss, then, can be expressed as

$$\delta(T_0 < t \le R_E)\lambda[(A_C(g) - A_C(b)) - (L(g) - L(b))],$$

where λ is the proportionality factor and R ($= R_E - T_0$) is the length of the recession, which may differ from T, the length of the period for intervention actions.

The parameter λ can be proxied by (the inverse of) a marginal capital–output ratio from a production (input–output) relation. The recession length, R, can be taken as the historical average length and a prototypical dynamic pattern over time can be imposed. For example, recessionary effects can be assumed to build steadily to a maximum at R/2 and then to decline.

Avoided disruption to the payments system

As discussed earlier, these avoided costs can be divided into those that arise from loss of deposits and those that arise from the forced holding of currency as the medium of exchange and can be expressed as

$$\delta(T_0 < t \le T_E)[(\mu D(g) - A(b)) + vA(b)].$$

D(g), deposits at the start of the crisis, are observable. The liquidation value of banking system assets, A(b), is equal to the observable precrisis level, A(g), less liquidation losses on marketable and nonmarketable assets:

$$(12) \quad A(b) = A(g) - \varepsilon M(g) - \Sigma Max[0, L_i(g) - (1-\Lambda)A_{C,i}(g)].$$

The parameter μ reflects the output loss stemming from the deposit loss with wealth held constant. Wealth effects are accounted for in the avoided losses of asset values. The loss that arises from the destruction of deposits here is a "pure" payments system effect. This effect is related to the role that bank deposits play as the medium of exchange in the modern economy. In that regard, deposits have the character of an "input" into aggregate production. Consequently, μ can be proxied by the estimated coefficient that captures the effect on output of money balances in an aggregate production function.

The parameter v reflects the loss that arises from economic agents being forced to hold the medium of exchange as currency rather than as bank deposits. It is legitimate to say that economic participants are forced into this state, since they must take this action to preserve the value of their monetary assets under the extreme condition of panic. The economic loss imposed by this condition can then be estimated as the loss of consumer surplus from a quantitative restriction—to hold more currency than desired. The loss from this restriction can be estimated as an area under a demand curve, similar to techniques used in international trade studies to estimate the loss from imposition of a quota.

Profit on asset disposition and reprivatization
Any expected profit to the government from the disposition of acquired assets and the reprivatization of publicly recapitalized banks is a benefit of intervention, or, more precisely, an offset to its costs. Since the government will recapitalize banks and acquire the assets of the banks at the depressed values that prevail during the crisis, it can have a rational expectation of profit on these transactions. This expectation is based on the asymmetry of knowledge between the market and the government about actions to resolve the crisis. The market's expectation of a continued unresolved crisis is priced into the risk premium on bank assets. The government knows that it will take steps to resolve the crisis, which will restore a normal risk premium and allow it to realize increased value on any assets that it acquires.

The expected profit to the authorities on reprivatization of public recapitalization of banks is given by the expected capital gain on equity. If equity is treated as an investment of infinite duration, the expected percentage capital gain, dP/P, can be approximated by the change in interest rates implied by the restoration of the normal risk premium, which is

$$(13)\ dP/P = -\rho(\mathbf{g})/(r(0) + \rho(\mathbf{g}))$$

where $r(0)$ is the precrisis interest rate (incorporating the precrisis risk premium) and $\rho(\mathbf{g})$ is the observable risk premium at the start of the crisis. The expected capital gain to the government is

$$(14)\ \delta(t > T_E)\Pi_E(\rho(\mathbf{g})) = \delta(t > T_E)[-\rho(\mathbf{g})/(r(0) + \rho(\mathbf{g}))] \times \sum_{C_G} (A(0) - A[\mathbf{g}, x(T)]),$$

where the last term is the amount of public equity put into the banking system.

The expected profit on asset disposition depends on the duration of purchased assets, $Dur(A(\mathbf{g}))$ and the expected change in interest rates, which is given by the elimination of the crisis risk premium, $\rho(\mathbf{g})$. The change in interest rates, then, is

$$(15) \; \Delta r = -\rho(\mathbf{g}).$$

The corresponding present value of the expected gain on asset disposition is

$$\delta(t > T_E) \Psi(\mathbf{g}) \sum_{C_P} A[\mathbf{g}, \mathbf{x}(T)] \times Dur(A(\mathbf{g})) \times (-\rho(\mathbf{g})).$$

Efficient restructuring

This benefit, expressed as

$$(\gamma \delta(t > T_E)(A(0) - A_L(0)),$$

represents the avoided set-up costs of reconstituting an entirely liquidated banking system. The parameter γ is a fraction of the assets of the banks that avoid unnecessary liquidation. This fraction will be reported to the authorities by their investment bankers and is, therefore, predetermined. As a first practical cut, we will take it to be roughly equivalent to an investment banking fee.

Costs of intervention

Fiscal-related costs

Deposit guarantees
Fiscal-related costs associated with a deposit guarantee arise when funds have to be paid out to depositors. This payout occurs when insolvent banks are liquidated. The undiscounted dollar amount of the payout is given by

$$\sum_{C_L} (D(\mathbf{g}) - A[\mathbf{g}, \mathbf{x}(T)]).$$

The average asset value over the intervention period, $A[\mathbf{g}, \mathbf{x}(T)]$, can be set equal to a fraction of the asset value at the beginning of the period:

$$(16) \; A[\mathbf{g}, \mathbf{x}(T)] = d \times A(\mathbf{g}),$$

where d is an estimate of the average rate of deterioration in asset value during the crisis period. With d known, the payout amount is known after monitoring that identifies the set of insolvent banks to be liquidated, C_L.

The value of d will depend on the rate of deterioration of banking system assets that results from delaying resolution actions. Frydl (1999) reports an estimate from a cross-section of banking crises based on Caprio and Klingebiel (1996) that the fiscal costs of crisis resolution rise by 0.8 percent of GDP per year of resolution horizon length. Assuming that assets deteriorate to the same extent resolution costs rise, this estimate will generate a rate of asset loss from which d can be constructed as a geometric mean:

$$(17) \quad d = (\prod_{i=1}^{T} (0.92)^i)^{1/T}.$$

The economic cost of the deposit guarantee is given by the discounted payout multiplied by θ, which represents the economic cost to the government of distributing losses from depositors to taxpayers. This parameter is difficult to estimate. If the government considers both groups equivalent, θ will be near zero and there will be few economic costs that arise from the fiscal costs of intervention. Since θ is likely to increase directly with both the tax burden, τ, and the government's debt burden, which is related to the future tax burden, a simple-minded approximation is to set $\theta = (\tau + i) / Y$, where i is government interest payments and Y is GDP.

Other fiscal-related costs

(1) *Monitoring costs*: Total monitoring costs (mCI) are predetermined. The number of intervened banks to be monitored, C_I, is known and the per bank fee is set by the auditors.
(2) *Search costs*: Search costs, $\delta(T_0 < t \leq T_E)s(\sigma, (C_4 + C_{5+}), T)$, reflect the effort that the government engages in to find private investors to restructure banks. They are determined by the government's own policy decisions. The terms σ and T are choice variables for the authorities. The authorities' investment bank will provide a schedule based on market knowledge linking σ, a measure of the intensity of the search effort for private investors, and T, the length of the resolution period, with n, the fraction of banks that has to be recapitalized by the government. The authorities will choose the values of σ and T that maximize net benefits. This choice, in turn, determines n, the fraction of banks with positive franchise value recapitalized by the government, and C_G and C_P, the number of such banks publicly recapitalized and privately restructured, respectively.
(3) *Support for private restructuring*: The economic cost generated by the fiscal costs of support for private restructuring is given by

$$\delta(T_0 < t \leq T_E)(\Psi(\mathbf{g}) \underset{C_P}{\Sigma} A[\mathbf{g}, \, x(T)] + \theta \underset{C_P \cap C_{I+}}{\Sigma} (D(\mathbf{g}) - A[\mathbf{g}, \, x(T)])).$$

As a first approximation, Ψ—the fraction of assets of privately restructured banks that is purchased by the government in order to facilitate the restructuring—can be taken to be the fraction of bank assets at the start of the crisis that are subject to some degree of supervisory classification. The second term in the expression represents the economic cost of payments to fill the hole in the net worth of insolvent but privately restructured banks. This amount is multiplied by θ since it is equivalent to a payout under a deposit guarantee.

(4) *Temporary public recapitalization*: The amount of funds expected to be committed to public recapitalization of banks, given by

$$\delta(T_0 < t \leq T_E) \sum_{C_N} (A(0) - A[\mathbf{g}, \mathbf{x}(T)]),$$

is determined when d, n, and T are known.

VIII. A case study: Sweden

This section applies the framework developed above to the Swedish banking crisis of 1991–92 as an illustrative case study.[28] The Swedish episode exhibits many key features of crisis and resolution as presented in this chapter: issuance of an emergency universal deposit guarantee, transference of assets to an AMC, official recapitalization and reprivatization. Of course, not all features of the framework apply in a specific historical example. In the Swedish case, the deposit guarantee was granted after the generally accepted start of the crisis and no bank liquidations or guarantee payouts occurred.

In dating the Swedish intervention, we relied on the expert opinion of those involved in planning and executing the intervention actions. We date the crisis from 1991-Q3 to 1993-Q4; this is consistent with the dating in earlier studies.[29] To calculate the net benefit of intervening in the Swedish crisis, we utilize ex post fiscal costs and benefits, assuming that they are the realized outcomes of ex ante expectations. These fiscal costs and benefits are presented in Table 2.5, along with the discount factors applied to all future values relative to the start of the crisis, 1991-Q3.[30] No banks were liquidated and no payouts were made in the Swedish case on the deposit guarantee.[31]

The remaining benefits and costs are calculated according to the formulas presented in Tables 2.2 and 2.3 and Appendix 2.II. The values of parameters and variables used for those calculations are in Table 2.6. Values for outstanding balance sheet data are taken at end-1990, the closest precrisis point for which consistent data are available. A two-year horizon is assumed for the recessionary shock arising from the forced liquidation of bank loans. In the absence of direct estimates, "reasonable" values are assumed for needed parameters.

The resultant estimates are presented in Table 2.7. They show a net benefit for the Swedish intervention of SKr 365 billion (25 percent of base year GDP). The avoided loss on marketable securities is calculated assuming a unitary price elasticity of demand in the absence of a direct estimate. The loss is assumed to reverse at a five-year horizon.

Table 2.5. Fiscal Costs and Benefits of Government Intervention in the Swedish Banking Crisis

(In SKr billions)

	91 Q3	91 Q4	92 Q1	92 Q2	92 Q3	92 Q4	93 Q1	93 Q2	93 Q3	93 Q4	1994	1995	1996	1997	Totals	PDV[a]
Costs																
Recapitalization—bonds	-4.2		-2.1	-10.0						-24.0					-40.3	-34.1
Recapitalization through purchases of impaired assets						-24.0									-24.0	-21
Other costs/revenue											-1.0		3.8		2.8	1.6
Total															**-61.5**	**-53.5**
Benefits																
Revenue from reprivatization												8.4	2.5		10.9	8.7
Increase in value of bank shares held														36.8	36.8	17.6
(Net value of bank shares outstanding)	(5.5)													(42.3)		
Total															**47.7**	**26.3**
Net fiscal costs	**-4.2**		**-2.1**	**-10.0**		**-24.0**				**-24.0**	**-1.0**	**8.4**	**6.3**	**36.8**	**-13.8**	**-27.2**
Discount rates	10.27	10.40	10.48	10.56	10.53	10.50	10.47	10.43	10.40	10.36	10.36	10.38	10.39			
Discount factors	0.975	0.950	0.925	0.900	0.877	0.855	0.833	0.812	0.792	0.744	0.671	0.604	0.545			

Note: Discount rates for 3 and 6 months, and 1, 3, 5, and 7 years are from the *Quarterly Review* of the Sveriges Riksbank. Other maturities are estimated by linear interpolation.

Fiscal costs and benefits are from Jennergren and Naslund (1998).

a Present discounted value.

Table 2.6. Parameters and Variables Used to Calculate Benefits and Costs of Intervention in the Swedish Banking Crisis, 1991–Q3 to 1993–Q4

Parameters and Variables	Symbol	Value	Date	Source	Comment
Deposits	D(g)	SKr 656.0 Bil.	end-1990	SA	Deposits by nonbank public
Bank holdings of marketable assets	M(g)	SKr 172.3 Bil.	end-1990	SA	Bonds and shares[a]
Bank loans to business	L(g)	SKr 521.2 Bil.	end-1990	SA	Including unincorporated business
Bank assets	A(g)	SKr 1604.9 Bil.	end-1990	SA	
Assets in business sector	$A_C(g)$	SKr 3053.4 Bil.	end-1990	OECD, SC	Capital stock plus financial assets[b]
GDP	Y	SKr 1447.3	1991	IFS	
Recession length	R	2 years			By assumption
Time horizon	T	9 quarters			1991-Q3 to 1993-Q4
Inverse of marginal capital–output ratio	λ	.33			By assumption
$\partial Y/\partial(M/P)$ from production function	μ	.10			By assumption[c]
Area under currency demand curve	ν	0			By assumption
Price elasticity of demand for marketable assets	ε	1.0			By assumption
Liquidation loss rate on business sector assets	Λ	.33			By assumption
Growth shortfall per year of resolution delay	k	.007		Frydl (1999)	Fraction of base year GDP

Sources: *International Financial Statistics*, IMF; Finansrakenskaper, 1986–90, Statistiska Centralbyran; Statistisk Arsbok, 1991, Sveriges Riksbank; and Flows and Stocks of Fixed Capital, 1971–1996, Organization for Economic Cooperation and Development (OECD).

a Securities of domestic issuer; nonlisted shares excluded.

b Net capital stock (from OECD) excludes government capital and dwellings; financial assets of nonfinancial enterprises (from SC) are net of domestic intergroup company claims and domestic trade credit.

c This assumed value is consistent with a range of estimates from various studies; see Laumas and Mohabbat (1980), Nguyen (1986), and Sephton(1988).

Table 2.7. Estimates of Benefits and Costs of Intervening in the Swedish Banking Crisis

Benefit/Cost	Formula	Value
Benefits		
(1) Avoided loss on:		
(a) marketable assets	$(1-\delta(t=5))M(g)/\varepsilon$	68.2
(b) nonmarketable assets	$(1+\delta(t<2)\lambda)[A_C(g) - A_C(b)] -$	
	$\delta(t<2)\lambda \, (L(g) - L(b))]$	346.7
(c) payments system disruption	$(1-\delta(t=5))\mu(D(g) - A(b)) + \mu A(b)$	0
(2) Profit on reprivatization and		
held bank shares	Ex post value, Table 5	26.3
Total benefits		**441.2**
Costs		
(1) Fiscal costs	Ex post value, Table 5	−53.5
(2) Short-term moral hazard	$kTY = (.007)(2.25)(1447.3)$	−22.8
Total costs		**−76.3**
Net benefits		**364.9**

The avoided loss on nonmarketable securities, equal to SKr 346.7 billion, dominates the calculation. This amount is composed of a permanent loss in business capital value of SKr 260.6 billion and a recessionary shock of SKr 86.1 billion. The significance of the permanent loss depends on the size of bank business loans relative to GDP and Λ, the loss liquidation rate. We assumed a loss liquidation rate of .33, since the liquid assets of Swedish nonfinancial enterprises (deposits and short-term securities), at SKr 183 billion, covered only 35 percent of the sector's loans from Swedish banks. For a country like Sweden, with a relatively developed bank credit market, potential liquidation of business loans poses a large threat, especially since the value of these asset losses is not discounted.[32]

The size of the recessionary shock is assumed to be proportional to the loss in business sector net worth induced by asset liquidation. To calculate the size of the recessionary shock, the loss in business asset value must be allocated between a loss in net worth for the enterprise sector and a loss in loan value for the banking system. Data on the distribution of bank loans across businesses are not available; but since the ratio of bank debt to assets in the business sector was low—17 percent—we assumed a slight loss on bank loan values equal to 10 percent of the loss in business sector asset value.

The avoided losses on payments system disruption are calculated in the Swedish episode at zero, because (1) the estimated liquidation value of bank assets, $A_C(\mathbf{b})$, far exceeded the value of deposits, $D(\mathbf{g})$, since Swedish banks relied to a significant degree on funding with nondeposit liabilities; and (2) we assume that currency demand is inelastic, so that the deadweight loss parameter, ν, is set equal to zero.

Realized values are used for proceeds on reprivatization and accrued capital gains as of the reprivatization date for remaining bank shares held. Realized fiscal costs are used and short-term moral hazard costs are calculated as in Section VI (but discounted).

An alternative way of looking at this calculation is the approach taken in Section VI: to assume that there is some probability of panic occurring and to use the expected benefits of avoiding it, that is, to multiply the gross benefits by the probability of panic. The benefit and cost values in Table 2.7, then, yield a break-even probability of panic of 17 percent, which can be set against the authorities' prior view of an acceptable risk of panic.

IX. Concluding remarks

A banking crisis is identified by the combination of a high risk of panic and widespread systemic distress produced by asset loss and capital deficiencies, including insolvencies. Intervention to address a crisis involves liquidity support actions, notably a universal deposit guarantee and resolution actions, liquidations of failed banks, assistance for private restructurings, and public recapitalizations. The principal benefits of intervention include the avoided costs of panic-induced asset liquidation and payments system disruption and the elimination of distorted incentives in the banking system and elevated risk premiums in financial markets that generate economic costs. The principal costs of intervention include the fiscal costs of paying for intervention actions and the economic costs of delay in resolving banking system distress.

The government should adopt the policy that maximizes net benefits. When intervening, the government's principal decision concerns the length of the resolution horizon—whether to adopt a deliberate or an aggressive resolution strategy. An aggressive strategy will reduce the economic costs of delay, but a deliberate one may reduce fiscal costs by relying more on private restructurings and less on liquidations and public recapitalizations.

A careful accounting of these benefits and costs allows a quantification of the net benefits of intervening in a crisis, in both an ex ante sense of evaluating a current policy decision on intervention and in an ex post sense of evaluating a previous decision. While many factors affect the net benefits of intervention, dominant considerations are likely to be the size of banking system relative to the economy, especially, in terms of advances to the enterprise sector, and the loss liquidation rate on business assets financed by bank loans. These factors are important because the loss from a panic liquidation is borne immediately and not discounted, while the fiscal costs of intervention actions (and other costs) are spread out over the future.

Appendix 2.I. The condition of banks before intervention

Table AI.1 presents a taxonomy of conditions in the banking system after an initial shock but before intervention actions. The classification distinguishes between private and state-owned banks and lists banks by their capital and liquidity conditions and their risk behavior.

Table AI.1 Conditions of Banks After an Initial Shock

Type of Bank	Capital Condition	Liquidity Condition	Risk Behavior
Private	Capital-adequate	Liquid	Risk-normal/risk-averse
State-owned	Capital-adequate	Liquid	Risk-normal/risk-averse
Private	Capital-deficient	Liquid	Risk-averse
Private	Capital-deficient	Liquid	Risk-taking
Private	Capital-deficient	Illiquid	Risk-averse
State-owned	Capital-deficient	Liquid	Risk-averse
State-owned	Capital-deficient	Liquid	Risk-taking
Private	Insolvent	Illiquid	Risk-taking
State-owned	Insolvent	Liquid	Risk-taking

Assumptions: No state-owned banks are illiquid because of a credible implicit guarantee on deposits. All capital-adequate banks are liquid but may be either risk-normal or risk-averse. Private insolvent banks are illiquid.

Making the distinction between private and state-owned banks is important because state-owned banks often operate on noncommercial criteria, such as providing subsidized lending to favored sectors. Indeed, the accumulated losses from such noncommercial lending can themselves become the trigger for a systemic crisis when they reach a high enough level.

The capital and liquidity conditions of banks and their risk behavior fall into different categories. Banks are classified as capital-adequate, capital-deficient, or insolvent in terms of their capital condition after the initial crisis shock. Capital-adequate banks exceed or meet regulatory minimum capital ratios, while capital-deficient banks fall below the minimum requirement. Insolvent banks show a negative book value of net worth.[33] The capital condition of a bank is based on accountable claims and obligations. It typically does not incorporate the franchise value of a bank, which reflects the present value of the institution as an ongoing concern. Positive franchise value will arise from the economic benefits to the bank of established customer relationships, the existence of a geographically extensive branch network that allows the bank to have access to a relatively inexpensive deposit base, and so forth. The capital condition of a bank can be readily observed by banking system participants, but the franchise value can be known only by paying a monitoring cost.

Banks are categorized as either liquid or illiquid; illiquid banks experience a net outflow of deposits but do not have ready access to interbank funds as a replacement. Banks that can replace deposit outflows with interbank funds are considered liquid.

Banks are rated either risk–normal, risk–averse, or risk–taking. A risk–normal bank makes investment decisions on the basis of the risk–return trade-off that is characteristic of a bank operating under normal conditions, i.e., without problems of liquidity, profitability or capital deficiency. Such a bank may be strictly risk-neutral, making investment decisions solely on the basis of expected net returns and ignoring the risk characteristics of assets. It is more likely, however, that a risk-normal bank will exhibit some degree of risk aversion, i.e., that it will forgo some investments with positive expected returns.

If risk aversion in investment is a consequence of the asymmetric information problem that arises between borrowers and lenders, the assumption that risk-normal banks are risk-neutral is equivalent to saying that they provide a full solution to that problem. This is a restrictive assumption, since even strong banks may exhibit some degree of risk aversion.[34]

Risk-averse banks are so characterized relative to the risk-normal state. If risk-normal banks operate with a minimal degree of risk aversion, risk-averse banks exhibit abnormally large risk aversion. Finally, risk-taking banks will undertake some investments with negative expected returns.

The number of possible states that banks may be in after an initial shock can be limited by a few reasonable assumptions:

(1) *Deposits at state-owned banks are assumed to carry a credible implicit guarantee, which protects any state-owned bank, even an insolvent one, from experiencing liquidity problems.* Of course, if the financial condition of the government is so weak, because of, say, heavy foreign indebtedness or a degraded ability to collect taxes, that a guarantee is not credible, the strategy of intervention becomes much more complicated. Steps to restore the government's own financial status will have to be taken prior to or simultaneously with actions to resolve the banking crisis. State-owned banks can also wind up in an intermediate liquidity position. The implicit guarantee on their deposits may be viewed as applying to deposit levels before the crisis hit. New depositors may have less confidence that they will be protected. As a consequence, state-owned banks will not serve as an effective source of supply in the interbank market able to channel back funds lost by illiquid banks during a crisis.

(2) *All capital-adequate banks are liquid but may behave in either a risk-normal or risk-averse manner.* Even a well-capitalized bank, of course, can experience an idiosyncratic liquidity problem, e.g., one arising from a computer disruption, but will likely be free of a distress-related liquidity squeeze, at least until the system crosses into the panic zone, where the interbank market fails and deposit outflows become systemic.

If the increase in the risk premium generated by the crisis is sufficiently large, even capital adequate, liquid banks may turn risk-averse because of a pervasive adverse selection problem. This problem can arise at high interest rate levels if uncertainties about the quality of borrowers remaining in the market override the increased returns.

(3) ***Private insolvent banks are illiquid.*** In the absence of a full deposit guarantee, depositors will have a clear incentive to withdraw funds from a private insolvent bank. Central banks are generally precluded from extending LOLR assistance to insolvent banks.[35]

The further evolution of the banking system without official intervention depends on the condition in which banks have been placed by the initial shock. Capital-adequate banks will continue to operate without distorted incentives, i.e., in a risk-normal condition. Insolvent banks face inevitable closure or liquidation, unless they can rapidly restore their condition in the limited time that they have to operate. As a consequence, insolvent banks are biased toward assuming risk. Capital-deficient banks can be broadly divided into moderate net worth and low net worth institutions. We categorize moderate net worth banks as adopting a risk-averse posture. Such banks have a reasonable expectation of restoring compliance with regulatory capital requirements quickly through a strategy of retaining earnings on relatively safe assets, thereby avoiding any regulatory interventions that could affect their operations.

Low net worth institutions, on the other hand, do not have reasonable expectations of being able to restore their capital position to regulatory compliance through following a conservative strategy. For such banks, the cost of further losses is low, since most shareholder wealth has been depleted and they already face the prospect of relatively severe regulatory intervention. They have a strong incentive to undertake risky, uneconomical projects that have some chance of a high payoff in the hope of a fortunate outcome. Low net worth banks, although technically solvent, face incentives that are very similar to those faced by insolvent banks. In other words, for moderate net worth banks the lure of returning to full regulatory compliance and maximum freedom of action dominates their decision-making; for low net worth banks, the threat of insolvency dominates.

At the same time, low net worth banks are more likely than moderate net worth banks to face liquidity problems since risk-averse depositors and other liability holders will be sensitive primarily to a bank's own capital condition and only secondarily to conditions throughout the system. There is the logical possibility of low net worth but liquid private banks. This condition could arise for banks that have a passive base of liability holders, for example, small, relatively uninformed retail depositors. Low net worth state-owned banks are, by assumption, liquid and will be less constrained from taking risks.

A hierarchy of bank conditions

In circumstances in which the set of capital-deficient, liquid, risk-taking banks is narrow—say, where state-owned banks are a relatively small part of the banking system and banks have broadly similar liability structures—banks can be partitioned into a hierarchy of conditions on the basis of their capital–asset ratios alone. This system of classification is represented in Figure AI.1. A bank can take on one of three liquidity states: liquid (L_{Liquid}), illiquid ($L_{Illiquid}$), or subject to a run (L_{Run})—and one of three risk preferences: risk-neutral (R_{Normal}), risk-taking (R_{High}), or risk-averse (R_{Low}). Assume that: (1) the switch points between states depend only on the bank's own capital–asset ratio when the system is outside the panic zone; (2) the bank switches from risk-normal to risk-averse to risk-taking (along the lines discussed above) and from liquid to illiquid to bank run as its capital ratio falls, and (3) no further switches occur. Since capital-deficient, liquid, risk-taking banks are precluded by assumption, the first liquidity switching point, k_{L1}, must lie between the two risk preference switching points, k^* and k_R.

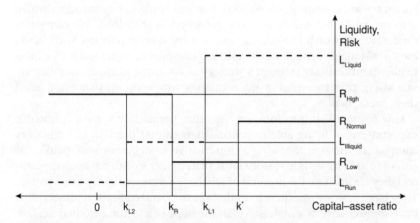

Figure AI.1 Conditions of Banks Before Intervention

Low net worth banks face incentives to take risk similar to those faced by insolvent banks but are subject to less extreme liquidity pressures. As an example, assume that there are two classes of depositors, risk-averse and risk-neutral. Risk-averse depositors will begin to withdraw funds from a bank if its capital–asset ratio drops below k_{L1}. Risk-neutral depositors have no incentive to withdraw funds if they have an expectation of positive net worth for the bank. However, a rational risk-neutral depositor must consider that a low net worth illiquid bank is in a condition of disequilibrium. A risk-neutral depositor may not know which other depositors of the bank are risk-averse but will assign some probability to the bank being in an illiquid state and, therefore, under pressure to liquidate assets. Additionally, the depositor will assign some probability to the bank undertaking risky projects of negative expected profitability. As a consequence, a rational risk-neutral depositor will expect that the accounting value of a low net worth bank overstates its true net worth and will begin to withdraw deposits before insolvency occurs, as indicated by the second liquidity switching point, k_{L2}.[36] At capital–asset ratios below k_{L2} a bank is subject to a run as both classes of depositors pull out funds.

This schema, presented in Table AI.2, allows banks to be grouped into five classes. Illiquid banks that are capital-deficient but still solvent will generally qualify for LOLR assistance. But incentives to seek such assistance vary among the classes of banks that qualify, because the LOLR will typically closely monitor borrowing banks, inducing them to behave in a risk-averse manner. Class 3 banks may be expected to seek LOLR assistance, since they are already inclined to be risk-averse as a strategy to restore their regulatory compliance. Class 4 banks, however, will pass up LOLR funds in order to maintain their preferred strategy of risk-taking. Class 5 low net worth (but still solvent) banks with capital ratios between 0 and k_{L2} may shift back to seeking LOLR assistance as the last hope to avoid insolvency and closure brought about by a bank run. Such a pattern of shifting incentives may help explain why LOLR assistance is provided so often to banks that eventually fail. Risk-taking banks have no incentive to seek LOLR funds until they are in a deteriorating condition so near insolvency that their true net worth is difficult to assess.

Table AI.2   Bank Conditions Ordered by Capital–Asset Ratios

	Capital-asset ratio	Conditions
Class 1 (C_1)	$k \geq k^*$	Capital-adequate, liquid, risk-neutral
Class 2 (C_2)	$k^* > k \geq k_{L1}$	Moderate net worth, liquid, risk-averse
Class 3 (C_3)	$k_{L1} > k \geq k_R$	Moderate net worth, illiquid, risk-averse
Class 4 (C_4)	$k_R > k \geq k_{L2}$	Low net worth, illiquid, risk-taking
Class 5 (C_5)	$k_{L2} > k$	Low net worth/insolvent, illiquid, risk-taking

Appendix 2.II.

Procedures for estimating economic benefits

Benefit	Formula	Ex Ante Procedure	Ex Post Procedure
Avoided loss on marketable assets	$\delta(T_0 < t < T_E)N(M(\mathbf{g}) - M(\mathbf{b}))$	For each marketable asset class, the percentage change in price equals the price elasticity of demand times the percentage change in quantity: $$dP/P = (1/\varepsilon) \times dQ/Q.$$ The price elasticity, ε, can be derived from estimated demand functions for each asset class. Since the banking system must liquidate its asset holdings, the percentage decline in demand is given by $$dQ/Q = M(\mathbf{g}) / M = M(\mathbf{g})/NM(\mathbf{g}) = 1/N,$$ where M is the total of marketable assets. Therefore, the loss in asset value from fire-sale liquidation is given by $$N(M(\mathbf{g}) - M(\mathbf{b})) = dP/P \times NM(\mathbf{g}) = (1/\varepsilon) \times dQ/Q \times NM(\mathbf{g})$$ $$= (1/\varepsilon) \times (1/N) \times NM(\mathbf{g}) = (1/\varepsilon) \times M(\mathbf{g}),$$ the price elasticity of asset demand times the banking system's holdings of marketable assets. If the government is uncertain whether demand is elastic or inelastic, it can simply assume $\varepsilon = 1$, so that the estimated benefit of preventing liquidation of marketable assets is simply equal to the banking system's holdings of such assets, $M(\mathbf{g})$.	Ex post valuations also require estimation of counter-factual outcomes. Ex post procedures are the same as the ex ante ones.

Avoided loss on nonmarketable assets	$(1 + \delta(T_0 < t < R_E)\lambda)(A_C(\mathbf{g}) - A_C(\mathbf{b}))$ $- \delta(T_0 < t < R_E)\lambda(L(\mathbf{g}) - L(\mathbf{b}))$	Same.

The potential loss from the liquidation of business sector assets, $A_C(\mathbf{g})$ $- A_C(\mathbf{b})$, represents a speculative counter-factual estimate of the loss arising from the disruption of productive investment projects. It can be estimated by applying a liquidation loss rate, Λ, to an amount of business sector assets, whose value is sufficient to cover the book value of outstanding bank loans, $L(\mathbf{g})$. This loss in asset value is given by:

$$A_C(\mathbf{g}) - A_C(\mathbf{b}) = L(\mathbf{g})/(1-\Lambda) - L(\mathbf{g}) = \Lambda L(\mathbf{g})/(1-\Lambda).$$

For the liquidation loss on banking system loans, $L(\mathbf{g}) - L(\mathbf{b})$, note that for firms that cannot cover their loan calls,

$$L(\mathbf{b}) = (1-\Lambda)A_C(\mathbf{g}).$$

If the balance sheet leveraging of individual firms can be observed, the loss on banking system loans is

$$L(\mathbf{g}) - L(\mathbf{b}) = \Sigma \text{Max}[0, L_i(\mathbf{g}) - (1-\Lambda)A_{C,i}(\mathbf{g})],$$

which is the sum of losses over all firms.

Finally, the parameter λ, which represents the recessionary effects arising from the capital destruction caused by the banking system collapse, can be proxied by the inverse of the marginal capital–output ratio in a production (input–output) relation. If this quantity cannot be estimated directly, an estimated value for an economy of similar structure can be substituted. The recession length, R, can be taken as the historical average length for recessions. The dynamic pattern can be taken as a prototypical profile. For example, the recessionary effects can be assumed to build steadily to a maximum at $t = R/2$ given by the marginal capital–output calculation and then to decline steadily.

Benefit	Formula	Ex Ante Procedure	Ex Post Procedure
Avoided disruption to the payments system	$\delta(T_0 < t < T_E)[\mu(D(\mathbf{g}) - A(\mathbf{b})) + vA(\mathbf{b})]$	The liquidation value of banking system assets, $A(\mathbf{b})$, is equal to the precrisis asset value, $A(g)$, less the liquidation losses on marketable and nonmarketable asset $$A(\mathbf{b}) = A(\mathbf{g}) - [M(\mathbf{g})/\varepsilon N] - \Sigma Max[0, L_i(\mathbf{g}) - (1-\Lambda)A_{C,i}(\mathbf{g})].$$ The parameter μ, which reflects the output loss stemming from the deposit loss with wealth held constant, can be proxied by the estimated partial derivative of output with respect to money balances in an aggregate production function. If this term cannot be directly estimated for the country, an estimated value from a structurally similar economy can be substituted. The parameter, v, reflects the loss that arises from economic agents being forced to hold the medium of exchange as currency rather than bank deposits. An estimate of this loss can be derived from a currency demand function, say, $$C/M = a - br,$$ where C/M is the currency share of the money stock. Forcing $C/M = 1$ (which destruction of the payments system does) is equivalent to imposing a quantitative restriction. The loss in consumer surplus from this restriction can be estimated as an area under the demand curve (Harberger triangle).	Same.

Profit on asset disposition	$\delta(t > T_E)\Pi_A(\Delta[g, x(T)])$	The expected profit on the disposition of purchased assets depends on the rise in asset prices consequent on the resolution of the crisis, which is given by duration of purchased assets times the change in interest rates: $$Dur(A(g)) \times \Delta r,$$ with $\Delta r = -\rho(g)$. The present value of the expected capital gain on asset disposition is, then, $$\delta(t > T_E)\Psi(g \sum_{C_P} A[g, x(T)] \times Dur(A(g)) \times (-\rho(g))$$	Recorded in fiscal accounts. Economic profits represent gains in excess of opportunity cost, so they must be discounted at the alternative return, the cost of government debt.
Profit on reprivatization	$\delta(t > T_E)\Pi_E(\Delta[g, x(T)])$	The expected profit to the authorities on reprivatization of public recapitalization of banks is given by the expected capital gain on equity. If equity is treated as an investment of infinite duration, the expected percentage capital gain, dP/P, can be approximated by the change in interest rates implied by the restoration of the normal risk premium, which is $$dP/P = -\rho(g)/(r(0) + \rho(g))$$ where r(0) is the pre-crisis interest rate incorporating the pre-crisis risk premium. The expected capital gain to the government is $$\delta(t > T_E) \times -\rho(g)/(r(0) + \rho(g)) \times \sum_{C_G}(A(0) - A[g, x(T)]),$$ where the last term is the amount of public equity put into the banking system.	Recorded in fiscal accounts.

Benefit	Formula	Ex Ante Procedure	Ex Post Procedure
Efficient restructuring	$(\gamma\delta(t > T_E)(A(\mathbf{0}) - A_{I-}(\mathbf{0}))$	This benefit represents the avoided set-up costs of reconstituting an entirely liquidated banking system, expressed as γ, a fraction of the assets of the banks that avoid unnecessary liquidation. These costs are pre-determined. As a first practical cut, we will take it to be roughly equivalent to an investment banking fee, say, 50 basis points on assets, or $\gamma = .005$.	Should be observable from the accounts of de novo banks.
Deposit guarantee			
Fiscal-related	$\theta\delta(T_0 < t < T_E) \sum_{C_{I-}} (D(\mathbf{g}) - A[\mathbf{g}, \mathbf{x}(T)])$	The summation term is the payout made on deposit guarantees for liquidated banks during the intervention period. The average asset value over the intervention period, $CA[\mathbf{g}, \mathbf{x}(T)]$, can be set equal to a fraction of the asset value at the beginning of the period $$A[\mathbf{g}, \mathbf{x}(T)] = d \times A(\mathbf{g}),$$ where d is the average deterioration over the intervention period. With d known, the quantity $\sum_{C_{I-}} (D(\mathbf{g}) - A(\mathbf{g}))$ is known after monitoring. The value of d will depend on the rate of deterioration of banking system assets that results from delaying resolution actions. Frydl (1999) reports an estimate from a cross-section of banking crises based on Caprio and Klingebiel (CK) (1996) that the fiscal costs of crisis resolution rise by 0.8 percent of GDP per year of resolution horizon length. Assuming that assets deteriorate to the same extent resolution costs rise, this estimate will generate a rate of asset loss from which d can be constructed. The parameter, θ, which represents the economic cost to the government of distributing losses from depositors to taxpayers, is difficult to estimate. If the government considers both groups equivalent, θ will be near zero and there will be few economic costs that arise from the fiscal costs of intervention. Since θ is likely to increase directly with both the tax burden, τ, and the government's debt burden, which is related to the future tax burden, a simple-minded approximation is to set $\theta = (\tau + i) / Y$, where i is government interest payments and Y is GDP.	Reported in fiscal accounts.

Long-term moral hazard	$\delta(t > T_E) \int_0^\infty [y(r_1, \omega(p_1), t)$ $- y(r_0, \omega(p_0), t)]dt$	As per argument in the text, this quantity can be taken as equal to zero. Same.
Resolution actions		
Monitoring costs	mC_1	Predetermined by the authorities' investment bank.
Search costs	$\delta(T_0 < t < T_E)s(\sigma, (C_4 + C_{5+}), T)$	The terms σ and T are choice variables for the authorities. The authorities' investment bank will provide a schedule linking σ and T with n, the fraction of banks that has to be recapitalized by the government, and the authorities will choose the value that maximizes net benefits.
Support for private restructuring	$\delta(T_0 < t < T_E)(\Psi(g)\Sigma A[g, x(T)]$ $+ \theta \sum_{C_P, C_{L-}} (D(g) - A[g, x(T)]))$	As a first approximation, Ψ is assumed to be the fraction of assets classified at the start of the resolution period.
Temporary public recapitalization	$\theta\delta(T_0 < t < T_E) \sum_{C_G} (A(0) - A[g, x(T)])$	This quantity is determined when θ, d, n, and T are known.
Short-term moral hazard	$\delta(0 < t \le T) \int_{f(z)=0} Y'(Z)dZdt$	Any growth shortfall in the economic forecast at the start of the crisis will reflect the economic cost of the initial crisis shock. Assume that this forecast incorporates a resolution horizon of one year, which is the mode of crisis lengths in the CK sample of crises with definite length. Frydl (1999) presents an estimate of 0.7 percent of GDP per year of resolution horizon length as the rate of deterioration in the growth shortfall. This estimate allows a calculation of the economic costs of delay in resolution beyond that assumed in the consensus forecast.	Attribute any increase in the growth shortfall beyond that forecasted at the start of the crisis to delay in resolution.

Notes

1. The authors would like to thank R. Barry Johnston, Liliana Schumacher, and Göran Lind (Swedish Riksbank), as well as participants of two MAE seminars and a Policy Research Group (MAE) meeting for their helpful comments and suggestions.
2. Experience with bank restructuring is reviewed and analyzed in Sheng (1996), Alexander and others (1997), Santomero and Hoffman (1998), Enoch and others (1999), Hawkins and Turner (1999), Lindgren and others (2000), and Woo (2000).
3. See Lindgren and others (2000).
4. For a discussion of the detailed modalities of blanket guarantees, as well as country experiences, see Garcia (2000), Ingves and Lind (1996), and Lindgren and others (2000).
5. See also, among others, Federal Deposit Insurance Corporation (FDIC) (1998), Lindgren and others (2000), and Enoch and others (1999).
6. See FDIC (1998) for a discussion of several types of P&A operations.
7. For a list of advantages and disadvantages of centralized public AMCs, as opposed to private arrangements, see Lindgren and others (2000) Box 8.
8. Blanket guarantees may also entail a regressive wealth distribution effect because taxpayers' funds are used to protect not only small savers, but also large depositors and creditors, including external creditors (Lindgren and others, 2000).
9. The shape of the contours $0a$ and $\alpha^K b$ depends on the distribution of capital and assets across banks. They are represented for convenience in Figure 2.1 as straight lines, which assumes that capital and assets are uniformly and continuously distributed across banks; in other words, the banking system is assumed here to be purely competitive with a large number of small equally-sized banks.
10. Although the discussion generally refers to a loss in asset values, what matters, of course, is a loss in asset values relative to liability values that negatively impacts bank net worth. This condition can arise from an increase in liability values, e.g., where a bank holds foreign currency-denominated deposits in a mismatched position.
11. These expectations will depend on the specific conditions that banks are in after the initial shock. Before the shock, participants will have an unconditional expectation about how the system will evolve from any starting point, say, point **d**, based on the probable distribution of distress across banks at that point. After the shock, when the starting point and conditions of distress are actually revealed, participants will form revised conditional expectations about the path **de**.
12. The lower boundary of the panic zone can be defined as a definite threshold that depends only on the aggregate values α and β but not on the conditions of individual banks. At this boundary the behavior of all depositors abruptly switches. The boundary between the crisis zone and the distress zone, however, has to be defined in a probabilistic sense in terms of (α, β) combinations that have an unconditional expectation of being the origin points of paths that will reach the panic zone. After the initial shock is revealed, the origin point and the conditions of distress are known. New conditional expectations about the path that the system will follow from the origin point are formed. It may turn out that these revised conditional expectations yield a path that starts in the distress zone but crosses into the panic zone or one that starts in the crisis zone but does not reach the panic zone. This ambiguity results from the two-dimensional nature of Figure 2.1. If the dimensions were expanded to include the percentage of bank assets held by banks in each state in Appendix Table AI.1, all potential events

(post-shock states) and the evolution of the system from any starting point could be specified unconditionally.

13. State-owned banks may retain their precrisis level of deposits because of the implicit guarantee but not attract new deposits. Whether this outcome will avoid major payments system damage will depend on the extent of such deposits.

14. An alternative action is to freeze deposits. While such a measure, unlike deposit guarantees, would create no actual or potential fiscal exposure for the government, it would create extensive disruption to the payments system, since the design and administration of efficient exemptions to the freeze would be very difficult. Countries whose government does not have sufficient financial strength may be unable to issue a credible guarantee unless accompanied by a program of actions to resolve banking system distress, limit future exposures and finance guarantee liabilities. Such a comprehensive program often requires time to be designed and enacted. Under the time pressure of an incipient panic, such countries may be forced to resort to a deposit freeze.

15. In general, of course, comprehensive deposit guarantees can affect not just the rate at which the system moves along a path like **fh**, but the magnitude and direction of such a path as well.

16. Suppose, for example, that the conditional probability of systemic insolvency given α^i is uniformly distributed over feasible states. Then, the conditional probability of panic is **ij/ic**.

17. The level of distress $x(T)$ is reached at some time between T_0 and T_E. At T_E, resolution is completed and the system has returned to a normal state of zero distress.

18. This assumption is superior to having set-up costs be proportional to the number of liquidated banks, since an efficient reconstitution of the banking system may require changes in bank size. In general, both the capacity of the reconstituted system and the number of *de novo* banks will affect set-up costs.

19. Actual disbursements of funds may be viewed as more costly than off-balance sheet guarantees because they need to be financed by on-balance sheet increases in debt that have a greater negative effect on the government's perceived credit standing.

20. The conditions of distress in the banking system are detailed in Appendix 2.I.

21. Risk-normal conditions are discussed in Appendix 2.I.

22. The government may also provide more clear-cut subsidies, in terms of tax advantages, for example, to encourage private restructurings.

23. The decision not to intervene but to allow a panic to run its course can be represented by setting $T = 0$.

24. Some payouts under a guarantee may be made on deposit losses that arise because the guarantee removes liquidity constraints on risky banks that are then able to take actions that generate new losses. This effect is an aspect of short-term moral hazard.

25. They also depend directly on the size of the initial crisis shock, since a greater level of initial distress will produce more distorted incentives that will, in turn, generate a faster rate of deterioration in the economy and the banking system.

26. This procedure will considerably underestimate the economic cost of a banking system panic because it ignores the lost value on business assets liquidated to pay bank loans that is not reflected in losses to banks.

27. See Frydl (1999).

28. The Swedish crisis is discussed in Ingves and Lind (1996, 1997), Backstrom (1997), Drees and Pazarbasioglu (1998), and Jennergren and Naslund (1998).
29. Although the deposit guarantee was extended in September 1992, we date the start of the crisis as 1991-Q3, when recapitalization funds were first extended. Earlier studies date the Swedish crisis in the 1990–93 range and estimate gross fiscal costs at 4–5 percent of GDP. See Caprio and Klingebiel (1996); Kaminsky and Reinhart (1996); Lindgren, Garcia, and Saal (1996); Dziobek and Pazarbasioglu (1997); and Demirguc-Kunt and Detragiache (1998).
30. Discount factors in Table 2.5 were derived from the market rates on government coupon-bearing securities for the listed maturities that held at the start of the crisis. This procedure introduces an error since precise calculation requires that zero-coupon rates be applied to future cash flows. However, when the yield curve is relatively flat, as in the Swedish example, the error is small (Hull, 1993).
31. The Riksbank also deposited a part of its foreign exchange reserves in the banking system in September 1992. Although this action represents a type of extraordinary liquidity support, we do not account for it as an intervention cost. We account for that part of public recapitalization funds that covers the net worth "hole" in intervened banks at face value, implying θ = 1.
32. We do not take account of potentially significant liquidation losses on other kinds of loans, such as mortgages; banks loans to the household sector at end-1990 totaled SKr 244 billion.
33. Marketable assets, such as securities or real estate, are considered to be booked at market values; nonmarketable assets, such as loans, are marked down in an appropriate manner to reflect their impairment.
34. Whether risk-normal banks are risk-neutral or risk-averse has important consequences for assessing the costs of long-term moral hazard arising from intervention in a banking crisis, as discussed in Section VI.
35. Central banks, of course, often lend to distressed banks that later fail.
36. If a bank's net worth could be continuously accounted, a risk-neutral depositor could react only to accounting values. Since there is an accounting lag, however, a rational, risk-neutral depositor must use all present information that affects the expected net worth of the bank.

Bibliography

Alexander, William E., and others, eds., 1997, *Systemic Bank Restructuring and Macroeconomic Policy* (Washington: International Monetary Fund).
Backstrom, Urban, 1997, "What Lessons Can Be Learned from Recent Financial Crises? The Swedish Experience," in *Maintaining Financial Stability in a Global Economy*, Federal Reserve Bank of Kansas City.
Caprio, Jr., Gerald, and Daniela Klingebiel, 1996, "Bank Insolvencies: Cross Country Experience," Working Paper 1620 (Washington: World Bank).
Demirguc-Kunt, Asli, and Enrica Detragiache, 1998, "The Determinants of Banking Crises in Developing and Developed Countries," *IMF Staff Papers*, Vol. 45, No. 1 (Washington: International Monetary Fund).
Drees, Burkhard, and Ceyla Pazarbasioglu, 1998, *The Nordic Banking Crises: Pitfalls in Financial Liberalization?*, IMF Occasional Paper 161 (Washington: International Monetary Fund).
Dziobek, C., 1998, "Market-Based Policy Instruments for Systemic Bank Restructuring," IMF Working Paper 98/113 (Washington: International Monetary Fund).

Dziobek, C., and Ceyla Pazarbasioglu, 1997, "Lessons from Systemic Bank Restructuring: A Survey of 24 Countries," IMF Working Paper 97/161 (Washington: International Monetary Fund).

Enoch, Charles, Gillian Garcia, and V. Sundararajan, 1999, "Recapitalizing Banks with Public Funds: Selected Issues," IMF Working Paper 99/139 (Washington: International Monetary Fund).

Federal Deposit Insurance Corporation, 1998, *Resolutions Handbook: Methods for Resolving Troubled Financial Institutions in the United States* (Washington: FDIC).

Frydl, Edward, 1999, "The Length and Cost of Banking Crises," IMF Working Paper 99/30 (Washington: International Monetary Fund).

Garcia, Gillian, 2000, "Deposit Insurance and Crisis Management," IMF Working Paper 00/57 (Washington: International Monetary Fund).

Hawkins, John, and Phillip Turner, 1999, "Bank Restructuring in Practice: An Overview," (Basel: Bank for International Settlements, August).

Hull, John C., 1993, *Options, Futures, and Other Derivative Securities* (Englewood Cliffs: Prentice Hall), pp. 84–6.

Ingves, Stefan, and Goran Lind, 1996, "The Management of the Bank Crisis—In Retrospect," *Quarterly Review*, Sveriges Riksbank, No. 1, pp. 5–18.

——, 1997, "Loan-Loss Recoveries and Debt Resolution Agencies: The Swedish Experience," in Enoch, C., and Green, J., (eds.), *Bank Soundness and Monetary Policy* (Washington: International Monetary Fund).

Jennergren, Peter, and Bertil Naslund, 1998, "Efter Bankriesen: Vad Blev Notan for Skattebetalarna?," *Ekonomisk Debatt*, Vol. 26, No. 1.

Kaminsky, Graciela L., and Carmen M. Reinhart, 1996, "The Twin Crises: The Causes of Banking and Balance-of-Payments Problems," International Finance Discussion Paper No. 544 (Washington: Board of Governors of the Federal Reserve System).

Laumas, Prem S., and Khan A. Mohabbat, 1980, "Money and the Production Function: A Case Study of France," *Weltwirtschaftliches Archiv*, Vol. 116, No. 4, pp. 685–96.

Lindgren, Carl-Johan, and others, 2000, *Financial Sector Crisis and Restructuring: Lessons from Asia*, IMF Occasional Paper 188 (Washington: International Monetary Fund).

Lindgren, Carl-Johan, Gillian Garcia, and Matthew I. Saal, 1996, *Bank Soundness and Macroeconomic Policy* (Washington: International Monetary Fund).

Nguyen, Hong V., 1986, "Money in the Aggregate Production Function: Reexamination and Further Evidence," *Journal of Money, Credit, and Banking*, Vol. 18, No. 2, pp. 141–51.

Santomero, Anthony M., and Paul Hoffman, 1998, "Problem Bank Resolution: Evaluating the Options," (Philadelphia: The Wharton School, University of Pennsylvania, October).

Sephton, Peter S., 1988, "Money in the Production Function Revisited," *Applied Economics*, Vol. 20, No. 7, pp. 853–60.

Sheng, Andrew, ed., 1996, *Bank Restructuring: Lessons from the 1980s* (Washington: World Bank).

Woo, David, 2000, "Two Approaches to Resolving Nonperforming Assets During Financial Crises," IMF Working Paper 00/33 (Washington: International Monetary Fund).

Part II
Options for Bank Restructuring

3
Techniques of Bank Resolution

Steven A. Seelig

I. Introduction

Banking, as with other businesses, involves taking risks. However, given the high leverage in banking, adverse outcomes can more readily translate into insolvency. While bank supervision is designed to monitor and curtail the level of risk taken by bank managers it cannot prevent problems that result from weak economies, fraud, or mismanagement. Consequently, countries need to have mechanisms in place to handle the exit of a bank from the system, due to its insolvency, with minimum economic disruption and loss of confidence in the banking system.

Banks do not typically become insolvent overnight. Typically there is a gradual erosion of capital that requires a series of supervisory responses. If a bank's capital has declined to a positive but inadequate level, supervisory action is called for. The focus of the supervisory response should be to get the shareholders to increase the capital of the bank. This may take the form of a direct capital infusion by the shareholders or their diluting their interest by having the bank sell new shares to different investors.[1] If this is not successful, the supervisor may facilitate a merger with a healthy bank without using public funds. Nevertheless, despite the best efforts of supervisors banks will become insolvent and fail, giving rise to the need to resolve them.

The goal of bank resolution is to remove an insolvent bank from the system while assuring that investor discipline is maintained and, most importantly, public confidence in the banking sector is maintained.

II. Insolvent bank resolution

In order to successfully resolve insolvent banks countries need legal structures that allow for alternative resolution techniques and are conducive to recoveries on nonperforming loans. There must be an existing capacity, or the capability to create one, to deal with the nonperforming assets from the insolvent bank. Lastly, there is a need for the administrative capability to take quick decisions and execute them in a timely manner.

Guiding principles

In developing bank resolution strategies it is important to determine who will suffer losses and who will be protected. Alternatively, following on the framework for bankruptcy that exists in many countries, a priority of claims can be established. However, there are some guiding principles that should govern this prioritization. Within this framework countries may add other groups to receive priority treatment, consistent with their own bankruptcy regime.

The first principle is that shareholders should suffer the first loss. Shareholders have made an equity investment and placed their capital at risk. They receive all or most, of the up-side if the bank is profitable and lose when the bank suffers losses. It is only appropriate that they take the first loss if a bank is insolvent and thus will be the last to recover anything in the event that recoveries exceed creditor claims.

Subordinated creditors should take the next loss. Since these creditors have voluntarily agreed to be subordinate to other creditors (general creditors) in the event the bank experiences difficulty, it is only appropriate that they suffer losses before other creditors (but after shareholders). The Basel capital standards recognize the distinction between subordinated debt and other forms of debt by counting it as part of Tier 2 capital.

General creditors typically take the last loss. This group usually includes depositors, trade creditors, employee claims, and bond holders. It will also include secured creditors who are discussed later. This group constitutes the bulk of the liabilities of a bank and frequently incurs losses as a result of the insolvency. The guiding principle is that they should be repaid in full before either subordinated creditors or shareholders receive any payment. If a country has deposit insurance, insured depositors receive their funds from the deposit insurer up to the insurance limit. The deposit insurer will bear the losses instead of the insured depositor. In effect, the deposit insurer takes the place of the insured depositor in the claims scheme.

If a bank has secured creditors, these creditors are typically paid first up to the value of their collateral. Such payment is made either through the liquidation of the collateral or by transferring ownership of the collateral to the creditor. In the event the collateral is worth more than the claim, it is in the interest of the other general creditors to have the secured creditor claim paid in full so as to preserve the excess value for the estate of the failed bank.

In a number of countries, various groups are accorded preference over other general creditors. In particular, taxes and employee claims for salary earned but not paid is often given super priority status. This means that these claims are paid before all others. In some countries, such as the United States, depositor preference has been adopted. Under this regime, depositors come ahead of all other general creditors.

The important thing is that the priority of claims is spelled out clearly and ex ante so that there is no confusion when a bank fails. Moreover, with this information, various creditors can properly determine their minimum satisfactory return commensurate with risk. It is equally important that it be clearly understood that shareholders are to take the first loss, meaning that they are the last to be paid and only after all other claimants have been paid in full. Without this latter principle, as well as a lower status for subordinated creditors, there will be no market discipline and bank managers will be faced with moral hazard leading them to take excessive risks.

Critical factors in designing a strategy

In choosing a resolution strategy it is critical that the strategy enhance public confidence in the banking system; avoid disruption to the payment system; minimize losses to depositors, the government, or the deposit insurance fund; and minimize adverse economic effects. The dual goals of bank resolution should be to maintain confidence while minimizing the losses faced by creditors as a result of bank insolvency.

Maintaining public confidence is critical if contagion effects of bank failures are to be contained. If the public has confidence that the insolvency will be handled in a manner that assures them access to liquidity and availability of banking services they will only be concerned with any loss they may suffer. In countries with deposit insurance this is not an issue for the vast majority of depositors. Providing depositors with speedy access to their funds is critical to maintaining public confidence. Similarly, assuring that the public has alternative banking services available is also an important element in the choice of a strategy since it too will affect public confidence and local economic activity. The loss of banking services is often seen as a sign of economic decay. Transparency is also critical to maintaining public confidence. The public needs to know what is happening, that decisions are being made objectively, and that there is accountability. This is best accomplished by full disclosure by decision makers through the public media and ongoing financial reporting of results, where appropriate.

Maintaining the payment system is a key factor in the design of a bank resolution strategy. Key components to be considered are the role of the insolvent bank in the payment system and the availability of alternative sources of payment services to the public. If a bank is very large and plays a significant role in the payment system, a straight liquidation of the bank may not be an option and alternative strategies will have to be considered. Clearly, it is critical that payment services be maintained, though the availability of alternative banks may address this problem. Alternatively, the payment system role of the insolvent bank may need to be maintained in the resolution.

Addressing the failed bank's loans, both those that are performing and those that are not, is critical for several reasons. First, if performing loans are not serviced they will quickly become nonperforming with the associated loss in value to the estate of the failed bank. Similarly, nonperforming loans (NPLs) that are not worked will also lose value to the detriment of creditors of the estate of the insolvent bank, including depositors or the deposit insurance fund.[2] If a country is experiencing a banking crisis, the failure to address NPLs will undermine creditor discipline to the detriment of solvent banks and also slow the recovery in lending.

If not handled properly, bank failures can cause adverse regional economic externalities.[3] To reduce the adverse effect on regional economic activity, especially consumption, it is important to minimize the liquidity impact of an insolvency. This is accomplished by designing a resolution strategy that assures that depositors receive at least a portion of their deposits (for countries with deposit insurance this would be the insured deposit) as quickly as possible. In the United States this is usually accomplished within 48 hours. Similarly, assuring that performing loans are serviced by an operating bank permits local businesses to have the opportunity to maintain banking services. This is particularly important for firms that rely on working capital or inventory borrowing.

Key elements in any resolution strategy

There are four key elements that are needed in any resolution strategy. These are (i) the method to assure the speedy availability of funds for depositors; (ii) a strategy to minimize the loss of available banking services; (iii) a means to rapidly address the credits of the insolvent bank; and (iv) a plan to assure proper transparency of the process.

As discussed above, assuring that depositors have quick access to their funds is critical to maintaining public confidence in the system and avoiding runs on banks. It is also important for minimizing the adverse macroeconomic effects that can accompany bank failures. In particular, if consumers' liquidity is frozen for extended periods, consumption will fall with the attendant ripple effects on the local and regional economy. Consequently, any strategy chosen should incorporate the means to provide depositors with quick access to funds. This can be accomplished through a rapid claims process in a payout of insured deposits, through a merger type transaction, or by employing another local bank to act as a paying agent.

The availability of banking services is important both for maintaining economic activity and payment services for the public and for minimizing the losses from the failed bank. In determining the appropriate resolution strategy, it is important to know what banking alternatives are available to the customers of the insolvent bank. If there are alternative providers, the full range of options can be considered. However, if there are no other banks in the area, it may not be desirable to implement a resolution that eliminates the only bank. Alternative strategies that retain banking services will need to be considered. As discussed below, there are several strategies that make shareholders suffer the first loss but preserve banking services. Hence, the absence of banking services should not be an excuse not to resolve an insolvent bank.

Inasmuch as most banks become insolvent because of problem assets, it is necessary to address these assets in the resolution process. Both the problem assets, loans and other assets, and performing loans need to be dealt with so as to minimize the loss to the government and creditors and to minimize economic disruption for business borrowers. Consequently, a strategy must incorporate vehicles for dealing quickly with both performing and nonperforming assets. This may include sale, transfer to third party managers, or management by the resolution/liquidation staff.

As mentioned above, transparency is a critical factor in maintaining public confidence. Consequently, it is imperative that a communications strategy be part of the bank resolution strategy. Such a strategy should include communicating why the bank is insolvent, including any evidence of fraud, if applicable. It should clearly explain what the resolution is and how various stakeholders (depositors, borrowers, employees, and creditors) are affected. It should also contain an announcement of future plans to provide information on recoveries and the cost of the resolution.

III. Resolution techniques

Praying for redemption is not a legitimate bank resolution technique. Once it has been determined that a bank is insolvent the appropriate authorities need to take action to resolve the bank. Hoping that somehow the bank will be able to earn its way out of its problems, or that capital will magically appear, is not an acceptable alternative. Experience has shown that delay increases the cost of bank resolution and introduces market distortions by allowing insolvent banks to compete with banks that are required to meet capital requirements. One of the lessons learned during the Savings and Loan crisis in the United States is that allowing insolvent banks to continue to operate increases moral hazard; with the attendant significant cost to the deposit insurer or the taxpayers.

The following sections describe some of the broad techniques of bank resolution and the advantages and disadvantages of each. It should be noted that each of these can be modified to make them better suited to unique country and bank situations. In particular, the design of each strategy will have to reflect the legal system within a country and also the nature and extent of the problems in the banking sector.

Straight liquidation

In many ways the straight liquidation of an insolvent bank is the purest form of bank resolution and the closest to a bankruptcy liquidation process that is applied to other businesses.[4] Due to the lack of special bank resolution powers, the authorities in many countries are limited in their dealing with an insolvent bank to either government recapitalization or straight liquidation.

No deposit insurance

In a straight liquidation, once a bank is declared insolvent it is closed (ceases to operate) and placed into liquidation.[5] In some countries an independent receiver or liquidator is appointed to manage the process, while in others the bank supervisory agency or the central bank performs this function. The manager of the liquidation will sell or recover on the assets of the insolvent bank and creditors will receive periodic distributions from these recoveries. Distributions are made in accordance with the priority of claims, as discussed above.

The following example traces the process of a straight liquidation. Assume that Easy Bank was showing itself as solvent but slightly below the capital requirement of Country X. The bank supervisor ordered a thorough full scope examination due to suspicions that the bank had not been adequately provisioning for NPLs. The balance sheet for Easy Bank prior to the examination is shown in Table 3.1.

Table 3.1.   Easy Bank—Prior to Examination

Assets		Liabilities	
Cash	10	Deposits	90
Securities	10	Taxes due	1
Fixed assets	2	Subordinated debt	5
Net loans	78	Equity	4
Total assets	**100**	**Total liabilities and equity**	**100**

The examiners found that the bank had been underreporting problems in the loan portfolio and the NPL ratio was significantly higher. As a result of these findings the supervisor determines that the correct balance sheet for the bank is as shown in Table 3.2.

Table 3.2.   Easy Bank—Correct Balance Sheet

Assets		Liabilities	
Cash	10	Deposits	90
Securities	10	Taxes due	1
Fixed assets	2	Subordinated debt	5
Net loans	72	Equity	−2
Total assets	**94**	**Total liabilities and equity**	**94**

Based on these findings, the bank supervisor declares the bank insolvent and revokes its license. The bank is placed into liquidation and a liquidator/ receiver appointed. The first task of the liquidator is to verify the assets and liabilities. Once the liabilities are verified they are assigned a priority of claims in accordance with Country X's law. In Country X the law requires that tax claims and the administrative expenses of the liquidation have the highest priority, followed by depositor and general creditor claims. The lowest category of creditor claims is accorded to subordinated debt. All of these must be paid in full, including accrued interest before shareholders receive any payments.

The liquidator will dispose of the securities quickly and is assumed to recover 8 which when combined with cash provides the liquidation with 18 in quick cash. This allows the liquidator to satisfy the government's tax claim in full and the remainder is set aside for expenses and general creditor claims. Over time the fixed assets are disposed of for 1 and the performing loans yield cash recoveries, either from sale or settlements with borrowers of 50. This process takes several years and costs the liquidation 6. As a result the net recovery available to settle creditor claims is 63. Consequently, in this example the depositors will receive the entire 63, resulting in their taking a 30 percent loss on their deposits. Subordinated creditors and shareholders recover zero since there are insufficient recoveries to fully meet the principal claims of the general creditors. It should also be noted that this process can take anywhere from 5 to 15 years with creditors suffering the loss of forgone interest while waiting for their money.

With deposit insurance

A straight liquidation with deposit insurance is similar to one without it. The major difference relates to the treatment of depositors. When deposit insurance is in place, one can think of this as a deposit insurance payout. Under a well functioning deposit insurance scheme, insured depositors will receive payment of the insured portion of their deposits shortly after the bank is closed. The deposit insurance fund, or the insurer, takes the place of the insured depositor as a general creditor in the liquidation. The net result is that depositors are fully protected, up to the amount of coverage, and receive access to their funds sooner than they would if there were no deposit insurance. The deposit insurer bears the losses that the uninsured depositors would otherwise have taken.

In the example of Easy Bank, above, had deposit insurance been in place that covered deposits up to a maximum balance of 2, which covers 80 of the 90 in total deposits, all depositors would have received the insured balance and the deposit insurer would have replaced them as a general creditor. Given the outcome of the liquidation, the fully insured depositors suffered no loss. Depositors with balances in excess of the insured amount lose 30 percent of the uninsured balance (if a depositor had deposits of 4 it would suffer a loss of 0.6) and the deposit insurer will lose 30 percent on its claim, or 24.

Advantages of straight liquidation

With the straight liquidation of an insolvent bank, shareholders lose their investment unless the losses in the failed bank's estate are so small that other creditors receive full recovery. Since other creditors, including depositors, typically suffer losses the closure and liquidation of an insolvent bank should increase market discipline.

If a deposit insurance scheme is in place, small depositors are fully protected while larger depositors suffer some losses. If the deposit insurance limits have been set properly, this should not result in a significant loss in market discipline since smaller depositors typically are not capable of analyzing the condition of a bank and exerting meaningful discipline. Since wealthier individuals and firms, with large deposits, will suffer some loss they have the appropriate incentive to monitor the bank.

Disadvantages of straight liquidation

In many countries there are significant delays before depositors receive their funds.[6] This, in turn, undermines public confidence in the banking sector. In addition, the liquidation of the assets can stretch out for many years (often more than ten) delaying the return of funds to creditors and creating undue expenses that typically are paid ahead of creditor claims.

Given the nature of the resolution, borrowers lose their relationship with a bank. In some instances this can create macroeconomic impacts, since firms frequently rely on a bank for working capital and inventory financing. Given the unique credit information that is developed in a commercial borrowing relationship, it may be costly for borrowers to establish new banking relationships.

If depositors are protected by the government at the time of the insolvency, either through a government sponsored deposit insurance scheme or a blanket guarantee, the fiscal outlays will be higher under a straight liquidation than other resolution techniques. The reason is that at the time of the bank closing, the deposit insurer or the government will have to lay out the full amount of deposit claims to be covered. (In the case of Easy Bank, this was 80.) It should be recognized that, while the fiscal outlay may be maximized, this does not imply that the fiscal cost will be higher than other resolution techniques. Since the fiscal cost is the outlay net of recoveries, if the unprotected creditor class is larger relative to protected deposits, the ultimate fiscal cost will likely be lower than alternatives that protect all depositors.

Nationalization

Often authorities are reluctant to "close" a bank, as would be required in a straight liquidation. An alternative is to nationalize the bank with the goal of keeping it open but replace the existing shareholders with the government. However, it is critical that steps also be taken so that the government ends up owning a bank that has been cleaned-up and meets all prudential norms.

The nationalization of an insolvent bank entails several key steps. First, the bank must be declared insolvent by the supervisor and the law should allow the supervisor to wipe out the shareholders' interest. If this cannot be done, the government (or the deposit insurer) will have to negotiate with the shareholders to dilute their interest to zero. Next, the state must recapitalize the bank sufficiently to fill the hole, namely to wipe out the negative equity and to add additional equity to bring the bank into conformance with the supervisory capital adequacy requirements. Recapitalization of insolvent banks by governments can be accomplished with infusions of cash, government paper, government guaranteed paper, or a combination of these.[7]

Nationalization has appeal in many countries because the only alternative in the law is straight liquidation and there is no ability to quickly dispose of assets and provide funds to depositors. This is especially the case in countries without deposit insurance. However, there have been situations where nationalization has been used, even when deposit insurance exists and where the legal system allows for a whole range of resolution alternatives. Typically this has occurred in the case of the insolvency of very large banks. For example, Continental Illinois National Bank, at the time the eighth largest bank in the United States, was found to be insolvent. Rather than close the bank, a resolution was structured whereby the Federal Deposit Insurance Corporation (FDIC) assumed the $3.0 billion in liabilities to the Federal Reserve and took ownership of $4.5 billion NPLs from the bank. The FDIC also invested sufficient cash to bring the bank in compliance with the Office of the Comptroller of the Currency's capital requirements. The shareholders surrendered their ownership interest in the bank for a residual claim against the pool of NPLs. In the event that recoveries on the NPLs exceeded the required payment of principal and interest to the Federal Reserve, they would get the excess. If recoveries did not cover the obligation to the Federal Reserve, the FDIC was obligated to cover the shortfall. Over a period of years the FDIC sold its equity interest in a series of secondary offerings to the public. The original shareholders were wiped out and the net cost of the transaction to the FDIC was less than 3 percent of the total assets of the bank.

Advantages of resolving a bank by nationalization

Clearly, with adequate planning this type of resolution can be handled very quickly. While it may require several months of planning and negotiations, the execution can occur very quickly and avoids the delays associated with a straight liquidation of a large bank. Even with deposit insurance, unless the deposit insurer has the latest in technology tools, the verification of deposits and claims can be a lengthy process for a large bank.

Nationalization of an insolvent bank protects all of the creditors of the bank. This is a benefit during periods of shaky public confidence and is an alternative to announcing a blanket guarantee for all bank creditors since, in effect, it is granted on a case-by-case basis.

Since the bank continues to operate, paying customers are able to maintain their lending relationships with the bank. This is particularly beneficial in situations where there are not alternative sources of credit. Similarly, there is no disruption to the payment system.

One of the disadvantages of a straight liquidation is that if deposit insurance exists and a large bank becomes insolvent, the fiscal outlay (or deposit insurance fund outlay) is very large. With nationalization the fiscal outlay is limited to the amount of funds needed to bring the capital level up to supervisory norms (the size of the hole plus additional capital).

Disadvantages of bank nationalization

Clearly, protecting all creditors of a bank erodes market discipline. If depositors and other creditors believe that the government will step in and protect them anytime a bank fails, they will have no reason to monitor the bank and impose discipline. There is also a risk of moral hazard since the management, knowing that all creditors will be protected, may be willing to take excessive risk in an effort to recapitalize the bank.

Many large insolvent banks, besides problems on the credit side, have been operated inefficiently. Nationalizing such a bank is likely to perpetuate such inefficiencies since governments have not shown much interest in taking what are likely to be politically unpopular decisions to reduce staff.

A nationalized bank may have significant competitive advantages relative to other banks because it will be perceived as having a full government guarantee on its liabilities. This may allow it to attract deposits at a lower rate than the market, and in turn price loans below market. This drawback can be mitigated by requiring the bank to set its prices at the average of the market. However, the competitive advantage of the perceived government guarantee cannot be eliminated.

In many countries, any time the government owns a commercial entity it invites political interference in the operations of the firm. This is especially true for banks. Once the bank has been nationalized, there will be a temptation on the part of politicians to direct lending to certain sectors or even individual borrowers. Staff reductions, branch closings and openings, and foreclosures on collateral all may become politicized to the detriment of the viability of the bank. This in turn will affect the end fiscal cost, since if the bank is privatized the proceeds to the government will be directly related to the performance of the bank.

Purchase and assumption transactions

The goal of a purchase and assumption transaction (P&A) is to have the insolvent bank cease to exist but avoid the disruptive effects of a straight liquidation. To utilize this resolution technique, another bank that is interested in acquiring all or part of the business of the insolvent bank is required. The basic structure is for the acquiring bank to purchase the good assets of the failed bank and assume its deposit liabilities. The deposit insurer or the government provides cash or government paper to make up for the difference between the good assets purchased and the liabilities assumed.

The liquidation/receivership seeks to recover monies for the government and other creditors by disposing of the assets of the failed bank. With a P&A transaction, the good assets are disposed of at book value and an offsetting amount of liabilities are satisfied. The liquidator/receiver will subsequently dispose of the "bad" assets, either through sale or by managing them. In the event there is more than one potential acquirer, the choice of acquirer is made based on choosing the bidder willing to pay the highest premium. This premium reduces the amount of cash needed to fill the shortfall between assets purchased and liabilities assumed.[8]

To illustrate a P&A transaction, let us assume that after the supervisor has determined that Failed Bank is insolvent, and restated its books, its balance sheet is shown in Table 3.3.

Table 3.3. Failed Bank

Assets		Liabilities	
Cash and securities	10	Deposits	100
Performing loans	50		
NPLs	50	Total liabilities	100
Less provisions	–20	Total equity	–10
Total assets	**90**	**Total**	**90**

Several banks have expressed interest in undertaking a P&A transaction for Failed Bank. The transaction would involve the shaded assets and liabilities of the bank. After undertaking a bidding process, the bank resolution agency chooses "Acquiring Bank" who has bid a premium of 2 percent of deposits. Acquiring Bank's balance sheet is shown in Table 3.4.

Table 3.4. Acquiring Bank

Assets		Liabilities	
Cash and securities	50	Deposits	325
Performing loans	300		
NPLs	50	Total liabilities	325
Less provisions	–25	Total equity	50
Total assets	**375**	**Total**	**375**

The transaction involves the acquirer purchasing the cash and securities and the performing loans and assuming all the deposits of Failed Bank. Since the deposits equal 100 but the good assets are only 60, the shortfall, net of the premium, will be made up by the government or the deposit insurer.

Since the premium paid by the acquiring bank is 2 the government reduces the amount of cash it injects, and the size of its subrogated claim against the liquidation. The following T-accounts for the acquirer and the failed bank liquidation reflect the transaction (Table 3.5).

Table 3.5. Acquiring Banks and Liquidation

Acquiring Bank

Change in Assets		Change in Liabilities	
Cash and securities	+10	Deposits	+100
Performing loans	+50		
Cash and securities from government	+38	Equity	–2
Total assets	**+98**	**Total liabilities and equity**	**+98**

Liquidation

Change in Assets		Change in Liabilities	
Cash and securities	–10	Deposits	–100
Performing loans	–50	Government claim	+38
Total assets	**–60**	**Total liabilities**	**–62**

If the acquiring bank had not had excess capital it would have had to raise additional capital to cover the transaction. Assuming a 10 percent risk weighted CAR, the acquirer would have needed to raise an additional 5 in equity.

As a result of this transaction Acquiring Bank and the Liquidation will have the following balance sheets, as seen in Table 3.6.

Table 3.6. Acquiring Bank and Failed Bank Liquidation

Acquiring Bank

Assets		Liabilities	
Cash and securities	98	Deposits	425
Performing loans	350		
NPLs	50	Total liabilities	425
Less provisions	–25	Equity	48
Total assets	**473**	**Total liabilities and equity**	**473**

Failed Bank Liquidation

Assets		Liabilities	
NPLs	50	Claims of the government	38
Less provisions	–20		
Total assets	**30**		

If the recoveries on the assets remaining in the liquidation turn out to be 19 (38 percent of the gross claim against the borrowers) the loss suffered by the government/deposit insurer on its claim will be 19, or a 50 percent loss. Since the acquiring bank paid a premium of 2, this reduced the loss to the government/deposit insurer by about 5 percent.

Advantages of purchase and assumption transactions

Operational issues are among the greatest difficulties in undertaking bank resolutions. While still operationally complex, a major advantage of P&A transactions is that they can be executed quickly. In the United States these transactions are typically accomplished over a weekend. Speed is important since it is a critical factor in maintaining public confidence. Moreover, it is a relatively easy transaction to explain to depositors since, as far as they are concerned, nothing more has happened than their accounts have been transferred to a new bank.

Since one of the goals for a government may be to retain banking services in a sparsely served area, a P&A transaction potentially meets this goal. The acquiring bank initially will take on most of the branches of the failed bank and continues to provide services in the geographic markets served by the failed bank. However, if over time, these services cannot be provided profitably it is reasonable to expect a prudent banker to reduce its presence in the market.

If there are several potential buyers, the transaction allows the government, or the deposit insurer, to capture the franchise value of the failed bank for the benefit of its creditors, including the government. This helps reduce the ultimate fiscal cost of the transaction as well as the immediate fiscal outlay.

While the P&A transaction meets the objective of forcing shareholders to suffer the first loss and results in an inefficient bank leaving the system, its biggest benefit is that it avoids the disruption that can accompany a straight liquidation. Specifically, all depositors avoid the liquidity implications of loss of access to their funds since they have almost immediate access. Current borrowers continue a banking relationship with the acquiring bank, and there is minimum disruption to the payment system since the acquiring bank takes over the obligations of the failed bank and its role in the payment system.

Disadvantages of purchase and assumption transactions

The major drawback to these transactions is that all depositors of the failed bank are protected, including the large sophisticated ones who are not supposed to be protected under deposit insurance schemes. Therefore, if depositors believe that bank resolutions will be handled using P&A transactions, market discipline will be eroded. In response to this concern, variations of the P&A transaction have been developed that result in uninsured depositors receiving the same treatment as in a straight liquidation. This is discussed below; however, it must be recognized that such transactions are a bit more operationally complex to execute.

If a failed bank is allowed to operate for an extended period of insolvency, it is likely that the negative equity will grow and may be quite large relative to the size of the bank. If this is the case, a P&A transaction requires a significant contribution from the government/deposit insurer to fill the gap between total deposits and the assets purchased. Similarly, in countries where banks are suspended while being intervened prior to being placed into liquidation, there likely will be a serious deterioration in the performing loan portfolio that will increase the cost of a future resolution.

Variations on purchase and assumption transactions

Insured-deposit transfer

An insured-deposit transfer is similar to a P&A transaction *except* that only insured deposits are assumed by the acquiring bank. Hence, the transaction is the same as that outlined above, except a portion of the deposits is not assumed and remain as claims against the liquidation. In the above example, if 10 percent of the deposits of Failed Bank were uninsured and not transferred the outlay of the government would have been reduced by the same amount and its proportional claim on the receivership's assets would be reduced to 28 and uninsured depositors would have a pari-pasu claim for the remaining 10.[9]

In countries with a least-cost test it would appear, on the surface, that this would always be less costly than a straight P&A since the loss to a deposit insurer is the same as in an insured-deposit payoff. However, this is not always the case. If the acquiring bank places a high value on the uninsured deposits, and is willing to bid a high enough premium for them, then a traditional P&A may actually be cheaper.

It should be noted that there may be significant operational obstacles to this type of transaction. First, it only will work where the deposit insurer is also the receiver/liquidator of the failed bank. This is because the receiver/liquidator is charged with protecting the interests of all creditors and thus would find it legally difficult to enter into a transaction that favors one group of creditors over another (except where the law gives preference to insured deposits). Hence, this may not be a possible resolution strategy for those countries where the deposit insurer only serves as a lock box.

An operational obstacle, is that to execute this transaction quickly, requires that the deposit insurer is able to identify the amount of insured deposits relative to uninsured at the time the bank is put up for bids. Moreover, it is critical that individual deposits can be separated quickly after the legal closing of the bank. Both of these require that the deposit insurer have access to the bank's deposit files prior to suspension of the license and have the system capabilities to deal with account combinations in a speedy manner. Unless this transaction is completed quickly, the benefits of a quick resolution, discussed above, are lost.

De novo bank purchase and assumption

Frequently, authorities wish to resolve an insolvent bank but are afraid of the disruptive effects of liquidation, even if a blanket guarantee is in effect that would require the government to make payments to depositors and creditors. A P&A transaction is the ideal solution, however it requires that there be an acquiring bank.

If there is no ready acquiring bank, a de novo P&A resolution can be used to gain the benefits of a traditional P&A. Under this variation a new bank is created and it assumes the liabilities and acquires assets in the same manner as an existing acquiring bank. The net transaction is the same as that outlined above. The new bank can be privately owned and created by private investors (who have met the fit and proper requirements of the bank supervisor) or the government can create the bank. If the government creates the bank, its outlay is increased by the initial capitalization of the bank sufficient to meet all prudential requirements. However, in the future the government should recover this outlay by selling its shares to the public or to a strategic investor.

The advantage of a de novo P&A resolution is that it avoids losing a bank in a community. This may be crucial to maintaining confidence after a crisis or for protecting jobs of bank employees that would be lost if the bank were liquidated. Banking services will be maintained and there will be minimal disruption for borrowers and depositors. The only downside is the increase in the government's outlay and all of the political drawbacks associated with nationalized banks (see above).

Sometimes countries have resorted to variations on this structure when faced with either legal restrictions on bank resolution or the absence of either deposit insurance or the ability to protect depositors. A recent example can be found in Uruguay. The authorities there had placed three banks into liquidation but wished to preserve banking services and minimize the losses to the depositors left in the banks.[10] The government created a new bank, Nuevo Banco Commercial. They initially capitalized it with the minimum required paid-in capital. The new bank bids on packages of assets offered for sale by the liquidations and paid for the loans with new certificates of deposit (CDs). The liquidators, in turn, distributed these CDs to the creditors of the failed banks on a pro rata basis. The government, as owner of the de novo bank, converted a sufficient amount of its CDs into equity to fully capitalize the new bank, and gave most of the rest to depositors to top them off up to $100,000. The government succeeded to these depositors claims against the liquidation.

Whole bank transaction

A whole bank P&A is the same as the traditional one *except* that the acquirer purchases all of the assets of the failed bank. The good assets are typically purchased at book value or a market value, if one exists, and the bad assets are priced on a bid basis. In practice, rather than asking bidders to bid a premium for the bank, they are requested to bid on the bad assets and the winning bidder is selected based on the price that is offered. As in the traditional P&A the government or the deposit insurer fills in the difference with cash or government securities. Potential acquiring banks must have the ability, interest, and financial resources to purchase and manage a portfolio of NPLs for this strategy to be successful.

Using the example presented for the traditional P&A resolution, let's assume the winning bank bid 50 percent of the book value of the NPLs, net of provisions. The T-accounts for the transaction would be as shown in Table 3.7.

Table 3.7.   Acquiring Bank and Liquidation for Whole Bank Transaction

Acquiring Bank

Change in Assets		Change in Liabilities	
Cash and securities	+10	Deposits	+100
Performing loans	+50		
NPLs at purchase price	+15		
Cash from government	+25		
Total assets	**+100**	**Total liabilities and equity**	**+100**

Liquidation

Change in Assets		Change in Liabilities	
Cash and securities	−10	Deposits	−100
Performing loans	−50	Government claim	+25
Net NPLs	−30		
Cash from sale of NPLs	+15		
Total assets	**−75**	**Total liabilities**	**−75**

The balance sheet for the liquidation, after the whole bank transaction is as shown in Table 3.8.

Table 3.8.   Failed Banks Liquidations

Assets		Liabilities	
		Claims of the government	25
Total assets	0	**Total**	25

While the aggregate loss to the government is greater, than in the example above that assumed a 2 percent premium and a recovery on the NPLs of 19, it should be recognized that the fiscal outlay for the government/deposit insurer is reduced to 25 and it eliminates the interest cost on the difference in the outlays. This may be greater than the difference in recoveries on the NPLs, especially if a country does not have a well developed capacity to collect NPLs rapidly.

The major advantage of a whole bank transaction is that it avoids the need for a protracted liquidation of assets by the government or the deposit insurer. All borrowers have the opportunity to maintain banking relationships and the resolution minimizes the fiscal outlay at the closing.

There are several critical drawbacks to using whole bank transactions as a primary resolution technique. This technique requires sufficient lead time for potential acquirers to undertake the necessary due diligence to formulate a bid for the NPLs. It also may require the cooperation of the failing bank's management that may be difficult to obtain. (This requires the supervisor signaling that the bank will be declared insolvent and protecting against asset stripping by the owners and management during the interim time frame while due diligence is taking place.) The government must recognize that it may need to accept a large discount below net book value for the NPLs and this may be politically unacceptable. Lastly, if the acquiring bank does not have the expertise to manage the "bad" assets the transaction could create a larger new problem bank. This occurred in one of the first whole bank transactions in the United States and subsequently led to a second round failure.

Good bank—bad bank

When a large bank becomes insolvent it frequently has a large portfolio of NPLs. Splitting the failed bank into two banks, one with good assets and the other with the "bad" ones may facilitate the resolution of the bank and minimize some of the disruptions typically associated with the insolvency of large banks. This technique can be used in conjunction with the nationalization of a large bank or when the bank is being purchased by a private party or another bank. The good bank/bad bank technique entails separating the bad assets from the bank and funding them with deposits or government paper.

This technique can also be used to facilitate a resolution of a seriously troubled, but still solvent, problem bank. If new investors (or another bank) are interested in taking over the troubled bank, but are unwilling to take on the risk associated with a large portfolio of NPLs, a solution might be to separate the bank into two banks: a good bank, that only has the good assets, and a bad one that holds the NPLs. The shareholders of the troubled bank will receive the ownership of the bad bank and the new investors capitalize the good bank. If the volume of NPLs is so large that all creditors cannot remain in the good bank, subordinated creditors will have to become creditors of the bad bank. Beyond this, if the volume of NPLs is too great, the bank will have to be closed or government funds used to protect creditors.

The primary benefit of this type of resolution is that it allows the "good bank" to solely focus on the business of banking, including developing the franchise, rather than dealing with the NPLs. The management of NPLs requires specialized expertise and frequently banks that become insolvent also have numerous other management problems, including weak credit policies and internal control weaknesses, that require the full attention of senior management.

Within the context of a nationalization of a large bank, the Continental Illinois bank resolution was the first to use the good bank/bad bank framework. The FDIC pulled out the bad assets and put them into a separate pool managed by a special group within the bank. This "bad bank" was owned by the former shareholders of Continental Illinois and funded with liabilities to the Federal Reserve (but fully guaranteed by the FDIC), while the good bank was owned by the FDIC.

A more recent example of a good bank/bad bank resolution is the strategy used by the government of Uruguay to address problems in its large state bank, Banco de Republica Oriental de Uruguay. This bank had a significant portfolio of NPLs and high operating costs. A special vehicle in the form of a trust was created to purchase the NPLs from the bank. In return for the NPLs it sold to the trust, the bank received a note from the trust, guaranteed by the government for the net book value of the transferred assets. An asset management company was established, with incentive compensation schemes, to manage the assets and assure the trust made timely payments on the note. The benefit of this resolution strategy was that the balance sheet of the bank was cleaned up and the bank fully capitalized. Moreover the management of the state bank was able to focus its efforts on cost-cutting strategies and refocusing the business plan of the bank. Collection efforts were handled by experts, with the result that borrowers recognized that they were no longer dealing with the bank that had, in effect been giving forbearance by making no collection efforts. The result one year into the transaction has been quite positive.

Conservatorship

In some countries, a conservator is appointed to determine if the bank is insolvent and whether it can be rehabilitated. The conservator takes over the management and voting rights of shareholders, but not their economic rights. In other countries, the role of the conservator is performed when banks are intervened (by an intervener) and frequently these responsibilities are carried out by the supervisory agency. Conservatorship can be used as an alternative to the forms of intervention that involve suspending the activities of a bank.

During the Savings and Loan crisis in the United States, after the insolvency of the thrift deposit insurance fund, savings and loans were put in conservatorship as a holding action until such time as appropriations could be obtained from Congress to fund the resolutions of these thrift institutions. The role of the conservator was to replace management and allow deposit operations and loan servicing to continue but limit growth in the bank as well as predatory behavior that would exacerbate the problems faced by other savings and loan associations.

Conservatorships can also be a form of intervention that is appropriate to deal with management problems. For example, if it is discovered that the owners/managers of the bank are engaging in fraudulent transactions, the appointment of a conservator is a way of stopping the fraud until its magnitude is discovered. It is useful in cases where a bank's capital is greater than zero but less than that required by the supervisor. A conservator can replace management and address the problems in the bank if the shareholders were unwilling to. Lastly, as was done for savings and loans in the United States, conservatorship powers can be used to take control of a bank while the authorities are arranging a resolution.

There are several drawbacks to the use of conservatorships. They can unnecessarily delay bank resolutions and increase the cost of the ultimate resolution. Public uncertainty may increase after the announcement that a bank has been placed into conservatorship, and this could lead to deposit runs. Depending on weaknesses in the legal framework or corruption in the judiciary, shareholders may be able to interfere in the operation of the bank, despite its being under conservatorship. Moreover, efforts to defend against interference take away from efforts to deal with problems in the bank.

IV. State banks

State banks are particularly difficult from both a supervisory and a resolution perspective. Since the government is the owner of the bank, supervisors often feel constrained in their approach to the bank. In some countries, the powers of the supervisor are constrained if the bank is directly or indirectly a constitutional entity. For example, only the President and/or possibly the legislature can remove senior management of the bank. Moreover, wiping out shareholder interests and closing the bank may not be viable options should the bank become insolvent. Nevertheless, steps must be taken to assure that the bank operates in a safe and sound manner and if it does not that the problems are corrected promptly. From international experiences several observations can be made:

- **State banks should be supervised in the same manner as all other banks.** These banks should be subject to the same capital standards, examination frequencies, prudential norms and other measures as all other banks. This is critical to minimize the adverse financial effects of directed lending and political interference inherent in state banks.

Moreover, it is necessary to minimize the cost to the taxpayers associated with poor management and lax lending practices.

- **The resolution of an insolvent state bank will require the government to recapitalize the bank.** An insolvent state bank should not be allowed to operate. Doing so will lead to a loss in confidence in the banking sector and undermine the competitive position of solvent private banks. Either the government must recapitalize the bank with cash and/or government paper or it should privatize the bank.
- **Unless problem loan and operational issues are dealt with the bank will continue to be a problem**. It is insufficient to just recapitalize a state bank that has become insolvent or undercapitalized without addressing the problems that led to its financial condition. An analysis of the financial condition of the bank must be undertaken and various stress tests performed to identify the steps that need to be taken. Absent addressing the bank's underlying problems, it will need to be recapitalized continuously.
- **Governance issues must be addressed!** Frequently the problems at state banks result from weak governance, either in the form of poor management appointed through a political process that ignores banking knowledge in favor of political rewards, a board that is purely political, or weak approval processes. A state bank needs senior management and a board of directors who are knowledgeable in banking and financial matters and who can assure that proper procedures and controls are in place. The role of the state bank should be to generate dividends to the government and not serve as a vehicle for politically directed lending that becomes a drain on the country's treasury.

V. Asset management companies

Proper management and disposition of nonperforming assets is a critical element in the resolution of problem banks. Without a capacity within the system to handle NPLs, bank resolutions become excessively difficult. NPL management can be performed by a state entity, such as a national asset management company (AMC) or the deposit insurer, commercial banks, or private firms. Absent dealing with problem assets, any resolution is doomed to failure and will likely need to be repeated.

How well the nonperforming assets are handled has a direct implication for the cost of a bank resolution. In the examples above, one can see that the recovery rate on NPLs bears a direct relationship to the cost to the government of the resolution.

If the volume of NPLs in the banking sector reaches a certain size the way they are handled can have systemic implications. As mentioned earlier, one of the externalities of bank insolvencies is the implications for economic activity in the real sector. This not only comes from the consumption behavior of depositors but also from business borrowers. Strategies to maximize recoveries on NPLs must take into account economic realities. Consequently, there are times when litigation and foreclosure are the best option and others when financial restructuring of a business borrower is best. These decisions require experienced management and accountability that can only be found in asset management companies.

Asset management companies can become vehicles to promote corporate restructuring. Typically one thinks of debt restructuring as a tool of an AMC; however, it can also use debt for equity swaps as a means to force true corporate restructuring that addresses issues of operating expense, governance, and business practices.

A more detailed discussion of the role of AMCs in bank restructuring and the issues surrounding the creation of them can be found in Chapter 9 by Ingves, Seelig, and He.

VI. Concluding comments

Bank resolution is all about public confidence. In many ways the technique chosen to resolve a bank is less important than that an insolvent bank has been resolved and that the process was handled rapidly with minimum disruption.

Public confidence requires that there be firm supervision of banks that is applied in a consistent manner across banks. The policies and rules of the supervisor should be clearly understood and transparent.

For bank resolution to be effective there is a need for a supportive legal system. This is also a critical component in maintaining public confidence. The system must assure that the rights of creditors and shareholders are clearly spelled out and their application in the event of insolvency, must be uniform. If the public believes that the legal system differentiates in its treatment of creditors, nonperforming borrowers, banks, etc., based on wealth or political connections, confidence is undermined. The legal system must provide for creditor rights so that banks, and liquidators or AMCs, can pursue collateral on NPLs. Moreover, it is imperative that the priority of claims is clearly spelled out and not open to subjective interpretation at the time of a bank resolution.

Transparency in the dealing with insolvent banks is critical to maintaining public confidence and thus is a key element in executing any strategy to resolve them. Authorities need to explain to the public what the causes of the insolvency were, the steps being taken to resolve the bank, the time frames involved, and the expected costs. This can be done through press releases and public statements. The party responsible for the liquidation of a bank should also publish financial results and projections on a regular basis so that creditors know the value of their claim.

Notes

1. Aside from bringing about a recapitalization of the bank, supervisors will also need to address the underlying problems in the bank through a series of other measures.
2. In countries where public funds have been used in the resolution of an insolvent bank, failure to address the loan portfolio of the bank has increased the losses paid by taxpayers.
3. See Kaufman and Seelig, Chapter 6, this volume.
4. It is almost identical to a Chapter 7 bankruptcy in the United States.
5. In some countries, such as Georgia, the bank will be intervened and activity suspended prior to it being placed in liquidation. This is done so that a formal determination of insolvency can be presented to the courts. Sometimes the liquidation proceeds during the intervention period and the insolvency and license revocation comes at the end of the process.
6. This is also the case in many countries that have deposit insurance schemes. See Kaufman and Seelig, Chapter 6, this volume.
7. During the Asian banking crises some countries issued special recapitalization bonds for banks taken over by the government. In the United States, at different times, recapitalization has been provided by the deposit insurer assuming the bank's borrowings from the central bank, through cash infusions, or even the use of net worth certificates (for mutual savings banks).
8. Potential acquirers should be preapproved by the supervisor based on their financial and managerial capacity to undertake the transaction.
9. If a country has adopted insured depositor preference, the deposit insurer's claim comes ahead of the uninsured depositors and the loss to the deposit insurer will be reduced dramatically.
10. Earlier in the banking crisis the authorities had set up a fund to cover all sight and saving deposits. However, the time deposits at the banks had been frozen until the banks were placed into liquidation, at which point they were to become creditors of the liquidation. The government was required to protect the time depositors of the three banks up to $100,000 using the resources they received on their claims against the liquidations that resulted from covering the sight and savings depositors.

4
Issuing Government Bonds to Finance Bank Recapitalization and Restructuring: Design Factors that Affect Banks' Financial Performance

Michael Andrews[1]

I. Introduction

Bond issuance by a government, or a government agency such as a deposit insurance fund or a specially created asset management company (AMC), is used in many instances of systemic banking crises to finance bank restructuring and is also frequently used to finance the restructuring of state banks for privatization.[2] Although there are many variations in practice, bonds are issued for two generic purposes in bank restructuring:[3] to finance the government purchase of equity in banks;[4] and to finance the purchase of distressed assets from banks. The design of the bonds issued for these purposes can be a crucial determinant of the future financial performance of restructured banks, and thus an important factor in the ultimate success or failure of the restructuring efforts. Appendix 4.I notes some of the key design features in over 40 instances of the use of bonds for bank restructuring. Table 4.1 summarizes the implications for banks and governments of the issues discussed in this chapter.

There are many issues to be addressed in systemic bank restructuring, and this chapter focuses on those related to bond design. Fiscal, debt management, and other related issues, while noted to provide a broader context for the discussion of technical issues relating specifically to bank restructuring, are not fully developed in this chapter. Similarly, sovereign default is discussed only in the context of bank restructuring, without a full exploration of the impact of the costs of bank restructuring on debt sustainability.[5] The principal

Table 4.1.   Banks and Government

Issue	Banks	Government	Other Considerations
Bonds issued by a government agency	Sovereign guarantee can provide same zero risk-weighting as a government issue. Possibly greater liquidity if bond issues are part of a larger pool of generally homogeneous government debt.	Few advantages except in the rare case where a government agency has the infrastructure already in place for bond issuance, and the government itself does not.	Possibly better secondary market for government debt by having more homogeneous issues rather than some government and some government agency issues.
Direct placement of bonds with banks	Even if negotiable, special purpose bonds may be less liquid than other government debt.	Can be used even if government is unable or unwilling to access the bond market.	Central bank may provide special discount facilities for bank liquidity management.
Restrictions on tradability	Can restrict loan growth and ability to meet liquidity requirements.	May limit banks' ability to invest in risky assets. May be used to ensure banks are able to redeem subordinated debt at maturity.	Central bank may provide special discount facilities for bank liquidity management.
Below market interest rates	May provide insufficient income to ensure bank profitability.	Reduces fiscal cost.	Valuing below market rate bonds at par is inconsistent with International Financial Reporting Standards (IFRS).
Fixed or floating interest rates	Exposure to mismatch risk unless fixed rate assets can be matched with fixed rate liabilities.	Fiscal preference based on forecasts of future rates.	May be secondary market preference for fixed or floating rates.
Foreign currency issues	May be needed to close large open positions.	Government bears risk of adverse foreign exchange movements, and will require foreign currency for debt service and redemption.	Bonds indexed to a foreign currency may be used, matching the denomination of obligations to that of tax receipts.
Maturities	Prices of longer-dated bonds may be more volatile and carry higher risk premium in secondary market. May be a lack of long-term liabilities to match with long-term assets.	Longer maturities defer refinancing needs. Range of maturities avoids lumpy refinancing profiles.	Range of maturities may be desirable to establish a yield curve.

intent is to illustrate the impact that various options for bond design may have on successful bank restructuring.[6]

Compromises are required to address specific issues and concerns, but a successful program requires that bonds placed with banks for restructuring purposes provide sufficient interest income to enable the banks to be profitable, and do not make it difficult to manage exposures to interest rate, maturity, or foreign exchange risks. In general, this will require the use of bonds with market-related terms and conditions. If a restructured bank is insufficiently profitable or has an embedded risk exposure arising from its bond holdings, the likely result will be the loss of the public funds used for recapitalization and a need for subsequent intervention and more costly restructuring.

II. Context for bond issuance: the use of public funds

Decisions on bond design are technical issues dealt with after crucial policy decisions have been made to use public funds for bank restructuring, and to finance the expense with bonds issued specially for the purpose. An examination of the costs and benefits of using public funds for bank restructuring is beyond the scope of this chapter, which focuses more narrowly on the financing through borrowing of the government expense. The case for use of public funds to recapitalize and restructure banks is that the costs of such extraordinary action are less than the broad disruption in the real economy that might result from the failure of one or more systemically important banks.[7] The benefits from such expenses are difficult to quantify as they largely relate to avoiding disruptive effects, the magnitude and consequences of which are difficult to estimate.[8] However, in most cases of systemic crisis the government has generally opted for public expenditure to preserve some portion of a widely insolvent banking system to ensure that essential banking services continue to be provided to the real economy.

III. Special purpose bonds

Once the decision has been taken to use public funds for bank restructuring, the issue then becomes how to finance the expense. The option of government cash expenditures to purchase bank equity and/or distressed assets, while theoretically available, may be impractical as the macroeconomic conditions likely to exist in a banking crisis would constrain government revenues and financing sources.

There are clear advantages, such as the existence of broader and deeper secondary markets, if the financing of bank restructuring is part of a larger pool of generally homogeneous government debt. However, in a crisis the only practical solution may be direct placement of bonds with the banks being recapitalized.[9] A transition or developing country may not have an established government debt market with the requisite breadth and depth. Where such a market is established, there may be few domestic institutions able or willing to purchase the additional bonds required to finance bank recapitalization, and international interest may be limited or prohibitively expensive in the wake of a banking crisis. Issuance of treasury bills is another possible way to finance bank restructuring, but this has at least one major drawback. Government will be faced with the need for frequent refinancing of this short-term debt. Use of longer-term debt defers the refinancing needs, and provides time for some of the debt to be retired either from the proceeds of the subsequent sale of the bank equity purchased by government, or from recoveries on the bank assets purchased. Even if it is possible to meet the expense from general government revenues and financing activities, as discussed below there are reasons why it may be desirable to provide recapitalized banks with bonds rather than cash.

Special recapitalization bonds fall into three broad categories. The most common category consists of bonds issued by the government, but unlike a more usual government bond issuance sold to a wide range of purchasers, recapitalization bonds are placed directly with the banks to be recapitalized, usually as payment for an equity investment or to purchase distressed assets. The two other approaches involve the use of an agency, such as the deposit insurer, AMC, or bank restructuring authority, to issue the bonds and hold the government investment in banks. The bonds may be placed directly with the banks (Macedonia Bank Restructuring Agency 1994; Fondo Bancario de Protección al Ahorro, Mexico 1995–96) or alternatively the agency can use a bond issue to finance cash payments to banks being restructured (Korea Asset Management Company (KAMCO), Korea 1998–99; Danamodal and Danaharta, Malaysia 1998–99). A sovereign guarantee is desirable to enhance tradability of the bonds, and may be necessary to enable the agency to successfully issue bonds. Even when the bonds are placed directly with the restructured banks, a sovereign guarantee may be desirable to provide a zero risk-weighting for the assets (KAMCO, Korea Deposit Insurance Corporation (KDIC), Korea 1998–99).[10]

Arguments for and against special purpose bonds

An argument in favor of bonds placed directly with the banks to be recapitalized is that this can be accomplished even without an established domestic market for long-term government debt. Direct placement can also be used if a government is unable or unwilling to access the bond markets in the period following a crisis. The potential drawback to this approach is that the banks receiving payment in bonds for assets or equity may be liquidity constrained.[11] Even with solvency restored, banks may face failure if they have insufficient liquid assets to meet the demands of deposit withdrawals. Banks' ability to raise liquidity by selling bonds, even when the bonds have no trading restrictions and a rate and tenor viewed as attractive by the market, will be limited if there are not other banks with significant excess liquidity, other potential domestic purchasers, or significant interest from foreign investors. One solution sometimes used is for the central bank to provide special discount facilities for recapitalization bonds (Côte d'Ivoire 1991).

There is generally little to gain through the issuance of bonds by an agency rather than the government itself, except in the rare case where the agency may have the infrastructure for bond issuance already in place, and the government does not. One possible benefit is that having the deposit insurer, AMC or restructuring authority issue the bonds can clearly separate bank restructuring costs from other government activities. While it is often desirable in managing a systemic crisis to have a single public agency coordinating bank restructuring, it is quite common for government financing of the expense to be arranged outside of the restructuring agency. With adequate disclosure, either arrangement can provide the necessary transparency regarding the costs of recapitalization and restructuring. From the perspective of the restructured banks, it may not be relevant whether the government or an agency issues the bonds provided there is a broad and deep market. A government guarantee can be used to confer sovereign risk if an agency issues the bonds.

There is a risk that cash, or negotiable bonds that can quickly be turned into cash, might be used by the recipient bank to invest in highly risky assets. Sound governance and competent management are the only true protection against this risk, but the desire to protect the public investment in bank restructuring may lead to use of other measures. Strengthened supervisory oversight can provide some comfort, although at best this will detect reckless lending and investment after the fact. Another measure commonly used is to restrict the tradability of the bonds. At least initially, this keeps banks liquidity-constrained and less able to fund rapid loan growth. Restrictions on trading of bonds used to pay for equity or assets are sometimes relaxed over time (Indonesia 1998–2000; Poland 1991), providing scope for the banks to gradually use recapitalization bonds to access liquidity. When government purchases bank subordinated debt, the bonds used for payment may be nontradable to ensure that the bank is able to redeem the subordinated debt at maturity by returning the bonds to the issuer (Thailand 1999–2000; Turkey 2001). In these cases, the amount of subordinated debt is small relative to the size of the banks, so trading restrictions do not significantly inhibit the bank's liquidity management.

The exact opposite issue can also be a concern, as banks that hold a significant portion of their assets in recapitalization bonds may be slow to resume lending. Banks may prefer the risk-free return on recapitalization bonds to riskier returns from lending. Banks should not be coerced into lending they perceive as unduly risky, but having bond coupon rates well within the spectrum for government debt ensures that banks do not have an undue preference for holding recapitalization bonds rather than investing in loans. However, even if the bond income is not especially attractive, banks may be capital-constrained and thus still prefer zero risk-weighted bonds to corporate loans risk-weighted at 100 percent.

IV. Interest rates

The fiscal concern of minimizing the cost of public investment in restructuring can conflict with the need to ensure that restructured banks are sufficiently profitable to return to full health and not exposed to unnecessary financial risks. Fiscal concerns make attractive the issuance of bonds with below market coupons (Bulgaria 1993–94; Côte d'Ivoire 1991), or capitalizing rather than paying interest (Poland 1993–94; Mexico 1995–96). Even setting aside the valuation issues discussed in Section VII of this chapter, which could cause a bank stringently applying IFRS to report continued insolvency despite receipt of recapitalization bonds, low or zero coupon bonds do not provide an interest income stream to match with the recapitalized bank's ongoing interest expenses. The importance to a bank of the revenue from the recapitalization bonds obviously varies depending on the proportion of other earning assets and potential for noninterest income. If the bond holdings are small as a proportion of the total earning assets of a recapitalized bank, the bank may earn enough other revenue to be profitable even with a below market yield on recapitalization bonds.

In situations where recapitalization bonds are a significant portion of bank assets, failure to pay a market rate will doom the bank to further losses, consuming the public funds used to finance the recapitalization. This is a central point in bank restructuring: the resulting bank must be capable of generating enough revenue to be profitable. A recapitalization plan that does not lead to the bank earning a healthy interest margin merely creates a situation likely to lead to subsequent problems and further costly restructuring. However, as further discussed in Section VII of this chapter, revenue from bonds priced relative to the bank's cost of funds rather than to the bond market interest rates that might prevail during a crisis could be adequate for a viable restructuring plan. These circumstances, where the relevant interest rate is determined by reference to bank cost of funds, might provide an exception to the general desirability of using bonds issued on market terms and conditions for bank restructuring.

The fiscal preference for fixed or floating interest rates will be shaped by expectations of future interest rate movements. Since it is not uncommon for interest rates to be very high in the aftermath of a crisis, government may have a preference for floating rate bonds as these avoid locking into high fixed-rate coupons. However, given the time often required to move to the recapitalization stage of bank restructuring, it is also possible that by the time bonds are issued, the country is well into the post-crisis period with much reduced interest rates. In this case, there may be a greater inclination towards fixed rates as a means of protecting the budget from future interest rate fluctuations. The difficulty with this approach is that it passes the interest rate risk from government to the recapitalized banks. If the amount of fixed rate bonds is small relative to total assets, or if there are fixed rate liabilities (or equity) that can be considered matched against the fixed rate bonds, these risks may be manageable. However, the situation of fixed rate bonds comprising a large percentage of a recapitalized bank's assets should generally be avoided lest increasing interest rates squeeze the banks' margins and threaten the success of the recapitalization program.

V. Foreign currency bonds

Governments may be reluctant to take foreign currency risks; however, the need to deal with large open foreign exchange positions in the banking sector may argue in favor of foreign currency denominated or indexed bonds. It is not uncommon for banks, in the wake of a currency crisis, to be faced with foreign currency denominated loans that are severely impaired because unhedged borrowers can no longer meet their debt service requirements.[12] Even banks that had balanced positions before such a crisis may be faced with large net short foreign currency positions as they must still repay their foreign currency liabilities while the value of their foreign currency assets has been impaired.

If banks with large net short positions receive domestic currency denominated bonds, they remain exposed to significant foreign exchange risk.[13] Banks with sufficient liquidity may be able to close their position using domestic currency assets to purchase foreign currency denominated assets. However, purchase of large amounts of foreign exchange in a short time period by banks seeking to cover their positions could be significant enough to influence the exchange rate. To deal with these issues, governments (or government agencies) have assumed the foreign exchange risk in order to provide banks with foreign currency denominated recapitalization bonds (Bulgaria, 1994, 1997, 1999; Korea 1998; Mexico 1995–96; Poland 1991; Uruguay 1982–84).

An alternative to issuing foreign exchange denominated bonds is to issue bonds with the principal and interest indexed to a major foreign currency (Indonesia 1998–2000; Nicaragua 2000–2001). This avoids the need for foreign currency to pay coupons and redeem bonds, but provides the banks with an asset that effectively matches foreign currency liabilities, covering the banks' short position.[14] In the case of Indonesia, such "hedge bonds" were issued with a portion of the amount outstanding converted to nonindexed bonds each quarter. In this way, the recipient banks have a period of years to deal gradually with their foreign currency positions, either by running off foreign currency liabilities consistent with the quarterly conversion of the hedge bonds, or by raising foreign currency assets each quarter to replace the portion of the bond portfolios that would no longer be indexed to the dollar.

The fiscal impact of foreign currency or indexed bonds obviously increases if the domestic currency continues to depreciate. However, the alternative to this increased fiscal cost may be the failure of the recapitalization plan, since the recapitalized banks would have to bear this cost through their short foreign exchange exposure. At best this will result in a more protracted recovery period for the banking sector, and at worst will lead to a second round of public expenses for recapitalization. Thus, in designing the bond issue for recapitalization it is dangerous not to address the foreign currency exposure of the banking system.

VI. Maturity

A number of debt management considerations may influence the choice of maturities for recapitalization bonds. Long maturities defer the government's refinancing needs, and very short maturities are likely undesirable as it would be preferable to avoid the need to roll over large amounts of maturing debt shortly after the completion of a bank recapitalization program. If the recapitalization bonds are a significant amount relative to the stock of outstanding debt, a range of maturities will be desirable to avoid "lumpy" refinancing requirements (Ghana 1990; Hungary 1993–93; Kyrgyz Republic 1995–97).[15] A range of maturities may also be desirable to establish a yield curve. However, long maturities may create mismatch and loss exposure problems for the recapitalized banks.

Long dated bonds issued by developing and transition country governments may carry a substantial risk premium relative to ones with shorter maturities. Even if the bonds carry a floating market rate of interest, mitigating interest rate risk, they may trade at a significant discount as investors may require a premium to take longer term credit risk. If the banks trade or make the bonds available for sale, potential mark-to-market losses may jeopardize capital adequacy. Even if treated as held-to-maturity and thus not marked-to-market, these bonds could negatively affect the valuation of the bank in a sale or merger prior to maturity of the recapitalization bonds.

Aside from the maturity risk of long dated bonds, banks may have difficulty matching long-term liabilities with long dated bonds if they carry fixed rates. Also, the value of long fixed rate bonds will vary significantly as interest rates fluctuate, again raising the issue of either recognizing losses by marking to market, or carrying below market rate assets that may limit flexibility in divesting public ownership. Further, should interest rate fluctuations result in the fixed rate bonds paying below market rates, the resulting squeeze on the margins of the recapitalized bank could imperil the success of the restructuring.

VII. Bond valuation and bank viability

There may be instances where the valuation of bonds under IFRS does not result in a calculation of bank equity or regulatory capital that accurately reflects a restructured bank's medium-term prospects. Other considerations may be important for accounting and statistical conventions, but in bank restructuring the crucial issue is cash flow. In some cases, even below market rate instruments may provide sufficient interest income to make a bank viable. Similarly, even if other sovereign debt is in default, as long as the government continues to service the restructuring bonds, there will be no impact on the banks' expected revenue stream from the bonds.

This is a difficult and controversial issue. On the one hand, accounting for bank restructuring bonds using the market valuation approaches of IFRS could help to identify inadequate restructuring plans that are likely to fail because the shortfall in interest income over expenses makes the bank unviable. On the other hand, there may be circumstances when it will be appropriate for the banking regulator to prescribe an approach other than IFRS for the sovereign debt held by banks, provided that the actual interest income received by the bank is sufficient for viability.[16]

Accounting rules

Countries have sought to minimize the fiscal burden of bank restructuring by using low or zero coupon bonds, or bonds where the interest is capitalized rather than paid. Even though the value of such instruments, determined by the discounted present value of the expected cash flows would be significantly less than par, restructured banks have generally valued these assets at par. This accounting treatment can obscure the fact that these restructuring bonds do not provide banks with cash revenues to meet their cash expenses. Nevertheless, use of this accounting treatment has been viewed as attractive by country authorities because it reduces and defers the fiscal cost and financing needs associated with bank restructuring while permitting banks to report that solvency has been restored.

IFRS 39 generally precludes valuation at par of below market rate bonds.[17] Any previous ambiguity has been removed, so even when bonds are classified as held-to-maturity and thus exempt from mark-to-market requirements, initial measurement of assets will have to be made with reference to prevailing market rates of interest. If there is evidence that the market value of recapitalization bonds is below par, such as similar sovereign debt trading at a deep discount, IFRS 39 would require banks receiving such bonds to initially value them by discounting the future cash flows using the indicated market interest rate.

In order to avoid qualified audit opinions and to report solvent banks under IFRS, the authorities would have to provide bonds with market-related rates, or a larger quantity of below market rate bonds. This is the desirable and appropriate approach in most cases; however, in times of systemic stress the premium demanded on sovereign debt may be very high, with nominal interest rates of 50 percent or more easily required for a bond to be valued at par under IFRS. These circumstances may be an exception to the general principle of providing bonds with market-related terms, as a successful bank restructuring does not necessarily require the cash flow from bonds to reflect bond market interest rates so long as the cash expenses for the bank's funding are below bond market rates.

Regulatory capital issues

The question sometimes arises whether a zero risk-weighting for capital adequacy purposes is the appropriate prudential treatment for the sovereign debt of a country facing the threat of default, or which has actually defaulted. Almost all countries attach a zero risk-weighting to banks' holdings of government debt denominated in the national currency,[18] and a change to this approach will generally not be appropriate in responding to the crisis. Maintaining the preexisting risk-weighting avoids placing immediate capital adequacy pressure on banks that would be sound except for exposure to their national government's debt, and facilitates use of public funds for bank restructuring. It would likely be impractical to introduce a capital charge for sovereign debt during a crisis, as even sound banks would likely have difficulty raising additional capital. For banks to be restructured at public expense, the recognition of the risk of government default would serve to increase exponentially the investment required to achieve the prudential capital adequacy requirement. It may well be appropriate to consider capital requirements for sovereign debt in the longer term, however, this should happen after the banking system has been stabilized, and if adopted, a phase-in period should be used to permit sound banks, and banks recapitalized to a minimum level, to build their capital through retained earnings.

VIII. Valuation rules in banking crises

The valuation of sovereign debt of countries in default or likely to default has implications for all banks, but has special relevance in the case of bank restructuring. For all banks, sovereign default could trigger mark-to-market losses rendering the banking system insolvent. Following sovereign default, application of IFRS valuation rules to debt held by banks might make the policy option of committing public funds to bank restructuring prohibitively expensive. Depending on the circumstances, interpretations that could fall within the bounds of IFRS would facilitate restructuring, but other cases may require the banking regulator to permit accounting practices that might not conform to IFRS.

The situation of potential sovereign default could be dealt with through an interpretation of IFRS. Banks are not required by IFRS to write down the value or establish an allowance for an asset as long as no impairment event has occurred. A decline in market value of bonds due to threatened sovereign default is not necessarily an impairment event. Under IFRS 39 bonds might still be classified as held to maturity and thus not marked to market even if there is a significant downgrade by an external credit rating agency or the bank's internal rating system.[19] It might be argued that until there was actual default on bonds held by banks, the objective evidence of impairment required by IFRS prior to establishing an allowance for loss does not exist,[20] and thus there would be no need to provision against recapitalization bonds prior to actual default.

After sovereign default, a government still wishing to use the policy option of employing public funds to preserve some portion of an insolvent banking system may need its banking regulator to mandate a valuation approach that varies from IFRS. This is clearly a situation where all of the options have significant downsides. The alternative of having depositors bear all losses may be viewed as unacceptable politically and socially. Government will likely lack the fiscal resources to issue sufficient debt with market terms and conditions for bank restructuring. In these circumstances, a clear distinction might be made between new and old sovereign debt, much as is done in many judicial and nonjudicial workouts. Thus, the banking regulator might mandate a valuation approach requiring banks to recognize losses on old sovereign debt, but permitting new debt to be valued at par provided it paid an interest rate including a margin over the banks' cost of funds, and government continued to service the new debt.

Bonds paying a rate related to the bank's actual cost of funds, rather than a rate related to the sovereign bond market, should provide sufficient income for a successful restructuring. Using bonds with coupons priced relative to a banks' cost of funds and valued at par could lead to qualified audit opinions if there is a significant difference between the market rate of return of sovereign debt and banks' cost of funds. The alternative to comply with IFRS would be to provide restructured banks with greater income than is actually required for a successful restructuring, either from the use of a greater quantity of below-market interest rate bonds, or from bonds paying market interest rates. Moreover, issuing more debt could increase the likelihood of future sovereign default. In these circumstances, qualified audit opinions, or a regulatory directive that banks use accounting standards that differ from IFRS for the valuation of sovereign bonds, would likely be preferable to investing more public funds in banks than are actually required to restore solvency and profitability.

It would be preferable to have a consistent valuation approach for all statistical, accounting and prudential purposes; however, differing objectives sometimes lead to different approaches. While not an approach to be advocated in normal times, to facilitate dealing with a crisis the banking regulator might permit banks to use a valuation approach that does not recognize impairment on recapitalization bonds and other domestic sovereign debt unless there is a default or announcement of intention to default on those specific bond series held by the banks. This would likely lead to qualified statements under IFRS, as default on any domestic currency denominated sovereign bond would likely be taken as objective evidence of impairment for all domestic sovereign bonds.[21] However, the alternative of requiring provisions if there has been default on other similar sovereign obligations threatens the solvency of otherwise sound banks holding significant quantities of sovereign debt not yet in default. Provided that government continues to service debt held by banks, prudential supervisors could ensure that the accounting treatment matched the economic effect for banks by not considering default on other sovereign obligations as evidence of impairment of the bonds held by banks. Thus, regulatory authorities might prescribe for banks an accounting treatment for sovereign debt that does not require establishment of an allowance unless there has been an act of impairment related specifically to the bond series held by the bank.

IX. Conclusion

There are many factors that have to be considered when bonds are being designed for use in publicly funded bank restructuring. The ultimate success of a program cannot be ensured by appropriate bond design, but the converse is certainly true. Attempts to reduce the fiscal costs of bank restructuring by departing from market terms and conditions for recapitalization bonds will not only compromise the restructuring effort, but fiscal costs could ultimately be higher. Banks with insufficient interest income, or risk exposure embedded in their holdings of recapitalization bonds, are likely to suffer losses leading to the need for subsequent intervention and a renewed attempt at restructuring. Key elements of a good bond design from the perspective of the recapitalized banks' financial performance are:

- market rates of interest to provide sufficient income;
- use of floating rates to deal with interest rate risk and minimize mark-to-market losses;
- short to medium maturities to avoid the likely lack of matching long-term liabilities and to mitigate the volatility in valuation of long dated bonds arising from interest rate fluctuations;
- no trading restrictions to facilitate liquidity management;
- foreign exchange or indexed bonds to cover banks' open positions.

All of these features may not be compatible in the same instrument, leading to the use of several series of bonds that combine different features. Also, as some of the desirable features from the perspective of bank financial performance conflict with fiscal and other government objectives, there will be inevitable trade-offs. There may be circumstances in dealing with a systemic crisis where the banking regulator will permit variance from IFRS in valuing recapitalization bonds, provided that the expected cash flow from the bonds is sufficient to make the restructured bank viable. The features of the final bond design need to result in projections of satisfactory financial performance for the recapitalized banks even in scenarios using much less optimistic assumptions than the banks' business plans. This will generally require bonds with market-related terms and conditions. Anything less results in an unacceptable risk of poor financial performance leading to loss of the public funds expended and the need for further supervisory intervention.

Appendix 4.1 Bond issues for bank recapitalization and restructuring[a]

Country	Year	Issuer	Purpose	Currency	Marketability/ Special Features	Interest Rate	Maturity
Algeria	1992–93	Government	Purchase bad assets	Domestic	Nontradable	10 percent	12 years
Algeria	1996	Government	Recapitalize state banks	Domestic			20 years
Algeria	1997	Government	Purchase bad assets	Domestic			12 years
Bulgaria	1992	Government	Purchase bad assets	Domestic		Central Bank rate plus 1 percent	15 years, 4 year grace period
Bulgaria	1993 (July)	Government	Purchase bad assets	Domestic		Fraction of Central Bank rate	20 years, 5 year grace period
Bulgaria	1993 (Oct)	Government	Purchase bad assets	Domestic		Fraction of Central Bank rate	20 years, 5 year grace period
Bulgaria	1993 (Dec)	Government	Purchase bad assets	Domestic		Fraction of Central Bank rate	20 years, 5 year grace period
Bulgaria	1994	Government	Purchase bad assets	U.S. dollar		6 month LIBOR	20 years, 5 year grace period
Bulgaria	1995	Government	Purchase bad assets	Domestic		Central Bank rate	3 years, 4 year grace period
Bulgaria	1997	Government	Purchase bad assets	U.S. dollar		6 month LIBOR plus 3 percent	18 months
Bulgaria	1999	Government	Swap for dollar denominated bonds	Euro		6 month Euribor	19.5 years
Chile	1984	Central bank	Purchase bad assets	Domestic	Nontradable	7 percent real return	4 year
Côte d'Ivoire	1991	Government	Pay government arrears to banks	Domestic	Up to 90 percent discountable at concessional rate by central bank	3 percent	15 years, 2 year grace period

Country	Year	Issuer	Purpose	Currency		Interest rate	Maturity
Croatia	1996	Government	Recapitalize Rijeck banka and Splitska banka	Domestic		8.5 percent	10 years
Croatia	1996	Agency for Rehabilitation of Banks	Recapitalize Privrendna banka	DM		5 percent	15 years
Croatia	1996	Agency for Rehabilitation of Banks	Recapitalize Privrrendna banka	Domestic		7.5 percent	15 years
Croatia	1996	Agency for Rehabilitation of Banks	Recapitalize Privrendna banka	Domestic		5 percent	15 years
Croatia	1998	Government	Replace earlier bonds	Domestic	Currency clause	6 percent	10 years
Croatia	1998	Government	Compensate for increased London and Paris Club liabilities	Domestic		6 percent	10 years
Croatia	1998	Government	Compensate for increased London and Paris Club liabilities	DM		6 percent	10 years
Ecuador	1999–2000	Government	Issued to Government Deposit Insurance Agency to finance its activities-bank recapitalization, liquidity support, pay depositors of closed banks	U.S. dollar	Deposit insurance agency discounted bonds with the central bank to finance activities	First tranche 4 percent fixed; subsequent tranches 14 percent fixed	First tranche 15 years, subsequent tranches 7–12 years
Ecuador	2001	Government	Recapitalize state bank	U.S. dollar	Nontradable	Below market	3 and 5 years

Country	Year	Issuer	Purpose	Currency	Marketability/ Special Features	Interest Rate	Maturity
Egypt	1991	Government	Finance equity purchase	U.S. dollar		LIBOR	10 years
Finland	1991	Central bank	Purchase bad assets				
Ghana	1990	Central bank	Purchase bad assets	Domestic		7, 9, 15 percent	2 to 5 years, subsequently rolled over
Greece	1991–95						
Hungary	1992–93	Government	Purchase bad assets	Domestic		Average yield on 3 month treasury bills	20, 25, 30 years
Indonesia	1998–2001	Government	Purchase bank equity	Domestic	Initially 10 percent of bonds tradable, restrictions progressively relaxed until all bonds tradable	12 and 14 percent fixed, variable at 3 month central bank rate, variable at SIBOR for domestic currency bonds indexed to U.S. dollars	3 to 10 years
Korea	1998	KAMCO (AMC), government guaranteed	Purchase bad assets	U.S. dollar	Tradable		
Korea	1998–99	KAMCO, KDIC (deposit insurer), government guaranteed	Purchase equity or preferred shares	Domestic	Tradable	Variable U.S. dollars	

Country	Year	Institution	Purpose			Interest rate	Maturity
Korea	1998–99	KAMCO, government guaranteed	Purchase bad assets	Domestic	Tradable	Fixed (initially) and variable rate	10 and 20 years
Kuwait	1992	Central bank	Purchase bad assets	Domestic	Nontradable	Market related	
Kyrgyz Republic	1995–97	Government	Purchase bad assets	Domestic		5, 25, 50.64, 55.7 percent	6 months, 1, 5, 10, and 25 years
Lao People's Dem. Rep.	1994		Purchase bad assets	Domestic	Nontradable		
Latvia	1994	Government	Purchase bad assets	Domestic	Nontradable	20.4 percent first year, CPI plus 1.5 percent thereafter	Up to 7 years
Lithuania	1996–98	Government	Purchase bad assets	Domestic	Nontradable	Average term deposit rate plus 1 percent	10 years (redeemed before maturity—last tranche in 2003)
Macedonia	1994	Bank Rehabilitation Agency	Purchase bad assets	Domestic	Bonds subsequently acquired by Central bank	Central Bank rate	15 years
Macedonia	1999	Bank Rehabilitation Agency	Purchase bad assets	Domestic			
Malaysia	1998–99	Danaharta (AMC)	Finance the purchase of bad assets	Domestic	Zero-coupon discount bonds	Market-based yield	

Country	Year	Issuer	Purpose	Currency	Marketability/ Special Features	Interest Rate	Maturity
Malaysia	1998–99	Danamodal (bank restructuring agency)	Finance the purchase bank convertible preference shares and subordinated debt	Domestic	Zero-coupon discount bonds	Market-based yield	
Mauritania	1993	Government	Purchase bank equity, bad assets and compensate central bank for liquidity support losses	Domestic	Nontradable	Central bank rediscount rate	6 month and 1 year renewable
Mexico	1995–96	FOBAPROA (bank restructuring agency)	Purchase bad assets	Domestic	Nontradable, income from NPLs used to redeem FOBAPROA paper, at maturity banks write off 20–30 percent of FOBAPROA paper outstanding, government covers balance	Variable—3 month T-bill rate, interest capitalized, not paid	10 years
Mexico	1995–96	FOBAPROA (bank restructuring agency)	Purchase bad assets	U.S. dollar	Nontradable, income from NPLs used to redeem FOBAPROA paper, at maturity banks write off 20–30 percent of FOBAPROA paper outstanding, government covers balance	Variable—LIBOR plus 4 percent, interest capitalized, not paid	10 years

Country	Year	Issuer	Purpose	Currency	Tradability	Interest rate	Maturity
Nicaragua	2000–01	Central bank	Support sale of performing assets and deposits of failed banks	Domestic	Indexed to U.S. dollars, zero coupon	Market related—margin over Central Bank bill rate	2 to 4 years
Poland	1991	Government	Cover banks' foreign exchange losses after devaluation	U.S. dollar	Tradable first three years only with central bank consent, thereafter tradable among domestic financial institutions	1991–95; 6 month LIBOR plus 2 percent; from 1996, 6 month LIBOR plus 0.5 percent	1 to 13 years
Poland	1993–94	Government		Domestic		Central Bank rediscount rate, but only fixed rate of 5 percent paid, balance capitalized	1.5 to 15.5 years
Slovenia	1992–94						
Sri Lanka	1993		Purchase bad assets				
Tanzania	1992		Recapitalize state bank for privatization			11 percent	20 years
Thailand	1999–2000	Government	Purchase bank equity	Domestic	Tradable	Market related fixed rate	10 years
Thailand	1999–2000	Government	Purchase bank debentures	Domestic	Nontradable	Market related fixed rate	10 years
Turkey	2001	Government	Purchase bank equity	Domestic	Nontradable	Market related	various
Turkey	2001	Government	Purchase bank subordinated debt	Domestic	Nontradable	Market related	various
Uganda	1996	Government	Recapitalize state bank for privatization	Domestic	Nontradable	Variable-average 91 day T-bill rate	1, 3, and 5 years

Country	Year	Issuer	Purpose	Currency	Marketability/ Special Features	Interest Rate	Maturity
Uruguay	1982–84	Central bank	Purchase bad assets	U.S. dollar	Banks required to arrange external U.S. dollar financing to central bank as a condition of the first tranche ("portfolio purchase linked loans"); subsequent tranches provided by central bank to support purchase of failed local banks by foreign banks	LIBOR plus 1.5 percent	7 years, 18 month grace period

Sources: James A. Daniel, 1997, "Fiscal Aspects of Bank Restructuring" Working Paper 97/52 (Washington: International Monetary Fund); Claudia Dziobek and Ceyla Pazarbasioglu, 1997, "Lessons and Elements of Best Practice" in William E. Alexander and others, eds. **Systemic Bank Restructuring and Macroeconomic Policy** (Washington: International Monetary Fund); Charles Enoch, Gillian Garcia and V. Sundararajan, 2002, "Recapitalizing Banks with Public Funds: Selected Issues" in Charles Enoch, David Marston and Michael Taylor, eds, **Building Strong Banks Through Surveillance and Resolution** (Washington: International Monetary Fund). Pablo Graf, 1999, "Policy Responses to the Banking Crisis in Mexico" in Bank Restructuring in Practice, BIS Policy Papers No. 6 (Basel, Bank for International Settlements); Carl-Johan Lindgren and others, 1999, **Financial Sector Crisis and Restructuring: Lessons From Asia,** Occasional Paper 188 (Washington: International Monetary Fund); Kanitta Messook and others, 2001, **Malaysia: From Crisis to Recovery,** Occasional Paper 207 (Washington: International Monetary Fund); Karim Nashashibi and others, 1998, **Algeria: Stabilization and Transition to the Market,** Occasional Paper 165 (Washington: International Monetary Fund); Sergtio Pereira Leite and others **Ghana: Economic Development in a Democratic Environment,** Occasional Paper 199 (Washington: International Monetary Fund); Juan Perez-Campanero and Alfredo Leone, 1991, "Liberalization and Financial Crisis in Uruguay 1974 to 1987" in V. Sundararajan and Tomas Balino, eds, **Banking Crises: Cases and Issues** (Washington: International Monetary Fund); Andrew Sheng, ed., 1996, **Bank Restructuring: Lessons from the 1980s** (Washington: The World Bank); Helena Tang, Edda Zoli, and Irina Klytchnikova, 2000, "Banking Crises in Transition Countries: Fiscal Costs and Related Issues" Working Paper 2484 (Washington: The World Bank).

a This table has been compiled from the banking crisis literature and various IMF documents. Details of the bonds used to finance bank restructuring are frequently not available, and in some cases, different sources provide conflicting details. The author would be especially grateful for further information to complete or correct the cases cited above, and for details of bonds used in additional cases of bank restructuring.

Notes

1. At the time of writing, the author was Financial Sector Advisor in the IMF's Monetary and Financial Systems Department. He gratefully acknowledges helpful comments and suggestions from Luis Cortavarria, Fernando Delgado, Alessandro Giustiniani, Peter Hayward, David Hoelscher, Mats Josefsson, Tonny Lybek, Kenneth Sullivan, and the participants in an IMF Monetary and Financial Systems Department seminar who discussed an earlier version of this chapter, as well as reviewers from other IMF departments.
2. Dziobek and Pazarbasioglu (1997) identify bonds as a tool used in 19 of 24 banking crises. Bonds issued or guaranteed by the governments of Indonesia, Korea, and Thailand were the main instruments to finance governments' contributions to bank restructuring in the Asian crisis, and bonds have been used recently in Ecuador, Nicaragua, and Turkey.
3. A third use of bonds—the issuance of bonds to the central bank in payment for support provided to insolvent banks—will not be addressed in this chapter since it does not affect the future financial performance of restructured banks.
4. "Equity" is used here in its broadest context. In practice, government may purchase a range of instruments that qualifies as either Tier 1 or Tier 2 capital, including common shares, preference shares (convertible or nonconvertible) or subordinated debt. See Enoch, Garcia, and Sundararajan (2002, pp. 327–33).
5. Sovereign default also affects other holders of government debt, including institutional investors such as pension funds and insurance companies. Dealing with losses by these investors is beyond the scope of this chapter.
6. While nontradable bonds are statistically classified as loans pursuant to the 1993 *System of National Accounts*, this chapter reflects the common terminology in bank restructuring and generally refers to bonds, even when there are restrictions on marketability.
7. The case of government owned banks is somewhat different. Bond design is still crucial for the financial success of the bank, but the decision to recapitalize reflects the recognition and measurement of losses already incurred by government as owner of the bank, rather than a decision to commit government funds to cover a portion of the losses incurred by privately owned banks.
8. Frydl and Quintyn (2000, pp. 5).
9. Bonds were placed directly with banks in all cases noted in Appendix 4.I except Ecuador 1998–2000, Egypt 1991, and Malaysia 1998–99. In Korea 1998–99, some cash was also provided to banks.
10. Bonds that are not viewed as sovereign risk generally will carry a 100 percent risk-weighting under prudential capital rules, and thus increase banks' regulatory capital requirements relative to a portfolio of zero risk-weighted government bonds.
11. Another drawback is that bond design may be more influenced by considerations related to the building of a bond market, such as providing a range of maturities, or providing largely fixed rate bonds if these are seen as preferred by investors, rather than by concern for the financial performance of recapitalized banks.
12. A company with income only in the local currency may borrow in foreign currency, taking advantage of lower rates and the expectation that a currency peg will be maintained. If the local currency suddenly depreciates, the borrower is faced with the requirement to repay a foreign currency denominated loan that has become a much higher amount when expressed in the local currency.

13. Prudential requirements for the calculation of net open positions may exclude "structural" positions, but as a practical matter, recapitalized banks will be exposed to foreign exchange risk in the absence of foreign currency denominated assets to match foreign exchange denominated liabilities.

14. In calculating a bank's open currency position, an instrument with principal and interest indexed to a foreign currency could be considered exposure in that currency for purposes managing currency risk.

15. Alternatives to bonds with the full principal due at maturity are also an option, but have seldom been used in bank restructuring. Uruguay 1982–84 is an exception, where principal was repayable in equal semi-annual installments over the term of the bonds.

16. It is not uncommon for accounting treatments prescribed by a regulatory authority to differ in some respects from a country's more broadly applicable accounting standards. A common instance relates to provisioning for nonperforming loans, where prudential rules frequently require establishment of a general allowance for loss, for example, 1 percent of the total loan portfolio. Under IFRS, an allowance should only be established when an impairment event has occurred. Nevertheless, many regulators prescribe general allowances despite its contravention of IFRS.

17. The insertion into the standard of an example with respect to zero interest assets removes the possibility of an accounting interpretation that below market-rate instruments could be valued at par. See *Proposed Amendments to IAS 39*, paragraph 67.

18. The current Basel capital accord provides that claims on central governments denominated in the national currency are zero risk-weighted. The revisions to the capital accord will maintain this weighting. Sovereign debt of Organization for Economic Cooperation and Development (OECD) countries is also zero risk-weighted. There is an exclusion if the country has rescheduled its external debt within the last five years. Sovereign debt of non-OECD countries, excluding debt denominated in the national currency, is weighted at 50 percent for maturities of less than one year, and 100 percent for maturities of greater than one year. Countries are free to apply more stringent weighting in their national regulations. Mongolia is a rare exception in requiring a 100 percent risk-weighting for domestic currency sovereign debt.

19. *Proposed Amendments to IAS 39*, paragraph 86.

20. *Proposed Amendments to IAS 39*, paragraph 111.

21. IAS 39, paragraph 110.

Bibliography

Daniel, James A., 1997, "Fiscal Aspects of Bank Restructuring," IMF Working Paper 97/52 (Washington: International Monetary Fund).

Daniel, James A., Jeffrey M. Davis, and Andrew M. Wolfe, 1997, "Fiscal Accounting of Bank Restructuring," IMF Paper on Policy Analysis and Assessment 97/5 (Washington: International Monetary Fund).

Dattels, Peter, 1997, "Microstructure of Government Securities Markets," in *Coordinating Public Debt and Monetary Management*, ed. by V. Sundararajan and Peter Dattels (Washington: International Monetary Fund).

Dziobek, Claudia, 1998, "Market-Based Policy Instruments for Systemic Bank Restructuring," IMF Working Paper 98/113 (Washington: International Monetary Fund).

Dziobek, Claudia, and Ceyla Pazarbasioglu, 1997, "Lessons from Systemic Bank Restructuring: Lessons and Elements of Best Practices," in *Systemic Bank Restructuring and Macroeconomic Policy*, ed. by William Alexander and others (Washington: International Monetary Fund).

Enoch, Charles, Gillian Garcia, and V. Sundararajan, 2002, "Recapitalizing Banks with Public Funds: Selected Issues," in *Building Strong Banks Through Surveillance and Resolution*, ed. by Charles Enoch, David Marston, and Michael Taylor (Washington: International Monetary Fund).

Frydl, Edward J., and Marc Quintyn, 2000, "The Benefits and Costs of Intervening in Banking Crises," IMF Working Paper 00/147 (Washington: International Monetary Fund).

Graf, Pablo, 1999, "Policy Responses to the Banking Crisis in Mexico," in *Bank Restructuring in Practice*, ed. by John Hawkins and Philip Turner, BIS Policy Paper No. 6 (Basel: Bank for International Settlements).

International Accounting Standards Board, 2002, *Proposed Amendments to IAS 39 Financial Instruments: Recognition and Measurement*.

Lindgren, Carl-Johan, and others, 1999, *Financial Sector Crisis and Restructuring: Lessons From Asia*, IMF Occasional Paper 188 (Washington: International Monetary Fund).

Lindgren, Carl-Johan, Gillian Garcia, and Matthew Saal, 1996, *Bank Soundness and Macroeconomic Policy* (Washington: International Monetary Fund).

Nyberg, Peter, 1997, "Authorities Roles and Organization Issues in Systemic Bank Restructuring," IMF Working Paper 97/92 (Washington: International Monetary Fund).

Sheng, Andrew, ed., 1996, *Bank Restructuring: Lessons from the 1980s* (Washington: World Bank).

Tang, Helena, Edda Zoli, and Irina Klytchnikova, 2000, "Banking Crises in Transition Countries: Fiscal Costs and Related Issues," WB Working Paper 2484 (Washington: World Bank).

5
What Happens After Supervisory Intervention? Considering Bank Closure Options

Michael Andrews and Mats Josefsson[1]

I. Introduction

Debate over the closure of banks frequently runs the gamut from almost casual references to the need to immediately close and liquidate insolvent banks to impassioned arguments not to close any bank due to real or imagined systemic repercussions. One reason for the very divergent views regarding bank closure is the different meanings commonly ascribed to the term.

One narrow meaning is the immediate closing of the doors of an insolvent bank, laying off staff and repaying depositors and other creditors over time, either pursuant to a deposit protection scheme or from the realizations on loans and other assets. While having the advantage of immediately checking operating losses, padlocking the doors and only then focusing on how to repay depositors could be very disruptive if it causes a more general loss of confidence in the banking system.

Alternative approaches to closure minimize disruption using a range of options such as a merger, sale of all or part of the bank's assets and liabilities, or deposit transfer and payout. This broader approach creates a vision of an orderly exit, and underpins the arguments in favor of closure as an appropriate part of the "toolkit" for dealing with problem banks in both normal times and in a systemic crisis.

"Bank closure" is used generically in this chapter to mean the act whereby the preexisting legal bank entity ceases to carry on the business of banking.[2] Closure in this context is a tool to achieve supervisory objectives, and should not be construed with the specific legal connotation ascribed to the term in some banking laws. A closure may be partial, with the bank ceasing to do new business and running down its existing assets and liabilities over time, or the bank may be left with a rump of bad assets to be worked out after a purchase and assumption transaction. A well-planned closure can be part of the legal process of achieving the orderly exit of a weak bank through a range of resolution options including liquidation or a complete or partial transfer of its assets and liabilities to other institutions.[3]

The next section of the chapter provides an overview of the supervisory process that can lead to the conclusion that it is necessary to close a bank. Section III briefly reviews the special nature of banks and the rationale for regulatory oversight, noting that these do not provide compelling arguments against closing banks, and provides an overview of experience with bank closures around the world. Section IV examines the issues of closure as part of the response to a systemic crisis. While many of the same objectives apply as when dealing with an individual problem bank, the review and assessment process will necessarily be very different than the "normal times" supervisory approach. The last section provides brief concluding remarks.

II. The decision to close a bank

Closure of a bank is not capricious action taken to punish shareholders or the bank itself, nor is the decision to close a bank generally an isolated or sudden event. Although serious problems can suddenly come to light, in the "normal times" circumstance of dealing with one or a few problem banks in an otherwise sound system, the decision to close a bank is usually the culmination of efforts over time to remedy the problems of a weak bank. The situation in a systemic crisis, when many banks may suddenly face serious financial problems, is a specific case addressed in Section IV of this chapter.

Three sources of problems

At a conceptual level there are three underlying causes of problem banks: microeconomic; macroeconomic; and "system related," or structural issues.[4] The microeconomic causes are generally poor banking practices that lead to losses through inadequate management of credit and other risks, or fraud. While soundly managed banks can weather cyclical downturns, there can be unexpected macroeconomic shocks, such as the 1970s oil crisis, that threaten even the most prudent institutions.[5] The category of "system related," or structural causes, includes factors that are not conducive to the development of an efficient banking industry, such as market distortions from state banks, directed credits, inadequate legal framework, and inadequate supervision.[6] A cyclical downturn or macroeconomic shock may bring to the surface the underlying microeconomic or structural weaknesses in a banking system.

In dealing with weak banks, it is important that the solution address the underlying problem. Only in the rare case of a macroeconomic shock "sideswiping" otherwise sound banks is the injection of capital or a period of time to rebuild capital likely to be sufficient to restore the health of the bank without taking other actions to address the fundamental problems. A period of time to obtain new capital can be a part of a broader plan to achieve a turnaround, but failure to address the underlying microeconomic or structural causes of the problem makes it likely that capital injected will be at risk, and delay in supervisory action likely only serves to increase the ultimate loss.

Guiding principles for the resolution of weak banks

The need for speed, cost efficiency, avoiding market distortions and the creation of perverse incentives in the banking markets all mean that banking supervisors have to consider closing banks when depositors and creditors face imminent risk of loss due to insolvency (Box 5.1). The preferred resolution of a weak bank occurs long before this need would arise. In normal times well-managed banks will themselves take corrective action to deal with emerging financial problems or prudential violations, frequently before these issues come to the attention of the supervisor. However, owners and managers hoping that a general improvement in economic conditions will solve bank-specific problems, or that the bank may grow out of its problems, may have an incentive to try to conceal the true financial condition of the bank from the supervisor. The supervisor will have to take more formal action in these circumstances or in the case when the owners and managers of the bank, acting in good faith, are unable to remedy the problems.

Supervisory action prior to closure

Specific approaches vary among jurisdictions, but there are two generic legal approaches to dealing with weak banks: (1) discretionary; and (2) rules-based. In jurisdictions with a discretionary approach, the supervisor is generally bound by broad objectives such as taking timely remedial measures,[7] but has wide latitude regarding specific corrective actions and the timing of supervisory actions. In part to address concerns that banking supervisors may use discretionary powers to defer decisive actions, and in part to foster greater consistency in the approach to weak banks, some jurisdictions have a rules-based approach. An example of the rules-based approach is the prompt corrective action (PCA) provisions adopted in the United States and elsewhere (Table 5.1). PCA requires the banking supervisor to take certain minimum actions in response to specified trigger points, usually defined by capital adequacy ratios (CARs). Even with the PCA approach, the supervisor generally has wide latitude to take steps in addition to the minimum required. Thus, when the supervisor is of the opinion that the situation requires that management and shareholders be removed, there is no need to wait until capital is depleted to the level that would trigger mandatory conservatorship or receivership.

Box 5.1. Principles for Dealing with Weak Banks

Speed. Supervisors should act promptly. Experience from many countries shows that regulatory and supervisory forbearance has exacerbated the problems of a weak bank. By not dealing with the problems promptly, they have grown rapidly making the eventual resolution efforts more difficult and more expensive, with the possibility of becoming more widespread and systemic.

Cost-efficiency. A least-cost criterion should guide the supervisor when making choices between alternative actions consistent with achieving the supervisory objectives.

Flexibility. Legislation frequently adopts a rules-based approach. However, it is also helpful if the legislation permits the supervisor to exercise discretion in the deployment and timing of supervisory tools.

Consistency. Consistent and well-understood supervisory actions will not distort the competitive environment. Such an approach will also minimize confusion and uncertainty in times of crisis. Similar problems in different banks, large or small, private or state-owned, should receive similar treatment.

Avoiding moral hazard. Supervisory action should not create incentives for banks to act in a manner to incur costs that they do not have to bear entirely. Shareholders should not be compensated for losses when a bank gets into difficulty; otherwise it will encourage other banks to behave less prudently on the expectation that they will receive a similar bailout if problems occur. Equally, supervisory action should not protect the interest of the bank's corporate officers.

Transparency and cooperation. Inadequate or incorrect information from the bank increases uncertainty for everyone involved. It can lead to misplaced supervisory action and add to the costs of solving the problems. The bank and the relevant authorities should aim for a high degree of information sharing and transparency about their intended actions.

Source: Basel Committee (2002).

The range of responses to a weak bank may be viewed as a continuum of increasingly intrusive actions by the banking supervisor. A break point on the continuum occurs at the moment of supervisory intervention.[8] Up until this point, the owners and managers of the bank retain control of the institution, notwithstanding specific directions or restrictions imposed by the supervisor. During the period preceding intervention the existing shareholders have their opportunity to try to solve the problems facing the bank, and should be strongly motivated by the potential loss of their investment. Thus, when intervention becomes necessary it is almost certain that existing owners did not have the financial resources or the willingness to inject capital or institute needed reforms, and probably also failed to find new investors or a merger partner. This can be viewed as a clear confirmation of the poor financial condition of the intervened bank, which while not precluding the possibility of a turnaround after supervisory intervention, makes a closure option more likely.[9]

Table 5.1. U.S. Prompt Corrective Action

Early Warning Period → Increasingly Intrusive Supervision → Intervention			
Adequately Capitalized CAR < 10 percent	Undercapitalized CAR < 8 percent	Significantly Undercapitalized CAR < 4 percent	Critically Undercapitalized Equity/Assets < 2 Percent
• Cannot pay dividends or management fees that would lead to undercapitalization	• Close monitoring • Capital restoration plan required within 45 days • Restrictions on growth, prior approval required for acquisitions, branching and new lines of business	• Recapitalization required • Restrictions on transactions with affiliates • Restrictions on interest rates, growth and activities • Require new directors and officers • Restrictions on holding company • Require divestitures	• Conservatorship, receivership or other action required • Appointment of receiver required if other action fails to restore capital

Resolution after intervention

Despite the best efforts of the supervisor there will be cases where it becomes evident that the bank is unable to continue its operations without jeopardizing the safety of depositors' funds. In these cases, the supervisor must intervene. While other options may be available, as outlined above there is a strong likelihood that a closure option should result. The essential functions of a bank and confidence in the banking system can be preserved through a well-planned closure. Prompt closure can preserve any going concern value that would otherwise erode through ongoing operating losses. Decisive action can actually enhance confidence in the supervisory regime and banking system by ensuring that only sound banks are permitted to continue operating.

Following supervisory intervention it is crucial that well qualified and experienced staff take effective control of the bank and immediately assess the operations and financial condition of the bank, and undertake a review of available options (Box 5.2). Much of this work may have been completed prior to actual intervention if there had been an extended early-warning period, but in any event needs to be completed quickly. There is a risk of a run on the bank if uninsured depositors and other creditors fear they would have to bear some losses, and even without a run the realizable value of an intervened bank is more likely to decline than to improve. Ongoing operating losses, flight of remaining good commercial customers to higher quality banks not constrained in their ability to lend, and erosion of any remaining name and franchise value is likely to occur in banks operating for any extended period following supervisory intervention.

Box 5.2. Procedures for Supervisory Intervention and Takeover of a Bank

Supervisory intervention and takeover of a bank can take place with full cooperation with the existing owners and management or can be imposed against their will.

When existing owners and management accept that the best option to maintain the value of the bank is for the supervisory agency to assume control and find a solution, it normally should be sufficient if the supervisory agency appoints an administrator or management team, which will determine which of the senior staff of the bank may be retained, and which should be replaced. Depending on the legal requirements to exercise control in a specific jurisdiction, directors of the bank may be removed so the bank functions under the direct control of the supervisory agency, or the board may be replaced by appointees of the supervisory authority.

When existing owners and management have explicitly opposed the supervisory intervention, or if there is a possibility that confusion or temporary lack of full internal controls might provide an opportunity for owners or staff of the bank personally to benefit through asset stripping or destruction of records, the supervisory agency needs to take physical as well as legal control of the bank. In addition to removing the board and replacing existing management and other key persons as quickly as possible, the supervisory agency needs to secure the bank's premises and moveable assets. A summary of key steps in such an intervention follows. More detailed information, including guides to planning, staffing requirements and detailed checklists for task completion can be found in the *Closing Manual* of the Federal Deposit Insurance Corporation (FDIC). Supervisory agencies (or deposit insurers) with legal responsibility for bank intervention have (or should develop) similar generic contingency plans.

1. Appoint administrator and support team (size determined by the size and complexity of the bank). The first responsibility for the administrator and the support team is to get control of all the key functions in the bank as quickly as possible. New heads should be appointed for (i) credits; (ii) cash and vaults; (iii) accounting and reporting; (iv) computer systems; (v) external bank accounts; (vi) files and records; and (vii) staff and branches. If required, arrange for law enforcement agencies or private security firms to assist in assuming physical control. As far as possible, head office and all branch locations should be entered simultaneously.
2. Suspend authority of existing management immediately, particularly the powers to contract, sign, and move money. Advise clearing houses, payments system administrators, key counterparties, and correspondents of the change in control and make arrangements for items in transit to be either honored or returned. Staff should firmly be told to follow instructions from the administrator and the support team. All new transactions to be authorized by the administrator or persons designated by the administrator.
3. Issue statement to the press, important clients and the public. Preferably one person should be in charge of all external contacts.
4. Secure and seal swift and telex systems, dealing rooms and terminals. Locks and codes should be changed and access only allowed by a person authorized by the administrator. ▶

5. Secure cash and vaults both at headquarters and branches and freeze all balances with correspondent banks.
6. Secure computer systems and make sure there are back-ups with off-site storage and disaster recovery provisions.
7. Secure all documents, and particularly board minutes, loan files, and collateral agreements.

All the above should have been planned thoroughly and need to be completed within a few hours after the intervention. Once the administrator and support team has full control of the bank they should start addressing more time consuming issues such as assessing the financial condition of the bank, staffing needs, auditing, and reporting.

The review of an intervened bank may indicate that restructuring is feasible, but these conclusions need to be critically examined. A willingness to undertake more radical restructuring than was palatable to the bank's owners and managers may be sufficient to achieve the turnaround that escaped the shareholders during the early warning period. It is more likely, however, that the failure to fix the bank prior to intervention is an indication that new capital, not just restructuring and reorganization, was required, and that the expected return was insufficient to attract new equity investors, or a purchaser or a merger partner.[10]

Restructuring an intervened bank may improve its attractiveness to investors, but it may be more cost efficient to sell all or parts of the bank on an as-is basis, at a discount, or possibly by providing a stop-loss or some other guarantee to the new owner.

The supervisor, or contract management or consultants retained to manage the intervened bank may be able to make improvements, but the incremental costs of restructuring may not be fully recouped in a subsequent sale. Quickly disposing of the intervened bank has the benefit of checking ongoing operating losses and permitting a more precise estimate of the costs of resolution than a longer-term restructuring plan with uncertain results.

For even the largest banks where recapitalization or restructuring has not been successful prior to intervention, possible solutions to preserve the essential functions of the bank include:

- sale of individual businesses of the bank on a going concern basis;
- liquidation and piecemeal or en bloc sales of individual assets and business lines; and
- an outright sale of the bank to another financial institution.[11]

Particularly if the bank has a large share in certain business lines or regions, its assets should be attractive to purchasers. Another viable option may be to split the intervened bank's assets, liabilities, staff and branch network into perhaps one or two new banks, which would be offered for sale to potential investors. If a banking system is too concentrated and dominated by a few large banks this could be a good opportunity to split it up, increasing the number of competitors.

III. The special role of banks does not preclude closure

When considering the possible closure of a bank, it is useful to recall the oft-quoted phrase: "Banking is essential, banks are not." It is the function performed, not the existence of any particular bank or group of banks, which is vital to the economy. The special role played by banks is well known.[12] Banks are subject to prudential supervision both because of their important function and to counterbalance the tendency to increased risk-taking that might otherwise arise from the provision of public safety nets such as the lender-of-last-resort (LOLR) facility and deposit insurance.

Reluctance to close a bank can arise from concern that the action will be seen either as a failure of the supervisors or country authorities more generally, or that the closure may lead to a broader loss of confidence. The real failure of the supervisory apparatus is not bank closure, but failure to deal on a timely basis with identified problems. Loss-making banks may use aggressive pricing to attract deposits, distorting the market to the detriment of prudently managed banks. Loss-making banks do not properly perform their intermediation function, but instead consume deposits to cover their ongoing losses. The objective of prudential oversight therefore is not to prevent the failure of a bank, but instead to identify risks and inefficiencies in a timely way and to ensure that inefficient banks exit the market in an orderly manner with minimum disruption to the real economy. In resolving problem banks the objective should be to minimize disruption to the essential functions, not necessarily to save a bank.

Reluctance to close a bank can arise from an unwillingness to impose losses on shareholders, depositors and creditors. Politicians will be concerned about the impact on the large numbers of voters who will comprise the depositor base of even a small bank. Failure to resolve a problem bank defers the crystallization of the direct resolution costs, and thus may create the illusion that these costs have been avoided. Shareholders and creditors facing losses may have political influence. A truly independent banking supervisor will be better able to withstand the political influence of special interest groups.

Deposit insurance can play an important role in mitigating the impact of bank failures. This can make closures politically acceptable, by ensuring that the vast majority of small depositors suffer little or no loss. Similar protection for small deposits can arise from the preference given in many of the former Soviet countries to household deposits in claims against the assets of closed banks, or by the more general priority given to depositor claims in countries such as Australia. The effectiveness of priority claims as a means of protecting depositors is crucially dependent on decisive action by the supervisor to intervene and resolve a weak bank while the value of the assets is still sufficient to meet depositors' claims.

Even with the challenges posed by political influence and the difficulties in imposing losses on depositors, bank closures are widely used around the world to resolve problem banks. Much of the literature and research is based on the U.S. experience with thousands of bank failures, and it is sometimes argued that nondisruptive bank closures are not possible in countries lacking the unique structure of thousands of banks, well developed markets for the sale of banking and real assets, and broad and deep capital markets. The evidence does not support this position. Bank closures have been used as a resolution technique in economies at all stages of development, both in times of systemic crisis and in dealing with one or a few weak institutions in an otherwise sound financial system (Table 5.2). More than two-thirds of 37 deposit insurers responding to an FDIC survey indicated that troubled deposit-taking institutions are routinely closed and liquidated or otherwise reorganized when equity capital is exhausted.[13] In over 60 bank failures in non-U.S. G-10 countries since 1980 the most frequently used resolutions involved closure of the bank—sale of the whole bank or its assets, or liquidation.[14] In a study of measures to resolve banking crises in 24 countries, including 20 developing or transition economies, a strong correlation was observed between exit policies and progress in resolving the crisis.[15] Of countries making substantial progress in resolving the crises, 80 percent employed bank closures as one part of the resolution strategy, while bank closures were used in only one-third of countries making slow progress towards crisis resolution. In dealing with failing banks in 12 transition economies in the Baltic States, Eastern Europe and the Commonwealth of Independent States, literally hundreds of banks were closed in the 1990s, largely without contagion, high costs, or social problems.[16] In the case of the Kyrgyz Republic and Kazakhstan, the closures included the country's largest and fourth largest bank, respectively. In 1995 Latvia closed and liquidated banks accounting for about 40 percent of banking deposits, including the largest private bank. Nigeria has a notable record among African countries, having closed and liquidated 34 banks since 1993. In Uganda four banks were closed between 1998 and 2001, including the second and third largest domestically owned banks, with two resolved by liquidation and two by purchase and assumption transactions. Since 1997, 20 banks have been intervened in Turkey representing some 20 percent of total banking system assets. Of these 20 banks, 12 banks have exited the market, primarily through mergers with two transition banks that were subsequently privatized. Four banks (including the two transition banks) have been privatized while four others remain under the control of the supervisory agency.

Table 5.2. Bank Closure Options Available to Deposit Insurers[a]

	Purchase and Assumption		Deposit Payoff	
	Has Authority	Used In Last 10 Years	Has Authority	Used In Last 10 Years
Belgium	Yes	Yes	Yes	Yes
Canada	Yes	Yes	Yes	Yes
Czech Republic	...	...	Yes	Yes
El Salvador	Yes	No	Yes	No
France	Yes	No	Yes	No
Germany	Yes	No	Yes	Yes
Greece	...	...	Yes	Yes
Hungary	Yes	No	Yes	Yes
Isle of Man	...	...	Yes	Yes
Italy	Yes	Yes	Yes	Yes
Jamaica	Yes	No	Yes	No
Japan	Yes	No	Yes	No
Lithuania	...	...	Yes	Yes
Mexico	Yes	Yes	Yes	No
Netherlands	...	...	Yes	No
Nigeria	Yes	Yes	Yes	Yes
Oman	Yes	No	Yes	No
Peru	Yes	No	Yes	Yes
Poland	...	...	Yes	Yes
Portugal	...	...	Yes	No
Romania	...	...	Yes	Yes
Slovak Republic	Yes	Yes	Yes	Yes
Spain	Yes	Yes	Yes	Yes
Sweden	...	...	Yes	No
Taiwan Province of China	Yes	Yes	Yes	No
Tanzania	Yes	No	Yes	No
Trinidad and Tobago	Yes	No	Yes	Yes
Turkey	Yes	No	Yes	Yes
Uganda	Yes	Yes	Yes	Yes

Source: Bennett (2001).

[a] Subsequent to completion of the FDIC survey used to compile this table, Peru undertook two assisted purchase and assumption transactions, so is shown as having used the purchase and assumption authority in the last 10 years despite not having done so at the time the Bennett article was prepared.

A systematic cross-country study of bank resolutions would provide further insights, but there is already ample evidence that closure options have been effectively employed in a wide range of circumstances. Closure options have been more often used to deal with small and medium-sized banks, which in part reflect the larger universe of small banks, but also are indicative of the greater opposition and obstacles to closure of large banks. Avoidance of closure is especially prevalent in dealing with large state-owned banks. It would appear to be easier to muster the political will to close large banks in countries where the financial system is less well developed since even if there is disruption, the actual impact on the real sector is minimal (Kazakhstan, Kyrgyz Republic, Latvia, and Uganda).

The conceptual approach to dealing with a large problem bank is the same as dealing with a smaller bank, but the resolution will be more complicated and difficult. The prospect of complications and difficulty does not mean that large problem banks should go unaddressed, or that closure options should not be among the solutions considered.[17] The key is that the resolution after intervention should avoid disruptions in the essential functions of the bank, even if it becomes necessary to proceed to liquidation and piecemeal asset sales. Arranging an orderly transfer of deposits and fair treatment of other claims is essential to maintaining confidence in the system. With adequate planning, an orderly transfer can be accomplished in a closure as well as in a going concern resolution. With inadequate planning, even a going concern solution can result in disruption to depositors that could lead to a more general loss in confidence in the banking system.

Presumption against extraordinary measures to avoid closures

It is quite often argued that large banks are too big to fail, or more accurately, too big to close and liquidate, due to the negative impact on the rest of the banking system and the real economy. Arguments used are that remaining operating banks would not have the capacity to provide banking services needed, would not be able to absorb assets and liabilities of the failed banks, or that the closure of a large bank would lead to a more wide-spread loss of public confidence. Another argument is that a bank with a dominant role in providing certain bank services (i.e., foreign exchange or payment services), or a bank that is the only provider of services in certain regions, cannot be closed without depriving the real economy of banking services. It is also suggested that disruption of borrowing relationships built up over time will be a crippling blow to a bank's customers. Thus, it is sometimes argued that the authorities have no choice if a large bank runs into trouble but to recapitalize the bank, at any cost.

All these arguments should be questioned. First, it is important to remember that the functions performed by the bank may be essential, but the bank itself is not. It may be cheaper to hive off the important parts of the bank rather than trying to save the entire institution. This can preserve customer relationships without the costs of maintaining loss-making operations. A second important point to consider is that the alternative to intervening is to permit the continued operation of an insolvent bank. Sale of viable parts of the bank or closure and liquidation may be less costly than continued subsidization of a bank's losses. Clearly, there is a need to take action to stem the ongoing losses to avoid diverting economic resources to an inefficient bank, and requiring other better managed banks to compete against the distortions a loss-making bank can introduce in a market.

Delay in addressing problem banks increases costs and makes ultimate resolutions more difficult. International experience has shown that bank problems can worsen rapidly if not promptly addressed; however, in many cases supervisors have tended to postpone taking timely and adequate corrective action in the hope that the problems will rectify themselves.[18] The "wait and hope" strategy is seldom successful. It is rare for additional information to surface after intervention that reveals the problems to be less severe than had originally been identified, or for a delay in intervention to actually reduce resolution costs. This is the case in nonsystemic situations, where "experience has shown that unsound banks are invariably in worse condition than is indicated by their financial statements, and that the lowest cost way to keep the banking system sound is to force their exit."[19] Evidence is also found in cases of systemic crisis, where in almost 25 percent of cases repeated recapitalizations are required because the amount initially provided turns out to be insufficient to restore solvency.[20] However, each problem bank presents a unique situation and it is not possible to test and determine or predict with absolute certainty the results of alternative strategies. Thus, the judgment involved in estimating costs and benefits provides supervisory authorities with the scope to reach a determination that a nonclosure option is more cost effective. While sometimes true, the evidence is that more frequently the analysis and initial decision to provide open bank assistance or forbearance are subsequently proved incorrect, ultimately increasing the costs of resolution.

To offset this embedded tendency to defer action and overestimate the likely success of open bank resolutions, there should be a strong presumption against the use of forbearance or public funds to avoid closures. In normal times, the use of public funds[21] for bank restructuring should only be considered in the case of systemically important banks, where the disruptive effect of the closure would result in higher costs than the cost of the extraordinary measures to deal with the problem banks. The burden of proof for use of public funds or a period of regulatory forbearance to deal with problem banks should be very high, especially when dealing with one or a small number of problem banks in normal times. This burden of proof is more readily met in a banking crisis, where there is an evident need to preserve part of an insolvent banking system to provide core functions for the real economy.

Costs and benefits of using public funds

Public funds or forbearance for troubled banks can create perverse incentives similar to those created by an ill-founded deposit insurance scheme. Depositors who have the expectation of being made whole exert no market discipline on banks. Owners and managers who expect public support in times of trouble are encouraged to undertake more risky activities and be less vigilant in managing the bank's exposure. For these reasons, a well-designed deposit insurance scheme incorporates features like low coverage limits to mitigate the negative effects on market discipline.[22] Similarly, the availability of LOLR support should generally be limited to solvent banks in normal times.[23] To avoid the negative consequences similar to those that can arise from the formal safety net for banks, the process of dealing with a problem bank should involve measures to ensure that it is not insulated from the effects of market discipline. In normal times these can be expected to include ensuring that shareholders lose their equity investment and depositors will not receive more than the limits of an existing deposit insurance scheme. Management found at fault need to be replaced to send a message about the negative outcomes from managing poorly.

The principal benefit of using public funds to rescue an insolvent bank is avoiding disruptive effects, the magnitude and consequences of which are difficult to predict. Fears of contagion or payment system paralysis may cause the authorities to favor extraordinary measures to avoid closure even if the probability of such widespread disruption is low. Governments may be so concerned about the costs and risks that an expensive bailout may be viewed as attractive, particularly when the costs of the bailout are uncertain and equally as difficult to quantify as the costs of disruption. The fiscal costs of government expenditures for bank restructuring or extended liquidity support can be more easily estimated, but the nonquantifiable costs outlined above may be even more significant.

IV. Systemic crisis

The assessments needed to close banks during a systemic crisis differ in a number of respects from the process leading to closure in an individual bank failure. In both cases, however, unviable banks should be closed. While the determination of viable and unviable can be difficult in the midst of a crisis, the evidence suggests that a strong exit policy for insolvent banks is an important part of successful systemic bank restructuring.[24] Such action serves to stem operating losses, limit the extent of needed liquidity support, and can also be important in providing markets a signal of a break with past practices of forbearance.[25]

A number of immediate steps are required to stabilize the system after the onset of a banking crisis. Depending on the circumstances, these may include liquidity support to ensure continued functioning of the payments system, a blanket guarantee to prevent bank runs,[26] and the prompt closure of unviable financial institutions.[27] In the midst of a crisis it will be difficult to quickly identify all the unviable institutions, with the result that liquidity support will likely be extended to some institutions that subsequently must exit. Thus, there will likely be an initial round of closures involving those banks that are immediately identifiable as unviable, followed by further closures or consolidation once the system has been stabilized and the immediate post-crisis period of bank restructuring takes place.

Statement of principles

In a systemic crisis or if a number of banks have been intervened, a clear strategy is required to avoid magnifying problems through ad hoc reactions. No decision on the use of public funds or a policy of forbearance should be taken until a strategy, which can be made public in a statement of principles, has been developed. This should lay out the process for dealing with the banking problems, including clear decision rules as to which banks will be eligible for extraordinary assistance and which banks should be closed. To be eligible for public funds, at a minimum a bank should:

- have fit and proper owners and managers;
- recognize the full extent of losses based on realistic asset valuations;
- have a business plan to achieve full capital adequacy within a realistic time frame;
- commit to necessary operational restructuring to assure future profitability; and
- involve private sector owners with sufficient capital at risk to provide a strong incentive for them to work for the survival and success of the institution.

In addition, the terms of provision of public funds should provide safeguards for the funds invested and incentives for the bank to be returned to full private ownership as quickly as possible. Such measures usually include intensive supervision and reporting requirements, restrictions on dividends, and could also involve provisions for automatic intervention or changes in management if agreed restructuring and performance targets are not met. Also, the provision of some or all of the public funds in the form of equity or convertible debt enables government to realize some of the benefits of a successful turnaround as well as providing the private shareholders with an incentive to repay the investment of public funds at the earliest opportunity.

It is important that the initial announcement of bank closures should be part of a coordinated package of actions and announcements including details of how the closures will be affected, plans to ensure smooth deposit transfer and payment, and details on the treatment of the staff of the banks to be closed. Failure to position bank closures as part of a coordinated process to deal with the crisis and to ensure minimal depositor disruption risks a continuation rather than stabilization of the crisis (Box 5.3). A clear communications strategy ensuring that only predetermined individuals speak publicly and deal with the press is important to ensure that the public is not confused by erroneous or speculative statements by individual politicians or officials.

Box 5.3. Indonesia: Doing It Wrong and Doing It Right

Intensified bank runs soon followed the closure of 16 small deeply insolvent Indonesian banks on November 1, 1997. Partial guarantees of depositors of the closed banks, the perception that other weak banks remained in the system, a loss of confidence in the government's overall economic management and currency flight all fueled the runs. This experience underscores the need for closures during a systemic crisis to be part of a comprehensive restructuring strategy that is clearly explained to the public, with sound macroeconomic policies in place.

A second round of closures was undertaken on March 13, 1999 concurrently with the take-over of seven banks by the Indonesian Bank Restructuring Agency (IBRA), the designation of nine other banks as eligible for public contribution to recapitalization, and the announcement of "fit and proper" reviews of banks viewed as viable. These actions, which resulted from assessment of the condition of private banks that began in the fall of 1998, were taken against the background of the January 1998 three-point plan of a blanket guarantee, the creation of IBRA, and introduction of a framework for corporate restructuring.

This second round of closures involving 38 banks was managed so that most deposits were transferred over the weekend of March 13, resulting in minimal disruption for depositors. The interventions and closures were well publicized through the electronic and print media, with customers getting full information about how to access their funds at banks receiving the transferred deposits. The combination of decisive action clearly communicated to the public, the existence of a credible guarantee, and evidence of a comprehensive approach to the private banks all contributed to the orderly exit of insolvent banks with minimal disruption.

Source: Lindgren and others (1999), Appendix I.

Evaluating banks' financial condition

An immediate review of the banking sector will likely identify some clearly unviable banks that should be closed immediately. An additional period of evaluation will be required to determine which other banks should be eligible for public assistance, and which should be subsequently closed or exit the market through merger (Box 5.4). The triage process is complicated by likely uncertainty about the veracity of reported financial data, the absence of market prices for most distressed bank assets, and general uncertainty arising from volatile macroeconomic conditions.

A review of the quality of banking supervision as part of this triage process serves two purposes. First, it establishes the extent to which supervisory data and bank reports provide reliable information on which to base assessments of banks' viability. Second, a review of prudential regulations and their enforcement, with a focus on asset quality, including loan classification and

Box 5.4. Assessing the Financial Condition of Banks

In most cases of systemic banking problems there is a need to assess the financial condition of banks to determine the "hole" in their balance sheets and thus the amount of capital needed to bring the system back to solvency. Making such assessments when the banking system is distressed is difficult because typically markets cease to function in a crisis, making it hard to estimate both the repayment capacity of borrowers and realizable value of collateral. Although difficult to do, it is important to avoid being too conservative on the one hand, leading to overstated capital needs, or too liberal on the other, resulting in banks remaining undercapitalized. The following is a summary of the methodology adopted in Turkey to assess the financial condition and thereby the capital needs of private banks.

The assessments were done by the external auditors and linked to their audit of the banks' financial statements as of end-December 2001. This did raise the issue of a conflict of interest since the external auditors, who had provided opinions on previous financial statements, might have been reluctant to provide assessments that would indicate any possible inaccuracy in historical financial statements. However, the current auditors' in-depth knowledge of the respective banks meant that they could carry out the assessments more quickly and at a lower cost than a new firm. Moreover, the Banking Regulation and Supervision Agency (BRSA) issued detailed specific instructions on supplementary reporting requirements to be prepared by bank management and certified by the auditors. As a further check against the possibility of the auditors deliberately or inadvertently mis-stating the financial condition of the banks, the BRSA appointed another firm independent of both the bank and the auditor to verify for each bank that the assessments had been carried out according to regulations and guidelines issued by the BRSA.

The supplementary reporting requirements focused on the following four areas:

Capital adequacy: Detailed information was requested regarding all classes of asset, application of risk weightings, and verification of the source of funds for any recent injection of capital.

Credits and other receivables: Since this constituted the single greatest risk for most of the banks, extensive disclosure of information and assessments were required on both individual and group exposure basis, including: (i) borrowers' performance; (ii) ability and willingness to pay; (iii) risk classification (five categories) and provisions established. In order to provide comfort that the bulk of the risk exposure had been examined in depth, auditors were required to certify that credit risk had been individually assessed for the greater of the 200 largest exposures or 75 percent of the value of the loan portfolio.

Exposures to related parties: Banks were required to disclose all related party balances and transactions with entities and individuals, both onshore and offshore. Auditors were required to confirm completeness and to review pricing and the economic substance of all such transactions.

Valuation issues: The instructions required extensive listing of transactions and testing of rates, prices and review of legal documents to assess the economic substance and legal form of transactions. Standards were given to identify and correct accidental or deliberate nonmarket pricing in the valuation of securities and foreign exchange accounts. The auditors were given specific instructions regarding detection of artificial pricing and fictitious transactions intended to window-dress the accounts.

provisioning requirements; accounting standards; profitability; liquidity; and solvency will identify areas that require strengthening as part of the institutional reform that is a necessary part of a longer term recovery plan.

Minimizing the fiscal burden

The authorities should always pursue options that minimize the fiscal burden once the decision has been taken to use public funds to assist in the restructuring of banks. This may mean having to limit the number of banks eligible for public assistance, perhaps by requiring that banks raise new private capital in order to be eligible for public assistance. In evaluating options it is important to consider that in the aftermath of a systemic crisis recovery rates from the assets of closed banks may be quite similar to recovery rates for the assets of restructured banks. In both cases, an asset management company would likely undertake much of the collection on loan assets. In a closure there is the possibility of recoveries from other assets and deposits sold to other operating banks. The cost for closing and liquidating a bank would roughly equal the estimated net value (likely to be negative) of the bank plus liquidation costs such as severance payments for staff, and lease and contract termination costs. These costs may not vary greatly from the costs of a financially assisted merger or restructuring, as all options are likely to entail significant rationalization of both staff and facilities.[28]

Save only the viable banking franchises

Hard decisions will be required to minimize the number of banks to be saved at public expense, both to minimize the fiscal cost and in an effort to ensure that the post-crisis landscape is not populated with a large number of "banks" that only warehouse recapitalization bonds. As a general principle a bank should be closed and liquidated if there is not a very high probability that recapitalization and a short period of restructuring would result in a bank that could be easily sold to private investors. Making this determination for individual banks in the midst of a crisis will be difficult, but it is important to keep in mind that injection of enough capital could make any bank financially viable, but it will only be attractive to investors if it has a valuable banking franchise. Thus, a bank with a largely nonperforming asset portfolio, or one that loses most of its customer base through the transfer of nonperforming loans to an asset management company, will most likely not be a good candidate for restructuring. Building a new customer base on the asset side is a risky and lengthy exercise, and if built up too quickly could involve assuming a high degree of credit risk. This suggests that recapitalization and restructuring efforts should focus on those banks that retain the largest portion of unimpaired loans. For banks without a strong franchise, faster and lower cost resolutions may be achieved through the en bloc or piecemeal sale of any attractive businesses and a deposit transfer and payout.

V. Conclusion

Closing a bank becomes necessary when other measures have failed to resolve the problems of a weak bank. There are many reasons why supervisors often hesitate to close a bank: concerns about potential disruption to depositors, borrowers, creditors and the payment system; the possibility that closure might trigger runs at other banks; and reluctance to impose losses on depositors, especially in the absence of deposit insurance or a government guarantee. All these concerns can be mitigated by timely, well-planned closure options. There may be concern that closing a bank will be interpreted as a failure by the supervisory agency, but "bank failures are part of risk-taking in a competitive environment. Supervision cannot, and should not, provide an absolute assurance that banks will not fail."[29] Avoiding disruption is an important consideration, but it is equally important that there be a mechanism for inefficient banks to exit the market.

Governments may be tempted to avoid the repercussions of bank failures by using public funds for restructuring or to guarantee bank depositors and creditors. These extraordinary measures may be required in response to a systemic crisis, but should generally be avoided. In addition to the fiscal burden ultimately borne by taxpayers, use of public funds can distort the market and create perverse incentives, ultimately weakening rather than strengthening the banking system. The disruptive effects of bank failures are better addressed through well planned and executed closures of banks, involving some form of purchase and assumption or deposit transfer to preserve the essential functions performed by a failing bank.

Despite differences in legal frameworks and market structures, bank closures have been widely used around the world to resolve problem banks. Closure of a bank is not a decision to be taken lightly or in isolation. It will almost always be the culmination of a supervisory process attempting to resolve problems before closure became necessary, or in the case of systemic crisis, part of a broader plan that will preserve part of an insolvent banking system. The best solution to a problem bank occurs before the bank reaches a level of weakness that requires supervisory intervention. However, this will not always be possible, particularly in a systemic crisis when the whole sector becomes populated with problem banks. It also will not be possible in many "normal times" situations where, despite escalating supervisory action, restructuring attempts, and a search for new private sector investors, intervention is ultimately required to limit the exposure of the deposit insurer, uninsured depositors and other creditors. When intervention becomes necessary, closure options should be considered in both normal times and systemic crisis.

Notes

1. The authors are grateful to Philip Bartholomew, Warren Coats, Luis Cortavarria, Olivier Frécaut, Peter Hayward, David Hoelscher, Alain Ize, Carl Lindgren,

Christiane Nickel, Marc Quintyn, Steven Seelig, Hemant Shah, and Jan Willem van der Vossen for helpful comments on earlier versions of this chapter.

2. For definitions of other terms commonly used in the discussion of bank resolutions, see Basel Committee (2002), Annex 5.

3. The legal framework for dealing with problem banks and effecting closure varies significantly among jurisdictions. For example, license revocation can be the key legal step in closing a bank, or it may be a routine administrative action taken at the end of a liquidation, long after the normal business of banking has ceased. Detailed discussion of the legal process in various jurisdictions is beyond the scope of this chapter. For an overview of the issues, see Asser (2001).

4. Hawkins and Turner (1999), pp. 16–18.

5. Lindgren, Garcia, and Saal (1996), Chapter 4.

6. Hawkins and Turner (1999), pp. 17–18.

7. This is one of the essential criteria of Basel Core Principle 22.

8. The nature of "intervention" varies among regimes. In this chapter intervention is defined as the authorities assuming control of a bank, taking over the powers of management and shareholders. Intervention is differentiated from less intrusive supervisory action through the supervisor (or deposit insurer, or an agent appointed by the supervisor or deposit insurer) assuming full legal control of the institution. An intervened bank usually stays open under the control of the authorities, while its financial condition is better defined and decisions are made on an appropriate resolution strategy. In some regimes there is a concept of conservatorship where the supervisory authority may assume day-to-day control of a bank, but shareholder consent would be required for major decisions.

9. Sheng (1996, p. 36) notes that if private buyers cannot be found for a failed bank, it is generally cheaper to liquidate than to keep an insolvent bank open.

10. This is quite understandable given that the first part of an investment in an insolvent bank simply fills the hole. For example, injecting equity of 15 in a bank with a capital deficit of 5 results in a bank with a book value of 10. The immediate effect is that an investor has spent 15 to acquire an asset worth only 10, which is unlikely to be attractive unless there are good prospects for a rapid turnaround in the performance of the bank.

11. In order to meet the requirements of specific circumstances there can be an almost infinite number of variations on the general themes of (1) purchase and assumptions and (2) deposit transfer and payout. See Federal Deposit Insurance Corporation (FDIC) (1998b), pp. 19–44.

12. Banks provide an essential store of liquidity by providing deposits valued at par and payable on demand. They provide a mechanism to make payments that are essential to completion of financial transactions in the economy, and they play a key role in the transmission of monetary policy. Banks play the major role in intermediating savings and investment.

13. Bennett (2001), p. 5.

14. Bartholomew and Gup (1999), pp. 78–80.

15. Dziobek and Pazarbasioglu (1997), p. 14.

16. Tang, Zoli, and Klytchnikova (2000), pp. 15–17.

17. Of the three generic options presented in the FDIC *Resolutions Handbook*, two involve closure of the bank, and the third, open bank assistance, is seldom the preferred choice due to the requirement to pursue least-cost solutions (FDIC, 1998b).

18. Basel Committee (2002), p. 21.

19. Bartholomew and Gup (1999), pp. 47–48.
20. Honohan and Klingebiel (2002).
21. Deposit insurance payments up to established limits may be used—this will not normally result in fiscal costs borne by the taxpayers.
22. Garcia (1999).
23. He (2000).
24. Dziobek and Pazarbasioglu (1997), p. 26.
25. Lindgren and others (1999), p. 23.
26. Blanket guarantees have a number of drawbacks, including the fiscal exposure of an open-ended government commitment to cover bank losses. Nevertheless, when faced with runs in a systemic crisis, countries with the fiscal resources to make such a policy credible have generally opted to guarantee all bank depositors and creditors.
27. There are also other key elements to a stabilization action plan, including macroeconomic polices, the possibility of capital controls, and debt restructuring. For a fuller discussion see Lindgren and others (1999), pp. 16–23. These broader issues are outside the scope of this chapter, which focuses more narrowly on issues related to bank closure.
28. In some jurisdictions fiscal costs of closure may be lower than restructuring as a receiver or trustee may not be legally required to pay the full staff severance or lease termination costs that an operating bank might face. In these jurisdictions the authorities will have to make a determination as to whether these costs should be borne by the budget.
29. Basel Committee (2002) p. 30.

Bibliography

Alexander, William E., and others, 1997, *Systemic Bank Restructuring and Macroeconomic Policy* (Washington: International Monetary Fund).

Asser, Tobias M.C., 2001, *Legal Aspects of Regulatory Treatment of Banks in Distress* (Washington: International Monetary Fund).

Bartholomew, Philip F., and Benton E. Gup, 1999, "A Survey of Bank Failures in the Non-U.S., G-10 Countries Since 1980," *Research in International Banking and Finance*, Vol. 16, pp. 45–88.

Basel Committee on Banking Supervision, 2002, *Supervisory Guidance on Dealing with Weak Banks: Report of the Task Force on Dealing with Weak Banks* (Basel: Bank for International Settlements).

Bennett, Rosalind L., 2001, "Failure Resolution and Asset Liquidation: Results of an International Survey of Deposit Insurers," *FDIC Banking Review*, Vol. 14, No. 1.

Caprio, Gerald, and Daniela Klingebiel, 2002, "Episodes of Systemic and Borderline Banking Crises," Discussion Paper 428 (Washington: World Bank).

Dziobek, Claudia, 1998, "Market-Based Policy Instruments for Systemic Bank Restructuring," IMF Working Paper 98/113 (Washington: International Monetary Fund).

Dziobek, Claudia, and Ceyla Pazarbasioglu, 1997, "Lessons from Systemic Bank Restructuring: A Survey of 24 Countries," IMF Working Paper 97/161 (Washington: International Monetary Fund).

Enoch, Charles, Gillian Garcia, and V. Sundararajan, 1999, "Recapitalizing Banks with Public Funds: Selected Issues," IMF Working Paper 99/139 (Washington: International Monetary Fund).

Federal Deposit Insurance Corporation, 1998a, *Managing the Crisis: The FDIC and RTC Experience 1980–1994* (Washington: FDIC).

——, 1998b, *Resolutions Handbook: Methods for Resolving Troubled Financial Institutions in the United States* (Washington: FDIC).

Frydl, Edward J., 1999, "The Length and Cost of Banking Crises," IMF Working Paper 99/30 (Washington: International Monetary Fund).

Frydl, Edward J., and Marc Quintyn, 2000, "The Benefits and Costs of Intervening in Banking Crises," IMF Working Paper 00/147 (Washington: International Monetary Fund).

Garcia, Gillian, 1999, "Deposit Insurance: A Survey of Actual and Best Practices," IMF Working Paper 99/54 (Washington: International Monetary Fund).

Hawkins, John, and Philip Turner, 1999, "Bank Restructuring in Practice: An Overview," in *Bank Restructuring in Practice*, BIS Policy Paper No. 6 (Basel: Bank for International Settlements).

He, Dong, 2000, "Emergency Liquidity Support Facilities," IMF Working Paper 00/79 (Washington: International Monetary Fund).

Honohan, Patrick, and Daniela Klingebiel, 2002, "Controlling the Fiscal Costs of Banking Crises," Discussion Paper 428 (Washington: World Bank).

Lindgren, Carl-Johan, and others, 1999, *Financial Sector Crisis and Restructuring: Lessons From Asia*, IMF Occasional Paper 188 (Washington: International Monetary Fund).

Lindgren, Carl-Johan, Gillian Garcia, and Matthew I. Saal, 1996, *Bank Soundness and Macroeconomic Policy* (Washington: International Monetary Fund).

Office of the Comptroller of the Currency, 1988, *Bank Failure: An Evaluation of the Factors Contributing to the Failure of National Banks* (Washington: OCC).

Santomero, Anthony M., and Paul Hoffman, 1998, "Problem Bank Resolution: Evaluating the Options" Financial Institutions Center Working Paper 98–05-B (Philadelphia: Wharton School, University of Pennsylvania).

Sheng, Andrew, 1996, "Bank Restructuring Techniques" in *Bank Restructuring: Lessons from the 1980s*, ed. by Andrew Sheng (Washington: World Bank).

Tang, Helena, Edda Zoli, and Irina Klytchnikova, 2000, "Banking Crises in Transition Countries: Fiscal Costs and Related Issues," WB Working Paper 2484 (Washington: World Bank).

6
Post-Resolution Treatment of Depositors at Failed Banks: Implications for the Severity of Banking Crises, Systemic Risk, and Too-Big-To-Fail

George G. Kaufman and Steven A. Seelig

I. Introduction

Bank failures are widely viewed in all countries as more damaging to the economy than the failure of other firms of similar size for a number of reasons. The failures may produce losses to depositors and other creditors, break long-standing bank–customer loan relationships, disrupt the payments system, and spill over in domino fashion to other banks, financial institutions and markets, and even to the macro economy (Kaufman, 1996). Thus, bank failures are viewed as potentially more likely to involve contagion or systemic risk than the collapse of other firms. The risk of such actual or perceived damage is often a popular justification for explicit or implicit government-provided or sponsored safety nets under banks, including explicit deposit insurance and implicit government guarantees, such as "too-big-to-fail" (TBTF), that may protect de jure uninsured depositors and possibly other bank stakeholders against some or all of the loss.[1]

But even with such guarantees, bank failures still invoke widespread fear. In part, this reflects a concern that protected and/or unprotected depositors may not receive full and immediate access to their claims on the insolvent banks at the time that the institutions are declared insolvent and placed in receivership. That is, they may suffer post-resolution losses in addition to any loss at the time of resolution. Unprotected depositors may be required to wait until the proceeds from the sale of the bank's assets are received.

Protected depositors may also not be paid in full immediately if the insurance agency has no authority or procedures for advancing payment before receipt of the sales proceeds or if there is insufficient time to collect and process the necessary data on who the insured depositors are and how much is insured for each depositor. If depositors are not paid the full value of their claims immediately, some or all of the deposits are effectively temporarily "frozen." In the absence of an efficient secondary market for frozen deposits, both protected and unprotected depositors will experience losses in liquidity and, in addition, protected depositors will experience present value losses if they are paid the value of their claim after the date of resolution without interest. Indeed, a European bank analyst has recently observed that

> The issue is not so much the fear of a domino effect where the failure of a large bank would create the failure of many smaller ones; strict analysis of counterpart exposures has reduced substantially the risk of a domino effect. The fear is rather that the need to close a bank for several months to value its illiquid assets would freeze a large part of deposit and savings, causing a significant negative effect on national consumption. (Dermine, 1996, p. 680)

The potential magnitude of losses to depositors in bank failures is likely to effect both the supply of and demand for government guarantees and to influence the resolution options available to a deposit insurer. The larger the potential losses in bank resolutions are perceived to be, the greater the demand for government guarantees by depositors and other stakeholders is likely to be and the more likely that governments will bow to such political pressures and supply the guarantees. Thus, the way depositors are treated at insolvent institutions in terms of the magnitude of the losses they may incur and their access to the value of their deposit claims has important public policy implications.

This chapter examines both the sources and implications of potential depositor losses in bank resolutions—in particular, depositor losses due to delays in paying both protected and unprotected depositors at failed banks the full values of their claims in a timely fashion after a bank is officially declared insolvent and resolved. For de facto insured depositors, the value of their claims is the par value of the eligible deposits at the time of resolution less any explicit deductible or loss-sharing amount. For de facto uninsured depositors, the value of their claim is the present value of the estimated eventual pro-rata recovery value of the bank's assets, which is likely to be less than the par value. Although losses to depositors in bank failures at the time of resolution have been frequently analyzed in the literature, the implications of losses after resolution from delayed depositor access through the freezing of insured and/or uninsured accounts have not been thoroughly analyzed.

Because the magnitude and timing of the losses to depositors in bank insolvencies are in large measure under the control of the deposit insurance agency or the government, this chapter develops public policy recommendations on how to minimize all losses to depositors, in particular, the losses to depositors from delayed access to their funds after resolution. On the one hand, if this loss could be reduced, it could contribute to reducing both the demand for and supply of broad government guarantees, including reducing, if not eliminating, the need for TBTF. In the United States, the Federal Deposit Insurance Corporation (FDIC) currently pursues such a strategy. With only infrequent exception, it effectively makes the full value of their permissible claims available to both insured and uninsured depositors one or two business days after a bank is legally failed. Combined with faster resolution after economic insolvency that reduces depositor losses at the time of resolution, this strategy has made it politically possible to resolve even large insolvent banks with losses to uninsured depositors. But this practice is not followed in most other countries. Rather, in these countries, both insured and uninsured depositors are paid the value of their claims only through time after the resolution of the bank. These delays may at times stretch many months for insured deposits and many years for uninsured deposits. As a result, to reduce the potential adverse economic and political ramifications damage from such additional losses to depositors, governments in these countries are often reluctant to resolve insolvent banks with losses to uninsured depositors and permit the banks to continue in operation by effectively protecting all depositors.

On the other hand, reductions in potential losses and delays in payment could reduce depositor discipline on solvent banks, thereby increasing their banks' fragility and the probability of failure. Thus, either corner solution appears to have drawbacks as well as advantages and an intermediate interior solution in terms of delay time in paying depositors may be preferred in reducing the potential damage from bank failures and maximizing aggregate economic welfare. The chapter models the trade-offs between increased market discipline and increased probability of government bailout as the time delay by the insurance agency in paying depositors the full value of their claims is varied to solve for the optimal depositor access delay time.

The remainder of the chapter is organized as follows: Section II identifies and analyzes the sources of potential losses to depositors in bank failures. Section III discusses the implications of delayed depositor access to their funds at insolvent banks in terms of the effects on depositor discipline, on the one hand, and depositor pressure to protect all deposits, on the other. Ways that policymakers can reduce depositor losses from bank failures are discussed in Section IV. Section V describes the current policies of major countries with respect to providing depositors with access to their funds at resolved insolvent institutions and procedures available to provide depositors with full and immediate access to their claims at the time the institutions are declared insolvent and placed in receivership. Particular attention is given to the procedure currently used by the FDIC in the United States. Section VI looks at the history of immediate and full payments of depositor claims, and Section VII discusses the disadvantages of providing immediate depositor access to the full value of their permissible funds. The access timing decision is modeled graphically in Section VIII to solve for the optimal delay time. Section IX reports on a survey of depositor access practices across countries conducted by the FDIC in spring 2000. The final section of the chapter develops conclusions and "best practices" recommendations regarding depositor access to their funds at resolved insolvent institutions to enhance the safety and efficiency of banking systems.

II. Sources of potential losses to depositors

Past analyses have identified four potential sources of economic losses to depositors or the government deposit insurance agency, which stands in the shoes of the de jure insured depositors, in from the resolution of insolvent depository institutions:

- **Poor closure rule.** Embedded losses from a delay between the time when a bank becomes economically insolvent (where the market value of the assets declines below the market value of the liabilities—the present value of the maturity value of the deposits and other debt) and the time it becomes eligible to be declared legally insolvent.
- **Regulatory forbearance.** Embedded losses from a delay in the time from when a bank becomes legally eligible to be declared insolvent and the time it is actually resolved—declared insolvent by the regulators or other authorized party (official recognition of the insolvency), a receiver appointed, and the existing owners removed.
- **Bad market conditions after resolution.** Losses (gains) from delay in the receiver selling the bank as a whole or parcels of its assets and deposits after the bank is declared legally insolvent either because of operational problems or to wait for a better market.
- **Inefficient receiver.** Losses from delay in the receiver distributing the proceeds from the sales to the uninsured depositors and the deposit insurance agency.

These potential losses occur sequentially. The first two sources of losses occur before the date of resolution because economically insolvent banks are permitted to continue to stay open and operate under their existing owners and managers. The first loss arises from a poor legal closure rule that focuses on book or regulatory values that often overstate bank assets and understate bank liabilities compared to their economic or market values. In the United States, banks (although not bank holding companies), unlike other corporations, are not subject to the jurisdiction of the bankruptcy process and courts. Rather, they are resolved by their primary federal regulator.

The second loss reflects regulatory forbearance from fear of imposing losses and injuring favored parties associated with the insolvent bank (e.g., shareholders, management, other employees, borrowers, or uninsured depositors), injuring other financial institutions and the macroeconomy, or injuring the regulators' own reputation as public guardians against bank failures. In addition, until the date of official recognition of the insolvency and resolution of the bank, embedded losses from the continued operation of insolvent banks are not booked and accrue only to the deposit insurance agency. Both insured and uninsured depositors can withdraw their maturing funds from these banks at par value. Because they are not officially booked, the embedded losses to the insurance agency are generally difficult for much of the public to recognize and easy for regulators to disguise, hide, and deny. Only at and after the date of official recognition of insolvency are the total embedded losses booked and visible to all and a pro-rata share imposed on the remaining unprotected depositors. This encourages regulators to delay closure. As a result, regulators are often poor agents for their principals—healthy banks and taxpayers. The costs of forbearance in encouraging moral hazard behavior by the banks and increasing eventual losses to depositors in the United States and abroad have been amply documented (Kane, 1990; Kane and Yu, 1995; Kaufman, 1995 and 1997a; Barth, 1991; and Gupta and Misra, 1999).

The costs of a poor closure rule and forbearance include not only increased credit and market losses, but also increased losses from fraud and asset stripping, which is more likely at insolvent or near-insolvent institutions, and misallocating financial resources leading to misallocations of real resources and reductions in aggregate economic welfare.

The final two sources of loss occur after the date of official resolution and the institution is put in receivership. Losses to depositors from delay in liquidating bank assets may be either or both credit/market losses and/or present value losses. This delay generally arises because of time necessary to determine who the depositors are and certification of their claims and attempts—legitimate or not—by the receiver, to avoid fire-sale losses or depressing asset prices further by selling quickly into perceived temporarily weak markets and waiting for stronger markets, from self-dealing by the receiver, or legal obstacles that prevent the receiver from disposing of assets quickly. The fourth and last source of loss from delays in distributing the funds from the sale of the bank is primarily a present value loss to depositors from operational inefficiencies.

III. Implications of post-resolution delayed depositor access to funds

Unlike the two sources of losses at the date the institution is legally declared insolvent and placed in receivership, which have been analyzed frequently, the two sources of depositor losses afterwards have been analyzed only infrequently. As noted earlier, at the time of resolution, insured (protected) depositors have claims for the par value of their deposits (adjusted for any coinsurance) at the date of resolution and uninsured (unprotected) depositors for the present value of the estimated pro-rata recovery value of their deposits. In the absence of an efficient secondary market, delay in offering depositors full access to their permissible funds decreases the liquidity and, in the absence of interest payments, also the present value of the deposit claims, and greatly intensifies both public fears and actual costs of bank failures.

Moreover, the fear of such inaccessibility alone is likely to have important political as well as economic consequences. Affected depositors are more likely to demand full and immediate access to their funds and regulators and governments are likely to bow to the political pressures and both delay official recognition of insolvency (forbear) and fully protect more if not all depositors (too big to fail) if and when insolvency is finally declared. At the same time, the government itself is likely to view any loss in depositor liquidity as potentially detrimental to the aggregate economy and may be reluctant to permit conditions that would trigger this loss. Thus, it may maintain insolvent institutions in operation and protect all depositors and possibly other creditors in full. Such response further reduces market discipline and encourages additional moral hazard behavior by the banks.

IV. Reducing potential losses to depositors

The adverse effects from bank failure can be reduced by reducing losses from any or all of the above four sources to both depositors and the deposit insurance agency. Indeed, if troubled banks could be resolved before the market value of their equity capital turned negative, losses would be restricted only to shareholders. Depositors would be unharmed. Little, if any, more serious adverse effects would then be felt from bank failures than the failure of any other firm of comparable size. Failures could be freely permitted to weed out the inefficient or unlucky players. Deposit insurance would effectively be redundant. In the United States, the Federal Deposit Insurance Corporation Improvement Act (FDICIA) attempts to reduce the first two sources of losses through prompt corrective action (PCA) that both impose a more efficient closure rule—2 percent tangible equity to asset ratio—and reduces regulatory discretion to forbear by requiring mandatory sanctions. These include resolution, when the discretionary sanctions applied appear to be ineffective as reflected in a continued decline in the bank's capital ratio.

The third source of loss could be reduced by careful monitoring by the banking agency that appoints the receiver of the receiver's motivations or justification for delaying selling bank assets. This monitoring would verify both that the probabilities are sufficiently high that relevant asset markets are only temporarily depressed, and may be expected to recover shortly, and that the assets can be managed efficiently in the meantime, so that the present value of the projected sales proceeds to depositors and the deposit insurance agency will be higher than if the assets were sold without a delay. Recent experience in most countries, including the United States, suggests that delay in asset sales, although often politically popular, rarely produces financial gains (Kane, 1990 and Gupta and Misra, 1999). Thus, it may be desirable to specify timely sales schedules. The fourth source of loss could be reduced by requiring receivers to distribute their proceeds more quickly as they are received and monitoring and enforcing their compliance with this policy.

V. Procedures For immediate and full payment of depositor claims at resolution

If losses are incurred in resolving an insolvency, governments, out of fear of depositor bailout pressure or of systemic risk, may prefer to provide depositors with immediate and full access to their claims at the time of resolution when the institution is legally declared insolvent and placed in receivership. The government or deposit insurance agency can do so by advancing funds to the affected depositors before they are received from the receiver or encourage the development of an efficient secondary market in the claims.

The United States appears to be one of the very few countries that currently does not freeze accounts at failed banks and provides all depositors immediate and full access to the value of their claims, so that there is no loss of either liquidity or present value.[2] The FDIC advances the funds. Although it rarely receives full and immediate payment for all the assets in the resolution of a failed bank, the FDIC typically advances the pro rata present value of the estimated recovery value (advance dividend payment) to all depositors at domestic offices of the bank on or about the next business day after the official recognition of insolvency and its appointment as receiver. Insured depositors and de jure uninsured depositors that are fully protected ex post by the FDIC receive access to this amount plus the amount necessary to make them whole payable either at the bank that assumed the insured deposits of the resolved banks or, if the insured deposits are not assumed by another bank, at the site of the failed bank operating in receivership.[3] De facto uninsured domestic depositors receive access to the present value of the estimated recovery value at the failed bank, unless these deposits are assumed by another bank at par value.[4] However, since 1992, the least cost resolution provisions of FDICIA make assumptions of uninsured deposits by another bank unlikely, unless there is no or next to no loss to the FDIC in the transaction.[5] The FDIC can do this because it has both legal authority to advance the funds and has solved the technical problems that underlie delayed payments after resolution. To give the FDIC sufficient time to prepare for these payments and transfers, which includes identifying the owners and total of eligible accounts, banks are generally declared insolvent at close of business on Thursdays or Fridays and depositors given access to their funds the following Monday. This generally provides the FDIC with time to review the bank's deposit statements and process the information to determine each depositor's total insured balances.

Reliable estimation of recovery values of bank assets, however, generally requires longer than a weekend, and examiners and supervisors in the United States are typically provided with additional time. Under prompt corrective action, bank examiners and supervisors are effectively required to progressively increase their familiarity with a bank as soon as its financial situation deteriorates to the extent that it becomes classified as undercapitalized, including increasing the frequency of on-site visits. Moreover, when a bank is declared critically undercapitalized (or even if the bank is being resolved for other reasons) by its primary federal regulator, the FDIC is notified in advance and prepares for a possible sale of all or part of the bank to other institutions at auction at the highest price. To do this, it has to prepare detailed financial information on the bank to be provided on a confidential basis to potential bidders prior to the auction and to gather the information needed to make the determination as to which of several resolution alternatives will be least costly to it. Thus, the FDIC typically sends its resolutions staff into the bank some days prior to it being closed to collect the needed information (FDIC, 1998a). The data collected is used to arrive at both market valuations for the assets of the bank and estimates of the number and holdings of insured depositors and other creditor classes. As a result, except in the case of major fraud, the FDIC is able to reasonably accurately estimate recovery values before the bank is declared legally insolvent and put in receivership and the deposits need not be frozen after closure while the magnitude and impact of the payout is being estimated.

If, after recovery is completed, the proceeds to the FDIC exceed the amount it advanced the uninsured depositors, the depositors are paid the difference up to the par value of their claims plus interest. Any remainder is paid to more junior creditors and eventually to shareholders. If the proceeds fall short of the amount it advanced to the uninsured depositors, the FDIC bears the loss. Thus, to protect itself, the FDIC advances to the uninsured depositors only a conservative estimate of the present value of the recovery value.[6]

VI. History of immediate and full payments of depositor claims

Immediate and full access for all depositors, or even for only ex-post protected insured depositors, to their permissible funds has not always been the practice of federal deposit insurance agencies in the United States, and is not the current practice of deposit insurance agencies in most other countries. In large measure, the delayed access, particularly for protected depositors, reflects the inability of the insurance agency to advance payment to depositors before receipt from the receiver and to collect and analyze in a timely fashion the necessary information on what balances and which depositors are insured and on estimates of recovery values, as well as the ability to establish paying agents quickly. The information on eligible insured deposits is complex because of, among other things, poor and/or non-computerized records, and depositor ownership of multiple accounts at the same bank. These obstacles provide a physical rather than a policy reason for not providing immediate and full access to both protected and unprotected depositors.

Before the establishment of the FDIC in 1934, depositors at failed banks, even in states with state insurance programs, were generally paid only as the assets were liquidated and funds collected (FDIC, 1998b and Mason, Anari, and Kolari, 2000).[7] Before the mid-1960s, the former Federal Saving and Loan Insurance Corporation, which insured savings and loans associations (S&L) before the FDIC, often disbursed funds to insured depositors at failed S&Ls only slowly through time, and before the early 1980s, the FDIC did not advance payments to unprotected uninsured depositors (FDIC, 1998a). Likewise, state governments in Ohio, Maryland, and Rhode Island, states that experienced widespread failures of perceived state-insured thrift institutions in the 1980s, generally reimbursed "insured" depositors at these institutions in full, but only slowly over a number of years, so that depositors suffered significant present value losses and liquidity costs (Kane, 1992 and Todd, 1994). Thus, contrary to current FDIC practice, the insured depositors were insured in future or nominal values only, not in present values.

Full and immediate depositor access also does not exist in most other countries.[8] For example, Article 10 of the May 30, 1994 Directive of the European Union on Deposit Guarantee Schemes, which became effective on July 1, 1995, requires that each member country's national insurance agency pay insured depositors "within three months of the date on which the competent authorities make the determination" that the bank is unable to repay its deposits in full and deposits become unavailable to the depositors. But, this time period may be extended for two three-month periods to a maximum of nine months if necessary in "exceptional circumstances." These delay schedules appear to have been imposed to limit the maximum length of delay from obtaining and processing the relevant deposit data and encourage faster payment rather than to prolong delay in order to increase market discipline. No harmonizing directive applies to the treatment of uninsured depositors and other creditors. This is left to the laws of the individual countries.[9] The competent authority that can declare an institution insolvent and when it can do so also is determined by each country. In general, private receivers are appointed to sell or liquidate the bank. The uninsured or unprotected claimants are paid the recovered values as they are collected and distributed by the receiver. In most instances, this process is not fully completed for many years, so that the depositors do not have access to the full recovery value of their claims for an equal number of years. As a result, both the insured and, particularly, uninsured depositors attempt, often successfully, to exert political pressure on their government to delay declaring the bank insolvent and to make most, if not all, depositors whole when it does. Both outcomes are costly and inefficient. TBTF or broader appears alive and well in most countries outside the United States!

VII. Disadvantages of immediate and full payment of depositor claims

But providing immediate depositor access to the full value of their permissible funds may have an important disadvantage as well as advantages and, thus, be a two-sided sword. It may reduce market discipline on the banks. Knowing that they may have to wait, and at times a lengthy wait, to gain access to the full value of their claims after resolution and thus suffer liquidity and possibly present value losses in addition to any other losses unprotected depositors may incur, may provide both insured and uninsured depositors greater incentive both to monitor the financial health of their banks and to discipline them when necessary by charging higher interest rates commensurate with the greater perceived risk or transferring their deposits (running) to perceived safer banks. In addition, under full and immediate access, any unexpected losses from delays in asset sales and distribution of the sales' proceeds will accrue to the deposit insurer rather than to the uninsured depositors. This would further reduce the incentive for unprotected depositors to monitor their banks. The trade-off between the advantages and these disadvantages of full and immediate access is modeled in the next section to examine the implications more carefully and to identify the optimal time delay in providing depositors with full access.

VIII. Modeling the access delay decision

As discussed above, the primary basis for reducing the cost of failure to depositors by advancing them funds immediately after a bank failure is to minimize the economic disruption that can result from the loss of liquidity associated with freezing deposits. However, there is a clear trade-off with market discipline. The greater the perceived loss that depositors may potentially suffer, the greater the incentive for them to monitor the condition of their bank and discipline the bank for taking excessive risks, either by withdrawing funds or requiring higher interest rates to compensate for the increased risk. Given this trade-off, the problem is to solve for the optimal time distribution of payments on given depositor claims on a failed bank, assuming that the resolution loss is fixed at the time of failure. This trade-off can be modeled graphically. Because the government can affect, if not set, the delay time, including the time necessary to process the relevant deposit data and estimate the recovery values, it effectively serves as a policy tool.

The model is shown in Figure 6.1. The payment time delay (PD) set by the insurance agency after the resolution of insolvent institutions in providing depositors with full access to their claims is measured on the horizontal axis. Assuming a given loss at the time of resolution, the additional market discipline (AMD) from delayed payment resulting in possible present value losses to protected depositors and liquidity losses to unprotected depositors is measured on the vertical scale. AMD may be expected to increase with delay time. Likewise, bailout pressure (BOP) is also measured on the vertical axis. BOP may also be expected to increase with delay time. As long as AMD increases with delay time faster than BOP initially and then more slowly, as appears reasonable, so that the two schedules intersect, trade-offs will result and an optimal delay time derived. Also in Figure 6.1, the optimum delay time is Q. For shorter delay times—to the left of Q—enhanced market discipline is greater than bailout pressure and for longer delay times—to the right of Q—bailout pressure more than offsets increased market discipline. As noted above, it appears reasonable that the slopes of both the AMD and BOP schedules are affected by the magnitude of the losses at resolution when the institution is placed in receivership (sum of losses from sources one and two). In particular, the slope of the BOP schedule may be expected to become steeper with increases in losses at resolution, so that pressures for bailout rise quickly above gains from increased market discipline. Indeed, if the slope of the BOP schedule is sufficiently steep at the beginning, the optimal PD is *0*. If

AMD, BOP

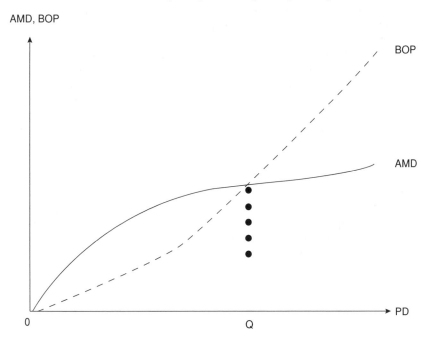

Figure 6.1. Additional Market Discipline and Bailout Pressure as Functions of Depositor Payment Delay Time

inability to advance payment or technical problems prevents the government from providing depositors with access at the optimal time, the government is likely to bailout all depositors at resolution. This reinforces the importance of both resolving institutions as quickly as possible with no or minimum loss and developing faster procedures for certifying protected deposits and estimating recovery values. It follows that by providing depositors with immediate and full access to their claims, as described in Section V, the United States implicitly assumes that bailout pressures immediately exceed gains from additional market discipline.

IX. The FDIC survey of depositor access practices across countries

In February 2000, the FDIC surveyed 78 deposit insurers in 64 countries outside the United States. The countries chosen were those that had explicit deposit insurance schemes in place. Thirty-seven surveys were returned providing insight into the deposit insurance practices of 34 countries. While the surveys covered a wide range of deposit insurance practices, this chapter examines only that portion of the survey relating to the availability of funds to depositors after a bank has been declared insolvent and differences in the treatment of insured and uninsured depositors.

When examining fund availability practices one must recognize the difference between policy intent and practice. A deposit insurer may wish to pay quickly, but not have the technical or informational capacity to do so. Conversely, they could believe in instilling market discipline by imposing costs on depositors through delay in making funds available, but not have the political resolve to carry out such a policy. Consequently, only the 30 responding countries that had actually experienced bank failures since 1980 were analyzed. Of these, three (Bahrain, Jamaica, and Sweden) did not specify a time frame within which they had paid depositors, since the failures occurred prior to the creation of a deposit insurance scheme.

Insured deposits

Two countries (Japan and Italy) provided immediate and full payment of insured deposits and one (Peru) immediate but not always full payment (Table 6.1). Japan has protected all depositors in those banks it has declared insolvent and used resolution techniques that provided for immediate access to funds. In Italy, the Interbank Deposit Protection Fund also provided insured depositors with immediate access to their insured deposits. Peruvian depositors have had access to some but not all of their insured deposits in some failures the day after failure, e.g., in the most recent failure in November 1999. In other failures, however, the depositors have had to wait as long as eight months for even the initial payment. According to the Peruvian Deposit Insurance Fund, the factors that determine the speed with which insured depositors get access to their funds are the potential systemic effects that would be triggered by the failure of a specific bank and the quality of information given to the insurer by the liquidation agency. Five other countries gave insured depositors access to their funds within one month of the failure and the majority of all respondents followed the EU guidelines and gave insured depositors access within no more than three months.

The Isle of Man Financial Supervision Commission was still in the process of attempting to pay off insured depositors more than six months after the failure of a bank in 1999. Three other countries, Poland, Czech Republic, and Greece, reported that they were able to make funds available to insured depositors within six months. It is interesting to note that almost all of the respondents provided insured depositors with all their funds at one time. Only the deposit insurers in Italy, Austria, Latvia, and Peru paid in installments.

The responses from Peru, and the experience of the Isle of Man, suggest that much of the reason for the delay in paying insured depositors may not be a conscious policy of promoting insured depositor discipline. Rather, it reflects the practical need for delay from the technical difficulties associated with paying off a bank quickly.

Uninsured deposits

The survey results, presented in Table 6.2, clearly indicate that the practice of advancing funds to uninsured depositors is unique to the United States. Twenty-three of the respondents indicated that uninsured depositors cannot be fully protected in their countries and only three deposit insurers (Canada, Japan, and Slovakia) indicated that they had the power to advance funds to cover uninsured depositors.

The timing of availability of funds to uninsured depositors is typically dependent on the type of resolution. Japan and Tanzania are notable examples of countries that have used resolution techniques to protect all depositors. In other countries, such as Italy and Brazil, uninsured depositors have immediate access to their deposits if a resolution results in the transfer of these deposits to another financial institution. In most countries, unprotected depositors will have to wait for the liquidation process to yield sufficient cash for payments to be made to them and the practices surrounding the liquidation of assets and payment of claims follows the national practices for bankruptcy, with discretion being vested with the courts or the liquidator, receiver, or administrator for the failed bank estate. In all cases where the uninsured depositors were dependent on a liquidation process for their proceeds, they received access to their funds in installments.

A review of the comments received from the respondents suggests that, while most deposit insurers have no discretion to protect uninsured depositors in liquidations or to advance funds from their deposit insurance funds to uninsured depositors, they can use resolution strategies that protect uninsured depositors. This suggests that these countries will probably resort to TBTF resolution strategies, nationalization of the bank (in whole or in

Table 6.1. Funds Availability of Insured Deposits

Country	Regulation or Laws?	Immediate Payment	Within Seven Days	Within a Month	Within Three Months	Within Six Months	Under Six Months	Payment
				(Countries with at least one insolvent bank since 1980)				
Austria (1)	Yes				Yes			Installments
Bahrain[a]	No							All at one time
Belgium	Yes			Yes				All at one time
Brazil	No			Yes				All at one time
Canada	No				Yes			All at one time
Czech Republic	Yes					Yes		All at one time
France	Yes				Yes			All at one time
Germany (1)	No				Yes			All at one time
Greece	Yes					Yes		All at one time
Hungary	No				Yes			All at one time
Isle of Man	No						Yes	All at one time
Italy (1)	Yes	Yes						Installments
Italy (2)	Yes				Yes			Installments
Jamaica[a]	Yes							
Japan	No	Yes						
Latvia	No				Yes			Installments
Lithuania	Yes				Yes			All at one time
Netherlands	Yes				Yes			All at one time
Nigeria	No							
Peru	Yes							Installments
Poland	Yes					Yes		All at one time
Romania	Yes				Yes			All at one time
Slovakia	Yes			Yes				All at one time
Spain	Yes			Yes				All at one time
Sweden[a]	Yes							All at one time

176

Country				
Tanzania	No	Yes		All at one time
Trinidad and Tobago	Yes		Yes	All at one time
Turkey	No		Yes	All at one time
Uganda	Yes		Yes	All at one time
United Kingdom			Yes	All at one time
Austria (2)	Yes			
El Salvador	Yes			
Germany (2)	Yes			
Mexico	Yes			
Oman	Yes			
Portugal	Yes			
Taiwan	No			

(Countries without insolvent banks since 1980)

a Denotes countries whose failures occurred prior to the establishment of the current deposit insurance scheme.

Table 6.2. Funds Availability of Uninsured Deposits

Country	Regulation or Laws?	Can Uninsured be Fully Protected?	Can Deposit Insurer Advance Funds?	Length of Time Before Accessing?	Payment Schedule?	Does the Resolution Method Affect Payment Schedule?
				(Countries with at least one insolvent bank since 1980)		
Austria (1)	Yes	No		5–6 months.	Installments	No
Bahrain[a]	Yes	No			Installments	Yes
Belgium	No	No		Several months.	Installments	No
Brazil	Yes	No	Yes	Dependent of the intervention process.	Installments	Yes
Canada	Yes	Yes		Not permitted.	Neither	Yes
Czech Republic	Yes	No		No bankruptcy proceedings have been finished yet.		
Germany (1)	No	No	No		Installments	Yes
France	Yes	No			Installments	No
Greece	No	No			Installments	
Hungary	Yes	No			Installments	Yes
Isle of Man	No	No		2 years.	Installments	Yes
Italy (1)	Yes	Yes		In case of assignments of assets and liabilities to another depository institution, they may have immediate access to their deposits; otherwise they have to wait until the receiver allocates the bank's liquidated assets.	All at one time, and in installments	Yes
Italy (2)	No	No				
Jamaica[a]	Yes	Yes	Yes	All deposits have so far been protected.		
Japan	Yes	No			Installments	No
Latvia	No	No		12 months.	Installments	No
Lithuania	Yes	Yes		This is done under normal bankruptcy laws between the receiver and the uninsured depositors. If funds are available for creditors of their rank, they will be paid out in due course.	Installments	Yes
Netherlands	No	Yes			Installments	Yes
Nigeria	No	Yes		There is no provision for depositors of insolvent banks to be paid from the Deposit Insurance Fund.		Yes

Country						
Peru	Yes	Yes	No	0–1 year.	Installments	Yes
Poland	Yes	No	No		Installments	Yes
Romania	Yes	No	Yes	No case.		No
Slovakia	Yes	Yes		Approximately 12 months.	Installments	Yes
Spain	Yes	No				
Sweden[a]	No	No				
Tanzania	No	Yes	No	In our experience: There was full compensation and the depositors had access to their deposits within the shortest period available.	All at one time	No
Trinidad and Tobago	Yes			Whenever there are sufficient funds from the realization of assets available for making distributions.	Installments	Yes
Turkey		No		Since 1980, depositors were not able to access their explicitly uninsured deposits.	All at one time	
Uganda	Yes	No				
United Kingdom			No	Handled by liquidators or administrators.		
				(Countries without insolvent banks since 1980)		
Austria (2)	Yes	No	No	No bank failure.	All at one time	Yes
El Salvador	Yes	No		There were bank failures but we did not have the insured deposits system.		No
Germany (2)	No	Yes		No bank failures.		Yes
Mexico	No	No				
Oman	Yes	No				
Portugal	Yes	No	No	No explicitly uninsured depositors prior to 1999.		No
Taiwan	No	No		In Taiwan, the competent authority, the Ministry of Finance, has never issued an order to close a financial institution during the past 15 years.	Installments	Yes

[a] Denotes countries whose failures occurred prior to the establishment of the current deposit insurance scheme.

179

part), and/or extend blanket guarantees to depositors while the insolvent bank continues in operation.

X. Summary and best practices recommendation conclusions

This chapter identifies and analyzes the four potential sources of losses in bank failures, two at the time an insolvent bank is resolved and placed in receivership and two afterwards. The two sources of post-resolution losses arise from delayed payment of depositor claims. The effective freezing of some or all of the deposits by the deposit insurance agency until reliable data are available on what deposits and depositors are protected and/or the proceeds from the sale of bank assets are received has two conflicting effects. On the one hand, fear of delayed payment increases depositor monitoring and discipline. On the other hand, fear of delayed payment increases depositor pressures for protection and government willingness to provide such protection to reduce the chances of systemic risk.

This chapter models these effects for a given loss from delayed resolution and solves for the optimal delay time that equates the gains from additional market discipline with the losses from increased bailout pressure. Different countries follow different practices with respect to delaying payment with different consequences for market discipline and resolution policies. In the United States, the FDIC does not freeze deposits at resolved institutions. Rather, it advances the proceeds to depositors before it, acting as the receiver, collects them from asset sales. Thus, insured depositors receive near immediate payment of the par value of their deposits and uninsured depositors receive near immediate payment of the present value of their pro-rata share of the estimated recovery value. This practice may reduce market discipline, but is likely to more greatly reduce pressures for bailout. Thus, given the loss at resolution, insolvent institutions are more likely to be resolved and uninsured depositors not protected. In contrast, most other countries freeze deposits and delay payments to both insured and uninsured depositors, according to a schedule or until the funds are collected from asset sales, both because of the inability to estimate quickly the amount that needs to be paid out and because of restrictions on advancing funds before collection of the sales proceeds.

These differences in the treatment of depositors at insolvent institutions have important implications for a country's bank resolution practices, in particular, for banks considered TBTF. The smaller the overall loss in bank failures, the easier it is economically and politically to resolve insolvencies with losses to de jure unprotected depositors. In the United States, if regulatory PCA is successful in limiting losses (negative net worth) at insolvent institutions to relatively small percentage amounts, say, to not more than 5 percent of assets at large banks (the loss experienced by the Continental Illinois National Bank in 1984 was near 3 percent), and uninsured depositors have immediate and full access to their funds, losses to large uninsured depositors should be restricted to a loss rate that is well within the boundaries that most of these depositors can tolerate without panicking, e.g., losses they appear to be willing to bear in investments in commercial paper or other short-term debt instruments. Moreover, since enactment of depositor preference, which subordinates deposits at foreign offices and other creditors to domestic deposits and the FDIC, losses at failed banks can be charged to these accounts before domestic depositors. Thus, losses to domestic depositors and the FDIC may be even smaller. As a result, if the losses are both small and access to the remaining deposits is immediate, uninsured depositors are less likely to exert political pressure on the government to extend the safety-net to them, and to be made whole, and governments are less fearful of systemic risk and too-big-to-fail protection may thus be avoided. The combination of the FDIC's payment practices and the improved closure rule under FDICIA helps to explain why uninsured depositors at almost all recent failed banks in which the FDIC suffered losses have been required to share pro-rata in the losses (Benston and Kaufman, 1998). However, because no large money center bank has failed since FDICIA, it is too early to declare TBTF dead in the United States.

In contrast, because losses in resolving insolvencies are not necessarily minimized and uninsured deposits are often frozen until payment is received from private receivers, most other countries find it difficult to resolve large insolvent banks with losses to depositors. They are thus under great pressure to protect all depositors and are fearful of igniting systemic risk if they do not. Thus, TBTF appears to be alive and healthy in these countries and large taxpayer losses in bank failures may be expected to continue.

Because cross-country differences in access of insured depositors to their funds affects both the intensity of market discipline and the probability of bailout, cross-country studies of the effectiveness and efficiency of alternative deposit insurance structures that specify the existence of such programs, or differentiate between explicit and implicit programs, only by a single yes/no (or 1/0) variable, and thus omit reference to access delay, are likely to be incomplete and inaccurate.[10]

The analysis in this chapter suggests that the best strategy for achieving aggregate bank stability, characterized by efficient exit of inefficient or unlucky banks through failure at no or least cost to the economy, involves resolving these banks before or shortly after their net worth turns negative and providing full and immediate or near-immediate access for insured depositors to the par value of their deposits and for uninsured depositors to the present value of their pro-rata share of the estimated recovery value. Such a strategy minimizes the potential for systemic risk and permits otherwise TBTF banks to be resolved just like any other insolvent bank. However, the ability to provide full and immediate or near-immediate depositor access may be constrained both by lack of legal authority for regulators to advance payment to depositors before receipt of the funds from asset sales from the receivers and by physical problems that interfere with this outcome, such as the unavailability of accurate and accessible account data and facilities for speedy analysis of the data and inability to estimate recovery values accurately and quickly. If this is the optimal policy, procedures for reducing the delays caused by these problems in each country need to be addressed.

Notes

1. "Too-big-to-fail" in the United States does not imply that the bank is not failed, but that it is "too-big-to-liquidate" or "too-big-to-impose losses on uninsured depositors" (Kaufman, 1990). This was recently reinforced by Federal Reserve Chairman Greenspan, who said, "the issue is that an organization that is very large is not TBTF, it may be too big to allow to implode quickly. But certainly none are too big to orderly liquidate" (Greenspan, 2000, p. 14).
2. Nevertheless, casual evidence suggests that at least some depositors are concerned that they may find their deposits at failed banks temporarily frozen.
3. In those instances where no bank acquires the insured deposits and there are a large number of depositors, the FDIC will either arrange for another bank to act as its deposit transfer agent or the FDIC will mail depositors checks for the insured amounts.
4. Under the Depositor Preference Act of 1993, unsecured depositors at foreign offices of U.S. banks and other creditors, such as Fed funds sellers, have claims junior to those of domestic depositors and, unless the TBTF provision of FDICIA is invoked, will be paid the recovery value of their claims only as the bank's assets are sold and all senior claimants have already been paid (Kaufman, 1997b).
5. Before FDICIA, the FDIC generally protected all depositors, including de jure uninsured depositors, particularly at larger banks, through merger (purchase and assumption) with another bank that assumed all deposits at par and received a payment from the FDIC (Benston and Kaufman, 1998 and FDIC, 1998a).
6. Because the FDIC pays the full par amount of insured deposits, misestimates of the recovery values affect only the final allocation of its costs, not the total cost of these payouts.
7. Note holders at failed national banks were paid the par value of their notes immediately by the U.S. Treasury (FDIC, 1998b).
8. As reported by the *Financial Times* in November 2000, Nicaragua resolved its second bank in 100 days and guaranteed deposits of only less than 20,000 cordobas (about $1,500) at the second bank. But only 10,000 cordobas would be paid within five days; the rest would be paid as the bank's assets were sold. "Angry customers gathered outside the closed branches of Bancafe yesterday shouting 'thieves' and 'vampires'" (*Financial Times*, November 21, 2000). As discussed later, only two (Canada and Peru) of the 25 countries other than the United States that responded to a survey by the FDIC and that had experienced at least one bank failure since 1980 reported paying its insured depositors immediately.
9. Only three countries in the FDIC survey (Canada, Japan, and Slovenia) report having authority to advance funds to uninsured depositors at failed banks, but few countries responded to this question.
10. For example, a recent study by Demirgue-Kunt and Huizinga (1999) reports finding evidence of some market discipline on banks in countries that have government-provided safety nets, but does not mention delays in payment as one of the possible reasons.

Bibliography

Barth, James R., 1991, *The Great Savings and Loan Debacle* (Washington: American Enterprise Institute).

Benston, George J., and George G. Kaufman, 2/1998, "Deposit Insurance Reform in the FDIC Improvement Act: The Experience to Date," *Economic Perspectives* (Chicago: Federal Reserve Bank of Chicago), pp. 2–20.

Dermine, Jean, December 1996, "Comment," *Swiss Journal of Economics and Statistics*, pp. 679–82.

Demirgue-Kunt, Asli and Harry Huizinga, July 1999, *Market Discipline and Financial Safety Net Design*, Working Paper (Washington: World Bank).

Federal Deposit Insurance Corporation, 1998a, *Managing the Crisis: The FDIC and RTC Experience* (Washington: FDIC).

——, 1998b, *A Brief History of Deposit Insurance in the United States* (Washington: FDIC).

Financial Times, November 21, 2000, "Managua Faces Crisis with Collapse of Another Bank."

Greenspan, Alan, May 2000, "Question and Answer Session," *The Changing Financial Industry Structure and Regulation: Bridging States, Countries, and Industries* (Chicago: Federal Reserve Bank of Chicago), pp. 9–14.

Gupta, Atul, and Lalatendu Misra, Winter 1999, "Failure and Failure Resolution in the U.S. Thrift and Banking Institutes," *Financial Management*, pp. 87–105.

Kane, Edward J., July 1990, "Principal Agent Problems in S&L Salvage," *Journal of Finance*, pp. 755–64.

——, 1992, "How Incentive-Incompatible Deposit Insurance Plans Fail" in George G. Kaufman, ed., *Research in Financial Services, Vol. 4* (Greenwich, CT: JAI Press), pp. 51–92.

Kane, Edward J., and Min-Teh Yu, November 1995, "Measuring the True Profile of Taxpayer Losses in the S&L Insurance Mess," *Journal of Banking and Finance*, pp. 1459–78.

Kaufman, George G., Summer, October 1990, "Are Some Banks Too Large to Fail? Myth and Reality," *Contemporary Policy Issues*, pp. 1–14.

——, May 1995, "The U.S. Banking Debacle of the 1980's," *The Financier*, pp. 9–26.

——, Spring/Summer 1996, "Bank Failures, Systemic Risk, and Bank Regulation," *Cato Journal*, pp. 17–45.

——, 1997a, "Preventing Banking Crises in the Future: Lessons From Past Mistakes," Independent Review, pp. 55–77.

——, 1997b, "The New Depositor Preference Act," *Managerial Finance*, Vol. 23, No. 11, pp. 56–63.

Mason, Joseph, Ali Anari, and James Kolari, May 2000, "The Speed of Bank Liquidation and the Propagation of the U.S. Great Depression," *The Changing Financial Industry Structure and Regulation* (Chicago), pp. 320–45.

Todd, Walker F., May 1, 1994, "Lessons from the Collapse of Three State-Chartered Private Deposit Insurance Funds," *Economic Commentary* (Federal Reserve Bank of Cleveland).

7
The IMF/World Bank Global Insolvency Initiative—Its Purpose and Principal Features

Ross Leckow[1]

I. Introduction

Bank insolvency can threaten financial stability. The failure of a large, important bank can bring about the collapse of a country's financial system and its economy. There are far too many examples of single or multiple bank failures that have sent shock waves through a country's economy and sparked a balance of payments crisis. It is, therefore, essential that a country's financial supervisors have the necessary tools to effectively prevent and resolve bank insolvencies. Foremost among these tools is a strong legal framework.

The question, therefore, arises: what should this legal framework look like and what are its principal elements? This issue has, in recent years, received considerable attention in the international community—amongst international organizations like the IMF and the World Bank, and the authorities of their member countries. A particularly important development in this area is the IMF/World Bank Global Bank Insolvency Initiative (the "GBII" or the "Initiative").[2]

This chapter provides an overview of the GBII. The chapter first examines the purpose of the Initiative and process under which it was developed. It then reviews the GBII's principal features before discussing the more challenging legal questions which the Initiative confronted. It ends with a brief conclusion.

II. Background—what is the Global Bank Insolvency Initiative and how was it developed?

The GBII is, first and foremost, a report, drafted principally by IMF and World Bank staff,[3] that describes a legal and institutional framework which countries could put in place to address cases of bank insolvency.[4] The Initiative builds on important work done by other organizations[5] and was a product of extensive cooperation within the international community. It was launched in January 2002 by the IMF and World Bank—in coordination with the Bank for International Settlements, the Financial Stability Institute, the Basel Committee on Banking Supervision, and the Financial Stability Forum. It benefited from the work of a "Core Consultative Group" of experts from international organizations, national institutions and the private sector who reviewed and commented on successive drafts of the report.[6] The report is still in draft form. It will be finalized after further experience is gained in applying its principal recommendations.

The report describes international "sound practices" that countries may employ in designing a legal and institutional framework for bank insolvency.[7] It does not propose a "one-size-fits-all" approach. There is no single, universally-accepted legislative model for bank insolvency. Countries take different approaches to the same problems. Moreover, the report does not seek to establish an international "standard" that would be used by the IMF or the World Bank for assessments under their standards and codes initiatives.[8] Rather, the report will be used by the two institutions primarily in providing technical assistance.

III. The Global Bank Insolvency Initiative—the legal and institutional framework

The legal and institutional framework described in the GBII recognizes two important principles: (i) bank insolvency is different from corporate insolvency; and (ii) the legal and institutional framework for bank insolvency needs to be built upon an effective regime for banking supervision more generally. Each of these principles is examined below.

Bank insolvency and corporate insolvency

Bank insolvency is, in several important respects, different from corporate insolvency. The legal framework for corporate insolvency is essentially designed to intermediate conflicts between private parties. It facilitates the maximization of value of an insolvent enterprise's estate and, to the extent possible, the satisfaction of claims. In contrast, the legal framework for bank insolvency serves a broader public interest—to protect the stability of the financial system. A bank's failure can produce a wider array of problems than can that of a nonfinancial enterprise. An insolvent bank's inability to execute payments instructions may disrupt the operation of payments and securities transfer systems, and may cause losses to counterparties in the interbank markets and to the depositing public. In a worst-case scenario, a bank failure may give rise to a systemic crisis. The bank insolvency framework, therefore, seeks to protect the smooth functioning of payments and settlements systems, and the depositing public.

It is for these reasons that many countries put in place rules governing bank insolvencies that differ from those applicable to corporate insolvencies. In some countries, the authorities may rely upon corporate insolvency law with appropriate modifications. In other countries, the authorities may put in place a special legal regime for bank insolvency, entirely separate from the corporate insolvency framework. Regardless of the approach taken, the bank insolvency framework will often differ from that applicable to corporate insolvencies in at least three important respects. First, a special role will be reserved to the supervisory authorities (the "banking authorities") in commencing and conducting insolvency proceedings; in contrast, the creditors normally play the leading role in corporate insolvency proceedings. Second, the bank insolvency framework will frequently allow insolvency proceedings to be commenced at a relatively early stage of a bank's difficulties in order to facilitate prompt intervention by the banking authorities. Third, special rules may apply to the collection and/or payment of financial claims.

The framework for banking supervision

A country's bank insolvency framework forms part of a broader regime for banking supervision. It cannot be expected to be effective if other aspects of the supervisory framework are not.[9] In particular, the legal and institutional framework for banking supervision needs to ensure that the banking authorities have a sufficient degree of autonomy in their operations but are accountable for their actions.[10]

To preserve their autonomy, the banking authorities should have the legal powers and the resources necessary to do their job effectively, subject to clear objectives set out in legislation. The framework should specify rules that, on one hand, shield the banking authorities' senior officials from undue interference (e.g., rules on their appointment and dismissal) and, on the other hand, subject them to the highest professional standards (e.g., rules respecting conflict of interest, financial disclosure, and use of confidential information). The banking authorities and their staff should be given adequate legal protection from liability for actions taken in the course of their duties.

To ensure their accountability, the banking authorities should, in particular, be required to regularly publish reports on their operations, including audited accounts. In certain circumstances, their actions should be subject to challenge in the courts (more about this below).

The bank insolvency framework—insolvency proceedings

Against this background, the question arises: what are the principal features of an effective legal and institutional framework for addressing cases of bank insolvency? As explained in the GBII, the primary legal mechanism through which insolvent banks are dealt with in most countries may be referred to as "insolvency proceedings." Insolvency proceedings comprise those forms of official action which involve the removal of management and/or the imposition of limits on, or suspension of, the rights of shareholders and the assumption of direct control by the banking authorities or other officially-appointed person over a bank that has crossed an insolvency-related legal threshold. Such proceedings can be administrative in nature or court-based. They may be distinguished from situations where the authorities take control of a bank for reasons unrelated to its insolvency (e.g., where the bank's management has engaged in criminal activities). The initiation of insolvency proceedings may result in the bank's survival as a legal entity or its liquidation.

The GBII describes two types of insolvency proceedings: (i) official administration; and (ii) liquidation proceedings. Not every country's bank insolvency framework provides for both types of proceedings, although most countries do have a form of liquidation proceedings. In some cases, the two proceedings are combined. Each is reviewed below.

Official administration

Official administration[11] refers to those forms of insolvency proceedings in which an officially-appointed person assumes direct managerial control of an insolvent bank with a view to protecting its assets, assessing its true financial condition and, to the extent possible, restructuring the bank's business and restoring it to soundness. It continues until the bank has been restored to soundness or placed in liquidation.

Official administration consists of two phases: (i) a diagnostic phase; and (ii) a restructuring phase. Under the diagnostic phase, the official administrator engages in due diligence, assesses the true financial position of the bank, and decides how to proceed. Under the restructuring phase, the official administrator engages in restructuring operations with a view to restoring, to the extent possible, the bank's business to soundness.[12] Where appropriate, the official administrator, on the basis of his assessment of the bank's financial condition, may refrain from conducting any restructuring operations and, instead, make arrangements for the commencement of liquidation proceedings.

The legal framework for official administration needs to address a number of important issues. In particular, it should clearly specify the moment at which control of a bank is transferred from the owners and managers to the official administrator and should allow for no "interregnum" that would permit the dissipation of the bank's assets.[13] The official administrator should, at a minimum, be authorized to exercise full control over the bank's management and day-to-day operations, and to pursue the bank's claims, protect its assets, and defend against claims made against the bank. In this regard, the bank will remain open during official administration.

The fact that a bank will remain open raises another important point: official administration should be temporary and short. A timetable should be specified for an assessment of the bank's financial condition and the completion of official administration. The rules governing official administration should not permit an insolvent bank to be kept open for an extended period.[14]

Liquidation proceedings

A bank's business that cannot be restored to viability should be liquidated. In liquidation proceedings, an insolvent bank is dissolved after a liquidator assumes legal control of its estate, collects together and realizes its assets, and distributes the proceeds to creditors, in full or partial satisfaction of their claims, in accordance with the applicable rules on priority. Upon the commencement of liquidation proceedings, the bank will continue to exist as a legal entity but will no longer be a going concern.[15] Upon the completion of the proceedings, the bank will cease to exist as a legal entity.

There are many important questions that need to be addressed in the legal framework governing liquidation proceedings. In particular, clear rules should be established for the formal placement of a bank in liquidation, the termination of its banking activities, and the assignment of the bank to an officially-appointed person to liquidate its estate. Immediately upon appointment, the liquidator should be given full control of the bank's assets, become its sole legal representative, and succeed to all governance rights and powers of its shareholders and directors. The law should specify the degree of supervision and oversight to which the liquidator will be subject.[16] The liquidator should be required to report periodically on his actions.

The liquidator must also be given the necessary power to preserve and maximize the value of the bank's assets. He should be able to exercise all rights of the bank in the assets, make payments directly out of the value of the estate, and advance funds to protect collateral supporting the bank's assets. The liquidator should be authorized to enter into contracts to employ various professionals to assist him in his functions, terminate certain executory contracts (i.e., for the purpose of "cherry-picking"), and apply to court for the avoidance of certain transactions and transfers that are unfair and prejudicial to creditors (e.g., fraudulent transactions).

A particularly important issue concerns the imposition of a moratorium. The placement of a bank in liquidation should lead to an automatic moratorium or suspension of all collection activity against the bank. The moratorium should, inter alia, provide for a stay on all current legal actions against the bank and a bar against the filing of new actions, except with the permission of a court or another appointing authority.

In the context of a bank insolvency, a moratorium raises three important issues: (i) the effect of the moratorium on depositors; (ii) the timing of the moratorium; and (iii) the treatment of netting and set-off provisions in financial contracts. Each of these is reviewed below.

With respect to depositors, the moratorium will invariably preclude depositors from gaining access to their savings. Where no system of deposit insurance exists, there will be hardship. To deal with these cases, the liquidator may be authorized to make immediate distributions, up to a specified proportion, against the bank's deposit liabilities. Moreover, depositors may be given a preferential position on the distribution of the proceeds of liquidation.

On the timing of the moratorium, policymakers will need to decide how to deal with transfer orders for payments and securities that are entered in a payment or securities settlement system on the day on which a bank's insolvency is declared, including those that are settled before the issuance of declaration. Some legal systems employ the "zero hour" rule in which the effects of the initiation of liquidation proceedings are dated back to the beginning of the day on which the bank's insolvency is declared. As a result, all outgoing and incoming payments and transfers of securities taking place on that day (including those which preceded the declaration) could be rendered void or unenforceable and would need to be unwound. Given the adverse consequences which such a rule can have for an insolvent bank's counterparties and for the stability of the financial system, some countries have introduced rules which promote "settlement finality." Under this approach, the commencement of liquidation proceedings gives rise to only prospective effects; it cannot lead to a reversal of settlements of transfer orders which precede a formal declaration of insolvency (or, in some countries, the moment at which the payment or securities settlement system is informed of the declaration of insolvency). A few countries go even further by establishing that the moratorium only takes effect at the beginning of the day following the declaration of insolvency or at a moment to be determined in the insolvency decision itself.

A third question which needs to be resolved is whether netting and set-off arrangements should be recognized in liquidation proceedings. Payments and settlement systems often operate on a net-settlement basis. Similar arrangements involving netting, set-off, novation, and/or close out arrangements can often be found in financial contracts (e.g., foreign exchange contracts, repurchase agreements). Upon the insolvency of a counterparty to such a contract, the application of such provisions by the solvent counterparty will permit it to apply the total amount of its claims on the insolvent bank against the total amount of its obligations to the bank; in this manner, the solvent counterparty will be able to satisfy its claims up to the total amount of its obligations. If such arrangements are not recognized in liquidation proceedings, the solvent counterparty will need to pay its obligations to the insolvent estate in their full amount and file for what is owed to it as an unsecured creditor and, probably, never recover a significant portion of its claims. In deciding whether or not to recognize such arrangements, a country's policymakers will have to weigh the preferential treatment which such arrangements accord to financial-sector counterparties against the need to minimize contagion risk in financial markets.

Liquidation proceedings result in the realization of the bank's assets and the distribution of the proceeds to creditors in accordance with priorities specified in the law.[17] The legal framework will need to provide for notice to creditors to file their claims, the verification of such claims by the liquidator, and the distribution of the proceeds of liquidation. Once the liquidator has completed the realization of assets of the estate, made a final distribution to creditors, and prepared final accounts and his report, the liquidation ends.

IV. The Global Bank Insolvency Initiative—important challenges in designing a framework

In the design of a bank insolvency framework, a number of questions will arise for which there is no universally-accepted solution. Participants in the GBII confronted a number of these issues. Several are set out below.

Administrative versus judicial proceedings

Policymakers must choose between bank insolvency proceedings that are administrative in nature (i.e., under which the proceedings will be conducted by the banking authorities without the involvement of the courts) and those which are conducted through the courts. For countries that rely upon the corporate insolvency law (possibly with a few modifications) to deal with bank insolvencies, insolvency proceedings will invariably take place in the courts.[18] In contrast, where a special regime for bank insolvency is established, the proceedings may be either administrative in nature or court-based. There are also systems in which some forms of insolvency proceedings (e.g., official administration) are administrative while others (e.g., liquidation proceedings) are judicial.

There is no universally-accepted model. Policymakers must choose between the need to resolve an insolvent bank quickly and efficiently, on one hand, and the need to protect the rights of affected parties, on the other hand. Avoiding the delays that often characterize general corporate insolvency proceedings is a major motivation for transferring responsibility from the insolvency courts to the banking authorities. Given the potentially systemic nature of a bank insolvency, the authorities must be able to respond more quickly than court-based proceedings might permit. Moreover, the necessary expertise is, in many countries, found with the banking authorities rather than the courts.

At the same time, bank insolvency proceedings will normally suspend or extinguish property rights—in particular, those of the owners. In many countries such action can only be taken in a judicial proceeding. Moreover, even where the conduct of bank insolvency proceedings is vested in an administrative agency, it will often prove difficult for legislators to completely exclude the courts. The banking authorities' actions to resolve an insolvent bank in administrative proceedings may subsequently be reviewed and possibly overturned in court. Where the banking authorities' actions are subject to judicial review, it is not clear that an administrative proceeding is always more efficient than a judicial one.

While one can find examples of both systems in developed and developing countries, it may be argued that an administrative proceeding is particularly useful in a country with a weak institutional environment. In such countries, the general corporate insolvency legislation may be poorly-structured and ineffective. The courts may be slow and inefficient. The judiciary may be poorly trained and unable to deal with the complex financial issues that often arise in a bank insolvency. In a worst-case scenario, the judiciary may be corrupt.

In such circumstances, it may prove advisable to remove cases of bank insolvency from the courts' competence and to entrust them to the banking authorities who possess the expertise necessary to resolve them efficiently. However, a word of caution is in order. Where a country's judicial institutions are weak and inefficient, it will not necessarily be the case that the banking authorities will be any better. There may be equally valid concerns over the competence and integrity of administrative agencies, including those responsible for supervising the banking system. There is also a danger that, by giving broad powers of intervention and resolution to administrative agencies, policymakers may undermine the status and prestige of the courts, and the legal system's respect for the rights of the country's citizens.

Threshold for commencement of insolvency proceedings

A second challenging question concerns the choice of the legal threshold that must be crossed before insolvency proceedings may be commenced. Different legal systems often employ different tests for this purpose. The GBII focussed on three of the most important.

The first such threshold may be termed the "liquidity threshold." Thus, insolvency proceedings may be commenced where the bank is unable to pay its obligations as they fall due. While appropriate in the context of corporate insolvency, this test is not sufficient in the context of bank insolvency. A bank can have temporary liquidity problems without being fundamentally insolvent. It can be insolvent without having liquidity problems. Liquidity problems in a solvent bank can, in most cases, be addressed through interbank borrowing or the lender-of-last-resort function of the central bank.

A second threshold may be termed the "balance sheet threshold." Thus, insolvency proceedings may be commenced against a bank whose balance sheet shows that its liabilities exceed its assets. This test is, perhaps, a more accurate "yardstick" than is the "liquidity threshold" for the true financial position of a bank. However, the "balance sheet threshold" is a necessary but insufficient test. Exclusive reliance upon the balance sheet threshold gives rise to a basic problem. A key purpose of a bank insolvency regime is, in many cases, to ensure early intervention by the banking authorities, if possible, to restore the bank to viability. If insolvency proceedings can be commenced only when the bank's liabilities already exceed its assets, it may be too late to take any action other than to liquidate the bank.

It is for this reason that some legal systems establish a third, lower threshold which allows the authorities to commence insolvency proceedings at an earlier stage. Under the "regulatory threshold," insolvency proceedings may be commenced when the bank still has positive net worth but its net financial position has fallen below a specified level. While the purpose of the threshold is clear, the fact is that many legal systems would not recognize this as "insolvency" in the classic sense. Moreover, some countries employ different thresholds for different types of insolvency proceedings. The regulatory threshold may be appropriate for the imposition of official administration but not for the commencement of liquidation proceedings; the latter may only be commenced after the bank is "balance sheet insolvent."

Mandatory versus discretionary systems

Policymakers must also decide whether the initiation of insolvency proceedings should, after a particular threshold is crossed, be mandatory or discretionary. On the one hand, mandatory systems can limit the exercise of regulatory forbearance and opportunities for political interference, and provide a clear signal to banks and to the public that action will be taken when a bank is insolvent. On the other hand, a discretionary system is inherently more flexible and may facilitate a more calibrated response to address individual cases.

While some industrialized countries lean towards a mandatory approach, such a system may be particularly appropriate in countries with weak institutional environments. In such cases, the supervisor may be under undue pressure to exercise forbearance and avoid proceeding against an insolvent bank. A system which requires the commencement of insolvency proceedings in certain circumstances may limit moral hazard and prevent the further accumulation of losses that would otherwise spread throughout the banking system.

Powers of the official administrator

In the context of an official administration that is conducted without judicial involvement, policymakers need to decide on the precise scope of the powers to be given to the official administrator. More specifically, what should the official administrator be permitted to do to restructure a bank and restore its business to viability? In some countries, the official administrator is empowered only to take control of the bank, assess its financial position, and manage its day-to-day operations; to the extent that the official administrator wishes to engage in restructuring operations (e.g., the transfer of assets and liabilities of the bank), the consent of other parties (e.g., the shareholders) will be required. Under another approach, bank insolvency legislation will empower the official administrator, even though he acts without judicial oversight, to restructure the insolvent bank (e.g., by transferring assets and liabilities to other banks) without the consent of the shareholders or of other affected parties. While the conferral of such broad powers on an official administrator facilitates a prompt and efficient response to a bank insolvency, the legal systems of many countries will not permit their exercise by an administrative agency without judicial oversight.

Standards for judicial review

Another important question concerns the standard of judicial review to be applied by the courts in reviewing (and possibly overturning) actions taken by the banking authorities in the context of insolvency proceedings. Such cases will generally arise only in the context of insolvency proceedings of an administrative nature. Where the banking authorities have exceeded their legal powers in taking action against a bank, affected parties should be able to challenge such action in the courts. At the same time, the exercise of discretion on the part of the banking authorities should be respected. A court should not be able to substitute its own policy decisions for those of the banking authorities. The legal framework should only "seek to ensure that the banking authorities act legally and within the limits of their powers, and should not allow a reassessment of their actions on substantive grounds."[19]

Two important questions respecting judicial review will need to be addressed: (i) the timing of judicial review; and (ii) the remedy available. On timing, judicial review should generally be available only after the fact. A request for judicial review should not, in most cases, result in a stay of the relevant insolvency proceedings; otherwise, the banking authorities may be prevented from taking actions that are essential to preserve the stability of the financial system. Such an approach will limit the remedies available to affected parties. As affected parties will be generally unable to seek redress before supervisory action has been taken, it will seldom be the case that the restoration of the previous situation will be possible, even where the banking authorities are found to have exceeded their legal powers. When the courts intervene, the relevant bank may already have been closed and its assets and liabilities transferred to other institutions. Under such a system, damages will be the only effective remedy.

V. Conclusion

The GBII, although a work in progress, represents a major step forward in the efforts of the international community to address the problems of bank insolvency. Throughout the world, there is a growing awareness of the threat which bank insolvency can pose to financial stability. It has also been recognized that bank insolvencies cannot be resolved effectively without a strong legal and institutional framework. While different countries often adopt different approaches to the problems of bank insolvency, international cooperation in this area is increasing. Policymakers worldwide are becoming increasingly aware of the approaches and experiences of their peers in other countries. As international cooperation grows, the bank insolvency frameworks of countries throughout the world will be strengthened. By drawing on the collective experience of the international community, the GBII will serve as a major catalyst in this process.

Notes

1. A previous version of this chapter was presented at the Seventh Meeting of Central Bank Legal Advisers organized by the Center for Latin-American Monetary Studies in Buenos Aires, Argentina in September, 2005. The views expressed in this chapter are those of the author and should not be attributed to the International Monetary Fund, its Executive Board, or its management.
2. *Global Bank Insolvency Initiative: Legal, Institutional, and Regulatory Framework to Deal with Insolvent Banks* (in draft form).
3. For both the IMF and the World Bank, questions of bank insolvency and financial stability are of paramount importance. In the case of the IMF, the promotion of the stability of the international monetary system is a central pillar of its mandate. See *Articles of Agreement of the International Monetary Fund*, Article I.
4. The GBII's principal objectives are (i) to identify the appropriate legal, institutional and regulatory framework for addressing cases of bank insolvency; (ii) to build progressively an international consensus towards the acceptance of this framework; (iii) to provide guidance for the evaluation of national bank insolvency regimes; and (iv) to provide a basis for a policy dialogue between international financial institutions and countries on these issues and to facilitate the provision of technical assistance to countries.
5. Important initiatives include the report of the task force of the Basel Committee on Banking Supervision on "Supervisory Guidance on Dealing with Weak Banks," the task force of the Financial Stability Forum on deposit insurance, and the Group of Ten "Report on Legal and Institutional Underpinnings of the International Financial System."
6. The report also benefited from consultations with the authorities of different countries which took place in a series of seminars held in each region of the world.
7. The report discusses these issues in the domestic context and does not address issues of cross-border bank insolvency. It also identifies the type of bank insolvency regime that would be most appropriate for countries with weak institutional environments. While the report discusses changes that would need to be made to a country's legal and institutional framework in the context of a systemic crisis, these issues will not be discussed in this chapter.
8. See *Standards and Codes; the IMF's Role* (IMF Issues Brief (01/04)).
9. Of course, the bank insolvency framework also needs to be based upon a strong legal framework in the country more generally that provides, inter alia, for well-defined property and contractual rights, and effective procedures for the enforcement and collection of financial claims.

10. The law should also ensure timely and effective coordination between different public authorities responsible for bank insolvencies (e.g., the central bank, the bank supervisor if this is not the central bank, the operators of payments and settlement systems, the deposit insurance agency). In particular, there should be a sound legal basis for the exchange of information between the public bodies involved, both within the domestic context and with foreign supervisory agencies, while protecting the confidentiality of this information.

11. In some countries, what the GBII refers to as "official administration" may be known as "bank intervention," "temporary administration," or "trusteeship."

12. Restructuring operations can include the merger of the insolvent bank with another bank, the conduct of "purchase and assumption" transactions, "bridge bank," and "good bank–bad bank" techniques.

13. The law should specify qualifications for appointment and rules of conduct (e.g., fit and proper criteria, avoidance of conflicts of interest) that ensure observance of the highest professional standards.

14. As noted in the draft GBII Report, "official administration does not imply that the bank should be kept open against all judgment or for an indefinite period of time. Especially, in a weak institutional environment it may not be feasible or even advisable to keep the bank open." Moreover, "keeping the bank open under official administration may give rise to expectations of a general bailout of creditors, which will often be inappropriate."

15. As their primary objective is to ensure the maximization of value and optimal collection of the bank's assets and their distribution to creditors, bank liquidation proceedings in many countries closely resemble liquidation proceedings applicable to corporate insolvencies.

16. While the liquidator should not be required to seek the appointing authority's permission for every action, he can be subjected to the appointing authority's instructions on the general direction of the liquidation and possibly to the appointing authority's prior approval for certain important decisions.

17. The liquidation framework needs to recognize that an insolvent bank's estate will largely comprise financial claims with respect to which traditional means of sale (e.g., public auction) may not be appropriate. Accordingly, the liquidator needs to be given sufficient flexibility to dispose of assets, either individually or in bulk, using techniques that ensure minimal loss of value. As such assets will often take the form of contractual interests and entail corresponding obligations, the liquidator should be permitted to transfer contractual relationships without the consent of the counterparty.

18. A country should rely upon its corporate insolvency framework only if it is effective. To the extent that the corporate insolvency regime is considered to be weak or out-dated, or if the authorities responsible for its application (e.g., the courts) are considered to be inefficient or possibly corrupt, the case for a special regime becomes more compelling.

19. Draft GBII Report, Chapter 2.

Part III
Options for Asset Management

8
Prudential Treatment of Restructured Loans

Inwon Song[1]

I. Introduction

Bankers are occasionally involved in troubled loan restructuring with borrowers who are experiencing financial difficulties that are likely to affect their repayment prospects. Such restructuring, if carried out in a way that is consistent with prudential lending practices and in accordance with accounting standards in force, can greatly improve a bank's prospects for collection. Troubled loan restructuring should be relatively infrequent. If not, the bank is probably experiencing significant difficulties.

The appropriate treatment of restructured loans is an important component of maintaining bank soundness, not only under normal circumstances but also in the event of a systemic crisis. In a systemic crisis situation, supervisory authorities and banks might be more inclined to resort to providing preferential treatment for restructured loans through establishing favorable provisions that will alleviate the impact on the capital adequacy of the related banks.

Banks should develop a policy regarding restructured loans to ensure that such loans are clearly designated, monitored, and properly handled from both accounting and loan review standpoints. The bank supervisors should provide prudential guidelines on the treatment of restructured loans and monitor the extent of these loans carefully. This chapter surveys country practices in classification and provisioning for restructured loans and suggests good practices on this issue.

This chapter is structured as follows. After the introduction, Section II discusses the definition of restructured loans. Section III addresses bank accounting for restructured loans. Section IV considers good practices for classification of restructured loans, while Section V presents good practices regarding provisioning for restructured loans. Section VI discusses the role of banks and supervisors in dealing with restructured loans, and Section VII concludes. G-10 and non G-10 country cases are surveyed in Appendix 8.I.

II. Definition of restructured loan

Bankers commonly use the term "rescheduling" to mean the deferral of principal repayments on a loan (usually regarding the periodicity of payments), or some modification of the terms of the loan with respect to the face value (the amount), or a combination of several other elements. A more precise term, "troubled loan restructuring," is generally used in place of "rescheduling."

According to the definition of the Basel Committee's 1999 Loan Accounting Paper, a loan is "a restructured troubled loan when the lender, for economic or legal reasons related to the borrower's financial difficulties, grants a concession to the borrower that it would not otherwise consider." The restructuring of a loan or other debt instrument (hereafter referred to as a "loan") may include (i) the transfer from the borrower to the bank of real estate, receivables from third parties, other assets, or an equity interest in the borrower in full or partial satisfaction of the loan; (ii) a modification of the loan terms such as a combination of the following factors: a reduction in an agreed-upon interest rate; an extension of the final maturity; a reduction of principal; or a reduction of accrued interest; or (iii) acceptance by the bank of the conversion of the borrower's debt into equity to be held by the bank, in full or partial settlement of a debt.[2]

A loan renewed at a stated interest rate equal to the current interest rate for new debt with similar risk is not to be regarded as a restructured loan as long as interest continues to be serviced on time, in cash, and without capitalization of interest.

When loans are classified and heavy provisions are required by accounting standards or banks' supervisors, some banks may engage in extensive troubled loan restructurings in case this treatment minimizes the impact of nonperforming loans on their net income. However, such treatment could be often interpreted as "cosmetic accounting" by supervisors in the context of postponing recognition of the true extent of their portfolio losses.[3]

III. Bank accounting for restructured loans

When banks engage in troubled loan restructuring, they should develop appropriate credit policies/procedures and comply with accounting standards in their jurisdictions. Usually, accounting standards such as International Financial Reporting Standards (IFRS) and the U.S. Generally Accepted Accounting Principles (GAAP) are very specific about a restructured troubled loan in terms of both valuation and disclosure.[4] Because the lender grants a concession to the borrower in view of the borrower's financial difficulties, a restructured troubled loan is regarded as a technically "impaired" loan until it is upgraded to a normal loan and/or placed on an accrual status.[5]

Troubled loan restructuring may include both a modification of terms and an acceptance of property in partial satisfaction of the loan. When the terms of the loan are changed, the bank shall not change the book value of the loan, unless the book value exceeds the present value (PV) of expected future cash flow (including related accrued interest).[6] The PV of the loan and interest income of the loan shall be calculated by using the loan's effective interest rate based on the original contractual rate, not the rate specified in the restructured agreement. If the PV of expected future cash flow of the loan is less than the book value, the book value should be written down to the PV of expected future cash flow. Thereafter, all subsequently received cash will reduce the book value of the loan and will not be credited to income (the U.S. "Financial Accounting Standards" FAS 15 and FAS 114).

When a bank receives additional assets to satisfy the loan in the restructuring process, the bank shall account for these assets at their fair value at the time of restructuring. The difference between the fair value of an asset (less cost to sell)[7] and the book value of the loan (including accrued interest), will be added to net income only when it is a realized gain. If it is a loss, the difference should be written off against any provisions for loan losses and the balance against net income of the accounting period during which the restructuring is undertaken (FAS 15 and FAS 114).

A restructuring may involve the substitution or addition of a new debtor for the original borrower. The treatment of these situations depends on their substance. If the substitute or additional debtor is controlled by, or is under common control together with the original debtor, then the bank shall account for the loan as a "restructured troubled loan." If after restructuring, the substitute or additional debtor and the original debtor are related by an agency, trust or other relationship that in substance earmarks certain of the original debtor's funds or fund flow to the bank (even though the payer may be the substitute or additional debtor), then the bank shall also account for the loan as a "restructured troubled loan." If, however, the substitute or additional debtor does not have any of the relationships with the original debtor described above, then the bank may account for the restructuring on an arm's length basis. The loan should be accounted for as a receipt of a "new" loan in full or partial satisfaction of the original borrower's loan.

Interest on impaired loans should not contribute to net income if doubt exists concerning the collectibility of loan principal or interest. Therefore, for impaired loans, a bank should cease the accrual of interest in accordance with the original terms of the contract.[8] Nevertheless, a loan that has been restructured so as to be reasonably assured of repayment and of performance according to its modified terms need not be maintained in nonaccrual status, provided the restructuring and any write-off taken on the asset are supported by a current, well-documented credit evaluation of the borrower's financial condition and prospects for repayment under the revised terms. Otherwise, the restructured loans must remain in nonaccrual status.

The evaluation must include consideration of the borrower's sustained historical repayment performance for a reasonable period prior to the date on which the loan is returned to accrual status. A sustained period of repayment performance generally would be a certain minimum period of demonstrated payments (for example, for six months or three consecutive timely payments in compliance with the new terms) and would involve payments of cash or cash equivalent.

It is imperative that the reasons for restoration of a restructured loan to accrual status be documented. Such actions should be supported by a current, well-documented credit evaluation of the borrower's financial condition and prospects for repayment under modified terms.[9]

If a restructured loan, which has been returned to accrual status, subsequently meets the criteria for placement in nonaccrual status as a result of its past-due position based on its modified terms, the loan must again be placed in nonaccrual status.

IV. Classification of restructured loans

All restructured loans should be subject to an assessment of risk according to criteria to determine their collectibility at the time of the restructuring. They should, thereafter, be identified in the bank's internal credit review systems regularly and monitored by bank management. When analyzing restructured loans, the credit reviewer should focus on the ability of the borrower to repay the loan in accordance with its modified terms both under normal circumstances and in the event of a systemic crisis. Although international best practices do not exist on this issue, the following elements could be regarded as good practices.

A restructured loan should generally be classified as "substandard" or no better than its category prior to restructuring, such as "doubtful."[10] Otherwise, banks can exaggerate their credit quality by granting terms to borrowers that are considerably easier than normal commercial terms. A borrower's compliance with the terms and conditions of the restructured loans for a certain specified period of time gives a fair indication of the improvement in the borrower's debt repayment capacity, and warrants the restoration of the loan to a regular category.[11]

After a reasonable period of demonstrated payment performance, banks could upgrade a restructured loan. Clearly, a period of sustained performance is a very important factor in determining whether there is a reasonable assurance of repayment and performance according to the loans' modified terms. Nevertheless, in certain exceptional circumstances, evidence may exist regarding other characteristics of the borrower that may be considered to demonstrate a relative improvement in the borrower's condition and debt service capacity. For example, substantial and reliable sales contracts obtained by the borrower or other important developments, which are expected to significantly increase the borrowers' cash flow and debt service capacity, may be considered to provide this assurance. When there is ample evidence to support this assurance of the borrower's improved debt service capacity, a conservative upgrading of the restructured loan may be warranted. However, if the restructured loan again runs into difficulties, it would also be appropriate to reclassify it in accordance with the formulated classification grades.

If the substitute or additional debtor is related or affiliated to the original debtor, then the original loan classification cannot be changed unless subsequent debt servicing by the borrower improves sufficiently to warrant a fresh review of the classification. If the substitute or additional debtor is totally unrelated to the original debtor, then the subjective loan classification criteria can be applied to the substitute or additional debtor. This should be done in accordance with the general principle of the borrower's ability to repay his/her debt in the normal course of business. If the new debtor is able to clear all interest arrears, then the loan classification can be upgraded accordingly.

If the substitute or additional debtor is only able to offer liquid assets as collateral, then the loan classification remains. Loan classification will be reviewed and loans will be reclassified in accordance with the substitute or additional debtor's debt service record at the next classification review exercise.

The great majority of supervisors in G-10 countries do not provide a definition of restructured troubled loans, and they have not issued guidelines on how such loans should be classified. Many supervisors in non G-10 countries, by contrast, provide specific criteria for banks to classify loans as restructured, and give more detailed guidance. Definitions of a restructured loan involve extending the loan's maturity or lowering its interest rate (or both).

Regarding the minimum time period before restructured loans are upgraded, country practices vary widely. Although most G-10 and non G-10 countries do not specify a minimum time period, several countries do so. In Bulgaria and Singapore, restructured loans may be upgraded if they comply with their new restructured terms for at least one year. In Malaysia, restructured loans can be reclassified as performing after the borrower services the loan for six months. In the Philippines, after the borrower has serviced the restructured loan for three consecutive months, the loan can then be reclassified.[12]

Some countries specify the upgrading requirements in terms of the number of repayments rather than the minimum period of remaining restructured loans. In Turkey, before a restructured loan can be reclassified as performing, at least three consecutive repayments should be realized, while six consecutive payments are required for related parties. In Lithuania and Indonesia, a restructured loan may be upgraded after three timely repayments are made. In Thailand, a borrower has to make three consecutive payments or at least three months of timely payments before a restructured loan could be classified as performing.

Good practices of classification of restructured loans would include: (i) a restructured loan should generally be classified as "substandard" or no better than its category prior to restructuring, such as "doubtful"; (ii) a reasonable period of demonstrated payment (for example, at least six months or three consecutive timely payments in compliance with new terms) should be shown before a restructured loan can be upgraded; and (iii) if the substitute or additional debtor is totally unrelated to the original debtor, then the subjective loan classification criteria can be applied to the substitute or additional debtor.

(See Appendix 8.I for G-10 and non G-10 country cases.)

V. Provisions for restructured loans

When troubled loan restructuring is arranged under more favorable conditions compared with market ones or the original terms of the loan, a cost should be assigned to this difference and provisioned in its full amount. To the extent that a substitute or additional debtor is able to offer additional liquid assets as collateral, the provisioning can be reduced by the fair value of the liquid asset offered as collateral. In addition, if a restructured loan is a collateral-dependent loan, the fair value of collateral should be reassessed in the process of restructuring and provisions should be adjusted considering the fair value of the related collateral.

When available information confirms that a specific restructured loan or a portion thereof, is uncollectible, this amount should be written off against the provisions for loan losses at the time of restructuring. Thereafter, the bank should regularly evaluate the collectibility of the restructured loan as a part of the impairment assessment process and so as to determine whether existing provisioning is adequate and whether any additional amounts should be charged to provisions.

Arguments could arise regarding the different treatment of restructured loans and associated provisions in a crisis situation as opposed to normal circumstances. Although there are no international best practices on this issue, it is suggested that prudential norms and practices for the classification and provisioning for restructured loans be the same under normal circumstances as in the event of a systemic crisis. In classifying restructured loans even in a systemic crisis, the emphasis should be placed on the quality of the restructured troubled loan and the prospects for repayment. Problem loans have to restore first their track record of payments to be upgraded, even under a systemic crisis.

Some considerations should be addressed regarding the treatment of specific provisions that were established for restructured loans. The criteria to reverse the provisions set up for restructured loans should depend on the conditions of the restructuring program. Specific provisions for restructured loans should remain until such time that borrowers have been able to show that they can service the loans (principal and interest) and fulfill all restructuring commitments and conditions.

VI. Role of banks and supervisors

A formal strategy for troubled loan restructuring should be established by each bank to ensure that such restructurings are identified, monitored, and properly handled. The highest level of management should be directly involved in formulating this strategy. The strategy should encompass not only troubled loan restructurings, but should also set forth policies regarding loan collection, loan recovery and write-offs. The strategy should form part of the bank's written credit policy.

The strategy should include clear, time-based objectives, measures for monitoring and reporting on performance against those objectives, and a plan of action. Guidelines should be developed with respect to troubled loan restructuring mechanisms based on the following factors: the nature of the credit, the approval process, decision-making bodies, accounting procedures, reporting requirements, and supervision. Before such concessions on restructuring are made to a borrower, it is a good practice to have the transactions approved by the board of directors or committee thereof; all such transactions should be reported to the board of the directors upon enactment.[13]

Bank supervisors should issue guidelines on troubled loan restructuring to assist bank management in determining the appropriate treatment, especially in terms of loan classification and provisioning. The bank supervisor should monitor the extent of troubled loan restructuring regularly, preferably on a quarterly basis, and the impact of troubled loan restructuring on the income of the bank and the quality of its own portfolio. Loan classification rules could include criteria for banks to assess the prospects and viability of the restructured debtor and the adequacy of banks' workout plans for distressed borrowers.[14]

The bank supervisor should note that extensive troubled loan restructuring could be an indication of both borrower liquidity and solvency problems. Extensive rescheduling by large borrowers or any identified economic sector is an early warning of potential problems of bank asset quality.[15] The bank supervisor should require banks to make a public disclosure of restructured loans in accordance with international accounting standards. Nondisclosure of restructured loans might have the effect of disguising the true embedded asset quality problems of a bank or the banking sector.

Since a lower interest rate or extended repayment schedule (or both) may help the debtor repay the debt, banks offer these mechanisms to safeguard their assets. In such cases where banks may offer new terms to borrowers who can no longer pay their debts, the new terms may provide temporary relief to the debtor and lead the way to additional concessions. In doing so, banks may try to conceal the extent of impairment. On the other hand, some "evergreening" practices, which include extending the credit facilities without amending the contractual interest rate, are difficult to track unless bank supervisors implement a proper reporting system or investigate this issue thoroughly during on-site examinations.[16]

In a systemic crisis situation, sometimes banks might be more willing to give preferential treatment for restructured loans, in terms of their classification and the establishment of provisions, in order to alleviate the impact on their income and capital adequacy. Such treatment would distort the soundness indicators of the banking sector and thus could aggravate systemic problems. Therefore, supervisory authorities should not allow such preferential treatment.

VII. Conclusion

The prudential treatment of restructured loans is an important component of maintaining bank soundness not only under normal circumstances, but also in the event of a systemic crisis. Banks should develop policies to identify, monitor and handle restructured loans properly from the prudential loan review and impairment assessment standpoints. Banking supervisors should provide prudential guidelines on the treatment of restructured loans and require banks to disclose restructured loans timely in accordance with international accounting standards. Further international good practices in classification and provisioning for restructured loans should continue to be developed.

Appendix 8.I. Some G-10 and non G-10 country cases

Country	Classification of Restructured Loans
G-10	
Italy	Only the portion subject to restructuring is classified. Restructured loans are those for which a borrower who was granted a moratorium on repayment in the previous 12 months and renegotiated the debt at a below-market rate. If more than a year has elapsed, banks are required to verify whether restructured loans should be classified as "substandard" or "bad debt."
Japan	If lending conditions have been relaxed or modified, then the loan is classified as a "special attention" loan.
United States	U.S. supervisors rely on the definition of a restructured loan provided by generally accepted accounting principles (FAS 114 with its amendment and FAS 15). Under the definition, debt is considered as troubled restructuring if the creditor, for economic or legal reasons related to the debtor's financial difficulties, grants a concession to the debtor that it would not otherwise consider. The restructured loan may include (i) the transfer from the borrower to the bank of real estate, receivables from third parties, other assets, or an equity interest in the borrower in full or partial satisfaction of the loan; (ii) or modification of the loan term or (iii) a combination of the above.

Non G-10 countries	
Australia	Australian supervisors consider a loan to be restructured if there has been a reduction in its principal, in the amount due at maturity, in the interest rate (to below-market level), or in accrued interest (including interest capitalization). A loan must also be regarded restructured if it involves an extension of the maturity date at an interest rate lower than the current market rate for new loans with similar risk. If the loan's yield is less than the average cost of funds after restructuring, the loan should be classified as nonaccrual.
Brazil	Restructured loans are also classified as nonaccrual or in a higher risk category and a better grading cannot be given until a significant amortization of the outstanding loan is achieved and sufficient evidence is provided to justify that decision.
Bulgaria	An exposure shall be deemed restructured where the original terms of the agreement have been modified by extending the terms for repayment of principal and interest, a reduction of the interest rate, a reduction of principal, refinancing, substitution of a debtor by a third person or subrogation of the debt by a third person, partial redemption by debt/equity swap or other financial concession by the bank. A restructured exposure will be eligible for reclassification as standard, provided that it has consistently met the conditions for not less than a year.
China	In 2002, the authorities introduced a new five-category loan classification system and corresponding provisioning requirements. However, the definition of restructured loans did not include such descriptions as the transfer from the borrower to the bank of real estate, receivables from third parties, other assets (as additional collateral), or an equity interest in the borrower in full or partial satisfaction of the loan.
	Strengthening the loan classification rule—including by specifying a minimum time period before restructured loans are upgraded to normal—would be beneficial. Loan classification rules could include criteria for banks and supervisors to assess the prospects and viability of the restructured debtor and adequacy of banks' workout plans for distressed borrowers.[a]
Czech Republic	A loan is considered restructured if the bank grants a new loan so that the customer can repay an impaired loan; a restructured loan cannot be classified better than substandard.
Estonia	A loan restructured due to solvency problems shall not be considered a standard loan until the circumstances that have caused the decrease of the borrower's creditworthiness have been removed.
Hong Kong	Restructured loans are classified as substandard or worse.
India	Losses incurred on restructured loans must be fully provisioned.
Latvia	A restructured loan shall be assessed, taking into account the borrower's ability to meet his/her liabilities to the bank in accordance with the modified condition of the agreement. Where any loan is restructured after specific provisions have been made, the reduction in the carrying amount of a loan shall be offset by the reduction in the volume of specific provisions.

Country	Classification of Restructured Loans
Lithuania	A loan that has been restructured must be attributed to the grade not lower than that before restructuring and not lower than the "substandard" grade. If a loan has been restructured in such a way two or three times, it must be attributed a grade not lower than "doubtful." Such loans may be transferred to the grade of lower risk (except the standard grade) if after the loan restructuring, the borrower timely repays the loan within three repayment terms fixed in the loan agreement and there is no evidence testifying to the possibility of the borrower's default in the future. If a loan has been restructured more than three times and the debt of the borrower during that period did not decrease or increase, such a loan shall be ascribed to a "bad" (estimated loss) grade. These loans may be classified as "doubtful," provided that after the loan restructuring the borrower made three timely repayments in compliance with the terms fixed under the loan agreement and there was no evidence testifying to the possibility of the borrower's default in the future.
Malaysia	Restructured loans stay at the same classification as before. After the borrower has serviced the loan for six months, the loan can be reclassified as performing.
Malta	Once a credit facility has been so rescheduled or restructured, credit institutions are expected to retain that facility in the grading allocated to it prior to its being rescheduled or restructured. Should the identified weaknesses be rectified and the new repayment program be honored, credit institutions may reclassify such facility accordingly. Credit facilities that were repeatedly rescheduled should be graded doubtful and provided for accordingly.
Philippines	A restructured loan generally stays at the same classification as before. After the borrower has serviced the loan for three consecutive months, the loan can be reclassified as performing.
Russian Federation	All loans that have been restructured more than once—regardless of whether the initial loan agreement has been revised—should be classified as substandard or risky (doubtful for loans rescheduled twice within amendments of the initial contract).
Singapore	Restructured loans are classified as substandard or lower, but may be upgraded to unimpaired if they have complied with their new restructured terms for at least one year.
Slovak Republic	Any claim that was restructured is to be considered at least as substandard; if it was restructured several times, it is deemed to be doubtful. The claim may be reclassified as special-mentioned if the borrower repaid all principal and interest installments during the first quarter of the term of payment according to the agreed repayment schedule and the bank is not aware of any reason to doubt that in the future the borrower will not comply with the repayment schedule. A claim that was restructured only by lowering the interest rate applied, is assigned the same category as before restructuring, except where before restructuring, the claim was standard. Such a claim is to be considered as special-mentioned.

Slovenia	Restructuring claims are classified into C, D, or E grade. The bank shall establish specific provisions with reference to the new balance of restructured claim, whereby the existing percentage used in establishing specific provisions may not be lowered in this process.
	The bank shall not reclassify the restructured claims into a higher grade than the one in which they were classified before restructuring until full repayment. The bank may lower or cancel the specific provisions only in the event that it acquires a security, which is deemed prime security.
South Africa	Restructured loans are classified in the two top categories only if all principal and interest have been paid continually for a reasonable period.
Spain	Restructured loans must remain as doubtful, except in the case of additional acceptable collateral and payment of interest.

[a] Nonperforming Assets in the Chinese Financial System in Selected Issues, IMF, 2003.

Sources: IMF (2002), Bank Supervision Regulatory Database, World Bank (2002).

Appendix 8.II. Some country cases which experienced systemic banking crises

Country	Measures taken for restructured loans
Argentina	The central bank had specific rules for restructured loan classification and upgrading their classification. Restructured loans usually should be maintained below the "substandard" category. When at least 50 percent of a restructured loan has been paid and there were promptly executable guarantees, the market value of the restructured loan could be upgraded (Central Bank of Argentina Communication A 2950, July 16, 1999). However, in 2003 the central bank temporarily allowed banks to immediately upgrade restructured loans after modest loan repayments. For example, a restructured loan which was classified as grade 5 (loss: worst grade) could be upgraded to grade 4 (doubtful)— if 4 percent of the loan had been repaid. If an additional 4 percent of the loan had been repaid, that restructured loan could be upgraded to grade 3 (Central Bank of Argentina Communication A 3918, April 4, 2003).
Bolivia	In August 2003, Bolivia embarked on a systemic corporate/bank restructuring process. At that time, restructured loans were allowed to be reclassified by up to two grades at the time of restructuring, with specific provisions in the profit and loss account. In preparation for the regulatory framework to support the systemic corporate restructuring, the Fund mission recommended that the restructured loans be gradually reclassified after the borrower demonstrated good performance through several repayments. When the reclassification took place, the specific provisions being released should be set aside as general provisions. It should not be allowed to be distributed as dividend.

Country	Measures taken for restructured loans
Indonesia	The financial sector restructuring program called for banks to maintain the classification of restructured loans for a minimum three payments under the restructured terms before upgrading and provisions could be reduced. A restructured loan was classified based on the borrower's ability to repay under the new terms, but substandard at best.
Korea	In 1999, the Fund agreed with Korea's financial sector program, as an interim measure, that restructured loans would be classified as "special mention" or "substandard" subject to provisioning within the range of 2 percent to 20 percent. In 2000, when the Korean authorities adopted forward-looking criteria (FLC) in loan classification, they applied this FLC to restructured loans. Thus, a restructured loan was classified as "substandard," "doubtful," or "loss" based on the FLC used.
Thailand	A borrower should show for three consecutive payments or at least three months that the loan had been serviced before a restructured loan could be classified as performing. However, a restructured loan could immediately be classified as performing provided that the Corporate Debt Restructuring Advisory Committee or court approved the restructuring.
Turkey	Turkey applies a special regulation about classification and provisioning rules for restructured loans. For restructured loans, there were no grace periods for interest payments. The loans had to remain classified and subject to specific provisioning in the same way as before the restructuring for at least six months to verify the repayment performance of the debtor. Before a loan could be reclassified as performing, at least three consecutive payments must have been made and repayments of interest should be made based on the contracted terms; for related parties six consecutive payments were required.

Notes

1. I would like to thank Mr. Jorge Cayazzo and Ms. Alicia Novoa for their detailed comments on the first draft and Mr. Colin-Jones for his editorial assistance.
2. Basel Committee on Banking Supervision (1999).
3. Banks are subject to specific mandatory disclosure requirements for troubled restructured loans in accordance with international accounting standards whether restructuring is for cosmetic purposes or not.
4. It is beyond the scope of this chapter to discuss the detailed accounting arrangements for restructured loans regarding valuation and disclosure in terms of IFRS or GAAP.
5. Loan "impairment" represents deterioration in the credit quality of one or more loans such that it is probable that the bank will be unable to collect, or there is no longer reasonable assurance that the bank will collect, all amounts due according to the contractual terms of the loan agreement(s). (BIS 1999.)
6. Present value is one of several methods that can be used to measure the impairment of a loan.
7. The fair value of assets transferred between debtor and creditor is "the amount that the debtor could reasonably expect to receive for them in a current sale between a willing buyer and a willing seller, that is, other than in a forced or liquidation

sale. Fair value of assets shall be measured by their market value if an active market for them exists. If no active market exists for the assets transferred but exists for similar assets, the selling prices in that market may be helpful in estimating the fair value of the assets transferred. If no market price is available, a forecast of expected cashflow may help in estimating the fair value of assets transferred, provided the expected cashflows are discounted at a rate commensurate with the risk involved (FAS 15, paragraph 13).

8. In the United States, if interest on a loan is not received within 90 days of the due date, the loan is placed on nonaccrual status. Interest cannot be accrued on a nonperforming loan.

9. Commercial Bank Examination Manual, Federal Reserve System (1994), Section 2040.1.

10. Under no circumstances should interest capitalization be permitted if the restructured loan has been classified as nonaccrual, substandard, doubtful or loss by external auditors or banking supervisors.

11. Some could argue that prohibiting banks from upgrading restructured loans after a loan restructuring process would have an adverse impact on the rehabilitation of the debtor. Because the debtor of the restructured loans should be maintained at a lower loan classification category for a certain period of time, the debtor might have difficulty in getting additional credits from the financial market.

12. World Bank (2002).

13. Commercial Bank Examination Manual, Federal Reserve System (1994). Section 2040.1.

14. World Bank (1992).

15. World Bank (1992).

16. World Bank (2002), p. 18.

Bibliography

Basel Committee on Banking Supervision, 1999, *Sound Practices for Loan Accounting and Disclosure* (Basel).

Federal Financial Institution Examination Council, 1994, Glossary (Washington: FFIEC).

Federal Reserve System, 1994, *Commercial Bank Examination Manual* (Washington: Federal Reserve System).

Financial Accounting Standards Board, 1977, Financial Accounting Standards No. 15: Accounting by Debtors and Creditors for Troubled Debt Restructurings (Connecticut: Financial Accounting Standards Board).

——, 1993, Financial Accounting Standards No. 114: Accounting by Creditors for Impairment of a Loan (Connecticut: Financial Accounting Standards Board).

International Monetary Fund, 2003, "People's Republic of China—Selected Issues," SM/03/317 (Washington: International Monetary Fund).

World Bank, 1992, *Bank Supervision Guidelines; Asset Classification and Provisions for Loan Losses* (Washington: World Bank).

——, 2002, "Bank Loan Classification and Provisioning Practices in Selected Developed and Emerging Countries: Survey of Current Practices in Countries Represented on the Basel Core Principles Liaison Group" (Washington: World Bank).

9
Issues in the Establishment of Asset Management Companies

Dong He, Stefan Ingves, and Steven A. Seelig

I. Introduction

This chapter discusses the role of asset management companies in facilitating bank restructuring and derives some lessons from recent experiences. It reviews various options and cross-country experiences in dealing with impaired assets during periods of financial crises. It argues that there are alternative strategies for managing and disposing of impaired assets, depending on factors such as the type of asset, size and distribution, the structure of the banking system, and available management capacity in the banks and in the public sector. The chapter concludes that there is no single optimal solution but rather a combination of solutions for each country that may vary over time and for each bank resolution. There are, however, common factors that contribute to the success of asset management companies (AMCs). These include supporting legal and regulatory environment, strong leadership, operational independence, appropriately structured incentives, and commercial orientation.

The chapter is organized as follows: Section II discusses the objectives of asset management companies (AMCs) in the context of a systemic bank restructuring strategy. Section III discusses the pros and cons of different approaches to the structure and organization of AMCs, and analyzes the factors that should be considered in choosing the right structure. Section IV discusses governance and incentive structure issues in different types of AMCs. Section V discusses the operational issues of AMCs, and Section VI provides some concluding remarks.

II. The objectives of AMCs

Asset management and bank restructuring

Proper management and disposition of nonperforming assets is one of the most critical and complex aspects of financial sector crisis management. Successful bank restructuring entails preserving the payment system, assuring that there are functioning banks, and that the residual troubled assets are managed and disposed of appropriately. While loan workouts are part and parcel of normal banking business, if the size of bad assets reaches systemic proportions, there are a number of reasons why setting up separate AMCs becomes necessary, not the least of which is to assure that corporate restructuring occurs. When AMCs hold a large percentage of financial sector assets, corporate workouts and restructuring should become a key part of their mission.

Probably the most important purpose of having AMCs is the managerial factor. The handling of bad loans and assets require other skills than are normally available in a bank. Real estate specialists, liquidation experts, and people with insights into various industrial sectors may be needed. In addition, managing the bad assets would interfere with the daily running of the bank. Importantly, both the good bank and the AMC could be given independent and transparent profit goals if separated. That would provide incentives for managers and staff.

Country experiences show that AMCs have been set up for a number of reasons. These include the facilitation of (a) the resolution of insolvent and nonviable financial institutions; (b) the restructuring of distressed but viable financial institutions; and (c) the privatization of government-owned and government-intervened banks. Examples of (a) include the Resolution Trust Corporation (RTC) in the United States and the Thai Financial Sector Restructuring Agency (FRA). Examples of (b) include the Swedish Securum and Cinda Asset Management Company in China. The mandates of the Korea Asset Management Corporation (KAMCO) and the Malaysian Danaharta encompassed both (a) and (b). Examples of (c) include the French Consortium de Realization, which was created as a subsidiary of Credit Lyonnais in 1995 to take over nonperforming assets from the bank before its privatization in 1999, and the AMC owned by the Financial Institutions Development Fund in Thailand for the sale of Radanasin Bank. The Indonesian Bank Restructuring Agency (IBRA) combined all three elements.

Operational goals for AMCs

For an AMC to operate effectively it is imperative that it have clearly defined goals and a governance structure that is both supportive of these goals and assures that management meets the goals. Different countries have taken different approaches to defining the goals for their AMCs.[1] AMCs in different countries may have different focuses. In some countries the AMCs operated with a focus on disposing of the assets acquired/transferred to the government. These AMCs functioned as rapid disposition vehicles quickly selling assets to the private sector. In all cases the goal was to dispose of the asset as quickly as possible so as to avoid further deterioration in value and to minimize the carrying cost of the government. It should be recognized that rapid disposition requires the AMC to have good information about the assets it is attempting to dispose of and that a market for these assets exists. Countries such as Korea and the United States in the case of the Federal Deposit Insurance Corporation (FDIC) signaled the market of the seriousness of their intent by initially conducting small sales and completing them successfully.

In other countries the government set up vehicles whose focus was on restructuring. In some cases, the emphasis was on restructuring the nonperforming loans (NPLs) so as to make them marketable. In others, the goal was to achieve broader corporate restructuring of the borrowers and the government-owned banks.

Regardless the focuses of different AMCs, their operations should be guided ultimately by the objective of profit maximization or loss minimization, taking into full account market conditions as well as the funding cost to the AMC. Experience has shown that AMCs with clearly defined, focused, and consistent goals are more likely to be effective. In some instances, such as the United States, social objectives were added to the asset management objectives of the AMC. The RTC was required to promote social goals in the areas of affordable housing and historic preservation by developing programs and giving preference to buyers who would meet program goals. The practice of mixing goals, and especially establishing conflicting objectives, is not recommended. Fortunately in the case of the RTC, the vast majority of the assets were not subject to social objectives and it was able to pursue its rapid sale strategies with success.

III. Structural and organizational issues

Ownership

Various approaches to the structure and organization of AMCs can be adopted to achieve the authorities' objectives. In terms of ownership, AMCs can be either public or private and within these there are alternative structures. Similarly, the sellers of assets to the AMC can be private or public entities. When a substantial amount of bad loans and assets has to be transferred to an AMC over a short period of time, it is often difficult to find a private investor willing to own such an AMC without asking for far-reaching government guarantees covering the future value of the asset portfolio. In this situation, the government is in a more favorable position owning the AMC itself rather than providing guarantees, since it might then benefit from any future upward price movements of the AMC's assets. In addition, it is difficult to formulate guarantees that would give a private owner strong incentives to sell the assets at the best prices. This could lead to further losses for the state.

When a single bank has a medium to large amount of bad loans and assets, an option is to set up an AMC as a subsidiary of the same bank. In doing so, the bank would benefit from its knowledge and close contacts with borrowers. However, it is important to guard against the AMC becoming the focus of the bank's management who should be working on restructuring the "cleaned-up" bank. In addition, certain types of assets, such as real estate, may be better handled by nonbank professionals. If the government has provided financial support to the bank, it may ask for a share in the "upside" of the AMC subsidiary.

Public AMCs can be freestanding entities or may be a responsibility of an existing public agency, such as the ministry of finance or the deposit insurer. It is preferable, however, that AMCs not be set up as a unit within the central bank, or as its subsidiary, since the central bank's primary responsibility is to achieve and maintain price stability, and its balance sheet should not be made unwieldy by taking on large amounts of nonperforming assets of the banking system.

The number of AMCs

Although there are no clear-cut rules as to the superiority of having a single AMC monopoly (the centralized approach) versus having a number of competing AMCs (the decentralized approach), there are advantages and disadvantages associated with each of them (Box 9.1 and Table 9.1).

Box 9.1. Advantages and Disadvantages of a Centralized Public Asset Management Company

Advantages

- Serves as a vehicle for getting NPLs out of troubled banks, based on uniform valuation criteria.
- Allows government to attach conditions to purchases of NPLs in terms of bank restructuring.
- Centralizes scarce human resources (domestic and foreign).
- Centralizes ownership of collateral, thus providing more leverage over debtors and more effective management.
- Can better force operational restructuring of troubled banks.
- Can be given special legal powers to expedite loan recovery and bank restructuring.

Disadvantages

- Management is often weaker than in private structures, reducing the efficiency and effectiveness of its operations.
- Such agencies are often subject to political pressure.
- Values of acquired assets erode faster when they are outside a banking structure.
- NPLs and collateral are often long-term "parked" in an AMC, not liquidated.
- If not actively managed, existence of public AMC could lead to a general deterioration of credit discipline in financial system.
- Cost involved in operating an AMC may be higher than a private arrangement.
- If dealing with private banks, determining transfer prices is difficult.

A very large AMC may obtain economies of scale but could also become unwieldy, which might hamper the ability to react swiftly, such as in sales transactions. In addition, problem loans and assets require far more work than a similar number of performing loans. In general, the choice of a particular organizational structure for AMCs depends on a number of factors, including types of assets, magnitude of the problem, depth of markets, and characteristics of debtors. For instance, when the types of impaired assets in different banks differ substantially, there may be some rationale to group assets by types and to transfer them to AMCs specializing in the management of a particular type or types of assets. When there is lack of depth in markets for certain assets, there may be stronger rationale for a centralized approach in the disposition of such assets.

Table 9.1.   Considerations for Decentralized Asset Management

	Within Banks	**In Private AMCs**
Advantages	Knowledge of the borrower may facilitate debt restructuring. Access to borrower through branch network.	Specialized skill mix. Focus on restructuring function. Creation of an asset management industry and secondary market for distressed assets. Upfront loss recognition. Cleans up the bank's books.
Disadvantages	Lack of skills for restructuring of troubled debt, operations of companies, debt-equity swaps, etc. Hampers "normal" banking functions (lending activities), particularly if the NPL portfolio is large. Less upfront loss recognition. Does not clean up the bank's books. May be problems of conflicts of interest with the parent bank as well as governance issues.	Lack of knowledge of the borrower. Bank may not have sufficient capital to recognize upfront losses associated with selling to an AMC.

During the Asia financial crises, each country considered the advantages and disadvantages of dealing with impaired assets in a centralized or decentralized AMC structure and related ownership issues in the context of its own circumstances. Centralized AMCs, which typically are state owned, have been used in Indonesia, Korea, and Malaysia. This does not exclude privately owned banks from setting up their own AMCs. For example, in Thailand a more mixed approach was used. While encouraging each commercial bank to establish its own separate AMC, a public AMC was established to purchase residual assets from the FRA.[2] In Indonesia private AMCs to deal with failed banks were ruled out due to governance concerns.[3]

Legal powers of AMCs

An important issue in setting up AMCs concerns their legal powers. The legal basis of the AMC should provide for clean transfers of titles (and the associated priority) in all asset transactions of the AMC. Similarly, legal obstacles for the transfer of assets, such as the requirement that the permission of the debtors be obtained before the transfer of loans be effected, should be removed. The legal basis should ensure that the AMC "stands in the shoes" of the former bank at least in the eyes of the law. In addition, asset disposition by public AMCs could be retarded by perceived potential legal liabilities accruing to the AMC management.[4] In this situation, legal protection for the employees of the AMCs in the execution of their responsibilities in good faith should be considered.

A legal system that includes an orderly and effective insolvency process is where bank and corporate restructuring meet. An effective insolvency system with well-designed vehicles for rehabilitation and liquidation can lead to an efficient maximization of resources in both the banking and the corporate sectors, and the economy as a whole. In this environment, efforts should be made to coordinate the design and implementation of bank and corporate restructuring strategies so that they do not work at cross purposes. For example, if the goal of corporate restructuring is to maintain viable companies, then the strategy of the AMC should not be rapid conversion to cash but rather focus on corporate workouts and possible equity ownership positions.

Another issue is whether special legal powers are needed for the AMC to facilitate the recovery process. Effective asset management and disposition requires the support of an effective legal system. Such a system should clearly define the rights of ownership as well as the legal obligations between debtors and creditors and provide for the orderly resolution of disputed claims, including debt recovery and realization of collateral for unpaid debt. Such a system should also balance the protection of creditors and that of debtors. However, when the existing legal system is not equipped to deal with the magnitude of the nonperforming assets (e.g., when the court system is inexperienced and does not have enough resources), or when endeavors to reform the system are excessively time-consuming, there may be a case to grant special legal powers to AMCs to facilitate asset recovery and restructuring. In Malaysia, for example, Danaharta is able to make use of three such powers: (i) special vesting powers insulate Danaharta and subsequent purchasers from undisclosed claims made after Danaharta acquires the NPL from the selling bank; (ii) Danaharta is able to appoint special administrators without having to go to court; and (iii) Danaharta can readily foreclose on collateral. The drawbacks of this approach, including potential abuse of these special powers and further weakening of legal due processes, should be carefully examined when considering granting such powers to AMCs.

IV. Governance and incentive issues

Governance

As with any type of organization, good governance is necessary to assure the effective operation of an AMC. Especially in the case of a government-owned AMC, governance issues are critical because the AMC is, on the one hand, subject to potential political pressure and, on the other, is accountable to the public for its actions and performance. Therefore, it is essential that an AMC be both independent and transparent with regard to its operations. Its stakeholders—the public, government, and shareholders—must be able to evaluate its performance.

Because AMCs handle large volumes of assets, and in some countries may control a significant percentage of the wealth of the nation, it is important that they be insulated from political interference in the disposition and restructuring of assets. The very nature of the asset management process invites political interference. If delinquent borrowers feel they may get more favorable treatment by contacting their elected officials, it is likely that they will do so. One must also expect elected representatives to make inquiries on behalf of their constituents. The critical balance is to assure that the AMC does not take inappropriate actions as a result of pressure, but at the same time is responsive to the public.

Because it is likely to be subject to political pressure, steps should be taken to shelter the AMC from this pressure. One approach is to establish the AMC as an independent entity. Part of this protection is to give it independence from the budget appropriations process in the same manner as that of central banks. Rather, the AMC should fund its operating expenses from within its own balance sheet.

The structure of the AMC within the government is also an important issue. The closer the AMC is to being a regular executive branch entity, the more it is subject to political pressure and the more difficult it becomes to be creative with compensation incentives. The goal should be to make the AMC distinct from a typical government agency and to distance it from normal government operations. One approach that worked well in Sweden is to create a holding company type of structure with different layers of governance and possibly multiple AMCs focusing on distinct asset types. This structure provides greater flexibility in managing the assets, creates competitive incentives, and provides greater political insulation.

Along with independence, however, comes transparency and accountability. Transparency with respect to all of its operations and its performance is critical for the AMC's political independence. It is also key to maintaining public confidence that the liquidation process is being carried out in a fair and objective fashion. Transparency promotes accountability of the managers and the board vis-à-vis the public and reduces the perception of, and possibly tendencies for, corruption.

To assure transparency, AMCs should be required to publish regular reports describing their performance in pursuing their goals. The financial statements should be prepared in accordance with accepted liquidation and fund accounting practices. In addition to making detailed financial information public, the AMCs should be audited regularly to assure that their financial statements are accurate, that representations as to the value of assets are reasonable, and that the AMC has proper internal controls in place to safeguard the assets under its management. Independent auditors chosen by the government should undertake such audits.

To help strengthen the independence of a government-owned AMC, it should be governed by a board of directors and, following principles of corporate governance, the majority should be outside independent directors. These directors should be sufficiently independent so as to be able to assist the AMC in resisting pressure from borrowers and prospective purchasers of assets seeking preferential treatment. The board should have a clearly defined mandate and it should be responsible for assuring that the AMC carries out its mission and meets performance goals. The board should have the flexibility to establish all policies and procedures for the AMC. These include policies for staff compensation, asset disposition strategies, credit and restructuring, budgets, and financial reporting.

Since asset management often involves contentious transactions, it is imperative that the governance structure of AMCs not be so limiting that the AMC loses its ability to deal with unforeseen circumstances. Experience has shown that managerial flexibility is extremely important to the effectiveness of AMCs.

A critical factor in assuring an AMC's success and independence is the ability of its stakeholders to evaluate its performance. This requires proper accounting for the assets at the time of transfer and for cash flows over time. Unfortunately, when AMCs have carried assets at their old book value, they typically show low recoveries leading the public to believe that the AMC has been a failure. Performance should be measured against either a "mark-to-market" value or an estimated recovery value at the time of transfer. If assets transfer at book value then appropriate provisions should be established as soon as possible after transfer, so that the initial shortfall is clear to everyone and performance is measured against original book value net of provisions.

In situations where privately owned and decentralized AMCs are used, there are also governance issues that must be addressed. If the government has ownership of the assets, or retains a significant financial exposure to the performance of the assets, it must assume regulatory oversight responsibility for the AMC. The challenge is for the government to assure itself that the assets are being managed and disposed of in an appropriate manner consistent with stated objectives, while at the same time not imposing an inefficient and overly burdensome oversight process. There are four key components to this process: (1) The agreements with the AMCs should clearly spell out the objectives, measurable performance requirements, and the delegations of authority from the government to the AMC; (2) AMCs should be required to prepare detailed reports on their actions and performance and provide all needed financial data to the government; (3) the government should audit the records and reports of the AMC and assure the same level of transparency as would be required of a public AMC; and (4) if the government has retained authority over certain actions, it must provide staff with appropriate authority to act quickly to approve or deny actions. These staff can also be the liaisons with the government agency having public accountability for the performance of the AMC. Variations on these approaches were used in the United States with great success.

Incentives

AMCs face an inherent incentive problem. Most commercial operations assure their continued existence by being successful. However, asset management operations are in the business of going out of business. If they are successful, they will liquidate the assets under their management through restructuring and disposition and cease to exist. Consequently, it is important to design AMCs so that they do not become "warehouses" of NPLs. There is a need for a structure of incentives that are designed to ensure effective and efficient asset management and disposition. These incentives need to address both the issues of the limited life of the entity and the performance of the staff.

One approach to the problem of the AMC being a self-liquidating entity is to develop incentives for the board members so that they will counterbalance the motivations of the staff to prolong the life of the AMC unnecessarily. These incentives can take the form of political rewards, such as higher office or public recognition of a job well-done or financial incentives to the directors. Another option that has been successful in several countries is to limit the life of the AMC at the time it is created. This approach worked well, and contributed to the success of the RTC and some of the private AMCs established by acquiring banks to manage assets for the FDIC. If the AMC is a public entity it helps to have senior career managers but rely on employees on term appointments, with terms that are tied to the expected life of the work. The use of term employees helps to alleviate political pressure to keep the AMC going in order to protect the jobs of its employees.

The other critical incentive issue is how to motivate employees and managers to maximize outcomes consistent with goals. As contrasted to many types of governmental activity, the work of an AMC is essentially commercial. Consequently, it is essential that the AMC be able to attract and retain employees with appropriate skills and motivate them to maximize recoveries on impaired assets as quickly as possible. One option is to have two components in the compensation package: salary and performance-based bonuses. It should be recognized that governments might have to pay salaries higher than those paid to civil servants in order to attract individuals with the necessary skills. Because these jobs are of limited duration, paying a premium over the civil service pay scale should be defensible. In addition, bonuses are a powerful tool to encourage both recovery maximization and speedy recoveries. A risk is that assets will be disposed of regardless of price just so employees can get a quick bonus. However, this can be mitigated by having proper approval procedures and establishing appropriate goals for individual assets. Just as an AMC's performance should be judged based on its recoveries compared to the original estimated recovery value, a similar approach should be used for establishing performance goals for employees and managers.

V. Operational issues

Even though AMCs in different countries may have different organizational structures, a common factor that is critical to satisfactory performance is the commercial orientation of an AMC's operations. Commercial orientation, in turn, depends critically on policies regarding selection of assets to be purchased or transferred, pricing of such assets, funding, and strategies for asset recovery.

Selection of assets

One of the first operational questions an AMC faces is whether it should buy assets from all banks, and what types of assets to buy from those banks. The ownership of the assets and the banks is often the key element in the decision. Some countries have chosen to acquire and sell assets only from banks that are being resolved by liquidation or merger, and hence under the ownership or control of the government. This was the case in Thailand[5] and the United States. Other countries also provide assistance to banks that are to remain open by buying their bad assets. For example, Indonesia, Korea, Malaysia, and Mexico have bought bad assets from open banks. When the government "owns" the selling bank and the AMC, the transaction is straightforward. Similarly, a private bank selling assets to an independent private AMC is involved in an arm's-length transaction that should be devoid of conflicts. The issue becomes more difficult when the transactions are between private banks and public AMCs.

When a public AMC purchases assets from open banks, a potential conflict arises between economizing limited resources and being fair to all banks. Buying bad assets only from troubled banks that are to receive government assistance could prejudice the competitiveness of those better banks that are still struggling unaided to handle their portfolio of bad loans. One way for the government to resolve this dilemma is to buy some, but not all, of the bad assets of assisted banks. The assisted banks should be left with roughly the same proportion of bad loans as the rest of the surviving industry. This was the compromise adopted by Sweden.[6] However, the structure of the banking sector also matters. For example, in countries where the assisted banks have relatively small market share the amount of loans purchased may not be an issue. In addition, in open bank assistance, it should be made clear that the purchase is a one-time deal, not to be repeated. An open-ended transfer arrangement could create moral hazard problems, undermining the credit discipline of the banks.

When handling all of the assets of failed banks, it is important to differentiate between the better quality loans and the impaired assets. Unimpaired performing loans will retain their value if left in the banking system and, consequently, should be transferred to other operating banks as quickly as possible. In the United States, the FDIC typically transfers the good loans to an assuming bank at the time of failure resolution. In Korea this was done through bridge banks, while in Thailand the assets of the closed finance companies were sold through public auctions.

If public AMCs have discretion in the choice of assets to purchase or take over, they should apply strict criteria in the selection of the assets. In principle, they should only take on those assets they are likely to manage more effectively. For example, fixed assets such as foreclosed properties and loans that require foreclosure or settlement with debtors are good candidates for transfer to AMCs. On the other hand, loans with potential for restructuring and those whose obligors are customers with whom the banks would like to maintain long-term relationships should be kept within the banks. Also, small credits whose recovery can be undertaken more efficiently by the bank branches where the credit originated should also be left with the banks. Danaharta in Malaysia, for example, applies a minimum threshold of RM 5 million (approximately $1.5 million) to the loans it will purchase. All banks are eligible to sell their impaired assets to Danaharta, but those with NPLs in excess of 10 percent of assets are strongly encouraged to reduce their NPL ratios.

Pricing

A realistic valuation/pricing of assets based on market pricing, sound accounting norms, strong loan classification and provisioning standards, and/or discounted present values, is crucial to the success of AMCs. The rigorous recognition of loan losses is the first and most important element of an effective strategy for dealing with problem assets, as it creates the right incentives for banks to restructure their loans, foreclose on collateral, and precipitate bankruptcy reorganizations.

The transfer of assets to AMCs, regardless of the methods of transfer, should be executed at fair market value. There are a number of reasons for doing so. First, private AMCs set up as subsidiaries of banks should not serve as a means by which the banks boost their capital by transferring their nonperforming assets at above market value to their AMCs.[7]

Second, AMCs should not serve as a means by which the government bails out private financial institutions by buying their nonperforming assets at above market value. Such a transaction helps recapitalize the institution, which, in effect, conceals the cost of recapitalization from the public and violates the principle of transparency and accountability. In addition, when the purchase price is above market value, financial institutions may end up selling to AMCs too large a number of their nonperforming assets.

Third, transferring assets to government-owned AMCs at fair market value provides a clear goal for the management and staff of the AMC. If they can return some of the original equity capital in the AMC, they have done a good job, assuming that market prices do not move in unexpected directions.

While it is often difficult to price nonperforming assets (especially in the midst of financial crises), an approximation of their value, based on the probability of recovery, cash flow projections, and appraisal of collateral, should be carried out and used for the purpose of the transfer. When timing is an issue, and there are a great number of assets involved, the transfer can take place at an initial price with the explicit agreement that the final price of the transaction be established after the value of the assets has been estimated or the assets have been sold. The drawback of this approach is that it may reduce the willingness of the sellers to part with the assets since they will still maintain their exposure to the final price of the assets. In this situation, some form of profit-loss sharing arrangement can help partially overcome this problem. This has been the practice of Danaharta in Malaysia.

Danaharta purchased impaired loans at an average discount of 55 percent. Banks selling to Danaharta retain a right to receive 80 percent of any recoveries in excess of their acquisition cost the AMC is able to realize from the loans. While banks retain the option of keeping NPLs on their balance sheet rather than selling to Danaharta, if they do so they must make a provision that brings the value of the NPL down to 80 percent of the offer price. There have been some cases in which banks have rejected the Danaharta offer, believing themselves better able to effect recovery of the loan.

Funding

It is important that public AMCs are sufficiently funded in order to perform their intended functions. At the same time, they should also be subject to hard budget constraints. Striking the right balance is a key consideration of the funding process. To achieve transparency, the operating budget of the AMCs should be separate from its funding for asset takeover. If the AMC is set up as an ordinary corporation the structure of its balance sheet determines both its funding requirements and longevity.

Funding for government-owned AMCs often comes from the proceeds of either government bond issues or AMCs' own bond issues backed by the government, with the proviso that, whenever the AMCs realize losses, the losses be directly absorbed by the budget. Although the latter expedient is sometimes preferred because it is more transparent, it is important, in countries where the government bond market is small, that the bonds issued by the AMCs do not lead to segmentation in the secondary markets for government and government-backed bonds. To avoid that situation, bonds issued by the AMCs should carry the same characteristics as existing government bonds and any issues should be closely coordinated with other government bond issues. When the financing needs of the AMC are large, representatives of the AMC could usefully take part in the government debt management committee.

The bonds that are issued to fund the AMC should have maturities that are consistent with both the legal life of the AMC and reasonable expectations about the cash flow generation capabilities of the AMC. To a large extent these will be influenced by the types of assets the AMC hold and economic conditions. If the bonds are to be tradable, one issue that will need to be considered is their tax treatment. If the bonds are government guaranteed and pay the same rate as government securities, investors will review them on a tax equivalent basis, thus suggesting they be given the same tax treatment.

An example of good funding practices are those of KAMCO where tradable bonds, paying interest semiannually, are issued with a government guarantee. Danaharta's funding is in the form of five-year maturity zero coupon bonds that carry a central government guarantee. There is an active secondary market in these bonds. By contrast, the funding structure for the Bank Fund for the Protection of Savings (FOBAPROA) in Mexico was not market based and was illiquid. The FOBAPROA was funded by ten-year promissory notes. Although these were backed by the government, they were not tradable instruments, and while interest accrued on the notes it was not payable until maturity.

Asset management and disposition

Strategies of asset management and disposition should be primarily a commercial decision and be guided by the goal of maximizing the value of assets by taking into account of market conditions as well as the funding cost of the AMCs. A number of countries established the goal of **maximizing the recovery value** on the transferred assets. A potential weakness in this approach is the lack of clarity with regard to the meaning of "recovery value." One interpretation is the maximization of the market value of the assets, regardless of the ultimate loss, and the other interpretation is the maximization of the book value of assets. The United States, when confronted with its Savings and Loan crisis, adopted by statute the goal of **maximizing the net present value** of the assets to be managed by the RTC and FDIC. This was an attempt to force the asset managers to recognize the time value of money in making decisions regarding the assets.

In Sweden, AMCs had to do the following calculation for each asset: if property prices are expected to climb gradually, what rate of yearly price increases are needed to compensate for the financial and other costs of holding on to the assets? If the required rate of increase is not judged to be realistic by property market experts, then the asset should be sold immediately. This simple method facilitated taking decisions leading to more rapid sales and also radically altered the time frame for the dismantling of the AMC.

There have been significant differences in the speed of disposition of assets among AMCs. Spain and the United States were relatively successful in disposing acquired assets rapidly. Similarly, Securum of Sweden disposed of 98 percent of its assets in the five years of its existence. By contrast, the fragile state of the Indonesian economy and the scale of the assets acquired by IBRA are among the factors that prevented the rapid disposition of assets in that country in early years. While IBRA did close down operations, in accordance with the sunset provision in the law, it transferred significant work to the ministry of finance.

VI. Conclusions

Proper management and disposition of nonperforming assets is one of the most critical and complex aspects of successful and speedy bank restructuring. The government's overarching objectives should be to maximize the value of the impaired assets in the system, while at the same time preventing credit discipline of borrowers from deteriorating. AMCs, with proper governance and incentive structures and sound operating strategies, could play an indispensable role in achieving the government's objectives.

In summary, this chapter makes the following arguments:

- As part of the crisis management process, AMCs provide a useful vehicle for the authorities to remove nonperforming loans from the banking system quickly, so that the banking system can resume its normal functions, including providing payment services which are crucial to all economic activities, as soon as possible.
- Probably the most important purpose of having AMCs is the managerial factor. Management of impaired assets requires banks to have commercial skills different from those needed for lending. Banks may also have to become actively involved in the management of firms and properties, a task that in many cases banks have neither the expertise nor the resources to undertake.
- No single model of AMCs would fit all country circumstances. The optimal strategy could also vary over time. There are, however, common factors that contribute to the success of AMCs. These include supporting legal and regulatory environment, strong leadership, operational independence, appropriately structured incentives, and commercial orientation.

- An AMC should have a strict profit-maximizing goal. In all its operations, it should act as a normal market participant. This goal should guide all its operational policies, including the valuation of assets, funding strategy, and speed of asset disposition.
- A critical factor in assuring an AMC's success and independence is the ability of the public and the government to evaluate its performance. This requires proper accounting for the assets at the time of transfer and for cash flows over time. Performance should be measured against either a "mark-to-market" value or an estimated recovery value at the time of transfer.

Notes

1. See Klingebiel (2000) for a listing of objectives for AMCs in different countries.
2. Subsequent to the crisis, a government-owned centralized AMC, the Thai Asset Management Corporation, was set up in 2001 to purchase NPLs from open banks.
3. This was done to prevent associates of some of the failed banks from setting up private AMCs, which could have circumvented rules for pricing and prudent governance.
4. They could personally be sued by borrowers or potential purchasers who are unhappy with the decisions of the AMC and wish to apply pressure to management.
5. This was the case during the crisis. However, the more recently established government-owned AMC can purchase assets from open banks.
6. See Ingves and Lind (1997).
7. Consolidated supervision is necessary to prevent private financial institutions from using their AMC subsidiaries as a means to boost their capital positions artificially by transferring their assets to the AMCs at too high a price.

Bibliography

Enoch, Charles, Gillian Garcia, and V. Sundararajan, 1999, "Recapitalizing Banks with Public Funds: Selected Issues," IMF Working Paper 99/139 (Washington: International Monetary Fund).

Ingves, Stefan, and Dong He, 2000, "Facilitating Bank and Corporate Restructuring: The Role of Government," in Adams and others.

Ingves, Stefan, and Goran Lind, 1997, "Loan Loss Recoveries and Debt Resolution Agencies: The Swedish Experiences," in Charles Enoch and John Green (eds.), *Banking Soundness and Monetary Policy* (Washington: International Monetary Fund).

Klingebiel, Daniela, 2000, "The Use of Asset Management Companies in the Resolution of Banking Crises: Cross-Country Experience," World Bank Policy Research Paper No. 2284 (Washington: World Bank).

Lindgren, Carl-Johan and others, 1999, *Financial Sector Crisis and Restructuring: Lessons from Asia* (Washington: International Monetary Fund).

Woo, David, 2000, "Two Approaches to Resolving Nonperforming Assets During Financial Crises," IMF Working Paper 00/33 (Washington: International Monetary Fund).

Part IV
Country Experiences

Part IV

Country perspectives

10
From the Front Lines at Seoul Bank: Restructuring and Reprivatization

Chungwon Kang[1]

I. Introduction

This chapter is a personal account of a banker who was given the rare opportunity to apply his knowledge of western banking and management practices to a distressed Korean commercial bank. Before joining Seoul Bank, I had worked at major international banks for two decades, mostly in Seoul—five years at Citibank, 15 years at Bankers Trust Company, and one year at Deutsche Bank after its acquisition of Bankers Trust in June 1999. Early in the 1997–98 financial crisis, the Korean government recapitalized Seoul Bank, effectively nationalizing it. Following several unsuccessful attempts to sell or transfer management responsibilities for Seoul Bank, the government appointed me Chief Executive Officer (CEO) on May 24, 2000. I became the first professional banker from a non-Korean bank to assume leadership of a Korean bank. My mission was to fix the bank and prepare it for reprivatization.

Two and a half years later, on November 1, 2002, I left Seoul Bank after signing a merger agreement with the Korea Deposit Insurance Corporation (KDIC) and Hana Bank, which bought 100 percent of the shares of Seoul Bank, at terms satisfactory to KDIC, the government shareholder. I was pleased that the fruits of Seoul Bank's two-year restructuring efforts attracted enough commercial interest that the government could finally negotiate the terms of sale from a position of strength. This was accomplished more or less within the time frame that I had set when I assumed the position. And I was grateful to the management team I had assembled at Seoul Bank and to the members of Seoul Bank's board of directors for sharing with me the sense of mission throughout the bumpy ride; and to those Seoul Bank employees and government officials who had trusted in my professional judgment and common sense, and persevered with me to the end.

To write about my Seoul Bank experience during a visit to the IMF in early 2003 seems a fitting end to that experience, partly because I took the job with a sense of public service. I am thankful to the IMF's Asia and Pacific Department and Monetary and Financial Systems Department, not only for this opportunity to record my experience but also for the keen interest Fund staff took in Seoul Bank's progress during my tenure. The continuing interest in the bank by the IMF Resident Representative office in Seoul and Fund missions to Korea was a source of significant encouragement to the management team at Seoul Bank, particularly in the early stage of our efforts.

What follows is mainly a record of Seoul Bank's restructuring efforts in the context of the Korean government's financial sector restructuring program, which was supported by the IMF after the 1997–98 crisis. I hope that this account of how a particular bank was turned around will be useful to policymakers and practitioners struggling to fix distressed banks in crisis situations.

II. Background

To understand the challenge of restructuring Seoul Bank, it is important to know some of the history of Seoul Bank and the previous attempts to deal with Seoul Bank's problems.

Seoul Bank before the crisis

In 1959, local entrepreneurs established the Bank of Seoul as a regional bank. Following a merger with Korea Trust Bank in 1976—the first bank merger in Korea—the new Bank of Seoul and Trust Company grew to become one of the largest commercial banks in terms of asset size by the late 1980s. However, the merger also left a lasting scar on the bank as cloak-and-dagger rivalry between the two factions continued well into the mid-1990s, disrupting management coherence and distracting employees from their work. The bank's name was changed to Seoul Bank in 1995, the year the bank recorded a small net income before sinking into a financial quagmire. A historical summary of Seoul Bank's financials and overall size is presented in Table 10.1.

Seoul Bank's financial problems surfaced in 1996 with the bankruptcies of several second tier business groups, for which Seoul Bank was the main creditor bank. At the end of 1996, Seoul Bank's stated nonperforming assets amounted to 9 percent of total assets, and it recorded a W 167 billion loss for the year.[2] In November 1996, the CEO of Seoul Bank was arrested on bribery charges and the managing director was appointed interim CEO. The fall of Daenong group in May 1997 further squeezed the bank. After nine months with an interim management team, the government appointed a former Deputy Superintendent of Banks as the new CEO in August 1997. The bank closed the year with a W 917 billion net loss.

Table 10.1. Seoul Bank: Historical Summary Table
(In billions of won; unless otherwise stated)

	1995	1996	1997	1998	1999	2000.6	2000.12	2001	2002.9
Total assets	35,000	38,300	40,900	32,800	26,800	24,200	20,400	23,400	26,100
Bank account	23,400	25,300	30,000	24,900	22,100	20,300	19,100	21,700	25,200
Trust account	11,600	12,900	10,800	7,900	4,700	3,900	1,300	1,600	1,600
KAMCO sale									
Face amount	...	...	1,960	1,040	4,560	...	...	868	...
Net proceeds	...	...	1,380	500	1,150	...	...	350	...
Net worth	1,372	1,202	702	266	1,044	798	551	686	903
Government recapitalization	...	...	...	1,500	3,320	...	611	...	...
Government contribution	...	...	...	...	...	...	222	...	...
Net income after tax	0	-167	-917	-2,242	-2,233	0	-520	101	136
Number of employees	8,668	8,303	7,511	4,809	4,707	4,643	3,920	3,886	3,848
Number of branches	347	363	365	295	295	295	295	294	290
(Overseas branches)	8	8	8	4	4	4	4	3	3
Memorandum item:									
Won–dollar exchange rate (end of period)	775.7	844.9	1,695	1,204	1,138	1,115	1,264.5	1,313.5	1,227.8

In the second half of 1998, two large construction companies—Dong-Ah Construction and Woobang Construction—were put into "voluntary" workout programs in the context of the government's corporate restructuring program. Seoul Bank was the main creditor bank for both, with exposures amounting to W 984 billion and W 171 billion, respectively, at the end of 1998, and only puny reserves set aside for both exposures. In August 1999, 12 Daewoo Group companies were also put into "voluntary" workout programs. The bank's net loss swelled to W 2.2 trillion in 1998 and stayed at that level in 1999 as charges related to nonperforming loans (NPLs) mounted. Accumulated losses from 1996 to the end of 1999 were W 5.5 trillion.

Seoul Bank's NPL-related charges in 1998–99 totaled W 4.7 trillion: W 3.4 trillion for higher provisioning requirements from more strict standards for loan classifications, including the introduction of forward-looking criteria in 1999 (W 1.7 trillion) and from new bankruptcies (W 1.7 trillion); and W 1.3 trillion loss from sales of under-reserved NPLs to Korea Asset Management Company (KAMCO). Two recapitalizations by the government in January 1998 and September 1999, totaling W 4.8 trillion, covered reserve shortfalls and losses from NPL sales.

Seoul Bank's failure may be traced to the accumulated damages from:

- structurally weak management from two decades of factional in-fighting;
- the tradition in Korean banking that emphasized the role of banks as providers of credit for industrial development, which resulted in banks with weak commercial orientation and limited risk management discipline for self-protection; and
- generally lax prudential regulations—for example, the Bank of Korea's Bank Supervision Office had general supervisory authority, but the legal lending limit for single obligor did not apply to banks' lending through Trust Accounts, which were supervised by the ministry of finance; and
- the absence of a governance structure for banking, except for the role of the government as supervisor, regulator, and policymaker. The government's ability to exercise control of the banking industry, including the ability to appoint bank CEOs, was facilitated by the Banking Law, which prevented controlling ownership by limiting single-investor ownership in banks to 4 percent.

Given the environment in which it operated, Seoul Bank was a not-so-innocent victim of unfortunate circumstances.

Seoul Bank in the IMF-supported program

Seoul Bank was singled out from the very beginning of Korea's IMF-supported program as one of the two most distressed nationwide commercial banks that needed to be nationalized first and then sold. In the addendum to the letter of intent (LOI) dated December 24, 1997, the Korean government committed to place Seoul Bank and Korea First Bank (KFB) under intensive supervision by the Bank Supervision Office, and to assume control of both banks and remove management responsible for losses by February 25, 1998.[3]

Both banks were nationalized through a mandatory reduction of capital and subsequent government recapitalization in January 1998. After an 8 to 1 reverse stock split, KDIC and the ministry of finance and economy (MOFE) injected W 750 billion each, for a total of W 1.5 trillion, to each of the two banks, resulting in 93.4 percent government ownership.

The first quarterly review of the program in February 1998 noted the following agreement between the Korean government and the IMF with respect to the two banks: "to appoint a lead manager/advisor to develop privatization strategy for the two banks by March 31 and to obtain bids for both banks by November 15, 1998, coinciding with the seventh drawdown date of the IMF facility and the Fourth Quarter Review date." In almost all subsequent quarterly reviews, the IMF and the government would address the timing issue regarding the reprivatization of the two banks, almost always setting a very tight deadline.

In May 1998, Morgan Stanley was appointed as lead manager/advisor for the privatization of both banks. KDIC and Newbridge Consortium signed a terms of investment agreement in September 1999 and the transaction was closed in December 1999. This was, in substance, a 51:49 joint-venture transaction with full management control of KFB given to Newbridge. KDIC, the government partner, provided full protection against the old loan portfolio of the bank—often referred to as a "put-back option"—for a maximum of three years. A new CEO for KFB—the first foreign CEO of a Korean bank—was appointed in January 2000. Coming two years after the nationalization of KFB, this was a relatively quick sale that required the government to protect Newbridge against the uncertain quality of the old portfolio.

In contrast, negotiations with the Hong Kong and Shanghai Banking Corporation (HSBC) for Seoul Bank, which started in February 1999, officially broke down in early September 1999, reportedly due to HSBC's insistence on taking much more than a 51 percent share in the bank and unbridgeable differences in the valuation and classifications of Seoul Bank's loan portfolio. In late September, the government injected a second round of new capital into the bank to fill the hole that had grown much larger since the initial recapitalization one and a half years earlier. With this second recapitalization, and in the absence of interested buyers capable of meeting the government's minimum requirements, Seoul Bank, by default, drifted slowly into a fix and sell mode.

In April 2000, Deutsche Bank was appointed as financial and restructuring advisor for Seoul Bank, and in May a new CEO was appointed. In the combined seventh and eighth reviews on July 12, 2000, which were the final reviews of Korea's IMF-supported program, the Korean government defined the role of the new management as follows: "The new management of Seoul Bank, on the basis of the review currently being conducted by Deutsche Bank, will prepare the bank for privatization." In the same review, the government also assured the IMF that: "While under government ownership, banks will be operated on a fully commercial basis and the government will not be involved in the day-to-day management."

However, as illustrated below, the trappings that came with government ownership did not allow the management to operate the bank on a fully commercial basis.

Seoul Bank in the context of banking sector restructuring

With the inauguration of the new President in late February 1998, the government's message to the weakened commercial banks was loud and clear: in order to receive government help and survive, they either had to raise new capital or merge, while undertaking serious internal restructuring. Based on the fifth LOI dated February 7, twelve banks not meeting the 8 percent Bank for International Settlements (BIS) capital adequacy ratio at the end of 1997 were asked to submit management improvement plans, including capital raising plans, by the end of April. Following a review by an independent management evaluation committee, the newly created Financial Supervisory Commission (FSC) closed five regional banks at the end of June by transferring their assets and liabilities to stronger banks in a purchase and assumption (P&A) transaction. These were the first bank closures in the country's history. Subsequently, there were four merger announcements and one FSC-ordered merger by February 1999. The largest merger during this period was between Hanil Bank and the Commercial Bank of Korea. KDIC injected W 3.3 trillion into the two banks in September 1998, and the merger was completed in January 1999, creating Hanvit Bank. This first stage of banking sector restructuring saw five bank closures and five bank mergers.

By early 1999, the Korean government had become a major shareholder of five nationwide commercial banks—Seoul Bank, KFB, Chohung Bank, Hanvit Bank, and Korea Exchange Bank. Seoul Bank and KFB, in agreement with the IMF, were on a separate track for an early sale to foreign investors. Of the three remaining banks, Hanvit Bank's new CEO, from Koram Bank, struggled during most of 1999 with integration issues; Chohung Bank's management was allowed to stay on and acquired two regional banks during the first stage of banking sector restructuring; and Korea Exchange Bank, which raised new capital of W 350 billion from Commerz Bank in July 1998, received matching support from the government in November, but struggled with its large exposures to the Hyundai Group.

In late August 2000, the FSC launched a second stage of banking sector restructuring by instructing six banks to submit management improvement plans by the end of September. The six banks were Hanvit, Chohung Bank,

Korea Exchange Bank, Peace Bank, Kwangju Bank, and Cheju Bank. These banks either had less than the 8 percent BIS capital adequacy ratio as of June 30, 2000, or had received public funds but were still considered weak. The majority of KFB had already been reprivatized, and Seoul Bank was exempted from this process because of the ongoing Deutsche Bank restructuring advisory process and in view of the rehabilitation plan being drawn up by the two-month-old management team. However, some time before October 2000 when the Financial Holding Company Act was legislated, Seoul Bank's journey on a separate track started to be challenged in the context of Korea's "graduation" from the IMF program with the early repayment of IMF loans in July 2000; growing criticism of the government for having sold KFB too cheaply to foreign investors; continuing pressure to consolidate banks; and the resulting new question: "Is Seoul Bank big enough to survive, even when it is sold?" Rumors that Seoul Bank might be put into a bank holding company started to circulate.

The review of the six banks' management improvement plans was completed in October. In early November, the FSC announced that Hanvit Bank, Peace Bank, Kwangju Bank, and Cheju Bank were nonviable without an additional injection of public funds. KDIC conducted a separate financial due diligence on Seoul Bank based on the end-September balance sheet to determine the amount of recapitalization necessary. Gyungnam Bank was also determined nonviable in an Financial Supervisory Service (FSS) inspection in late November. All six banks were determined insolvent as of end of September 2000 and KDIC injected a total of W 4.1 trillion at the end of 2000 to raise their BIS capital adequacy ratios to 10 percent, following a complete reduction of capital for each bank (Table 10.2).

Table 10.2. Recapitalization of Korean Banks—December 2000
(In billions of won)

	Hanvit	Seoul	Kwangju	Cheju	Peace	Gyungnam	Total
Capital injection	2,764.4	610.8	170.4	53.1	273.0	259.0	4,130.7
Contributions[a]	1,877.6	221.6	273.1	161.5	338.9	94.0	2,970.3
Total	4,642.0	832.4	443.5	214.6	611.9	353.0	7,101.0

[a] Contributions covered the deficiency in net worth as of end of September 2000 as well as any stock valuation and trading losses of each bank between end-September and end-November 2000. KDIC issued IOUs for the contribution portion and funded the IOUs in September 2001. This two-step recapitalization was required by the Special Law for Public Funds Management, legislated in December 2000.

Korea Exchange Bank and Chohung Bank, which did not ask for additional public funds in their management improvement plans, were given conditional approvals to pursue their plans.

The government announced in late December that, in conjunction with the upcoming recapitalizations for the six banks, a financial holding company would be established in early 2001, and that Hanvit Bank, Peace Bank, Kwangju Bank, and Gyungnam Bank would be included in it. The four banks became subsidiaries of Woori Finance Holding Company in April 2001.[4] Cheju Bank was put under management supervision of Shinhan Bank until Shinhan Bank created its own holding company.

In the same announcement, the government gave Seoul Bank a six-month window in which to escape inclusion in the financial holding company: if the bank was not sold to foreign investors by end of June 2001, Seoul Bank would be put in the financial holding company. Seoul Bank was coming off its separate track.

Korean government efforts to deal with Seoul Bank

Up until September 1999, when negotiations with HSBC for the sale of Seoul Bank broke down, the IMF and the Korean government treated both Seoul Bank and Korea First Bank as nonviable banks earmarked for early sale. The government's financial support to keep the two banks afloat was also similar in form and substance (Table 10.3).

On December 22, 1997, both Seoul Bank and KFB were placed under prompt corrective action in preparation for recapitalization. Later in December, the government purchased some subordinate debt issued by the two banks to raise the banks' year-end BIS ratios. The initial W 1.5 trillion recapitalization in January 1998 was made jointly and equally by KDIC (in cash) and MOFE (in shares of government-owned corporations). This was preceded by an 8 to 1 share reduction of existing public shareholders, resulting in post-recapitalization shareholding in each bank of 46.7 percent by KDIC, 46.7 percent by MOFE, and 6.6 percent by the public.

Morgan Stanley, appointed in May 1998 as the government's advisor for privatization strategy and sale of both banks, offered both banks for sale in the same auction process. Only HSBC and the Newbridge Consortium showed interest, but only in KFB. The potential investors considered KFB to have a better branch network, a better corporate client list, and better manpower than Seoul Bank. On December 31, 1998, a memorandum of understanding (MOU) was signed with Newbridge for the sale of KFB, and the transaction was closed at the end of December 1999. Newbridge paid about W 500 billion to take a 51 percent share and management control, while the government kept 49 percent and provided a put-back option for the existing portfolio of KFB. In February 1999, the government signed an MOU with HSBC for the sale of Seoul Bank. However, negotiations with HSBC fell through in August 1999.[5]

Seoul Bank was insolvent again by June 1999. And immediately after the breakdown of discussions with HSBC in August, the government undertook a second round of recapitalization, twice the size of the first one, in September

Table 10.3. Korea: Government Financial Support
(In billions of won)

	Seoul Bank				Korea First Bank			
	Recap.	NPL Purchase	Sub-Debt Purchase	Total	Recap.	NPL Purchase	Sub-Debt Purchase	Total
1997								
November[a]	...	1,383	...	1,383	...	1,527		1,527
December	...	...	270	270	...	...	142	142
1998								
January	1,500	...	...	1,500	1,500	...		1,500
July	...	499	...	499	...	607		607
1999								
July	3,320	1,154	...	4,474	4,209	897		5,106
September	...	...	...	...	...	...		...
Total	**4,820**	**3,036**	**270**	**8,126**	**5,709**	**3,031**	**142**	**8,882**

[a] The November 1997 purchase of NPLs by KAMCO from the two banks represented the first KAMCO purchases from the newly created "Nonperforming Assets Fund."

1999. Following a complete share reduction for public shareholders, KDIC injected W 3.3 trillion in Seoul Bank, resulting in a 93.6 percent ownership. MOFE did not participate in this recapitalization, and its share was diluted to 6.4 percent. The incumbent CEO resigned after the second recapitalization and his deputy was appointed as interim CEO. Not by design, the strategy for Seoul Bank was changing to something like "fix and sell."

In October, Morgan Stanley started to contact large international banks for interest in a management contract, with a small minority stake in the bank, to operate Seoul Bank. At the same time, Morgan Stanley subcontracted the search for a CEO to an international human resources firm. In the absence of any serious interest, the idea of a management contract was scrapped in January 2000, and the search for a CEO intensified. Also in January, Deutsche Bank began to market the idea of a restructuring advisory for Seoul Bank to the government. Deutsche Bank had already been engaged by the Indonesian government to restructure Bank Mandiri, a government-owned bank created by the merger of four banks. This track record gave credibility to its proposal.

On March 23, 2000, newspapers reported that President Kim had instructed the FSC chairman to achieve a prompt normalization of Seoul Bank. The following day, Seoul Bank's interim CEO resigned and the next officer in the hierarchy became the interim CEO. Having exhausted most alternatives, and under pressure from the very top to "normalize" the problem of Seoul Bank, the government decided to hire Deutsche Bank as restructuring advisors. On April 16, KDIC and Seoul Bank signed a Financial and Restructuring Advisory Agreement with Deutsche Bank. Deutsche Bank was also mandated to find a new CEO. Deutsche Bank contracted a human resources firm to search and evaluate the candidates. In late May a new CEO was appointed, after an eight-month vacuum in management.

What emerges from this background is a picture of a bank that had lacked stable management and direction since November 1996. There were three interim CEOs and one regular CEO in the four-and-a-half-year period to May 2000. Interim CEOs are by definition temporary caretakers without authority to provide a vision for the bank. Frequent changes at the top exacerbated instability. Since the initial bailout in January 1998, the bank had been completely dependent on the government's continuing financial support for its survival. Indeed, the government's commitment to the survival of Seoul Bank was the only positive attribute of the bank in the market place during this period. And the government shareholder, under pressure from, and in conjunction with the IMF and the World Bank, struggled to find a viable strategy and direction for the bank until the spring of 2000.

During this period of extreme uncertainty and instability, which lasted more than three years, the bank was bound to become alienated and inward-looking:

- The management became alienated from its shareholder government, particularly when the bank was headed by interim CEOs, and perhaps from the employees as well, because of its inability to provide direction.
- The uncertain future and tight conditions in the rehabilitation plans that preceded each recapitalization led to many interim decisions and an extreme cut back on investments, including in people.
- Customers became alienated from the bank due to the deteriorating quality of customer service and frequent postponements in announced target dates for the sale of the bank, for a management contract, and for a new CEO.
- A general feeling of helplessness and neglect prevailed, giving rise to an increasingly active labor union.

III. Restructuring in practice

The restructuring process began with the appointment of the new CEO and the formation of a new management team. The process encompassed all operational aspects of the bank, including relations with its employees and labor union; restructuring its balance sheet, which required a final recapitalization by KDIC in December 2000; and the creation of a new culture and image for the bank. The restructuring process was more or less complete by the middle of 2001 when the last Deutsche Bank credit specialist seconded to the bank left.

CEO selection and formation of the management team

Deutsche Bank initiated the search for a CEO for Seoul Bank in April 2000 through an international human resources firm, which defined the job description and evaluation process. The prospects were not promising. During Morgan Stanley's six-month search for the same position, everyone worth looking at—both Koreans and foreigners—was looked at. A few individuals whom the government wanted were not interested. The government rejected the initial list of candidates interviewed and evaluated by the human resources firm in late April. I volunteered to be included in the second round of interviews in early May. Reportedly, three new candidates were interviewed. Based on the recommendation of the human resources firm, I was selected. This was the first time that a CEO of a government-owned bank in Korea was selected through a process managed by an international human resources firm.

Although not in writing, I requested from my government counterpart—and was assured of—complete management autonomy, including selection of the new management team, and the prompt injection of the necessary amount of public funds based on Deutsche Bank's financial due diligence on Seoul Bank.

My decision to ask for an interview for the job was based on three considerations:

- I convinced myself that I had the necessary qualifications of management experience and exposure to international best practices in banking, as well as a sense of mission.
- Deutsche Bank had already been engaged as financial and restructuring advisors for Seoul Bank; I knew Deutsche Bank, and knew that I could rely on them for the nuts and bolts of restructuring.
- I was vaguely confident that I could bring together enough professionals with appropriate expertise, background in international best practices, and shared sense of mission into my management team.

I believed that the formation of the management team would be key to successful restructuring. I had learned the importance of having a like-minded and well-qualified management team for successful banking operations in the private sector. The challenge lying ahead required massive and speedy managerial input into every aspect of the bank's existing operations, including building a new culture focused on business and performance. It would be critical to bring in as many professionals with the necessary expertise as possible, and to maintain close and unwavering teamwork.

Having been notified of the government's selection in mid-May, I did not have enough time to lock in anyone before I moved into the bank on June 1. I recruited the first member of my management team from Citibank in mid-June, and during the following six months, one of my main preoccupations was to identify and speak to the candidates.

By early December, we had a professional management team of seven, not only with the necessary skill sets required at the bank but also with enough background and commitment to international best practices: two had over 20 years of experience at Citibank, one American had been a branch manager of First Chicago in Seoul, one had experience both at JP Morgan and at a trading company, one had extensive IT experience at U.S. insurance companies and a large Korean bank, and two had worked in rating agencies. Each additional member was "interviewed" by those who had joined earlier, and only those with unanimous backing were invited to join the team. We shared the goal of fixing the bank together and turning it around quickly, so that privatization could take place as soon as possible. We also shared, at least in the initial stage, the sense that our efforts at Seoul Bank, if successful, would make a meaningful contribution to the government's own efforts in the last phase of banking sector restructuring. This somewhat naïve thought evaporated quite quickly in the face of a seeming disregard of our efforts in most quarters of the government; but it was not altogether a false thought in hindsight.

The bank was not functionally organized before I joined. About six management team members shared the branch network based on seniority, with good areas or branches going to senior directors. Functional responsibilities were added to such geographic coverage, without much regard for required functional expertise. While such expertise was generally in short supply, the disregard for matching expertise to positions was, at times, extreme.

A week after I moved into the bank, I asked the existing directors to resign, except for one, who was kept for continuity's sake. In addition, I kept the standing auditor, who was also a member of the board and whose two-year term was to expire in March 2001. My first recruit joined in mid-June and we started to share responsibilities. In October, following a 640- person redundancy program, we made two in-house promotions to management positions. By December 2000, management responsibilities were more or less fully and functionally delegated, according to a functional organization chart drawn up with the assistance of Deutsche Bank advisors, to the management team composed of seven from outside and three from inside. The outside management team, however, frequently held separate meetings to discuss restructuring issues and kept much longer work hours.

By early 2001, the employees had generally accepted the new management team's dedication and expertise. Team work matured rapidly in the environment of intense work pressures and was effective, at least in the eyes of the employees used to factional in-fighting at the management level, and management's work hours became more normal.

Restructuring Seoul Bank required more or less a complete overhaul of the bank. In early group meetings with senior managers, I likened the work in front of us to transforming an old vacuum tube radio into a new transistor radio, referring to the need to change the control system, the circuitry, and the look and the size of the radio.

Operational restructuring

As an addendum to the April 2000 Financial and Restructuring Agreement, we signed an Implementation Services Agreement with Deutsche Bank on June 30, 2000. Based on this, about 20 Deutsche Bank commercial bankers with expertise in a variety of areas were mobilized throughout the month of July to camp out in Seoul Bank.

Our operational restructuring efforts were based on Deutsche Bank advisors and their close hand-holding of Seoul Bank staff members assigned to the project teams. The success of their efforts depended on the staff members' enthusiasm to learn quickly the new systems and procedures, and propagate the knowledge to others. The new management team was fully involved in the process and supported the employees with training sessions. Management also kept the board and the shareholder updated on the progress.

The Deutsche Bank advisory group consisted of a small team of investment bankers accountable to Seoul Bank's management for the quality of the restructuring advisory work and a large team of commercial bankers, headed by a senior banker as overall project manager. We endeavored to assign enthusiastic and smart Seoul Bank employees to the project teams. In mid-July, 13 project teams were launched with one or two Deutsche Bank advisors as project leaders and three to five Seoul Bank staff assigned to each team in the following areas: retail banking and operations, international banking, international trade operations, treasury and market risk management, trust banking, investment trust, securities service (share registrar), credit risk management, accounting and control, audit, compliance, logistics, and information technology.

We removed several items from the original list proposed by Deutsche Bank, such as strategy and branch reorganization, as we thought that we could address the items better by ourselves. Under the guidance of the project leader, each team reviewed existing procedures and organizations of the assigned department or function, mapped out new procedures and organizational structures, presented recommendations to management, and assisted the executive in charge to implement the recommendations signed off by management. In the process, the project managers worked on a "train the trainer" concept to transfer knowledge to members of the Seoul Bank restructuring team. Most projects were completed by early 2001. The accounting and control project, which included building a system for database management and a system for management information reporting, dragged into May when the implementation service agreement expired.

Credit risk management restructuring implementation was overseen by a team of three Deutsche Bank commercial bank credit specialists seconded to work inside Seoul Bank from July 2000 to July 2001. They provided legitimacy to the many changes made to the infrastructure and the process of credit risk management, and were used as a mechanism to defend the bank against several requests for credit extension under collective arrangements, such as the System of Prompt Underwriting of Corporate Bonds introduced in late 2000 to help Hyundai Group companies.

Until December 2000, the management team met with the Deutsche Bank project team heads every Thursday to update and fine-tune the work in progress. Each Deutsche Bank project team head also had free access to the management team member responsible for the department or function. In 2001, the joint meetings became bi-weekly, with more frequent discussions between the project teams and appropriate management members. Throughout the process, periodic updates were presented to the board and the shareholder on the progress being made in operational restructuring.

By early 2001, we completed implementation of the following key concepts of international best practice in banking:

- created a functional organization structure, consisting of three business divisions of retail banking, corporate banking, and trust business; and five support divisions of planning, operations, accounting, credit, and information technology;

- created an independent and consolidated credit department;
- segregated the duties between front office and back office;
- established specialized business lines, separating retail from corporate banking business;
- overhauled the system of branch banking by segregating front-office and back-office functions in each branch, and appointing one group of officers for corporate banking and one for retail banking business;
- instituted process mapping and manualization of operational functions for controlled back-office operations;
- introduced an audit system based on systems and procedures; and
- created a management information system and strengthened the risk management system.

Seoul Bank employees

Subsequent to the first government recapitalization in January 1998, the bank undertook several self-help measures. These included the sale of its training center, cutting the number of overseas branches from eight to four in 1998, and a massive redundancy program that reduced the workforce by some 35 percent from 7,500 to 4,800 by the end of 1998. The average headcount reduction among Korean commercial banks in 1998 was 34 percent. In June 2000, the total headcount of the bank was 4,643, of which about 80 percent were union members. The bank had an effectively closed union shop, and employees in grades 4 and below (those without authorized signing power) all belonged to the union, except for a few in sensitive positions such as the CEO's office and the human resources and planning departments. The leader of Seoul Bank's union was a key member of the Korean Federation of Financial Unions, whose influence grew during the crisis. It was obvious that we had to deal with this internal political force in order to effect change quickly.

In spite of the significant headcount reduction in 1998, the bank's ratio of loans (or assets) per employee was among the lowest in the industry, as the asset size of the bank had shrunk more than 40 percent, from W 40.9 trillion at the end of 1997 to W 24.2 trillion at the end of June 2000. There were internal talks about the bank being too top-heavy and a further reduction in headcount seemed generally expected. The questions were how many, who, when, and how. Answers to these questions were all subject to negotiations with the labor union.

At the first meeting with the union leader during my first few days in office, we agreed on the urgent need for a drastic change. This meeting of the minds was quite encouraging. However, the Federation of Financial Unions was organizing a general strike and a rally for July 11. The Federation's agenda was to seek a guarantee of stable employment, to stop government intervention in bank management, and to oppose the government's plan to form a financial holding company. To my surprise, Seoul Bank's union decided to participate in the strike, albeit with the assurance that the union would cooperate so that all of our branches would remain open and running during the strike. I could not understand how the labor union of a bank that was practically bedridden, despite two heavy shots of government recapitalization and a new CEO, and was making a last desperate effort to stand up, could join a street protest against the government and still expect customers to use the bank. The government and supervisors, on the other hand, were not surprised that Seoul Bank's union, which had earned a reputation as being very active, was participating.

Almost all commercial banks joined the strike on July 11, with banks having public funds and facing the possibility of being put into the financial holding company taking particularly active roles. The strike was over by the end of the day; the Seoul Bank union was one of the last unions to withdraw. This was a very frustrating moment for the new management. A few days later, we assembled senior managers in the Seoul area and I gave a "show-me-your-will-to-live" speech: the new management team was prepared to operate on the bank—a sick patient—but would not start the operation until the patient demonstrated a will to live. It was a very awkward meeting; I just had to shock them back to reality. They did not know what was expected of them and I did not know what to expect. The next day, the union leader came by to confirm his support for the new management's restructuring efforts, and we agreed in principle to implement an early retirement program (ERP) as soon as possible (Table 10.4).

Table 10.4.   Seoul Bank: Early Retirement Program, September 2000
(Number of employees; unless otherwise stated)

	Grade 1	Grade 2	Grade 3	Grade 4	Clerical	Others	Total
Pre-ERP	32	172	440	1,821	2,082	80	4,627
Number of reduction	30	78	135	345	56	1	645
Post-ERP	2	94	305	1,476	2,026	79	3,982
Reduction ratio (in percent)	94	45	31	19	3	1	14

The ERP included an informal arrangement in which all employees born in or before 1948—most of the head office general managers and regional managers—would take the redundancy package, which averaged about 15 additional months' pay. Cruel as it seemed, this was accepted as a practical way of avoiding the difficult process of selecting who was to stay and who was to leave among the most senior employees—most grade-one and quite a few grade-two officers. The program was completed in late September, preceded by a massive personnel change throughout the organization. Some 80 percent of the department heads left through the program and were replaced by younger grade-two or grade-three officers; 275 of 290 branch managers were replaced.

Toward the end of September, a training center in the head office building was completed, a project started in late July. Conveniently located on the second floor, the training center had a capacity for 340 people in eight rooms. It also had a mock branch layout for customer service training. With the new training center and the completion of the redundancy program, we were set to train staff. Initially, the training center offered a mandatory class in basic English for all head office department heads (as the bank was then supposed to be sold to foreign investors), and a four-hour class in international best practices, a program developed and tailored to Seoul Bank's needs by a professional corporate-culture building firm. The program was essentially an initiation course in market-orientation, highlighting the relationships among shareholders, management, employees, and customers—the key message being that the bank owed its existence to the shareholders and depended on customers for business and growth—and providing examples of international best practice organizations and behaviors that we needed to embrace going forward. In a room large enough to hold about 100 people, we started with the management team and head office department heads and then ran the program for the remaining work force, including security guards. In all, 40 sessions were held between October and early November. As a result, international best practice, or IBP, became a common phrase of substance among Seoul Bank employees.

Balance sheet restructuring

The speedy and thorough clean up of NPLs and minimization of market risks on the bank's balance sheet were top priorities for the management team, particularly the chief credit office and the chief financial officer. The bank had the highest NPL ratio among banks at the end of June 2000—20 percent—and insufficient reserves. To regain credibility in the market and earn customer confidence, we had to clean up the balance sheet quickly. This priority was also dictated by the need for additional and final recapitalization by the government, for which management had to prepare. After instructing to liquidate immediately W 50 billion worth of Korean stock in the trading portfolio in late June, it became my weekly routine for the remainder of 2000 to press the chief credit officer and the chief financial officer for speedy disposition of impaired assets, for strict loan classifications, and for provisioning of adequate reserves. During the second half of 2000, we charged close to W 1 trillion to credit reserves. The credit reserve balance for the whole year 2000 was W 1.4 trillion, enough to write off most of the bad assets in 2001. The July 2000 LOI with the IMF, which included termination of forbearance regarding loan loss reserves related to "voluntary" workout credits by December 31, 2000, also helped this process. By allowing a below-market rate of provisioning for workout credits—between 2 and 20 percent regardless of the true credit risk—the forbearance had encouraged banks to put bad companies into workout programs. As this forbearance was lifted, we began to reclassify workout credits and charge appropriate reserve amounts for the 2000 year-end book closing.

The first sale of impaired assets consisted of foreign currency loans and securities for non-Korean obligors. Through secondary-market brokers, an exposure of US$128 million to obligors in eight different countries was disposed starting in October, leaving US$104 million exposure in three countries, mostly yen exposure to Korean-Japanese businesses in Japan, with a 56 percent provision, by the end of 2000. In addition, US$128 million of securities issued by Korean companies was sold or redeemed during the second half of 2000, with the remaining balance in this portfolio category valued at US$52 million at the end of 2000.

In June 2000, Seoul Bank was a main bank for, and had exposure to, five companies in "voluntary" workout programs. These companies had been put into the programs between 1998 and early 1999. Creditor institutions followed a 75 percent consent rule regarding proposals by and for these companies. The lead bank for each company was expected to take a leading role within each creditor committee. Seoul Bank's total exposure to the five companies amounted to W 705 billion, against which W 241 billion was provisioned at the end of 1999. Dong-Ah Construction, which was managing the last phase of the Great Man-Made River project in Lybia, and Woobang Construction, which was the major surviving company in the Daegu area, were the two largest exposures among the five. No companies had been let go by bank creditors since the inception of the workout program.

Woobang Construction had total borrowings of W 1.2 trillion in June 2000. Seoul Bank was owed W 181 billion, and had a 26 percent voting share among bank creditors. Woobang suffered severe cash flow problems in late June, and in early July it requested new loans of W 155 billion from creditor banks. The bank creditor group decided to make a partial advance of W 44.4 billion to meet the company's immediate cash flow requirements and, in late July, engaged an accounting firm to issue a due diligence report that would be used to decide on the remainder of the request. The due diligence report in late August indicated that the company had not provided full accounting information requested by the due diligence team, and that the best-effort estimate of the survival value of the company was less than the liquidation value. It was also learned that the company's audit firm had refused to sign off on the company's first-half financials for 2000. On August 28, the bank creditor group voted to reject the remaining W 111 billion loan request, with only 54.8 percent consent votes, about 20 percentage points short of the required 75 percent. The company filed for court receivership a few days later, becoming the first company to be unplugged from the protection of a workout program.

Woobang Construction was the largest surviving company in the Daegu area, Korea's third largest city, which had been hit harder than most other major cities by the economic contraction during the crisis. Because of this, the case attracted press and political attention and was painted as a conflict between the social interests of the regional economy and the individual commercial interests of the creditor banks. And Seoul Bank, holding a pivotal 26 percent voting share, was put on the spot. It was a difficult, but necessary, decision to make in this context.

On September 27, President Kim Dae-Jung announced that the government would complete the second-stage restructuring in corporate and financial sectors by end of 2000. In early October, the FSS instructed banks to submit lists of nonviable companies that needed to be exited from the market. Instructions were quite specific: among companies whose borrowings from financial institutions amounted to W 50 billion or more, banks were instructed to select those firms whose loans were classified as precautionary and below on the basis of forward-looking criteria, and those whose interest coverage ratio was below 100 percent for the past three consecutive years. Banks were also asked to select companies that were classified as potential problems according to each bank's internal standards, regardless of the companies' borrowing size. The pool of companies selected based on the above criteria was then classified as one of the following: "Normal," "Temporary Liquidity Problem," "Structural Liquidity Problem," and "Exit." The FSS reviewed the initial lists submitted by banks in mid-October and asked them to redo the lists using tougher standards, warning the banks that they would be accountable for letting weak companies survive.

Under this new regulatory posture, the creditors met on October 30 to vote on Dong-Ah Construction's request for W 346 billion in new loans. With total borrowings of W 2.3 trillion, the company was much larger than Woobang Construction, and the decision was more decisive. The request received only 25.3 percent consenting votes. Seoul Bank had 16.7 percent voting share and did not consent. The outside directors of the board of Seoul Bank volunteered to be involved in the decision regarding Dong-Ah Construction. A few days before October 30, the board passed a resolution endorsing management's decision not to consent to Dong-Ah's request. At this point, the board had begun to get actively engaged for the protection of the bank and in support of management's restructuring efforts (Table 10.5).

Table 10.5. Seoul Bank: Disposition of Nonperforming Loans (In billions of won)

	2000 2nd Half	1Q	2Q	2001 3Q	4Q	Total
Sale to KAMCO	...	655.7	143.3	4.9	64.4	868.3
Sale to private owners	360.0	...	35.5	...	8.5	404.0
Write-offs	109.6	198.6	221.2	102.9	189.6	821.9
ABS issue	...	...	...	446.8	...	446.8
Collateral sales and others	274.5	80.6	124.7	166.5	48.6	694.9
Total	744.1	934.9	524.7	721.1	311.1	3,235.9

In December 2000, NPLs totaling W 404 billion were sold, through an auction, to Lone Star and GE Capital Consortium. Unlike the previous NPL sales to KAMCO, the bank did not incur any loss, as we had charged sufficient provisioning for the NPLs.

Despite the initial disposition of NPLs of more than W 700 billion during the second half of 2000, the NPL ratio did not fall at the end of 2000 because a significant amount of loans were downgraded from the categories of normal and precautionary to the categories of substandard and below during the same period. As companies in workout programs, both Woobang and Dong-Ah Construction, for example, had been classified as precautionary at the end of 1999. The bank's exposure to Woobang (W 191 billion) and Dong-Ah Construction (W 380 billion), both pending court receivership, was the main piece of a W 670 billion NPL sale for W 312 billion to KAMCO in January 2001, the first NPL sale to KAMCO by the new management. The bank again did not incur any loss against the net book value of the NPL sold.

Beginning in the first quarter of 2001, Seoul Bank also started to write NPLs off aggressively and created an asset-backed securities (ABS) structure in September to take W 447 billion of NPLs off our books. The credits transferred to ABS for W 158 billion had W 309 billion in reserve, resulting in a gain of W 20 billion, which we did not recognize as income but kept in reserve. Most of our NPL disposition took place during the first year and a half.

With these efforts, the NPL ratio declined rapidly from June 30, 2001. By the end of 2001, Seoul Bank's loan portfolio was among the cleanest in the market; and by the end of June 2002, its net NPL ratio was lower than that of all other banks. At last, Seoul Bank was a clean bank. In early 2002, we became confident that the bank was prepared to be sold, without the put-back option or protection of the legacy portfolio becoming an issue in upcoming discussions with potential investors (Table 10.6).

Table 10.6. Nonperforming Loans in Korean Banks
(In billions of won)

	June 2000		June 2001		September 2001		December 2001	
	NPLs	Ratio	NPLs	Ratio	NPLs	Ratio	NPLs	Ratio
Seoul Bank	2,285.3	20.0	1,027.6	8.6	435.7	3.6	320.0	2.4
Hanvit	7,288.4	14.0	3,686.2	7.7	2,950.1	6.0	981.4	2.1
Hana	1,713.7	5.6	1,154.3	3.9	988.0	3.2	650.0	2.5
Shinhan	1,316.3	4.0	924.1	2.7	1,279.5	3.6	868.6	2.4
Korean Exchange Bank (KEB)	3,455.7	10.3	1,535.9	4.7	1,662.0	4.7	1,186.0	3.6
Chohung	3,612.9	10.2	2,014.3	5.8	2,097.0	5.7	1,200.0	3.2
Hanmi	1,695.9	9.0	1,233.7	6.7	1,236.6	6.3	650.0	2.7
Industrial Bank of Korea (IBK)	1,398.3	4.5	1,286.2	3.9	1,414.7	4.1	1,240.8	3.5
Kookmin	3,833.4	7.0	3,161.9	5.4	3,347.8	5.7	4,000.0	3.5

Source: Financial Supervisory Service.

Rebuilding business: new focus, culture change, and new image

The simple vision that I brought to the bank, with the help of a communications consulting firm, and enunciated at the inaugural speech on June 1, 2000, was "Small but Strong and Clean Bank" (it sounds much better in Korean). Most employees did not seem to like the emphasis on small, as their remaining pride was associated with the bank having been one of the largest banks. But small was important because it meant we would be able to change more quickly than the larger banks and would be closer to our customers, providing more personalized services. Strength was to come from a new culture of working together toward the common goal of becoming Korea's first international best-practice bank. Cleanness was of the utmost importance, in view of the bank's tainted reputation and in view of the bad loans still in our portfolio. I appealed that we should recover the bank's reputation through clean practices, much improved customer service, and a clean balance sheet.

New business focus

Like most other banks in Korea prior to the crisis, Seoul Bank was principally in the business of extending credit to corporate clients. It traditionally had more than 80 percent of its portfolio in corporate loans. Even after a 30 percent decline in assets between end of 1997 and June 2000, mostly from sales and write-offs of corporate loans, the bank's loan portfolio was still 80 percent corporate as of end of June 2000. The bank once had a dominant market share of the custody business for local investment trust companies and foreign investors in the Korean market. The custody business for foreign investors practically disappeared with the onset of the crisis as the bank's rating plummeted. Local customers remained, but competition was growing and the bank had about a 30 percent market share. Seoul Bank's credit card business was small and was losing money. What we called investment trust business—effectively asset management business for a fee through the trust account—was still going through the last phase of clean up of the guaranteed trust accounts. With only four overseas branches, there was no advantage in the business of trade finance. The treasury was supposed to be active, but we could not expose our income to market risk.

Housing and Commercial Bank, which merged with Kookmin Bank in late 2001, was the dominant retail bank, due to its well-established franchise in the household mortgage loan market. Most banks were talking about focusing on retail banking, a natural focus in an environment of slow demand for loans from creditworthy corporations coupled with a culture of credit aversion at most banks. But action to change focus was slow. We decided early on that retail banking, particularly household mortgage loans, would be our primary business focus, followed by credit cards. We would brush up the custody business and prepare it to regain business from foreign investors, but that would be subject to a rating upgrade. In the meantime, custody business would be a "defend" business in terms of local market share. Market risk business was to be minimized. Corporate banking business was difficult to address. We soon found that, despite the traditional reliance on corporate credit business, only a few bankers had basic skills in corporate banking. We hired a former foreign bank corporate banker to train our people in financial analysis and other corporate banking skills for about a year. We transferred as many people as we could out of the Credit Department and into the branches to cover corporate banking.

With this business strategy, we built an organization for retail banking, starting with a separate Retail Banking Division headed by a former Citibanker with experience in branch banking and small and medium-size industry business. The Credit Card Business Department was made a part of the Retail Banking Division. Within the Retail Division, we built a new Marketing Department to create and coordinate marketing activities. Fortunately, a very able grade-four officer was managing the bank's small and neglected Call Center, which needed to play an important role in the expansion of retail business.[6] He had a long reporting line to the head office. We made him report directly to the head of the Retail Banking Division and supported him with people and investment to quickly increase volume. Perhaps as important as the new organization for the retail business was the role of the chief operations officer and her consolidated back office departments. The consolidation of back office functions under the chief operations officer allowed the Retail Banking Division to focus on business expansion. The Information Technology Division and Controllers also contributed to building this separate Division quickly. The management information system report with a separate line for retail banking became available in the first quarter of 2001 (Table 10.7).

Table 10.7. Retail Loan Growth in Korean Banks
(In billions of won)

	Total Retail Loans 2000	2001	Percentage Increase	Mortgage Loans 2000	2001	Percentage Increase
Seoul Bank	1,752.9	5,351.1	206	716.9	2,890.7	303
Korea First Bank (KFB)	5,032.6	7,887.4	57	188.0	1,465.5	680
Hanvit	7,068.5	11,823.2	67	2,595.0	6,488.4	150
Chohung	5,385.5	9,072.3	68	2,251.6	4,394.0	95
Shinhan	6,458.4	11,140.9	72	2,232.3	6,958.0	211
Hana	5,982.0	10,751.7	80	2,630.3	5,682.4	116
KEB	3,843.9	6,464.5	68	1,588.9	3,888.3	144
Hanmi	3,482.6	4,746.9	36	1,549.0	2,704.0	74
Kookmin	48,874.3	60,153.6	23	...	...	0

Seoul Bank was the fastest growing retail bank throughout 2001. By the middle of 2001, we overtook Hanmi Bank in household mortgage business volume. By the end of 2001, our loan portfolio was balanced between corporate and retail exposures, with about half of retail in mortgage loans. By the first quarter of 2002, only Housing and Commercial and Seoul Bank had a retail portfolio that was larger than their corporate portfolio. This was an attractive portfolio for any potential investor.

Achievement of the rapid growth in retail business and the rebalancing of the loan portfolio would have been more difficult without the underlying growth in the retail market. However, the fact that Seoul Bank outpaced all other banks during this period and was able to overtake other banks in volume while keeping a low NPL ratio may be proof that Seoul Bank worked harder, our new organization and systems supported the rapid growth, and due to the small size, we could effect the changes faster.

Culture change: to become a "small but strong and clean bank"

During the first months in the office, the new management team made the following changes to show that management was serious about change and that informality, open communication, transparency, and a relentless focus on work were the new values of Seoul Bank:

- opened the CEO's bank e-mail address to employees and encouraged them to provide direct input;
- abolished the tradition of an "accompanying" male secretary, who followed the CEO throughout work hours, including evening functions;
- reduced the CEO's office space by a third by converting an adjacent guest receiving room to an office for the chief financial officer and an adjacent mini-board room to an office for the chief credit officer;
- corrected the name of the daily management meeting from "management tea time" to "management meeting";
- freed the CEO-only elevator for general use;
- closed the executive dining room and converted it to a dining room for team lunches or lunches with guests; had executives line up in the general cafeteria to lunch with other employees;
- issued a CEO decree prohibiting stock trading and nonbusiness-related internet surfing during office hours;
- issued a CEO decree on "insider reporting" making the failure to report wrong-doing punishable (initially only real name reports were accepted, but this was later modified to include anonymous reports); and
- instituted an open door policy for all head office department heads' rooms and removed televisions since department heads should not have time to watch television.

In late July, after 50 days in office, I summarized my frank impression of the bank in a three-page memo to the staff. Although some progress had been made, the following issues persisted:

- there was still too much emphasis on formalities at the expense of substance;
- the bank continued to operate like a "public" institution, not a commercial bank;
- the bank was not yet attuned to the pace of change in the market and its demands—I reminded employees that some W 3 trillion in deposits had shifted from striking banks to nonstriking banks during the July strike; and
- the urgent need for change was not yet widely accepted. This was how it had looked in the beginning.

In the spring of 2001, we engaged a consulting firm specializing in employee perception surveys. Through questionnaires and interviews, this firm surveyed 840 employees and produced a report in June. The survey confirmed a good acceptance of the new leadership and the restructuring process, employees' support of the restructuring efforts, and general acceptance of the new branch system, in which employees were assigned specialized functions of relationship managers, personal bankers, and operation officers or clerks. It also showed that employees in grades three and below still depended on the labor union quite a bit.

There were some other interesting results. For example, respondents gave themselves higher marks on international best practice than they gave their peers, superiors, and even the management. In general, employees perceived that the bank had become more commercially oriented and customer oriented, had greater concern for employees' career development and equal opportunities, and showed longer-term concerns than before.

Shortcomings included lagging investment in equipment and premises, and not much change in employee welfare. These shortcomings were mostly due to cost-related restrictions imposed on the bank by the shareholder through memorandums of understanding.

New image

The bank had acquired a bad reputation even before the crisis as a result of factional infighting and poor service. The stigma of having received public funds during the crisis worsened the image of the bank. We addressed this problem first by changing the bank's logo. In October, we launched the "Green Square" logo: the square was for being a simple, no-nonsense bank; the green was for cleanliness and youth. It was intended to convey that Seoul Bank was a new bank, not the old Seoul Bank. Some board members even wanted to change the name of the bank, but we decided that the name was simple enough and had good representational value.

In late December, the renovation of the main branch in the head office building was completed in line with the new identity. Instead of one long counter for indiscriminate customer service, the new concept incorporated the restructured branch banking system, with separated space for corporate and retail banking as well as segregation of front office and back office. Glass walls surrounded the outside for a transparent look, and we built a small stage in the main lobby for customer events. A small coffee stand was also placed in the lobby, and free coffee was served to customers. Starting on January 1, 2001 we joined other banks by advertising on television for first time since 1997.

Final recapitalization and the memorandum of understanding

In mid-December 2000, the amount of recapitalization needed to increase the bank's BIS ratio to 10 percent was agreed with KDIC. In late December, the government announced that, with the recapitalization, Seoul Bank had to be sold within six months (the end of June 2001) or be included in the financial holding company. Although it seemed a mindless decision to us, this was considered a favor to the new management. Reportedly, some policymakers wanted to give only three months for the sale, before putting the bank in the financial holding company.

In accordance with the procedures for the governance of public funds, the management had to prepare a two-year MOU in order to receive the planned recapitalization. In late December, the management finalized a two-year financial projection of the bank, in consultation with Deutsche Bank investment bankers, who began to prepare an information memorandum for the sale of the bank. Based on the financial projection, we derived the key quarterly management indicators required in the MOU. The indicators were the BIS ratio, return on asset ratio, cost ratio, adjusted revenue per employee, NPL ratio, and net NPL ratio. The two-year projection as well as a draft MOU with KDIC was presented to the board on December 27 for approval. After a lengthy deliberation, the board approved the plans more or less as presented, and we submitted the draft MOU to KDIC. However, KDIC did not accept our key management indicators and sent a revised set of indicators to be used. The revised targets for the cost ratio and adjusted revenue per employee targets were simply impossible to achieve, even during the first two quarters of 2001. We first asked KDIC to take a closer look at the condition of the bank and come up with achievable indicators, but the discussion soon deteriorated into arguments. Their bottom line was that, as a bank injected with public funds, Seoul Bank should achieve such numbers as minimum requirements. My bottom line was that KDIC had to either change the numbers to what management could achieve or change the management.

Higher authorities intervened. They were sympathetic to our position that we could not commit to targets that were not possible to achieve, particularly as the upcoming sales process would require full disclosure of our financials and plans, including financial targets. With the blessing of the higher authorities and with the understanding from the management team and the board, a compromise solution was reached on December 30: KDIC agreed to accept the management numbers for the first two quarters of 2001, on the condition that if the sale of the bank is not successful by end of June 2001, the new management would resign from the bank, and the management agreed that KDIC's revised numbers would be used beginning in the third quarter of 2001.

This episode illustrates the extreme differences of opinion between KDIC, the government shareholder, and the commercially oriented management of Seoul Bank, and highlights the disregard of the board by the shareholder. The resulting compromise haunted management until the bank was finally sold in September 2002. As expected, from the third quarter of 2001, our cost ratio and the adjusted revenue per employee number fell short of the MOU targets. KDIC asked the management to stay after the unsuccessful first sales attempt, but did not adjust the MOU targets.

IV. Performance summary

From the first quarter of 2001, the bank started to show growing quarterly operating income, before provision for credit losses, while the bank's NPL ratio nose dived. By the first quarter of 2002, the bank had a very credible track record of consistent earnings and a relatively clean balance sheet.

Most of the new income came from the growing retail business (as interest income) and credit card business (as fee income). Net interest income fell in 2001 due to substantial reduction in interest paying NPLs and high cost deposits renewed in late 2000, despite the growth in retail loans. From late September 2000, the government's announced plan to revert to a limited deposit insurance scheme put pressure on the deposit gathering of distressed banks. During the fourth quarter of 2000, Seoul Bank had to pay significantly higher rates to roll over maturing deposits into 2001. By mid-2001, much of the high rate deposits had matured.

The main components of fee income were credit card business and trust business (custody and trust fees). The problem of guaranteed trust accounts, which required the bank to pay out from its capital, had been resolved by the end of 2000 through write-offs and reserves. The bank also showed a good balance between interest income and fee income.

The second half of 2001 saw the unfolding of Hynix's—the former Hyundai Semiconductor —difficulties, which almost wiped out the bank's 2001 income. Our policy was to reduce Hynix credit whenever possible. The bank did not participate in either the Citibank-arranged W 800 billion local-currency syndication loan in late 2000 or in the Rapid Bond Underwriting Program in December 2000, which was used to refinance Hynix's maturing bonds.

The board passed a resolution supporting the management's decision not to participate in the underwriting program for Hynix. Our Hynix exposure, about W 260 billion, was classified as precautionary, with a 19 percent reserve at the time of government recapitalization at the end of 2000. In June 2001, Hynix raised US$1.25 billion by issuing a global depository receipt, and its problem appeared to stabilize. However, with the rapid decline in semiconductor prices, the company's problems resurfaced around September, and in December another debt restructuring proposal was made. Creditors were given the choice of either participating in the new credit facility or forgiving 76 percent of outstanding loans and converting the remaining into convertible bonds. Again with the involvement of the board, Seoul Bank decided not to participate in the new credit facility but to take the haircut and write-off the exposure. Seoul Bank was the only bank among public-funds-injected banks to do so. As a result, the bank had to charge an additional W 150 billion to credit reserve in December; we were fortunate to show a small operating income in 2001. The loan exposure was completely written off at the end of 2001, and the bank was left with W 71 billion convertibles, which were converted in May 2001 and completely sold in the market with a small loss (Table 10.8).

Table 10.8. Seoul Bank: Profit and Loss
(In billions of won)

	1999.12	2000.12	2001.12	2002.3	2002.6	2002.9
Operating income before provision	329.4	91.2	283.4	78.3	162.7	238.3
Net interest income	284.9	387.7	337.2	98.6	198.7	306.0
Noninterest income	250.4	69.4	301.9	74.9	145.7	209.5
Operating expenses	363.9	365.3	355.7	95.2	181.7	277.2
Provision (new/refund)	440.2	942.1	277.3	21.2	59.0	95.8
Operating income	110.8	850.9	6.1	57.2	103.7	142.5
Nonoperating income (incl. tax)	2,343.9	331.1	54.6	0.6	4.6	6.1
Net income[a]	2,233.1	519.8	101.4	56.6	108.3	136.4

[a] For 2001.12, including deferred tax income of W 40.7 billion.

Quite a number of our efforts to implement international best practices at Seoul Bank were the first attempted by Korean banks (Table 10.9). We also received several International Organization for Standardization (ISO) certifications ahead of other Korean banks thanks to the clear procedures and systems established with the help of Deutsche Bank advisors:

- Segregated duties between the front office and the back office and consolidated backoffice functions in the chief operations officer (the first Korean bank to do so);

- Established an Operations Center in the head office (in June 2001), centralizing the branch backoffice functions of clearing, cash delivery, and management of delinquent assets (the first Korean bank to do so);
- Received the highest honor in Customer Satisfaction Management category (November 2001) and Best Quality Service Certificate (April 2002) from the Korea Management Association (the first time Seoul Bank had received customer service-related awards in the memory of most employees);
- Established the only ISO 9001-certified domestic call center (March 2002);
- Received ISO 9001 certification for Custody operations (the first for a Korean bank in June 2002);
- Received ISO 9002 certification for Share Registrar operations (the first for a Korean bank in September 2002); and
- Achieved the same rating as Korea First Bank and Hanmi Bank by early 2002 (in June 2000, Seoul Bank's rating by Moody's was two notches below that of Korea First Bank and one notch below that of Hanmi Bank).

Table 10.9.   Seoul Bank: Balance Sheet
(In billions of won)

	1999.12	2000.12	2001.12	2002.3	2002.6	2002.9
Total assets	26,797.3	20,437.4	23,373.8	25,868.1	25,881.6	26,724.2
Bank account	22,128.4	19,139.5	21,731.3	24,242.5	24,188.1	25,178.1
Trust account	4,668.9	1,297.9	1,642.5	1,625.6	1,693.5	1,546.1
Total loans	12,680.3	11,570.4	13,348.0	15,155.4	16,021.8	16,810.5
Corporate loans	9,207.1	8,660.2	6,822.7	7,033.2	7,266.9	7,357.3
Household loans	2,183.2	2,258.0	6,247.9	7,808.9	8,473.7	9,210.5
Mortgage loans	459.3	716.9	2,890.5	3,761.0	4,471.8	5,329.4
Other loans	1,290.0	652.2	277.4	313.3	281.2	242.7
Total shareholder's equity	1,043.6	550.8	685.6	958.1	918.2	903.0

Note: For 2002, valuations gains on FRN-typed KDIC balance—W 158.3 (March 2000), W 130.6 (June 2000), W 92.7 (September 2000).

As noted, the government and the IMF treated Seoul Bank and Korea First Bank similarly until mid-1999. A comparison of the two banks from the time new management was brought into each bank in 2000 is interesting because both banks faced similar strategic issues and restructuring needs, partly reflecting that they were two of the three smallest banks with a nationwide network.

Seoul Bank's new management consisted of mostly Koreans with a background in foreign financial institutions or rating agencies, while KFB's top management consisted mainly of foreign professionals with limited command of the local language. KFB's management was supported by commercial shareholders with full management control. Although the government shareholder had assured management autonomy, Seoul Bank's management was constrained by MOUs with the shareholder and the regulator. The prompt corrective action order was lifted from KFB at the time of the sale to Newbridge; Seoul Bank's new management lived with it until the bank was sold to Hana Bank in December 2002. However, the performance of Seoul Bank during the 2001–June 2002 period was generally better than KFB (Table 10.10).

Table 10.10. Comparison of Seoul Bank and Korea First Bank (As of June 30, 2001)

		Seoul Bank		Korea First Bank
Number of employees		3,861		4,282
Number of branches		294		392
Paid in capital (in billions of won)		610.8		980.6
Ownership (in percent)	KDIC:	100.0	Newbridge:	51.0
			KDIC/MOFE:	49.0
New management		June 2000		January 2000

KFB's higher cost ratio during 2001–02 may well reflect its commercial ownership, including freer investment decisions. Seoul Bank's initial investment plans for information technology and branch renovation had to be postponed or scaled back several times due to constraints imposed by the MOUs (Table 10.11).

Table 10.11. Key Management Ratios of Seoul Bank and Korea First Bank (In percent, unless otherwise noted)

	Seoul Bank			Korea First Bank		
	2000	2001	2002.6	2000	2001	2002.6
BIS capital adequacy	10.05	9.22	10.14	13.40	13.29	12.88
Return on assets	−2.53	0.51	0.94	1.13	0.86	0.39
Before deferred tax income	...	0.31	0.94	...	0.47	0.32
Return on equity	...	15.60	23.30	26.80	15.20	6.80
Before deferred tax income	...	9.30	23.30	...	8.40	5.50
Cost ratio	66.60	59.40	53.70	58.80	68.50	72.30
Revenue/Employee (in million won)	124.00	152.00	176.00	159.00	159.00	168.00
NPL ratio	19.75	2.44	1.97	10.38	2.51	4.57

On the business side, Seoul Bank staff generally pressed harder, and had a higher sense of urgency, as the management as well as the government made clear that the bank was on its final course of survival. This nervous energy was more or less captured through international best practice and the new specialized organization, resulting in a rapid growth in business volume and revenue. Relative to those of KFB, Seoul Bank's costs were suppressed, while its revenue and business volume were maximized during this period.

V. Sale process and reprivatization

The first pressure to "do something" in this area came some time in September 2000, when rumors circulated that Seoul Bank was one of the banks to be included in the financial holding company. Through a cabinet reshuffle in August 2000, both the minister of finance and economy and the chairman of the FSC were changed and, along with them, most key players involved in the banking sector restructuring. Through a few visits, I learned the changing agenda of the new policymakers. Some of them had a strong view that the banking sector still suffered from an "over-banking" problem, that most of the good-quality employees at Seoul Bank had left during the crisis (but not the new management, most of them would hasten to add), and that, even with a successful restructuring, Seoul Bank was perhaps too small to survive in a post-consolidation environment.

I made my position clear: I had no interest in managing the bank if it went into the holding company. I had taken the job at Seoul Bank confident that I could turn it around, partly because of its relatively small size. I had seen a US$200 billion American bank go belly up, and I did not think size was the problem in most Korean banks. To the new team of policymakers and regulators, it seemed that Seoul Bank was still an unresolved problem, and some of them were thinking about resolving it through the financial holding company. Only four months into the job and having shed 650 employees in the name of saving the bank, this was an exasperating way of learning the discrete nature of government policies.

Several close advisors, including some outside directors, suggested contacting a few potential investors to help keep Seoul Bank off the list of holding company banks. With a 20 percent NPL ratio and a promise of recapitalization at the end of the year, we had little to show investors except for our redundancy program and the five new management team members who had joined by the end of September. We presented these to a large American private equity firm in late September. Following a few meetings, including a meeting with the management team, we received a draft proposal in October. As expected, it indicated that the firm might agree to pay the net book value on the condition of full government protection against the NPLs, which was not acceptable to the government. For the sake of process transparency and in the interest of management time, Deutsche Bank, which had the right of first refusal under the Financial and Restructuring Advisory Agreement of April 2000, was engaged as financial advisor to prepare for either a capital raising or a partial sale of the bank.

Following the government decision to allow six months for the sale of the bank and the recapitalization in December, we went on a one-week road show in early February 2001 to several cities in the United States, followed by a visit to major Asian cities for one-on-one meetings. We met three strategic investors during the trips, with two of them actually showing interest.

On December 20, 2000, the Special Law for the Management of Public Funds was legislated, and under the law, a Public Funds Oversight Commission (PFOC) was established in February 2001 to deliberate on and coordinate matters involving the management of public funds. Within the PFOC was the Subcommittee for the Evaluation of the Sale of Public Funds Invested Companies. PFOC became the decision-making authority for companies with public funds, including Seoul Bank. In March, the subcommittee took control of the key processes of the sale, and KDIC assumed the principal role in the sale of Seoul Bank.

Under the newly formalized decision-making line-up, Deutsche Bank ran a controlled auction for the sale of Seoul Bank in the spring of 2001. The information memorandum dispatched to four parties in April included the bank's financials up to first quarter 2001 and projections for the year. Although the first quarter 2001 result showed a significant jump in quarterly operating income, the NPL ratio was still 12 percent. By May, the parties were either backing out or asking for protection against the NPLs. Only one party submitted a proposal letter toward the end of June. The proposal from Deutsche Bank Capital Partners (DBCP), a private equity arm of Deutsche Bank, included specific references to NPL protection. At the end of June, the PFOC decided to give KDIC three more months, until the end of September, to negotiate with DBCP. During the three months, the issue of NPL protection was the main point of negotiation, and it was not resolved by the new deadline. In early October, the PFOC announced that the discussion with DBCP had been terminated. Seoul Bank was to continue its normalization efforts and future sale of the bank would be open to domestic investors as well as foreign investors. Seoul Bank's management was to prepare a privatization plan by the end of the year.

Upon the announcement of the termination of the discussion with DBCP, I visited the higher authorities who intervened in the December 2000 MOU process with KDIC, and expressed my intention to be responsible for the failure of the sale by the extended deadline. Their response was that I was also responsible to finish what I had started. By this time, three of the seven new management team members had left, their positions were replaced by internal promotions, and another was preparing to leave. In the process, the management team came to have a good balance between the new and the original Seoul Bank staff. Business Divisions were headed by original Seoul Bank officers. The separate meetings among the new management team disappeared around this time. We were becoming a mixed team on the same boat.

Preparing a privatization plan entailed finding potential investors and introducing them to the government, even as the FSC was publicly expressing its preference for merging Seoul Bank with another bank. The government clearly indicated that its preference was a merger with a sound Korean bank, followed by a sale to qualified domestic or foreign investors, or, if this was not possible, a merger with another public-funds-injected bank. At least, Seoul Bank did not have to worry about being put into the financial holding company. The policymakers seemed to believe that the managers of the financial holding company had their hands full with the five entities already in it.

Around this time, MOFE was preparing a draft amendment to the Banking Act that would increase the single-shareholder limit in banks from the existing 4 percent to 10 percent, and would eliminate the limit altogether for a Korean business group qualifying as a specialized financial group. About three business groups would come close to qualifying as a specialized financial group. One of them showed a keen interest but withdrew from discussions later due to other concerns. Discussion with the second group was tentative from the beginning and did not go anywhere. A cold call on the third group, with four quarters of consistent earnings and clean balance sheet, led to follow-up meetings, and they became very interested. An unexpected, but seemingly genuine interest in the bank, came from an American private equity firm in November. The firm's managing director visited in December to confirm its interest. Another unexpected interest was shown by a consortium of some 30 Korean companies, organized by a business group for whom Seoul Bank was the main bank. By the end of December, written indications of interest were received from the three parties and delivered sealed to the government.

In late January 2002, in an announcement regarding the disposition of government-held bank shares, MOFE announced that the preparation for the sale of Seoul Bank would proceed simultaneously with discussion for a merger with a sound bank. My only comment was that we needed to put the two options in the same process to maximize the proceeds from the sale.

Parliament passed the amendment to the Banking Act in April. In May, Goldman Sachs and Samsung Securities were appointed as KDIC's advisors. With financials up to the first quarter of 2002 in the information memorandum, which showed one of the cleanest balance sheets among Korean banks and five consecutive quarters of consistent and growing operating income, the bank looked well prepared for sale. Three parties were selected for on-site due diligence in early July, but one dropped. Lonestar and Hana Bank competed till the last moment. This time, the government was prepared to sell 100 percent of the bank. Lonestar's final offer was W 950 billion cash, with the government sharing in the upside potential up to W 250 billion. Hana Bank's offer was W 1.15 trillion in shares of the new merged bank, representing about 30 percent of the new bank. Hana Bank also guaranteed to buy the government shares in the new bank within 18 months. Neither party asked for protection against the bank's NPLs.

Lonestar's valuation of Seoul Bank was W 7,776 per share, before the upside sharing, and Hana Bank's valuation was W 9,414. The government's recapitalization in December 2000 had been made at W 5,000 per share.

In August 2002, the PFOC selected Hana Bank as the preferred buyer of Seoul Bank, as recommended by the subcommittee. And in mid-September, the PFOC approved the sale of Seoul Bank to Hana Bank. A merger agreement between Seoul Bank, Hana Bank, and KDIC was signed on September 27.

VI. Broader issues

The restructuring of Seoul Bank raises a number of broader issues, including the roles of the government and board of directors, as well as governance issues.

Role of government

Five government entities were involved in banks receiving public funds:

- KDIC, the nominal shareholder and administrator of MOUs with the banks, performed at least four quarterly MOU audits a year. KDIC was a strict administrator, with a clear bias to minimizing downside risks. KDIC closely followed Seoul Bank's restructuring process since it was also a signatory to the restructuring agreement with Deutsche Bank.
- FSS, the regulator and administrator of rehabilitation plans prepared under prompt corrective action orders, performed regular prudential audits, program audits, and quarterly rehabilitation plan audits. FSS did not treat Seoul Bank any more leniently than privately owned commercial banks. In prudential audits, FSS auditors showed interest in the progress and results of our restructuring efforts.
- FSC, the government agency charged with regulatory policymaking, but also doubling as the policymaker for troubled financial institutions, had the power to grant, suspend, and revoke licenses, a power transferred from MOFE in April 1998.
- MOFE, the parent of KDIC, was responsible for overall policy for the financial industry. As policymakers dealing with industry-wide issues, both MOFE and FSC, but particularly FSC with its mandate to deal with troubled financial institutions, showed continuing concern with the bank as a potential problem. As indicated by several premature initiatives for the sale of the bank, particularly the first deadline of end of June 2001, it appeared that few policymakers appreciated the value of restructuring.
- Korea Board of Audit (KBA), the public sector watchdog with powers to audit and inspect all government ministries, agencies, and public

sector corporations, was required by the Special Law for Public Funds Management in December 2000 to audit all matters related to the management of public funds and to report to the National Assembly. It conducted an annual audit on public-funds-invested banks. In its audit of Seoul Bank, KBA regarded the bank as a public institution, rather than a commercial bank, by virtue of ownership through public funds. In this context, it took issue with the bank's television advertising.

Summarizing their roles: KDIC was the immediate shareholder under MOFE's control; FSS was the regulator and administrator of rehabilitation plans, FSC and MOFE were the policymakers; and KBA was the super auditor, not only of the public-funds-invested banks, but also of the activities of the four government entities with respect to such banks.

In terms of hierarchy, the government entities above may be lined up from the top as the policymaker (MOFE and FSC), the regulator (FSS), and the shareholder (KDIC)—with the super auditor (KBA) watching over all of them. The shareholder's position at the bottom of the hierarchy resulted from its relationship to the policymaker. KDIC reported directly to MOFE, making it a true nominal shareholder, or an administrator.

Although this arrangement ensured maximum flexibility for the policymaker, who deals with industry-wide issues (or who deals with individual bank issues on the industry level), it also eliminated the role of an active shareholder who tries to capture the upside of his equity by taking some risk, if necessary. A nominal shareholder with administrative responsibilities cannot be expected to perform this role. Instead, the arrangement has a built-in bias to minimize the downside risk of each shareholding: KBA's audits on the government entities ensured this bias, frustrating the efforts of the restructuring manager whose interpretation of his mandate was to make a damaged bank as commercially valuable as possible for privatization.

This passive bias is understandable. The shareholding came about in reaction to the need to keep the financial system from collapsing. Several injections of public funds had been wiped out, and there was not much confidence in the practices of weak banks regarding credit extension and otherwise. Public demands to guard against moral hazards in the use and management of public funds were constant. In this context, the best solution for both the government and the restructuring manager was for the bank to be sold as soon as possible.

Role of the board

The role of active shareholder was, in the case of Seoul Bank, provided by the board. In 1998, in an effort to improve corporate governance in the troubled banking sector, the government established a system of outside directors and an Audit Committee. Outside directors were required to make up more than half of each bank's board of directors and at least two-thirds of the Audit

Committee. Typically, outside board members were appointed for a one-year term, renewable for a maximum of three years.

During my tenure, the board consisted of five or six outside directors, at a time, and two inside directors, the CEO and the standing auditor. The outside directors, all of whom were appointed by the government, during this period included three corporate executives, two university professors (one of whom was an active member of a nongovernmental organization), one lawyer, two editorial writers of economic dailies, one accounting firm advisor, and two KDIC officers. Chairmanship of the board was held by an outside director.

Although their proper function was to oversee the CEO and his management, the outside directors soon understood the value of the restructuring efforts, recognized the seriousness of the new management, and provided enormous moral support to the new management team. The board did not have full management power to delegate to the CEO. They also had to sign the KDIC MOUs in conjunction with the recapitalization at the end of 2000, and were bound by them. But within this constraint, they not only performed management oversight but also prompted the management to increase the commercial value of the bank. In this regard, they were furious when our investment plans for branch renovation were delayed due to cost targets in MOUs. The board was required to meet four times a year. In 2001, there were 20 extraordinary board meetings, usually to report and discuss rather than to seek board resolutions. The attendance rate of outside directors was close to 100 percent throughout the period. Two members of the Audit Committee, including the committee chairman, came into the bank each week for three months in early 2001 after the standing auditor abruptly resigned, to review all documents signed by the CEO, among others, until the standing auditor's replacement was appointed in March.

The outside directors were well informed and committed. They did not behave at all as an agent of the government. However, not once during my tenure did either the nominal shareholder or the policymakers invite the outside directors to discuss the status of the bank in general or the timing of the sale in particular. For the government shareholder who appointed the outside directors, this board seemed a wasted resource. By taking the board seriously, the government—both as shareholder and as policymakers—could have benefited much with respect to timing the privatization of public funds banks, among others. In the case of Seoul Bank, premature attempts to sell the bank, which distracted management and employees from restructuring efforts, could have been avoided if the government had taken the opinions of outside directors seriously.

Governance issues

Two main governance issues arose during this period. One was the need to prevent the banks from making arbitrary credit decisions, so as to minimize future credit losses, and the other was the need to check and prevent potential moral hazard of the CEO and his management. The first concern was double-edged: arbitrary decisions could be made from the inside or pushed from the outside. Credit committees, headed by CCOs with complete independence from the CEO, were institutionalized in 1997–98. CEO's simply could not interfere in credit decisions. The outside influence, which was a part of the labor union agenda during the banking strike that took place on July 11, 2000, was symbolically addressed in a labor–government agreement following the strike: the government agreed in writing not to interfere in bank management. The government agreed to the same with the IMF in the July 2000 program reviews.

The moral hazard issue was addressed by the introduction of a board structure in which outside directors outnumbered insiders and by incorporating an audit committee with a standing auditor (a full-time auditor who was simultaneously a board director). This arrangement was intended to minimize the potential for the CEO to abuse his power. In addition, the bank's management was audited by KDIC at least quarterly, and by FSS on regular regulatory audits as well as quarterly audits on the rehabilitation plan (sometimes, they were done simultaneously). KBA started its audit from 2001.

This intense oversight reflected the politics of public funds. Public criticism and suspicion regarding the use of public funds became particularly acute during the second half of 2000 as the government had to seek congressional approval for W 40 trillion of additional public funds for the second-stage restructuring, which was partly used to recapitalize the banks at the end of 2000. The Special Law for the Management of Public Funds was drafted in order to assure the National Assembly of more transparency and accountability in the use and management of public funds. Thus, the PFOC was created with more civilian members than the three ex-officio government members, and KBA's audit of matters relating to public funds was institutionalized. The law did not forget to remind the government of its responsibility to seek claims from or otherwise hold accountable those deemed to have lapsed in management and supervisory responsibilities in distressed banks. A thick layer of governance was created to address the varied demands from the public—starting from the National Assembly and ending with the standing auditor, who was next to the CEO in status on the board of directors.

While this structure may have met the political demand for governance, it is questionable whether it also served the functional needs of bank governance. Governance is a systemic structure to create good checks and balances within the organization for all stakeholders, particularly the shareholder. The new board system based on outside directors and an audit committee, most likely, was meant to perform this function. However, the structure of governance developed for public-funds-invested banks limited the power of the board in many respects. For example, KDIC, the shareholder, by imposing quite detailed MOUs not only on the CEO but also on the board, relegated the board to the position of an "extra" management team. In addition, the governance structure was too top heavy on the function of checks, with the resulting dilution of accountability at the bottom. The standing auditor is typically exempted from any reprimands when bank management has been found guilty of mismanagement by regulators and/or the super auditor. An important issue is how to strengthen bank governance through the new board system, even for public-funds-injected banks.

VII. Retrospect and conclusion

Some time late in the process of writing the original version of this chapter, I was reminded of my own comments regarding the state of the bank before my arrival: "During this period of extreme uncertainty and instability, which lasted for over three years, the bank was bound to become alienated and inward-looking." With the exception of customer behavior and the quality of customer service, the bank continued to suffer similar symptoms and syndromes in varying degrees during my tenure. The new management became alienated from the government shareholder by the end of 2000. Alienation from the employees started in the middle of 2001, following the break-up of discussions with DBCP, when I became an interim CEO. Because of the constraints imposed by the MOUs, investments were cut back and some decisions were made on an interim basis starting in late 2001. From the middle of 2002, the labor union became active again in its opposition to a merger with Hana Bank.

However, there were also differences between the two periods. From early 2001, the bank started to operate on a restructured "transistor radio" mode. Although restructuring in a broad sense may be an endless process, by mid-2001, Seoul Bank's organization, main systems, and processes, as well as culture, incorporated most of the basic international best practices in commercial banking. International best practices settled into the bank more quickly as employees associated the rapid reduction in NPLs and equally rapid growth of retail and mortgage loan portfolios with best practices. The association of best practices with the growth of retail loans and mortgages was most obvious, as the growth followed the reorganization of the Retail Business Division and the rollout of the new branch system. The association of the cleanup of NPLs with best practices was more cultural: employees regarded management's early decisions to unplug from nonviable companies as important for the protection of the bank. In many respects, what kept the bank going from late 2001 was the power of the interim management to reinforce and maintain international best practices. The first period of uncertainty and instability did not have this benefit.

Finally, the bank was blessed with good timing. If our push for the retail and mortgage loan business had been late by as much as three months, the same result would have been difficult to achieve. If the restructuring efforts were delayed by even a month, the disruption at the end of December 2000 could have shattered what had been achieved by that time, including the newly formed management team. And the most blessed timing was the timing of the sale.

As Perlin (1996) has noted, "bank restructuring is a process, not an event." A former outside director of Seoul Bank has added that while the sale of a public-funds-invested bank is an event of political significance, restructuring is of secondary concern. These two observations summarize the experience of Seoul Bank during my tenure. Bank restructuring as a process requires time for management to implement restructuring and for the organization to digest it. It is a cumulative process whose value is not obvious until a critical mass of influence is achieved over the entire organization. In contrast, the timing for the sale of a public funds bank, as dictated by policymakers, can be arbitrary, with little regard for the restructuring in progress. An understanding of this seemingly inherent conflict, as it unfolded in Seoul Bank, offers a practical perspective for future "restructuring" managers as well as policymakers.

Notes

1. I am indebted to David T. Coe, Paul Gruenwald, and Peter Hayward of the IMF; to Dong-Won Kim of *Maeil Business Newspaper* for encouragement and useful comments; and to Maryse Dubé for assistance. I am also thankful to the Asia and Pacific Department and the Monetary and Financial Policy Department for inviting me to visit the IMF in early 2003 to write this paper.
2. This was not based on the forward-looking criteria (FLC) introduced after the crisis.
3. For a comprehensive background discussion on the causes of the financial crisis in Korea and the subsequent recovery, see Ajai Chopra and others (2002). The LOIs are available on http://www.mofe.go.kr and http://www.imf.org.
4. The market generally perceived Woori as a vehicle for collecting bad banks. As Seoul Bank had already started its restructuring efforts in June 2000 with a new management, Seoul Bank employees and management viewed inclusion in the holding company as self-defeating. For the employees, it meant heightened job insecurity. For the management, it meant compromised autonomy as it created another layer of management. For the government, the bank holding company was a way to reduce the number of problem banks in what is considered to be an "over-banked" sector, albeit at the cost of increasing the magnitude of the restructuring task.
5. For a detailed account of the government's negotiations with Newbridge and HSBC, see Su-Gil Kim, pp. 138–47.
6. As noted above, the hierarchy of employees is determined by grades. Grade four is the lowest ranking officer with authorized signing power; it takes between five to eight years to obtain this level. All employees in grade four and below are union members. When grade-one officers become executives, they get their accumulated severance payments and sign a new one- to two-year contract that may or may not be renewable.

Bibliography

Chopra, Ajaj and others, 2002, "From Crisis to Recovery in Korea: Strategy, Achievements, and Lessons," in David T. Coe and Se-Jik Kim, eds., *Korean Crisis and Recovery* (Washington: IMF; Seoul, Korea: Korea Institute for International Economic Policy).

Kim, Su-Gil, Jung-Jae Lee, Kyun-Min Chung, and Sang-Ryul Lee, "The vault is Empty: A Documentary of Korean Economy during Five Years of DJ Government," January 2003, Chung-Ang M&B.

Perlin, Gary 1996, "Foreword," in Andrew Sheng, ed., *Bank Restructuring: Lessons from 1980s* (Washington: World Bank).

11
Banking Crises and Bank Resolution: Experiences in Some Transition Economies

Charles Enoch, Anne-Marie Gulde, and Daniel Hardy[1]

I. Introduction

It has been estimated that in the past 20 years over half the members of the IMF have experienced banking crises.[2] Among these, much attention has been paid to the Nordic banking crises of the early 1990s;[3] more recently, the focus has been on the crises that hit several Asian countries in the late 1990s.[4] Between these two well-recorded episodes was a set of major banking crises that critically affected economic developments in a further group of countries: the transition economies. During the 1990s, most of the countries that were undertaking the difficult transition from a centrally planned to a market economy experienced banking crises of varying severity. These crises reflected in part factors specific to countries emerging from state socialism. Banks in transition economies were characterized by linkages to loss-making public and private enterprises, insider lending, absence of sound prudential practices, and legacy problems from the earlier regimes in their countries, all of which characteristics helped undermine the soundness of banking systems in these countries.[5] To a surprising extent, however, the experiences of the transition economies reflected factors common to banking crises across all types of economies—transition economies were clearly more vulnerable than others to the emergence of banking problems, but overall the factors contributing to systematic banking sector problems in these countries had a great deal in common with those found elsewhere. Similarly, the lessons that can be learned, in particular on how the authorities handled the crises, may also be of wider applicability.

Such considerations motivated this study of three particular episodes of banking crisis in transition economies. Bulgaria in 1996–97 experienced one of the deepest banking crises of any transition economy, in terms of impact on gross domestic product (GDP), reflecting the pervasive disruption caused by banking system failure in an economy where financial intermediation had progressed relatively far. Lithuania's banking crisis in 1994–95 was one of the earlier ones, and illustrates one of the first attempts by the authorities in a transition country to restore banking soundness. Lithuania had to address the banking crisis within the constraints of a currency board arrangement, whereas in Bulgaria the banking sector issues had to be addressed before a currency board could be adopted. Finally, Mongolia's experience in 1996 shows a crisis in a transition country similar in many ways to a developing country, and where financial deepening had hardly begun. In this case the authorities were able and willing to undertake forceful intervention at short notice to seek to address the crisis within a comprehensive framework. In each of these cases the authorities took appropriate action in some regards, but can be seen also to have made some mistakes.

During the 1990s financial sector issues came to be central in the work of the IMF and the World Bank—a centrality that was reinforced in the later Asian banking crises and with the establishment of new international financial architecture to seek to safeguard economies from financial crises more generally.

The following sections look at each of the three crisis episodes in turn. The final section presents some conclusions.

II. Bulgaria: the banking crisis of 1996

Economic and institutional background

Until the 1990s, the Bulgarian economy had been fully integrated into the socialist economic block and had specialized in agriculture and certain heavy industries complementary to those in other socialist countries. Bulgaria was correspondingly hit particularly hard by the break-up of the socialist system, in the form of a collapse of demand for its traditional exports and large terms of trade adjustment associated with the move to world market prices. Real output eventually declined by more than a third during the transition process, and inflation was persistently high. The enterprise sector had to be profoundly restructured and reoriented to respond to the new pattern of demand and costs. While there was substantial reform momentum in the first year after the break-up of the socialist system, through most of the early 1990s the reform process proceeded less quickly and smoothly than in other countries in central and eastern Europe; continued government subsidies, in particular to the enterprise sector, and lack of fiscal adjustment led to high levels of domestic and international debt. By 1993–94, output had stabilized, but recovery was slow and inflation remained high. Summary macroeconomic data are shown in Table 11.1.

Table 11.1. Bulgaria: Selected Economic Indicators, 1993–98
(In percent; unless otherwise indicated)

	1993	1994	1995	1996	1997	1998
Nominal GDP (in millions of leva)	299	526	880	1749	17,055	21,577
Real GDP growth	–1.5	1.8	2.9	–10.9	–6.9	3.5
Nominal GDP growth	48.8	75.8	67.5	98.6	875.3	26.5
CPI inflation (period average)	72.8	96.0	62.1	123.0	1082.2	22.3
			(End of period)			
Broad money (in millions of leva)	234	418	584	1,310	6,019	6,597
Growth in broad money	47.6	78.6	39.6	124.5	359.3	9.6
Broad money/GDP	78.3	79.5	66.3	74.9	35.3	30.6
Credit to the private sector (in billions of leva)	11.1	19.8	185.4	622.1	2,151.8	2,733.7
Credit to the private sector/GDP	3.7	3.8	21.1	35.6	12.6	12.7
Reserve money (in billions of leva)	55	89	154	352	2,174	2,387
Money multiplier	4.27	4.71	3.78	3.73	2.77	2.76
Money market interest rate	48.1	66.4	53.1	119.9	66.4	2.5
Exchange rate (leva per U.S. dollar)	27.6	54.1	67.2	177.9	1,681.0	1,760.7
International reserves including gold (in millions of U.S. dollars)	960	1,311	1,546	793	2,539	3,127
International reserves/reserve money	48.3	80.0	67.3	40.1	196.3	230.6

Sources: *International Financial Statistics*, and Fund staff estimates.

As part of the transition process, the Bulgarian financial system had to be transformed from one designed solely as an ancillary to the system of central planning to one playing an active role in the generation of savings and the allocation of investment. Before 1987, the Bulgarian banking system mirrored that in other central and eastern European countries. It comprised only three banks: the Bulgarian Bank of Foreign Trade, in charge of international reserve and external debt management as well as other foreign exchange transactions; the State Savings Bank (SSB), in charge of household deposit mobilization and housing loans; and the Bulgarian National Bank (BNB), in charge of currency issuance and commercial and investment banking operations with enterprises. As a result of the introduction of a two-tier banking system in 1987–90, seven specialized commercial banks and 59 new commercial banks were created, and the BNB was turned into a central bank. Three more commercial banks were licensed in July 1990, leading to a system of 71 relatively small banks, often with capital below the statutory minimum.[6]

In response to a view that regarded this fragmented system as inefficient, the incoming Bulgarian government set up a Bank Consolidation Company

Table 11.2. Bulgaria: Economic Standing of Banks at the Outset of the Banking Crisis

Banks	Number of Banks	Number of Banks Meeting Capital Standards	(In Millions of Leva, Dec. 95)		(In Millions of Leva, Apr. 96)		Asset Concentration Share in Total Banking Sector Assets (April '96)
			Total Assets	Net Worth	Total Assets	Net Worth	
State banks	10	1	661,584	−39,777	477,864	−93,532	66.3
Private banks	29	18	242,453	−13,853	236,118	...	32.8
Foreign banks	6	6	6,671	287	6,525	...	0.9
Total	**45**	**25**	**910,708**	**−53,343**	**720,507**	**−93,532**	...

Table 11.3. Bulgaria: Loan Portfolio of the Banking Sector by Ownership Group (April 1996)

	State Banks		Private Banks		Foreign Banks	
	In Millions of Leva	In Percent of Total	In Millions of Leva	In Percent of Total	In Millions of Leva	In Percent of Total
Government	106,531	29.0	22,663	10.8	627	10.6
State funds	20,648	5.6	141	0.1	0	0.0
Local government	28,349	7.7	1,398	0.7	0	0.0
Public enterprises	130,199	35.5	49,183	23.5	2,851	48.2
Private enterprises	80,342	21.9	130,820	62.5	2,418	40.9
Households	894	0.2	735	0.4	15	0.3
Nonbank financial institutions	102	0.0	4,299	2.1	0	0.0
Total loans outstanding	**367,065**	**100.0**	**209,239**	**100.0**	**5,911**	**100.0**

Sources: BNB; BCC; and Fund staff estimates.

(BCC) in 1992.[7] Its purpose was to serve as a temporary holding company for the shares of the state-owned banks, with a mandate to merge the existing banks and to strengthen them for privatization. Following these mergers, the numbers of state banks, excluding the SSB, fell to ten by 1996 (Table 11.2 on p. 271). At the same time, private banks—which were first licensed in 1991—grew in number, so that by 1996 more than 30 were operating. While most remained small compared to the public institutions, some—most notably the First Private Bank—had reached significant size by 1996 in terms of both assets and branch representation. By 1996 five foreign banks and bank branches were operating in Bulgaria.

In terms of business activities, by early 1996 about one-third of lending went to the government, one-third to public enterprises, and the remainder to private sector enterprises and households (Table 11.3). The state banks (excluding the SSB) catered to all sectors of the Bulgarian economy, including the newly emerging private sector, but lending public sector enterprises remained the largest component of their portfolio. Private banks concentrated on lending to the newly emerging private sector, yet they also lent a considerable amount to the government and to nonfinancial public enterprises.[8]

In spite of the structural changes in the banking landscape, certain key problems were evident from the beginning. These included, first, a high degree of concentration: by 1996 the five largest banks (four state owned, one private) held 60 percent of total assets. Second, most banks—especially the state banks—remained to a large extent sectorally and/or regionally oriented, leaving some highly exposed to vulnerable state enterprises (see Appendix 11.I). Third, more or less state-controlled banks were still dominant: in spring of 1996, the ten banks partly or fully state-owned held two-thirds of the assets of the banking sector (Tables 11.2 and 11.3).[9] In addition, the shares in these banks that were not directly held by the government belonged, for the largest part, to enterprises that most often were themselves state owned. The BCC acted also as the state oversight body for these banks. However, while adequate prudential regulations had by and large been put in place, they were largely not enforced. The BNB had almost no supervisory powers over the banks that fell under the BCC, and often exerted only limited authority over the private banks.

Early signs of banking sector weaknesses and initial response

Difficult macroeconomic conditions, combined with inadequate internal risk control procedures, and the absence of any loan repayment culture led to a rapid increase in nonperforming loans, soon exceeding 60 percent in a number of banks' loan portfolios. This derived in large part from the fact that banks allocated much of their lending under government-mandated credit plans, rather than commercial credit analysis, and the major borrowing enterprises were often hard hit by the economic transition. Even after the abolition of directed credit, strong interrelationships persisted between banks and major enterprises, leading to lax credit analysis. The lack of bankruptcies in the enterprise sector throughout the transition period reinforced the pressures on the banks to finance losses. Banking supervision, which was in its infancy, seems to have been ineffectual in preventing this deterioration, in part reportedly because of lack of effective authority of the supervising institutions (the BCC and BNB for the state and private banks respectively) in enforcing their mandates. Insider lending was widespread and there was a perception (evidenced in some high-profile examples) that organized groups were utilizing their influence over the banks and enterprises to profit at the expense of the state. In spite of the BCC's mandate in that regard, by 1996 none of the state banks had been privatized.

Of the state-owned banks, on the basis of information using Bulgarian accounting standards,[10] only one—Bulbank, the former foreign trade bank—showed positive net worth in early 1996 (Tables 11.2 and 11.4). While this bank was the largest in terms of assets, its particular business structure limited potential positive spillovers to other banks and the economy at large: the bank's activities were concentrated in the trade financing area, with no branch network and few retail banking activities, and it thus had only limited direct interaction with the mainstream of the Bulgarian economy.[11]

Table 11.4.   Economic Standing of the State Banks

	(Dec. 95)		(Apr. 96)	
	Assets	Net Worth	Assets	Net Worth
Bulbank	265,238	31,773	263,243	15,648
Biochim	70,344	–8,219	40,402	12,073
United Bulgarian Bank	63,805	–14,903	35,616	–17,476
Balkanbank	61,896	–14,400	29,161	–28,594
Mineral	48,123	–7,740	30,612	–9,133
Economic	41,895	–15,374	16,738	–20,028
Hebrosbank	38,876	–5,158	19,462	–9,482
Expressbank	30,580	–1,429	22,961	–3,133
Bulgarian Post Bank	22,955	–749	18,820	–5,096
Yambol	17,872	–3,578	843	–4,164
Total state banks	**661,584**	**–39,777**	**477,864**	**–93,532**
Private banks	**242,453**	**–13,853**	**236,118**	**...**
Foreign banks	**6,671**	**287**	**6,525**	**...**

Sources: Bank Consolidation Company; and Fund staff estimates.

The remaining nine state banks—all of which were predominantly engaged in domestic business—showed significant negative net worth at the end of 1995. On one estimate, in three of the state banks nonperforming loans exceeded 90 percent of their total loans. Excluding Bulbank, the average size of state banks' nonperforming loans relative to total loans was 70 percent at end-December 1995.[12]

According to BNB data, the economic standing of private banks in April 1996 was more mixed. A group of smaller private banks appears to have been relatively more successful in managing their business affairs: in December 1995, among the 20 banks with assets of leva 10 billion (about US$65 million) or less, only five reported negative capital. In contrast, more than half of the institutions above that threshold were insolvent.[13] Notwithstanding such differentiation, all private banks shared in the rapid loss of deposits between December 1995 and April 1996, an indication that the public was unable to distinguish between the relatively more healthy smaller private banks and the remainder of the system.

As a result of the above factors, liquidity and solvency problems emerged in the banking sector. In an earlier effort to address banking sector difficulties, the government had issued bank rehabilitation bonds, so called ZUNK bonds, in exchange for state banks' nonperforming assets in 1994.[14] Due to flaws in the design of the instrument—in particular their low yields—they only restored solvency in a technical sense, but did little to improve the actual economic sustainability to the banks that had received such bonds.[15] Instead, the BNB and the SSB increasingly acted as lenders of last resort by refinancing all illiquid institutions. The extent of such refinancing—whether through the BNB's lending facilities, placements by the SSB, or arrears in the payments system—had reached a point where the authorities' ability to conduct monetary policy was put in question.[16]

By the end of 1995 the Bulgarian authorities could no longer ignore the problems in the banking sector. In late 1995 a high-level interdepartmental committee had been established, reporting directly to the prime minister. It recognized the seriousness of the incipient crisis, although it could not establish consensus on the necessary remedial measures quickly enough. Nevertheless, a number of steps were taken. From January 1, 1996 substantial provisioning requirements were imposed upon the banks. With greater transparency in the banks' accounts, the situation of the banks was seen to be far worse than had earlier been estimated. Table 11.4 shows the economic standing of the state banks according to figures supplied by the BCC at end-December 1995 and end-April 1996. The deterioration in the position of the banks between the two dates reflects both weak performance in the first months of 1996 as well as, probably more importantly, the recognition of losses incurred earlier. The authorities had thus obtained evidence that a large number of institutions were technically bankrupt. The BNB apparently felt, however, that under the banking law it did not have a mandate to close failed banks, because the law at that time did not provide a legal basis for the BNB to place conservators in banks. At a more general level, the authorities faced a dilemma because all existing institutions were either infected, or too small, or too specialized to offer a viable continuation of banking services if a comprehensive approach to addressing banking sector weakness were to be adopted; any solution would have to go beyond closings to ensure the continued provision of banking services.

Around this time too the public became fully aware of the banking crisis: banks developed serious liquidity shortages, especially in foreign exchange, and lines outside banks became commonplace. There were widespread rumors about the failing health of the banking system, by itself a factor aggravating the problems. Deposit runs occurred against at least two banks of significant size. In addition, the sudden emergence of a large volume of items in arrears in the payment system caused system-wide liquidity shortages and accelerating loss of public confidence in the system. To keep the system afloat, the BNB injected leva 25 billion (or 16 percent of end-1995 reserve money) into the system in the first four months of 1996, and the SSB increased interbank lending by leva 12 billion (8 percent of reserve money). At the same time, the BNB's attempts to establish control over the situation were stymied: in the absence of an efficient bank bankruptcy law it was unsuccessful in trying to close two smaller banks, leading to a further erosion of confidence, and visible financial disintermediation.

Initial policy response

In May 1996, with widespread deposit runs on the banks, the authorities acknowledged the existence of the crisis and determined to take action.[17] Measures included amending the banking legislation and working out, in secret, the technical details of bank closures. A modified law, which allowed the BNB to suspend bank management and replace it by BNB-appointed conservators, was passed by the Bulgarian parliament. Following the establishment of the legal basis, the authorities took the decision to close the two most vulnerable large banks—First Private and Mineralbank—along with three smaller banks during the following weekend. A weekend was chosen to allow sufficient time for the complex logistical tasks involved, including the planning of the physical seizure of all bank branches, and notification of foreign central banks to close the respective branches abroad. In the event, the closures went relatively smoothly, although it appeared that the owners and managers of at least one bank—where the cash reserves were found to have been seriously depleted—had received advance warning. Depositors demonstrated at some locations, but in general remained relatively calm following an announcement that their domestic currency deposits would be available after two weeks at the SSB. Foreign currency deposits, the BNB announced, would be transferred to Postbank and paid in four installments over a two-year period.[18]

Restrictions were placed on the operations of the remaining weaker banks. These restrictions were laid down in memoranda of understanding (MOUs) between the BNB and each individual bank. A key element of the MOUs was to forbid any new lending prior to achievement of a viable capital asset ratio. In order to retain some control over macroeconomic liquidity targets, under the economic program being agreed between the Bulgarian authorities and the IMF, limitations were placed on the volume of the total unsecured refinancing that the BNB could provide, and commitments were made to enhance supervisory standards.

Evaluation of the initial response

The measures introduced in May 1996 had some initial effect, most notably reflected in a brief period in July when deposits in the banking sector stabilized. Thus, the closure in May 1996 of the most affected banks initially achieved a significant reduction in pressure on the BNB and the SSB. However, with a number of banks known to be insolvent still remaining in system, the measures essentially only bought time to address the underlying situation. In addition, problems emerged with the closure process itself and with the deposit insurance system. Specific issues of concern included:

- The BNB applied to the court system to request insolvency of the institutions in question, but failed to withdraw their licenses. All the banks opposed the BNB's applications, and—given the untested legal basis for the BNB's actions as well as inadequate preparation of the legal system for the challenges of bankruptcy procedures for banks—lengthy court procedures emerged, involving courts at all levels. The courts all failed to accept the BNB's assessment of the financial health of the institutions in question, and instead required a further "independent" assessment of the banks' balance sheets. Decisions on all banks involved were repeatedly postponed.[19]
- Failure of the system to act decisively on the question of insolvency, combined with the generous deposit insurance arrangements, allowed banks—most notably the previously largest private bank—to continue some operations. Given that their liabilities had all been taken over by the deposit insurance system, some institutions managed to create a public perception of having regained profitability. Using their newfound strength, they led intense court battles against the BNB to fight the closure decision.[20]
- The implementation of deposit insurance arrangements was unsatisfactory.[21] Thus the SSB, which was charged with paying out domestic currency deposits, received a relatively illiquid government bond to cover the new and, as it turned out, very liquid liabilities. In the event, deposit withdrawals were substantial—more than 70 percent of deposits were withdrawn in the first week after the deblocking of the accounts, which were overwhelmingly financed out of the liquid assets of the SSB. On foreign currency accounts, depositors were given a choice between withdrawal in leva cash or payments over two years in four six-monthly installments. However, as the choice was not made binding,

depositors could at any point opt for leva currency payments, on relatively favorable terms, which complicated liquidity management.

- The extent of government indebtedness limited its ability to handle the banking crisis in a more comprehensive fashion, either through bank recapitalizations or through recognition of prompt payment of deposit insurance liabilities as an explicit fiscal cost. The resultant nontransparencies undermined credibility in the authorities' efforts at resolving the crisis.
- The banking crisis and the authorities' inadequate attempts to respond to them had serious macroeconomic costs. The provision of substantial liquidity by the BNB over the period July to September 1996, without any ability to undertake equivalent sterilization of the liquidity effect, exerted continuous pressure on the exchange rate. The leva depreciated from around 70 to the U.S. dollar in September 1995 to around 230 in September 1996. The basic interest rate in early September 1996 stood at 108 percent (180 percent annualized with compounding), almost three times its level of late-1995.

Comprehensive approach to resolution

Relapse into crisis

As the initial round of bank closures fell short of what was needed to stabilize the system, the negative effects of maintaining undercapitalized banks in the system persisted and again became apparent. Among the problems were negative cash flow, mounting uncollected interest, and further declines in the quality of banks' loan portfolios.[22] Associated with this was widespread disintermediation from the banking sector, with significant declines in both leva and foreign currency deposits. Deposit outflows occurred from almost all Bulgarian banks, including Bulbank. Reflecting the inadequate liquidity of the banks, sizeable delays in payments of deposits occurred, lines outside banks again became a common sight throughout the country, and most banks had to resort to formal or informal queuing mechanisms to restrain the speed of outflows.

The banking crisis now spilled over into the public debt markets and the payments system. Participation of banks in the public debt market declined sharply as even those banks with adequate liquidity feared further pressure for deposit withdrawals and preferred to hold (domestic and foreign currency) cash. These preferences threatened to paralyze the government debt markets and required extraordinary liquidity injections by the BNB. In addition, and further derailing the BNB's ability to control liquidity, there were increasing delays in the payments system. By early September, payments queues as large as leva 10 billion had developed, despite several costly BNB attempts to clear them. In addition to the monetary consequences, these delays in the payments system threatened to lead to serious contagion effects, spreading the crisis even to the relatively stronger banks, which, through delayed receipt of payments due, themselves were experiencing liquidity problems. By early September the public was clearly expecting a further wave of bank closures.

Resolution strategy

The authorities began to plan to reestablish confidence through a comprehensive and wide-ranging restructuring of the banking sector. As a precondition, they developed criteria for a redesign of the sector, ensuring that the exercise would only leave open institutions that were clearly viable and could, if necessary, be supported by the authorities. The exercise was based on a bank-by-bank analysis of liquidity, earnings, net worth, and foreign currency positions. Based on these indicators, a simulation exercise using different assumptions regarding the progress of the crisis was undertaken, which suggested that 15 more banks (B-list banks) should be closed immediately, while the BNB should publicly declare its support for the remainder (A-list banks) of the system.[23] At the same time, it was recognized that the banking framework, in particular the supervisory system, needed to be strengthened substantially to allow the public to regain confidence in the financial sector.

Implementation

The authorities put nine further banks under conservatorship on September 23, 1996, which—together with the institutions closed earlier—meant that roughly one-third of the Bulgarian banking sector had been closed.[24] At the same time, in an attempt to reestablish tighter monetary control, the BNB increased the basic interest rate to 25 percent per month. Finally, reacting to the shortcomings of the previous deposit insurance system, the BNB decided that, for the second round of bank closings, deposit insurance payments would be deferred until the banks in question had been declared bankrupt by the courts.[25]

Reflecting the fragility of the situation, at least two of the A-list banks became subject to intense pressure during the first three weeks of October. Runs on these banks were initiated through rumors that the Customs Service was shifting its accounts due to the poor financial health of the institution in which its accounts were held. Following these rumors, intense demand for the withdrawal of foreign currency deposits developed, and banks lost about US$23 million (equivalent to about 1 percent of reserve money).

The BNB's policy was geared toward restoring confidence through firm signals of support for the remaining banks. To that end the BNB accommodated the banks' leva liquidity demand through its Lombard window and, later, conducted outright purchases of ZUNK bonds. Among the state banks, Biochim (the most heavily affected) was granted refinancing of leva 3 billion. Total outstanding claims on deposit money banks during this period increased by another leva 15 billion (about 10 percent). Although the BNB refrained from direct refinancing in foreign exchange,[26] its public announcements that the second wave of closures had been final would have to imply full support for the remainder of the system, thus posing significant risks to monetary stability. Although the BNB's instruments were thereby severely challenged, it is not clear that its policy was necessarily misguided; in almost all cases of systemic banking crisis, there has been similar testing of the surviving banks after initial bank closures, even if the effect of the closures was ultimately to help achieve the successful resolution of the crisis.[27]

By November 1996 the banking sector had stabilized to the extent that no insolvent banks remained in the system. Nevertheless, at least one of the state banks that had been subject to the runs in late fall remained extremely vulnerable. The BCC continued its attempts to increase confidence in the sector by privatizing at least one of the large remaining state banks. In the event, progress on the privatization of the bank in question was slow. During this period too, further active policy measures were hampered by inflationary pressures, an emerging political crisis and an intense debate about the possibility of switching the monetary regime to a currency board arrangement (CBA).[28] Thus, by late 1996 official intervention in the banking sector came to a halt, leaving the institutions to attempt their own stabilization efforts. Some of these were successful: a few smaller private banks managed to raise their capital. In addition, the solvency of the remaining institutions was helped by the rapid devaluation of the leva, given that banks mostly had long foreign exchange positions.[29] However, the remainder of the state bank system increased its profitability during the period as a result of returns from high domestic interest rates, exchange rate revaluation gains, as well as increased business due to a "flight to quality."

Banking sector restructuring and the introduction of a currency board
Banking sector considerations in designing the currency board

Starting in November 1996, the Bulgarian authorities began planning in earnest the introduction of a currency board, a monetary arrangement in which the central bank's ability to lend to the government and commercial banks is abolished or, at least, severely curtailed. Such arrangements have in other countries contributed to the reestablishment of public confidence in the domestic money and domestic economic institutions and proven instrumental in arresting high and hyperinflationary situations.[30] However, none of the other countries that introduced a CBA in the recent past had done so while facing banking sector challenges comparable to those in Bulgaria.

Notwithstanding the urgency of macroeconomic stabilization, there was concern that the reconstitution of the Bulgarian banking sector might be especially difficult within a currency board framework. The major considerations regarding the banking sector in the preparation for the CBA included:

- In view of the constraints on the provision of lender-of-last-resort support under a CBA regime, the soundness of all banks that would be in the system when the CBA was established was to be reevaluated using the latest data available. It was agreed that no unsound bank, that is a bank with negative capital, should be permitted to exist at the time of the change in the monetary arrangement.
- Given the need to maintain confidence in the banking sector, it was felt that even after the introduction of the CBA some limited lender-of-last-resort facilities should be available.
- Under a CBA, bank liquidity management, as well as system-wide liquidity distribution via interbank markets, was seen to take on an added importance. Availability of sufficient liquid assets, along with the institutional arrangements in place for effective interbank markets, became another focus of attention.
- Adequate capitalization of banks also acquired added importance. It was felt that given the strictures of a CBA the path toward achieving adequate capitalization (estimated to be at least 12 percent of assets in Bulgaria) should be accelerated.
- The banking law had previously hindered decisive and fast action by the central bank to cope with problem banks. Therefore, the "Law on Banks and Credit Activity" had to be amended to accord greater and more precise supervisory powers to the BNB, and to allow faster procedures for bank closure by limiting banks' recourse to judicial protection to a degree more consistent with international practice.

The currency board arrangement and bank soundness

At the time when a CBA was first considered, there was concern that Bulgaria's foreign currency reserves were far from sufficient to cover domestic monetary liabilities, as is required under a CBA, except at an extremely depreciated exchange rate, and that confidence in the banking sector was so weak that there would likely be runs on the banks that would quickly test the constraints of the CBA. At an early stage it was envisaged that the introduction of a CBA might well have to be accompanied by the imposition of exchange controls and/or controls on the withdrawal of deposits. These indeed might have served to undermine the credibility of the CBA at its outset and reduced the likelihood that it would be able to function effectively.

In the event, discussions over the introduction of the CBA were protracted; as the government seemed unable to handle the enfolding crisis in the winter of 1996, confidence collapsed, and the exchange rate fell dramatically as hyperinflation ensued. This hyperinflation, while disastrous for the well-being of many Bulgarians, served to severely erode the liabilities of the banking system, making their coverage by the country's foreign reserves much more feasible. At the same time, the resignation of the government and its replacement after elections, generated confidence in the country and its institutions, which served to substantially recapitalize the banking sector (by restoring positive market value to the state bonds that dominated their balance sheets), and rendered remote the likelihood of serious runs on the banking system.

With the new government in place, the authorities changed the central bank law to form the legal basis for a CBA. The currency board, linking the leva at 1,000 to the deutsche mark, was officially introduced on July 1, 1997.

The final currency board design has two features in particular specifically focused on the handling of the banking sector:

- The currency board consists of two distinct departments within the BNB, the issue and the banking department. While the issue department represents the currency board proper, the banking department's assets—which also are covered through foreign exchange—are available for emergency lender-of-last-resort support. It is expected that the existence of this facility should of itself help avoid a system-wide panic in case of difficulties of individual banks. The use of the facility and the operationalization of the criteria used in the law to justify such support were to be regulated by BNB ordinance.[31]
- To ensure a smooth transfer to the currency board environment, it was decided to retain banking supervision within the BNB. The new supervision department became the "third pillar" of the currency board organization, headed, as are the issue and the banking departments, by a BNB deputy governor.

At the time of designing the CBA, the authorities again reviewed the state of the banking sector and undertook several supporting measures to ensure that the banking sector was sound and seen to be sound at the outset of the CBA. Most notably, they engaged into a limited recapitalization of one state bank that was marginally undercapitalized prior to the shift in the monetary regime.[32] In addition, efforts toward privatization of the state bank sector were accelerated, leading to the sale of one large state bank to a group of three investors (European Bank for Reconstruction and Development, Bulbank, and Bank Oppenheimer). Privatization and/or management contracts for other state banks were also actively pursued, with clear prospects for the sale of at least one bank emerging at the time.[33] In addition, a reorganization of the banking supervision department of the BNB; a redesign of prudential regulations governing licensing, capital, liquidity, open foreign exchange positions; and an ambitious plan to increase on- and off-site inspections were implemented.[34]

Epilogue

The currency board to date has largely achieved its main macroeconomic targets—reducing inflation, limiting the budget deficit and restoring confidence in the Bulgarian economy—while avoiding any major testing due to renewed banking sector pressures. This outcome can be ascribed to a variety of factors, not least of which are the confidence-enhancing measures undertaken prior to, and at the time of, the introduction of the arrangement. In addition, the hyperinflation of the spring of 1997, during the political hiatus at the time of the preparation of the CBA, served to greatly deflate the real value of banks' liabilities, substantially improving the solvency of the banking system. Finally, the abolition of the minimum price on ZUNK bonds, together with increased demand for these bonds as confidence returned in response to the establishment of the CBA,[35] increased the value and the liquidity of the state banks' assets.[36]

Notwithstanding the initial positive developments in the banking sector under the currency board, challenges remained. The most important included:

- The subsequent privatization process was initially slow and subject to a number of setbacks. While these in part resulted from the changing business plans of potential investors, in part they seemed to derive also from bureaucratic red tape and somewhat unrealistic expectations on the side of the authorities. More recently, however, the process has been brought near to completion.
- The SSB for long operated as a quasi-fiscal organization, intermediating resources between household depositors and government borrowing. The process of changing the SSB from a "narrow bank," to which the authorities accord full deposit guarantees in exchange for a very limited and safe investment strategy, into a full-fledged commercial bank, now called DSK Bank, with its deposit insurance subject to the same limitations as those of the other banks in the system, is ongoing, with plans for divestiture of the state's ownership in the bank.
- Despite some economic recovery, banks in Bulgaria were initially slow to resume substantial lending.
- Banking supervision long suffered from deficiencies. Since the crisis a new regulatory framework for supervision has been put in place. The focus more recently has moved to compliance and enforcement.

In conclusion, a full recovery of the financial sector in Bulgaria remains closely linked with the prospects for stabilization and growth in the country. Once growth becomes more robust, the banking system will have greater potential to recover its strength. The prospect of EU accession provides a good medium-term framework both for macroeconomic policy and structural measures to further bring about the necessary strengthening and safeguarding of the banking system.

III. Lithuania: transition into banking crisis

Economic and institutional background

Lithuania is the southernmost and largest Baltic country, with a population of 3.7 million. From the period after the Second World War up to independence in the early 1990s,[37] Lithuania had been part of the former Soviet Union and shared its centrally planned economic and financial system. Output declined by 40 percent during the transition, and inflation peaked at an annual rate of about 1,000 percent.

The macroeconomic situation was transformed by the introduction of a CBA on April 1, 1994, under which the national currency was tightly pegged to the U.S. dollar and full convertibility was enshrined in law.[38] Inflation was reduced rapidly and began to converge to the level of the countries' main trading partners. Macroeconomic conditions have been relatively stable throughout the remainder of the period under consideration (Table 11.5).[39]

Table 11.5. Lithuania: Selected Economic Indicators, 1993–98
(In percent; unless otherwise indicated)

	1993	1994	1995	1996	1997	1998
Nominal GDP (in billions of litai)	11.6	16.9	24.1	31.6	38.3	42.9
Real GDP growth	–16.2	–9.8	3.3	4.7	5.7	5.1
Nominal GDP growth	240.3	45.8	42.6	31.0	21.4	12.0
Consumer price index (CPI) inflation (period average)	410.4	72.1	39.5	24.7	8.8	5.1
			(End of period)			
Broad money (in billions of litai)	2.7	4.4	5.6	5.4	7.3	9.6
Growth in broad money	100.4	63.0	29.0	–3.5	34.1	32.4
Velocity	23.1	25.8	23.3	17.2	19.0	22.4
Credit to the private sector (in billions of litai)	1.4	5.9	12.1	9.9	7.6	6.9
Credit to the private sector/GDP	12.1	34.9	50.2	31.4	19.8	16.1
Reserve money (in billions of litai)	1.3	1.8	2.4	2.5	3.3	4.3
Money multiplier	2.13	2.40	2.30	2.17	2.20	2.26
Money market interest rate	n.a.	69.5	26.7	20.3	9.6	6.1
Exchange rate (litai per U.S. dollar)	4.3	4.0	4.0	4.0	4.0	4.0
International reserves including gold (in millions of U.S. dollars)	412.2	587.3	819.0	834.3	1062.7	1460.0
International reserves/reserve money	140.0	128.8	133.9	133.5	128.5	137.1

Sources: *International Financial Statistics*; and Fund staff estimates.

In the banking sector, the former Soviet financial institutions continued to dominate for a period after independence, at first with unclear ownership relations between Moscow and Lithuania. The Bank of Lithuania (BOL) was founded in 1990 to become the central bank of the new republic.[40] However, its role initially differed from the classic model of a western central bank in at least two important regards: first, until October 1992 Lithuania was still part of the ruble zone, which left the central bank no room for independent monetary policy.[41] Second, in October 1990 the BOL took over the branches of two former Soviet State banks and was thus initially engaged in both central and commercial banking;[42] in 1991 it provided as much as 40 percent of total outstanding credit to the economy. In these circumstances, and in the absence of a relevant legal framework, the development of banking supervision was slow.

In the aftermath of independence, Lithuania, like most other transition economies, witnessed a sharp increase in the number of financial institutions. This development mainly reflected the fact that minimum capital requirements were not changed from their 1991 levels, in spite of high inflation and depreciation of the currency (see Table 11.5). By the beginning of 1994, 28 banks operated in Lithuania, some of which acted as lending agencies for one or two enterprises only. In addition, an undetermined number of enterprises were engaged in banking business without having obtained the necessary license.

Nonetheless, concentration remained high: in 1992 two of the old institutions, Agrobank and the Savings Bank, together with the commercial banking arm of BOL (which later became the State Commercial Bank) accounted for more than half of the banking systems' deposits and loans.[43] In late 1995 the five largest banks accounted for 77 percent of deposits and 71 percent of assets. Yet, given the relatively low level of financial intermediation (see Table 11.5), the transmission of financial sector developments to the rest of the economy remained limited.[44]

In light of the perceived weaknesses in the financial system and to form the basis for a modern banking sector, the authorities undertook a series of measures. Important steps included the enactment of the Bank of Lithuania and the Commercial Banking Laws in December 1994, which provided the legal basis for all banking activities, created a clear two-tier banking system, and defined the BOL's supervisory role. Prudential regulations put in place at that time included a higher minimum core capital requirement, a capital adequacy ratio, limitations on both connected lending and lending to a single borrower, as well as open position limits.[45] The new banking laws of 1994 created the necessary legal basis for a prudential framework to support a market economy, but significant restructuring within the BOL, as well as training of supervisors, was required to operationalize the framework.

Owing to the previous absence of prudential regulations, the formerly prevalent practice of directed lending, as well as the weak credit evaluation skills of commercial bankers, improved supervision alone could contribute little to a rapid change in the quality of the banking environment. At first banks profited from high inflation—which averaged more than 400 percent in 1993 (see Table 11.5). In the absence of indexation, inflation eroded the real value of both assets and liabilities. Inflation also masked the cash flow problems that would normally be associated with a similar level of nonperforming loans, allowing banks to continue imprudent lending practices longer than they could have in a more stable environment. However, once macroeconomic policies were tightened—most notably after the introduction of the CBA in April 1994—inflation declined and banks started to feel the liquidity and solvency consequences of their weak loan portfolios.[46]

Early signs of banking sector weakness and initial response

A number of banks failed to make progress toward compliance with the prudential norms established in 1994, most notably on capital requirements.[47] The continued violations of the prudential norms remained unsanctioned. In addition, the prudential norms themselves were not fully consistent with those in a market economy, as the law foresaw a stepwise adjustment toward international practice. As these regulations were progressively being phased in, banks already in breach of the old norms slipped even further into noncompliance.

The increasing stress on the banking system was first felt by the smaller institutions. Starting in 1994, a total of 14 smaller banks were forced into bankruptcy procedures. Yet, in spite of the large number of institutions involved, the economic impact initially remained modest, as these banks' combined assets accounted for only about 5 percent of the total assets of the banking system.

Signals of deeper banking sector problems arose during the summer of 1995. Aura Bank, a medium-sized institution, faced liquidity problems after deposit withdrawals that were caused by rumors questioning its solvency. To avoid a crisis, Aura Bank received support both from the government and the BOL. Still, banking problems continued to deepen during the fall of 1995, and public confidence in the system continued to erode. Deposit withdrawals were ongoing, bank capital diminished, and bank losses increased substantially. In the fall of 1995, the government had to provide liquidity support to Vakaru Bank, another medium-sized institution.

By late December 1995, banking sector fragility had developed into a full-scale crisis. An on-site inspection by the BOL revealed the insolvency of Innovation Bank, the largest private bank, and its would-be merger partner, Litimpex Bank, mainly due to serious portfolio quality problems. The two banks were put under moratoria, which suspended all their commercial banking activities, except for the collection of loans and other assets. Deposits held with both institutions were blocked. Vakaru Bank, which had obtained liquidity support earlier in the fall, again experienced liquidity problems and was now put under conservatorship by the BOL. With the extension of the crisis to these three institutions, about 30 percent of deposits in the system were affected.

Depositors reacted rapidly and shifted their deposits to the state-controlled banks, where individuals' deposits were fully guaranteed by the Civil Codes, thus liquidity shortages emerged even in relatively solid private banks. The interbank market came to a standstill, deposit withdrawals continued, and confidence in the banking system was shaken. In the event, from December 1995 to March 1996, about 25 percent of the existing household deposits left the banking system. Around this time the press increasingly started to question also the solvency of the three state-owned banks. Audits of two state banks (State Commercial Bank and State Savings Bank) revealed that both had made losses in 1995 and that they would need to be recapitalized in order to meet the capital adequacy ratio. When these audits were published by local newspapers, a systemic crisis appeared in prospect.

After the BOL's initial intervention no further action was being taken regarding the two commercial banks under moratoria. The attendant uncertainty caused a further loss in public confidence in the financial system as a whole. In an attempt to calm depositors' rising fears, parliament passed a law pledging state assets to guarantee in full the deposits and creditors at the two banks. This move, however, was not consistent with the deposit insurance law, passed in December 1995, which provided limited insurance of LTL 4,000 (US$1,000) per depositor, and only applied to litas deposits, excluding the large amount of foreign exchange deposits held with banks.[48] To restore interbank trading, parliament passed a law providing for the extension of government guarantees of one-year duration for interbank deals for a volume up to a total of LTL 300 million (US$75 million, or 12 percent of reserve money), albeit with little measurable impact. As a measure of last resort and in order not to weaken banks already in distress, the BOL decided not to enforce penalties on banks that did not meet reserve requirements.

Evaluation of the initial response

The early attempts of the government and the BOL to address the banking sector problems largely failed. In part, this was due to the CBA put in place in 1994—before the crisis—which severely limited the central bank's ability to pledge financial support.[49] In the event, funds of only LTL 19.3 million (about 0.8 percent of reserve money outstanding at end-1995) were lent by the central bank to commercial banks during the first quarter of 1996.[50] At the same time, the uncertainty associated with the banking crisis led to significant capital outflows. Net foreign assets of the central bank decreased by LTL 506.6 million (US$126.6 million), equivalent to 20 percent of reserve money at end-1995, associated with a concomitant decline in reserve money.

Uncertainty about the relative responsibility of the government and the central bank, coupled with fear of the political fallout from a crisis, also contributed to the absence of fast and decisive action. The ongoing political uncertainties eventually led to a change in both the leadership of the government and the central bank. The authorities also relied on the failed banks themselves to propose their own rescue packages. The absence of serious attempts to manage loan portfolios of banks under moratoria weakened creditors' morale; and by not enforcing penalties on some banks, incentives to maintain reserve requirements and other prudential norms weakened for all banks. This was not incentive compatible, and in the end further weakened the financial position of the institutions in question.

Thus, although the width and depth of the problems were recognized early in the crisis, the initial response was limited to a case-by-case approach and concerned only with mitigating the most pressing liquidity needs. No action was taken to assess the broader solvency issues and formulate steps toward a recovery of the system as a whole.

Comprehensive approach to resolution

By mid-1996, when banks holding more than three-quarters of the systems' assets and liabilities were insolvent or undercapitalized, it became clear that a resolution of the banking crisis would require a strategic plan. Key issues to be decided included whether to rehabilitate or liquidate banks in difficulties, the cost sharing of any rescue operations between shareholders and the government, as well as new "rules of the game" to minimize the likelihood of a recurrence of such problems.

Resolution strategy

After considering a number of options, the government decided in September 1996 to adopt a plan based on the following three principles: first, that no bank would be allowed to operate unless it met the capital adequacy requirement by the end of 1996; second, that any capital support from the government had to give the government a commensurate portion of share capital and voting rights as private contributors, ensuring that existing shareholders could not benefit unduly from a bank's rehabilitation; and third, that any government support was to be conditional on change of the top management of the bank.[51] These principles translated into the following plan:

Measures on individual banks[52]

- Aura Bank was to have its license revoked and be relicensed as a bank under the name Turto Bank with limited bank powers. The new bank's sole purpose was to become the asset management company (AMC, see below) for assets purchased from banks undergoing restructuring using public funds and be 100 percent owned by the government.
- Regular bankruptcy and liquidation procedures were to be initiated for Vakaru Bank.
- Innovation Bank was to be restructured by the end of 1996. If it failed to do so, the bank's license was immediately to be revoked and bankruptcy procedures initiated.

- Litimpex Bank had been allowed to restart operations on June 10, 1996 as the BOL had determined that the bank met all prudential regulations.[53] Certain safeguards, however, were put in place. The BOL was to examine Litimpex during October 1996 and in the event the bank failed to meet all prudential rules, the BOL was committed to immediately revoke its license.
- The State Commercial Bank and the State Savings Bank had already been recapitalized by the state, and the value of the stock of existing shareholders had been appropriately diluted.[54] The two banks' bad loan portfolios were to be bought by the AMC and the government was to make a specific public commitment to privatize the banks in the near future.

Legal and regulatory changes

- The law protecting all creditors in a bank had recently been amended by parliament, allowing the government to recapitalize a bank if at least 40 percent of the large private deposits were converted into equity by December 1, 1996.
- The government committed itself to pass new laws and regulations which were to set new "rules of the game," minimizing the possibility that similar problems were to recur. These included abolition of all socially- and politically-based lending; redefinition and tightening of lending limits to connected parties; strengthening personal liability of bank board members for deficient application of prudential regulation; lowering large exposure ratios and expanding the definition of borrower; revision of capital rules to comply with Basel standards; introduction of International Accounting Standards for all regulatory purposes; facilitation of foreclosure; revocation of the provisions in the Civil Code protecting in full individual depositors in the state-controlled banks. The government was to actively seek foreign participation in the banking market. Parliament also passed a law allowing foreign banks to open branches or affiliates in Lithuania.

The asset management company[55]

- In order to allow banks to reorient their businesses away from collecting on bad loans, as well as in the hope to maximize loan collection, the government decided to centralize loan collection in an AMC. It was hoped to minimize the time needed for the AMC to be operational by using an existing failed bank as the shell for the AMC, an approach sometimes termed "hospital bank." Aura Bank was chosen for the purpose and was renamed Turto Bank after it assumed its new role. The asset transfer relied on government injections in the form of special treasury bills, which would be given to the ailing banks in exchange for the bad loans that would be handed over to the asset management company.

Depositor protection

- No specific arrangements for depositor protection were put in place at the time of the design of the bank restructuring plan. The legal arrangements in place included a complete guarantee (under the Civil Code) of deposits in the three state-owned banks, as well as a scheme protecting deposits in private banks up to LTL 4,000 (equivalent to US$1,000).[56] In addition the Commercial Bank Law gave individual depositors claims on proceeds from the liquidation of a bank of up to LTL 5,000.

Implementation

The process of banking sector rehabilitation has, in its broad outline, followed the initial plan, albeit with some delays and modifications.

Regarding the state banks, which continued to dominate the system, rehabilitation and privatization proceeded more slowly than had been hoped for. There were no transfers of bad loans to Turto Bank, the asset management company, until the second quarter of 1998, which left the banks concerned weak and undercapitalized.[57] In an effort to assist the Agricultural and the State Commercial Banks, parliament passed a law in March 1997 exempting these banks from penalties arising from the noncompliance with prudential regulations. In the meantime, the authorities made several failed attempts at privatizing the State Commercial Bank, followed by the final closure of the institution in March 1998. In modifying the original plan, the privatization of the Agricultural Bank and the State Savings Bank were delayed for several years. The remaining private banks were profitable and in compliance with prudential regulations following the restructuring.

In the area of depositor protection, the authorities on several occasions during the crisis augmented the coverage available to depositors (see above), and on the basis of these laws all depositors in banks that failed prior to 1997 were paid in full, with coverage provided by the budget. The total of the proposed bank restructuring plan was estimated to be roughly US$261 million (3.5 percent of GDP), and a significant part of the cost was to be covered by special Treasury securities.

Epilogue

Indicators of financial sector health (Table 11.6), most notably the sharp increase in bank deposits, show that by end-1997 significant progress had been made in overcoming the banking sector crisis. Nevertheless, domestic and international challenges remained that had a potential to endanger previous gains, including the high level of nonperforming loans. Further events showed, however, that the system remained stable, even in the face of further challenges.

Table 11.6.   Lithuania—Indicators of Financial Sector Soundness and Market Development[a]
(In percent)

	Dec. 1996	Dec. 1997	Mar. 1998
Capital adequacy[b]	10.5	10.8	14.0
Returns on equity	–9.1	–8.3	3.4
Excluding state banks	15.4	10.8	5.9
Growth of deposits (annual rate)	–5.0	34.0	30.0
Growth of private sector credit (annual rate)	–4.0	19.0	26.0
Borrowing by banks from nonresidents/total liabilities	3.0	6.0	8.0

Sources: Bank of Lithuania; and Fund staff estimates.

[a]   Operating banks. March 1998 excludes the State Commercial Bank.
[b]   The methodology for calculating the ratio was adapted to international norms in the first quarter of 1997.

One challenge included renewed banking sector problems in 1997. It appears, however, that the shift to limited deposit insurance—where the new depositor protection regulations are based on EU standards, with a maximum of LTL 25,000 per depositor—has served well to improve confidence.[58] The new regulations were successfully applied in the case of Taurobank, which failed in July 1997. The limited amount of deposit coverage did not lead to any loss in confidence in the remainder of the system, although a "flight to quality" continues to be noticeable.

The second challenge was the 1998 Russian crisis, which caused a deep recession in Lithuania. The decline in output notwithstanding, bank performance did not deteriorate in the process. Since that time, the momentum for privatization has resumed. The Development Bank and Savings Bank were privatized in 2001; there was a tender also for privatizing the Agricultural Bank in 2001. Lithuania is now preoccupied with putting in place a prudential framework compatible with EU accession, which is likely to take place within a few years.

IV. Mongolia: the 1996 bank restructuring operation

Mongolia is geographically the largest but economically the smallest of the countries considered in this study. Many of the population of 2.5 million still follow a traditional lifestyle, and measured income per head is only about US$400 a year. The formal sector is dominated by the production of primary products, notably copper, cashmere, and gold, the prices for which can be volatile. Mongolia, while always formally independent, was closely integrated into the Soviet economic system, and formerly received large subsidies from the Soviet Union. The country was therefore very badly affected by the collapse of the Soviet economic bloc and the breakup of the Soviet Union. Real gross national product declined substantially between 1989 and 1992, and near-hyperinflation prevailed. However, by 1993, output had stabilized and new enterprises began to be established, especially in the gold mining, retail, and trade sectors (Table 11.7). Inflation moderated, although it remained high (at about 50 percent per year) and volatile. The national currency, the togrog, was allowed to float, although the authorities occasionally intervened and during some periods stabilized the rate.

Table 11.7. Mongolia: Selected Economic Indicators, 1993–98
(In percent except where otherwise indicated)

	1993	1994	1995	1996	1997	1998
Nominal GDP (in billions of togrog)	166	283	429	587	759	876
Real GDP growth	–3.0	2.3	6.3	2.4	4.0	3.5
Nominal GDP growth	251.4	70.4	51.5	36.8	29.3	15.4
CPI inflation (period average)	268.4	87.6	56.9	46.9	36.6	9.4
	(End of period)					
Broad money (in billions of togrog)	43	77	102	128	170	167
Growth in broad money[a]	227.6	79.5	32.9	25.8	19.8	8.8
Broad money/GDP	25.7	27.1	23.8	21.9	22.4	19.1
Bank claims on nongovernment sector (in billions of togrog)[b]	31	52	62	76	70	99
Claims on nongovernment/GDP	18.4	18.5	14.4	13.0	9.3	11.3
Reserve money (in billions of togrog)	14	29	38	51	65	73
Money multiplier	3.0	2.6	2.7	2.5	2.6	2.3
Money market interest rate	629	180	150	109	46	23
Exchange rate (togrog per U.S. dollar)	395	414	474	694	813	915
Gross international reserves including gold (U.S. dollar millions)	65	92	115	98	138	123
International reserves/reserve money	179.9	131.4	145.0	132.8	173.7	153.8

Sources: *International Financial Statistics*; Mongolian authorities; and Fund staff estimates.
[a] Adjusted for temporary increase in broad money at end-1997.
[b] Includes nonperforming loans.

Until 1990 Mongolia had a pure monobank system, without even the specialized banks found in other socialist countries. In 1991 new banking and central banking legislation was passed, and the monobank was broken up into seven institutions: Mongolbank, which is the central bank; two banks serving mostly retail clients and some enterprises, namely Ardyn Bank (also known as People's Bank) and Cooperative Bank; two banks that concentrated on enterprise financing, namely Insurance Bank and the Bank of Investment and

Technological Innovation (BITI); Agricultural Bank, which was represented mostly in rural areas; and Trade and Development Bank (TDB) specializing in foreign currency operations. All of the commercial banks except TDB were partially privatized already in 1991. Ownership became diffuse, although state enterprises gained dominant influence, especially in BITI. In addition to the descendants of the monobank, 11 new wholly private banks were founded during 1991–96. The data in Table 11.8 show that the banking system as a whole was highly concentrated, and certain individual financial institutions retained near-monopolies in their respective areas of specialization.

Table 11.8.   Mongolia: Structure of the Banking Sector

	Loans		Deposits	
	Amount (In Billions of Togrog)	Share (In Percent)	Amount (In Billions of Togrog)	Share (In Percent)
	October 1996			
Ardyn Bank	32.0	37.6	41.3	39.1
Insurance Bank	6.3	7.4	8.8	8.3
BITI	18.5	21.7	20.3	19.2
Agricultural Bank	10.0	11.8	9.2	8.7
TDB	9.1	19.7	18.0	17.1
Eight small banks	9.2	10.8	8.0	7.6
Total	**85.1**	**100.0**	**105.6**	**100.0**
	February 1997			
Savings Bank	...	...	23.1	23.2
Reconstruction Bank	6.6	13.4	21.6	21.8
BITI	17.1	34.8	13.2	13.3
Agricultural Bank	4.6	9.3	5.7	5.7
TDB	9.2	18.7	19.3	19.5
Eight small banks	11.7	23.8	16.3	16.4
Total	**49.2**	**100.0**	**99.2**	**100.0**
Memorandum item:				
Loans at MARA	30.0	...	...	...

Sources: Mongolbank; and Fund staff estimates.

The central bank developed comparatively quickly. It introduced reserve requirements in 1991, when also interest rates other than on household saving deposits were liberalized, but bank-by-bank credit ceilings were retained. Liquidity was provided to commercial banks under different facilities to accommodate their short-term liquidity needs to refinance their longer-term lending, and to finance lending to preferred sectors. In 1993 Mongolbank began auctioning short-term bills as a means to withdraw liquidity and in 1995 began auctioning refinance credits. The payment system was modernized starting in 1992 so that by 1996 most payment orders were being cleared within two days of submission. Some preliminary prudential regulations, notably on capital adequacy, were issued already in 1992, and a system of on- and off-site inspection established. Subsequently, prudential regulations were extended and strengthened. However, resource limitations, and the poor record keeping and internal controls at the commercial banks limited the effectiveness of supervision. When breaches of regulations were uncovered, Mongolbank was often unable or unwilling to impose sanctions or to force bank management to take corrective action.

The deterioration in bank soundness

It became apparent already in the early 1990s that the banking system was not functioning satisfactorily. In 1994 the government forced BITI to take over a small bank and Ardyn Bank had to take over Cooperative Bank.[59] BITI and Ardyn Bank were never compensated for implied reduction in their net worth, although they did receive special refinancing loans from the Mongolbank. This episode does not appear to have been decisive in undermining the soundness of these banks, but the strategy of merging weak banks proved at best a means of gaining time. By 1995 a report by an outside consultant who had inspected Ardyn Bank concluded that it was already insolvent and continuing to lose money.

The causes of the poor performance of banks were manifold. The macroeconomic conditions faced by the banks made sound operations difficult enough: inflation and interest rates fluctuated sharply, and many established enterprises suffered sharp drops in output. Bank management seems often to have been of poor quality or self-serving: reportedly insider lending was widespread, and banks were unwilling or unable to collect on many loans. Banks frequently preferred to capitalize interest on nonperforming loans rather than reveal the extent of losses, and may have made new loans to loss-making enterprises in the hopes of keeping them going and eventually recovering something. These adverse tendencies were compounded by certain government policies, notably the requirement that banks lend to certain privileged sectors and enterprises whose survival was judged to be of strategic or social importance. Such so-called inherited and directed credits were often extended on noncommercial terms, with little expectation that they would be repaid. In addition, banks reportedly came under political pressure not to force large employers into bankruptcy. Moreover, a minimum deposit interest rate was set with the aim of limiting dollarization and capital flight. At least during certain periods, the minimum rate was so high that banks attracted more funds than they could use to finance reasonably safe and viable projects.

During 1996 the state of the banking system began to deteriorate more rapidly. Several banks started to fail to meet prudential norms, credit ceilings, and reserve requirements, sometimes for extended periods. On occasion depositors were unable to withdraw funds on demand, and either had to pay a fee or received only payment orders that could not be cleared and that circulated as a means of payment. Among the major banks, Insurance Bank nearly ceased operating, and Ardyn Bank, Agricultural Bank, and BITI experienced periods of illiquidity and admitted to significant losses. On-site inspections by Mongolbank and reports by external bank auditors revealed an increasingly alarming picture of nonperforming loans, operational ineptitude and, in some banks, managerial complacency. For example, during the first nine months of 1996 Ardyn Bank repeatedly failed to meet reserve requirements, and suffered a decline of Mongolian togrogs (Tog) 6 billion (approximately US$12 million at the time) in its liquid assets, but the bank extended Tog 4 billion in new loans and continued to spend large sums on the construction of a headquarters building.

Mongolbank felt obliged to provide these banks with liquidity through the extension of ever-larger loans. These loans were not backed by collateral, nor were bank managers required to take immediate action to prevent the recurrence of illiquidity. In addition to explicit credits, some banks were exploiting delays in the clearing system to make payments even when they had no funds available. The government treasury operations were also affected because government deposits at commercial banks became unusable and some enterprises had difficulty paying taxes.[60]

The mounting difficulties of the banking system are illustrated in Figures 11.1 and 11.2. The real money stock, as measured by broad money deflated by the consumer price index (CPI), fell during the course of 1996, but real currency in circulation increased.[61] Thus, enterprises and especially households were fleeing the banking system. Bank liquidity, and especially bank reserve deposits with Mongolbank were also declining. The fall would have been greater and faster but for the extension of ever-larger refinancing credits from Mongolbank, and the build-up of government deposits at the commercial banks.

The situation of one small bank, Central Asian Bank (CAB), deteriorated to the point where in June 1996 Mongolbank decided to close it down. The value of the bank's deposits amounted to Tog 1,139 million (approximately US$2 million at the then prevailing exchange rate), owed to about 3,000 mostly small depositors. Although there was no deposit insurance in Mongolia, the authorities announced that depositors would be compensated for losses up to Tog 100,000, though interest accrued in 1995 and the first half of 1996 was annulled.[62] The assets of CAB were found to be almost entirely worthless, and indeed it was very difficult to identify assets because the bank had been run in a chaotic manner.

The failure of CAB contributed to a growing public distrust of the banks. Doubts about bank soundness became manifest in a number of forms: the real stock of togrog deposits began to fall; the exchange rate depreciated rapidly; TDB, which has a good reputation, experienced a strong inflow into dollar-denominated deposits.[63] There was however no acute run on the banks.

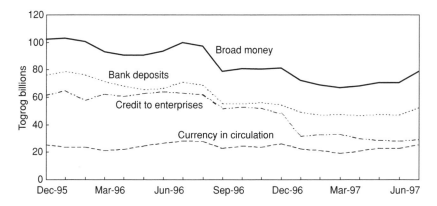

Figure 11.1.   Mongolia: Real Monetary Aggregates
(Deflated by end-1995 CPI)

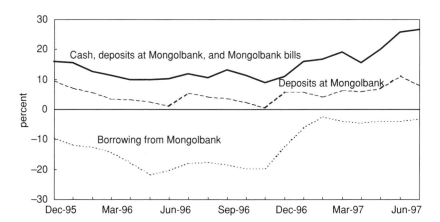

Figure 11.2.   Mongolia: Bank Liquidity
(In percent of bank deposits)

Sources: Mongolbank; and Fund staff estimates

The injection of liquidity by Mongolbank and falling demand for togrog-denominated assets accelerated the depreciation of the exchange rate, and led to a revival of inflation.

Initial attempt at restructuring

By mid-1996 the authorities clearly recognized that the state of the banking system was poor and deteriorating rapidly. The largest bank was illiquid, insolvent, continuing to lose money, and apparently under management that had no intention of altering its strategy. Of the other major banks, one was inactive and entirely illiquid, and two were technically insolvent and in breach of several prudential regulations. Only one major bank seemed to be on a sound footing, largely because of its very tight specialization in foreign exchange business. Many of the small banks were of dubious viability, but because their combined market share was less than 10 percent they were of little systemic importance. The available estimates of the magnitude of the losses were very approximate and probably too optimistic, but indicated that the negative net worth of certain banks was already large.[64]

A broad section of the population and most enterprises were already affected by the dysfunction of the banks, and would be exposed to large losses should the banks fail. Disintermediation, principally in the form of dollarization, was continuing. The rule of law was being undermined as borrowers were not sanctioned for nonrepayment; banks were restricting access to deposits and not paying penalties on breaches of regulations; and the Mongolbank was effectively compelled to extend liquidity-support loans to banks without the safeguards required by the new central bank law. The extension of liquidity-support loans, the disregard of reserve requirements, and the breakdown of the use of deposits as a means of payment undermined the implementation of monetary policy. Fiscal policy was also affected because many government deposits were effectively blocked in illiquid banks.

In late August the authorities began planning a comprehensive strategy to deal with all problem banks. In particular, they decided to move first against Insurance Bank, which by that stage was described as "comatose." Insurance Bank was widely known to be insolvent, and therefore its closure was expected to be met with little political opposition from vested interests, nor sharply to weaken confidence in other banks. Insurance Bank was also relatively small, so that the logistics of its closure would be manageable and the total volume of losses acceptable even if the government ended up bearing a disproportionate share of the burden.

While Mongolbank was in the midst of the preparations for the closure of Insurance Bank, Ardyn Bank applied for an additional liquidity support loan. The authorities realized that Ardyn Bank was also in a very precarious situation and decided to move against it immediately.

The implementation of this decision turned out to be difficult. It was hard to find anyone to assume the responsibilities of conservator. Eventually someone was appointed for Ardyn Bank, and officials entered both banks on September 18. There was no immediate public announcement of the action, nor any explanation of what would happen to the public's deposits or whether the banks would continue operating. Indeed, debate on these issues continued among the authorities even after the seizure of the bank. In practice household depositors were allowed to make withdrawals of up to Tog 100,000, and enterprises apparently could make withdrawals freely. Mongolbank supported Ardyn Bank with new liquidity-support loans at favorable interest rates.

The conservator for Ardyn Bank resigned after three days, citing a lack of official support for her actions. Ardyn Bank management had attempted to undermine her authority, and the existing staff had been hostile and uncooperative, while the conservator did not have available the support staff necessary to effect control of Ardyn Bank's numerous activities, which were often run with little systematic documentation. The practical difficulties of the operation combined, and the political pressure that Ardyn Bank management was able to exert forced the authorities to yield. Control was restored to the old management in both banks. The Governor of Mongolbank publicly apologized and resigned shortly thereafter.

The bank closure operation

The collapse of the attempt in September to place two problem banks in conservatorship did not cause the authorities to abandon strong action as politically impossible or resign themselves to "muddling through" in the hope that a general economic recovery would lift the strain on the banks. Rather, the experience led them to the conclusion that a more thought-through and well-organized strategy was necessary.

The authorities also recognized that they faced several constraints on their approach to bank rehabilitation. Implementation capacity was extremely limited. The central bank had only a handful of staff with training in financial analysis and on-site supervision. No pool of trained accountants and auditors, let alone receivers, was available in the country. The authorities had experience only in the closure of one small bank (CAB), which had turned out to be a drawn-out and laborious exercise. Skills in bank management and operations were also in short supply, and it was unclear whether the authorities could identify and attract the ablest bank managers. The judiciary and the legal profession were not fully familiar with market-based economic concepts and in particular banking practice, and in any case the courts were overburdened and reputedly liable to be open to influence.

The nongovernment sector generally could not be relied upon to discipline bank management or provide new capital, even if the banks were economically solvent. Rather, the nongovernment sector relied critically on the banking system to provide transaction services, extend loans, and offer savings instruments. The government also relied on the banks to conduct its business. In this sense the continued functioning of a banking system represented a kind of "public good." Any costs incurred in maintaining this public good would have to be borne at a time of great fiscal stringency, as the government faced myriad spending demands, diminished revenue, and limited financing.

Under these circumstances the authorities realized that they would have to seize back the initiative in rehabilitating the banking system. The government, including the central bank, would have to initiate intervention and in the end bear much of the financial burden involved. Any action to intervene in the troubled banks would have to be as comprehensive and rapid as possible. The constraints on implementation capacity implied that efforts would have to be concentrated on the most urgent problems; the resolution of less immediately threatening problems, and many of the specific issues that would arise from intervention would have to be delayed in the interests of decisiveness. The rehabilitation strategy would also aim to reestablish respect for the rule of law and to restore the effectiveness of monetary policy.

The strategy worked out in November 1996 was designed to accord with these principles. During the initial operation attention would focus on the two large banks that were in the worst condition, namely Ardyn Bank and Insurance Bank. Together, these banks accounted for 45 percent of deposits and loans. Both would be closed and liquidated by receivers. The accounts of their household depositors would be immediately transferred to a new "narrow" bank, the Savings Bank that would hold only safe assets. The accounts of their enterprise depositors in good standing would be transferred after being partially written down, together with nonimpaired loans, to a new commercial bank named Reconstruction Bank (RB). Their impaired loans would be transferred to a collection agency, the Mongolian Asset Realization Agency (MARA). This phase of bank restructuring would be financed by the issue of government bonds. The two other large problem banks (BITI and Agricultural Bank) would be obliged to sign MOUs with the government and the Mongolbank under which they committed themselves to raise capital, streamline operations, and improve their loan portfolio according to an ambitious timetable. Initially the small banks would be largely ignored. Subsequently attention could be directed toward recovering loans and strengthening financial discipline on both banks and borrowers, and improving the operational capacities and financial strength of the banks. Still later decisions would be needed on the further restructuring of the entire banking sector, for example, through additional closures, mergers, and eventually privatization.

The initial operation was planned in detail so that it could be carried out as rapidly and smoothly as possible. The steps that had to be executed included the following:

Organizational and legal issues

- A small high-level committee with representatives of the ministry of finance, Mongolbank, and the prime minister's office was formed to coordinate the preparation and implementation of the operation. As far as possible the plan of the operation was kept confidential so that the management of the targeted institutions would have less chance to prepare a defense or plunder their banks. However, other ministries and key parliamentarians were informed of the strategy so as to build consensus.

- A number of legal issues had to be resolved in preparing the closure operation. New laws on banking and the central bank had been passed in September 1996. It was verified that according to these laws the Mongolbank had the power to close a bank, appoint a receiver, and withdraw a bank license without necessarily first consulting existing shareholders or attempting to rehabilitate the bank through the appointment of a conservator. Mongolbank's actions could not be halted by a restraining order, but they could be challenged in court ex post.[65]

Institutional restructuring

- The Savings Bank was registered as a company and granted a bank license by Mongolbank after submitting the legally required documentation, including a business plan. The Savings Bank was designed to be a "safe haven" for household depositors, whose savings would no longer be illiquid or in danger of forfeiture, and who would continue to need transaction services. To this end the Savings Bank received household deposits as its only liability and was given only safe assets, specifically government restructuring bonds, Mongolbank bills, cash in vault, reserve deposits, and real property. Therefore, the Savings Bank needed only the minimum allowable capitalization (Tog 400 million), which was provided by the government. It was assigned most of the branch network and nonmanagerial staff of the closed banks and opened as soon as possible after the closing operation. Managers for the Savings Bank (and the other new institutions) had to be recruited, which proved difficult given the small pool of experienced bankers in Mongolia.
- Likewise preparations were made to establish the RB. The RB received the verifiably performing loans of the failed banks and the (written-down) deposits of enterprises that were not in arrears. In this way those enterprises did not suffer an immediate liquidity squeeze or a disruption of payment services. The enterprises could transfer their business to other banks, but that process would be drawn out because banks in Mongolia prefer to build up familiarity with clients over time. As the value of the transferred deposits exceeded that of the good loans, the RB also received enough restructuring bonds to ensure its adequate capitalization (its initial capital was Tog 1.8 billion). In addition, the RB took over all foreign operations of the failed banks, including a small volume of household foreign currency deposits.
- Under the agreed strategy the MARA would receive the impaired loans of the failed banks and try to recover as much as possible. The aim was not only to minimize the cost of the bank restructuring operation, but also to set an example of financial discipline and the enforcement of loan contracts. It could use a number of techniques to recover loans,

including netting loans against deposits, renegotiating loans, seizing collateral, and initiating bankruptcy proceedings. It had been proposed to make MARA an incorporated public enterprise, which would have facilitated the extension of performance-based contracts to MARA staff and enhanced its commercial, nonpolitical nature. The authorities opted instead to make it a government agency so that its actions carried the official imprimatur. It was made answerable to the ministry of finance, which set for it an ambitious timetable for loan recoveries. It was given a separate budget, which went largely for personnel, establishing regional offices, and the storage and deposing of collateral (some of which consisted of livestock).

Allocation of assets and liabilities

- Once appointed, the responsibility of a failed bank's receiver was to the creditors of the failed institutions, but according to the new laws he could satisfy classes of creditors by making payouts based on the estimated value of remaining assets, rather than on final verified amounts. The new laws also specified a certain schedule of priority for creditors, according to which the claims of high-priority creditors such as household depositors would be met to the full extent possible before any payout could be made to others. Mongolbank had estimated that the remaining assets of the failed institutions were sufficient to cover all household deposits, and indeed households were given immediate access to the full value of their deposits. The estimated remaining assets did not fully cover enterprise deposits, but were instead allocated pro rata: the value of enterprise deposits in Ardyn Bank were written down by 20 percent and those in Insurance Bank by 50 percent. The same rule was applied to the deposits of local government and the social security and pension funds. This allocation relied upon Mongolbank acknowledging that its claims on the failed banks were loans rather than deposits and thus of lower priority, and the central government accepting the role of residual claimant who bears the risks in case the value of loans turns out to be less than first estimated.[66]
- Several transactions were necessary to transfer the assets and liabilities of the failed banks to the new institutions while ensuring that all parties fulfilled their respective fiduciary responsibilities. The core of these transactions was that the receivers would sell nonperforming loans to MARA in exchange for restructuring bonds; the receivers could then transfer to the Savings Bank togrog household deposit matched with an equal value of assets in the form of bonds, reserve money, and real property; the receivers could make a similar transfer to the RB of enterprise business (deposits of enterprises in good standing, loans to them, foreign currency denominated assets and liabilities, other assets

needed for operations, and a balancing value of bonds). In this way the receivers could discharge their duty as rapidly as possible. In practice, a number of rounds of transactions were necessary before all balance sheets of all institutions were brought in order, for example, because it took some time to identify and assess all the loans recorded in the rural branches of the failed banks. To facilitate transactions, it was necessary to issue a larger volume of bonds than was eventually needed for the restructuring. However, since any excess would be distributed among wholly government-owned institutions, it did not constitute a net increase in government debt.

- The specification of the restructuring bonds needed to be adapted to circumstances, in particular the absence of a functioning bond market and the prevalence of high and very variable inflation and interest rates. In the initial period the bonds were issued with a maturity of just one month, with an assurance from the ministry of finance that they would be rolled over; the interest rate was set each month at a level slightly above the then current Mongolbank bill rate, which serves as a guiding rate in the economy. In this way the new banks could at least break even while offering attractive interest rates, and the budget would not be burdened with very high interest costs indefinitely if rates fell. During the first half of 1997 the rate was always set at 4 percent per month. The authorities decided to make the bills in general nonnegotiable and available only to banks.[67]

- The government decided to use the same bonds to fulfill its pledge to compensate commercial banks for losses on inherited and directed credits. The government accepted that it was responsible for these quasi-fiscal operations, and therefore agreed to swap bonds for inherited and directed credits in all banks. The amount involved was Tog 7.7 billion (US$11 million) at the end of 1996.

Intervention procedures

- Mongolbank made a number of special provisions to anticipate the possible effects of the bank closures and the opening of new institutions. A large volume of cash was distributed to Mongolbank branches so that withdrawals from reliquidified deposits could be met. Once the restructuring bonds were distributed banks were informed that, at least for a limited time, they would be rediscountable at face value with Mongolbank. In this way the new banks, and other commercial banks that received bonds in exchange for inherited and directed credits, could acquire the liquid resources to comply with reserve requirements. Several commercial banks, including some nonintervened banks, made extensive use of this facility in the months following the closing operation. Mongolbank also monitored developments in the foreign exchange market closely for signs of a run on the currency, but none emerged.[68]

- The actual closing operation was logistically challenging. The operation started shortly before the close of business on Friday, December 13, when the banks would be relatively empty of clients and few transactions would be under way. About 900 officials were deployed to enter all the nearly 100 branches of Ardyn and Insurance Banks simultaneously. These officials showed their credentials and required all senior bank management to leave the premises immediately before they could seize physical or financial assets or destroy records. The officials then set about securing property and means of payment. It was recognized that nonmanagerial staff would be needed to reconcile loan records and to start the operations of the new banks. They were therefore offered new employment contracts, which were almost universally accepted.

- Officials and some bank staff then worked through the weekend to identify the banks' assets and liabilities and organize the opening of the new institutions as soon as possible. Meanwhile the operation was explained to the public, who were reassured that all would be "business as usual" by Monday. According to the original plan the Savings Bank and the RB would initially operate out of the same premises and with the same staff, who would have had to identify household and enterprise clients and complete correspondingly different payment orders, etc. This proved impractical, and instead on Monday morning Ardyn Bank branches opened as the Savings Bank, and Insurance Bank branches opened as the RB; later the branches and other facilities were divided more rationally. The public response was indeed muted, with only a small surge in withdrawals, and the exchange rate remained stable. Depositors at Insurance Bank were reportedly pleased to have received anything, while enterprise depositors at Ardyn Bank complained only moderately about the write-down of their deposits. An effort by Ardyn Bank management to organize a strike by employees fizzled out. Ardyn Bank management also initiated court action against Mongolbank, which was eventually quashed.

Follow-up

Much time and effort was required to sort out the final balance sheets of the failed banks and the initial balance sheets of the new institutions. Revised, ex post estimates of the losses, shown in Table 11.9, were obtained in June 1997. According to these estimates, the total losses were approximately as large as had been estimated in November 1996, but only after numerous positive and negative adjustments had been made. For example, liabilities increased due to the recognition of certain amounts payable or in transit as deposit claims, but assets were increased by income accrued in 1996. The estimates are based on certain, perhaps optimistic, assumptions about how much MARA would be able to recover from the impaired loans that it had taken over.

Table 11.9. Mongolia: Estimated Bank Losses and Their Allocation
(In billions of togrog)

	Ardyn Bank	**Insurance Bank**	**Total**
Total loss to allocate	26.3	12.0	38.3
(As percent of 1996 GDP)	–4.9	–2.3	–7.1
Government	16.2	7.5	23.6
Government deposits	0.6	2.0	2.6
Other	15.6	5.5	21.0
Mongolbank	4.8	1.5	6.3
Enterprises	2.2	1.4	3.7
Offset to nonperforming loans	1.0	...	1.0
Deposit write-down	1.3	...	2.7
Shareholders	3.0	1.2	4.2
Others	...	0.5	0.5

Sources: Mongolbank; and Fund staff estimates.

Some of the revenue drain may be offset if the new institutions pay dividends or when they are eventually privatized. Interest paid on the bonds held by Mongolbank should also return to government in the form of dividends, and Mongolbank initially at least voluntarily accepted to hand back 80 percent of any interest it received, and interest due was not always paid in cash. However, Mongolbank itself suffered large losses which left it undercapitalized.

The MARA was not expected to recover very large amounts from the nonperforming loans that it was given, in part because many of the borrowing enterprises ceased to exist. By June 1997 it had recovered Tog 1.3 billion and seized approximately Tog 2.0 billion in collateral, while incurring expenses of only about Tog 100 million; the overall recovery rate was about 17 percent. One of the purposes of MARA was to set an example of financial discipline by pursuing defaulting borrowers by all legal means, and in this it has reportedly been diligent, within the limits set by an inadequate court system.

In the initial aftermath of the closing operation the situation in the banking system remained generally calm, and there were signs of a return of confidence. The real money stock recovered in 1997, led by a rise in the real value of deposits at commercial banks (see Figure 11.1). The exchange rate displayed some turbulence in the second quarter of 1997, which may largely be attributable to uncertainty surrounding presidential elections, but it was stable over the summer of 1997 after appreciating from its lows in May. Inflation in some months had been negative, albeit due in part to seasonal factors.

Aggregate bank liquidity was adequate, although certain banks were on occasion illiquid (see Figure 11.2). Among individual banks, the Savings Bank lost deposits in the second quarter of 1997 after it lowered interest rates on deposits, but recovered them when it restored rates. In some months it and RB failed to meet reserve requirements, in part because the government was occasionally late in paying interest on the restructuring bonds, and therefore Mongolbank waived penalties on the reserve shortfall. The process of dollarization was not reversed; dollar-denominated deposits at TDB, which was seen as the soundest bank, continued to grow rapidly in the first half of 1997. Some of this trend may be viewed as a stock adjustment as enterprises and households adjusted their portfolios once all deposits became freely available.

Table 11.8 shows that the structure of the banking industry in Mongolia was indeed transformed. No one bank is as dominant as Ardyn was before, although certain banks retain near-monopolies in their respective segments of the market. The small banks and TDB have expanded their balance sheets and gained market share at the expense of both the successors to Ardyn and Insurance Banks and also the distressed Agricultural Bank and BITI that are subject to MOUs.

Epilogue

It was realized at the time of the 1996 operation that the Mongolian banking sector would require substantial further restructuring. Indeed, the subsequent period was marked by the continued severe distress of some banks and the reemergence of large losses, which necessitated a second round of closures in 1999.

Two developments constituted the principal hindrances to the emergence of a sound financial system. First, the two banks under MOUs, namely Agricultural Bank and BITI, failed to meet their commitments, and in particular failed to raise sufficient new capital, improve credit quality, and reduce costs. Second, RB soon went beyond its original mandate and became a universal bank, taking deposits and expanding lending rapidly. Much of this lending seems to have benefited well-connected parties, and prudential supervision was clearly inadequate. At a macroeconomic level, Mongolia was severely affected first by the Asian financial crisis, which caused the prices of its main commodity exports to fall sharply, and then by two years of exceptionally harsh weather. In these circumstance, the share of loans in the banking system that were nonperforming rose to over 30 percent in 1998, and eventually almost all loans in the portfolios of RB and BITI became delinquent. The banking system made losses, and capital was eroded almost to zero; the losses of RB, Agricultural Bank and BITI in 1998 are estimated at Tog 4.1 billion, Tog 5.1 billion, and Tog 12.0 billion, respectively, totaling about 2.4 percent of GDP or more than 20 percent of total lending to nongovernment.

An initial attempt in 1998 to merge RB with a private bank, Golomtbank, was reversed due to political opposition to the way the transaction was carried out. However, in early 1999 RB, BITI, and Agricultural Bank were put into conservatorship, under which they could take no new deposits and grant no new loans. In the fall of that year, RB and BITI were placed in receivership and their licenses revoked; their residual assets were eventually passed to the MARA. Agricultural Bank had to be preserved in order to provide financial services to the population and government in the countryside. New, foreign-led management was installed, and an effort undertaken to reduce operating costs. Also in 1999, four small private banks went into voluntary liquidation, and three others voluntarily ceased banking operations.

By mid-2001 there were 13 banks operating in Mongolia. TDB was the largest, with more than 40 percent of all assets in a relatively well-diversified portfolio. TDB at this point appeared to be profitable and well capitalized. The Savings Bank was the second largest institution and held a majority of local currency deposits. However, its capital base was weak, the quality of its loan portfolio was not assured, and it remained dependent on the maintenance of an adequate spread between the interest rate it paid on deposits and that it received on government securities, which still made up three-quarters of its assets. Nonetheless, it was marginally profitable and liquid. The privately-owned Golomtbank had the third largest share of assets in the system. Agricultural Bank was just profitable after it resumed lending to small rural borrowers and the new external management made progress in limiting operating expenses, but it still has negative capital. The banking system as a whole appears to be sounder and more commercially oriented than before, but remains vulnerable to the exogenous macroeconomic shocks to which Mongolia is especially prone, and loan quality must remain a concern.

V. Common trends in the banking crises and their resolution

The previous chapters identified a number of similarities, and also key differences, between the three countries being studied, both with regard to banking sector developments and to the ways in which the authorities addressed the problems.

Sources of banking sector distress in transition countries
Initial development of the banking sector under transition

In all three countries the banking sectors had evolved out of the monobank systems that had operated throughout most of the planned economy period. As the socialist system was dismantled, development of the banking sector derived from two sources: first the establishment of banks out of the monobank; and second, the development of a private banking sector usually through the liberalization of banking laws in order to allow the entry of new banks. Already toward the end of the socialist period there were moves, particularly in Bulgaria, toward setting up a two-tier banking system through the carving out of a central bank and a number of commercial banks from the monobank. These commercial banks were generally not in competition with each other, since they were all state-owned and generally servicing specified sectors of the economy. Each country had an Agriculture Bank, an Economic (and/or Industry) Bank, and a Foreign Trade Bank. In all cases households saved predominantly through the Savings Bank, which during the socialist period had been used to finance the budget.

The private banking sector was formed on the basis of lax licensing procedures, and low capital requirements. With banking supervision barely functioning at this time, there was little pressure on these banks to develop sound banking practices after their establishment. The result of this initial liberalization was in most cases the creation of significant numbers of mostly small banks, often established largely in order to generate funds to lend to the owners' other business interests—these were therefore essentially "pocket banks," operating without the constraints of operative insider lending, or large exposure, limits.

In all these countries there was a substantial decline in economic activity in the first few years of the transition, reflecting a weakening in performance of the enterprise sector, particularly in the heavy industry sectors—these were often the main customers of the state banks, which were still the dominant element in the banking systems. With lending continuing to these sectors, often at the insistence of the government, there was a marked increase in nonperforming loans in these banks' portfolios. Indeed, the political influence on lending decisions increased as the fiscal position deteriorated, generally following the collapse of traditional sources of government revenue and the rapid accumulation of debt on the first few years of the transition. With governments no longer able to lend freely to favored sectors, the authorities relied on the banks for quasi-fiscal purposes. The banks' portfolios thus became determined by political rather than commercial considerations.

Meanwhile, the absence of any understanding of risk among depositors meant that high interest rates attracted depositors largely regardless of the riskiness of the institution.[69] With no financial institution having failed in the pre-transition period, there was an expectation of implicit government protection of depositors. Without high deposit rates being associated with greater riskiness, owners and managers raised rates they offered depositors above economic levels, further increasing the fragility of their institutions.

Poor infrastructure

In the period of central planning, the countries' accounting systems had been designed with the primary objective of monitoring achievement of the targets of the national plans. National accounting systems designed within this framework differed substantially from international accounting practices, with the banking sectors particularly affected by these differences. With no accrual accounting, and no proper accounting treatment for delinquent loans, the deteriorating position of the banks was not immediately obvious. High inflation in most of the countries for much of the transition period meant also, given existing accounting regulations, that valuation gains—for instance from foreign exchange positions—gave the impression of continuing profitability while the underlying position of the banks was already deteriorating markedly. There was a lack of understanding of the purposes of transparent accounting, i.e., that financial statements should reflect real developments, and that there would be substantive consequences from these statements.

The inadequacy or absence of minimum capital requirements contributed to the proliferation of small and vulnerable banks. The lack of appropriate prudential regulations, in particular the inadequate loan loss classification and provisioning regulations, distorted the banks' reporting of their positions. There was widespread decapitalization of the banks, as owners paid themselves dividends on the basis of reported income and unrealized revaluations.

The supervisory expertise at the central banks was severely limited—there had been no experience of operating supervision in a market environment, the central banks had limited supervisory authority, and they had few resources to build up a capacity quickly. The importance of the function was not generally recognized; neither the managers of the state-owned banks nor the owners of the private banks had any desire to see the role of the supervisors enhanced, and in the event of confrontation it was unlikely that the bank supervisor (a low-paid state functionary) would carry the necessary authority to challenge the banker. In practice the supervision function was generally exercised largely through the off-site and mechanical monitoring of compliance with regulations (a natural follow-on from decades of monitoring plan implementation). Even when appropriate regulations were in place and transgressions were identified, there were few instances of penalties being levied.

Underlying these issues was the political and economic power of the banks' owners and managers. These were frequently among the most powerful individuals in the country. At a time when the establishment of the rule of law was by no means secure, these individuals rarely felt that they had much to fear from the legal process. There were also frequent conflicts of interest, for instance, with politicians linked to the banks.

The role of banks as intermediating resources between lenders and borrowers was limited, with bank failure being the consequences of inadequacies in performing this intermediation, was not fully appreciated or institutionalized. Thus, in none of these countries was there a suitable exit mechanism in place. Without the prospect of such sanctions, the incentive for bankers to discipline themselves in the rates they offered depositors or pursue nonperforming debtors was limited.

Similarly, on the borrowers' side there was no traditional repayment culture. In centrally planned economies, credit management was essentially a bookkeeping exercise, designed to monitor compliance with the plan, rather than itself determining the allocation of resources. With banks not perceived as intermediaries of funds, nonrepayment was not seen as implying a real loss of resources to the original lender or to a potential alternative user of the funds. Meanwhile, with enterprises under severe strain in facing the challenges of the transition, debt repayment was frequently not seen as a priority. Indeed, with many of the credits in the state sector having been determined on noncommercial grounds in order to foster other goals, such as the preservation of employment in those sectors, with the economies continuing to decline, nonrepayment of debt was seen as a valid way to avoid disruptive adjustments.

None of the countries had an adequate legal framework, in particular as regards the authority of the central bank in enforcing supervisory requirements. Licensing was frequently the responsibility of a different agency, and with no viable exit strategy and derisory maximum penalties available, there were few sanctions available to the central bank. Bank insolvency laws were nonexistent, and general insolvency laws barely tested. As insolvency cases came to court, judges frequently showed themselves sympathetic to the debtors.

Linked to this was the lack also of a functioning collateral law. Thus, even when a debtor was in default and had pledged collateral there was no certainty that the banks would be able to seize the collateral. In any case, for many borrowers there was little collateral available, apart from real estate—which frequently had minimal value in the transition conditions.

Commercial banking expertise was often in short supply. A few bankers had had international experience and in some cases demonstrated considerable success for their banks even while the overall banking system of the country was in deep distress.[70] Mostly, however, state bank managers were government functionaries, sometimes redeployed from sectors where they had gained no financial expertise. Private bankers might have had some corporate experience, but they too had frequently not worked in commercial banks. Once banks started getting into trouble, authorities tried replacing managements, but this was largely a game of musical chairs. In Lithuania, for instance, there were several periods of rotation of management around the state banks. Each time the "new" management could disclaim responsibility for the problems in the bank they had just entered, while escaping also from responsibility for the problems of the banks they had just left.

Particularly in Bulgaria, considerable hopes were placed at the outset on the prospect that the newly-arriving foreign banks would boost the commercial banking culture for the sector as a whole and would thereby stimulate also the domestic banks quickly to make themselves competitive in international terms. However, evidence for a significant knock-on effect during this early phase cannot be found. The foreign banks were able to restrict themselves to "cherry-picking" the most profitable business, largely trade finance and a small number of flagship customers. They thus dampened the profitable opportunities open to the domestic banks. Perhaps even more seriously, they could identify the best local staff and were able to outbid domestic rivals. Even during the worst phases of the banking crisis, in most cases the foreign banks did well.

Many of these developments and characteristics are not unique to transition economies, but are found in some degree in most countries that suffered a banking crisis. This similarity obtains primarily because severe banking crises are predominantly caused by distress at the corporate level, which translates into credit risk, and such distress can arise in any economy. Thus, banking crises are often proceeded by a fall or marked slowdown in output, large variations in relative prices, and sharp fluctuations in inflation and real interest rates, all of which adversely affect the ability of borrowers to service their obligations. At a structural level, many banking crises can be traced to an excessive dependence of banks on corporate owners, or to politically-motivated lending to nonviable projects. Furthermore, the inadequacies of the legal framework and the judicial system in transition countries have parallels elsewhere, in particular with regard to the enforcement of property rights and the collection of collateral and the resolution of bankruptcies.

Emergence of banking sector problems

While problems in the banking sector had been building up for some time, they became evident as the economies started to stabilize, decapitalization reached its natural limit, and international accounting and provisioning standards were applied.[71] With inflation slowing markedly, and currencies no longer depreciating so rapidly, it was no longer possible for banks to live off their unrealized exchange rate gains.

Public awareness of the weakness of the banks developed when the authorities took their first partial measures to address the banking system problems. In Mongolia a small bank was closed; in Bulgaria the authorities tried to introduce a limited explicit deposit insurance scheme. The unthinkable quickly came to seem possible, and even likely—banks might be closed, and people might lose money.

With a loss of public confidence in the weakest banks—or those perceived to be the weakest or with least hope of a government bailout—liquidity problems emerged. To some extent the situation was kept in check by the fact that the bulk of household savings remained in the respective Savings Banks, so that there was no total panic, but there was nevertheless an atmosphere of surly disgruntlement. The central banks tried to alleviate the liquidity problems by financing the banks in difficulty, but the absence of adequate monetary instruments meant that there was little attempt (or ability) to sterilize such intervention. Monetary control was rapidly lost, the exchange rate depreciated, and inflation accelerated. Moreover, the liquidity support was generally provided unconditionally, and the affected banks made no adjustments in their behavior. With no restoration of public confidence, the banks' liquidity problems continued to mount, exacerbating the loss of monetary control.

Especially in Bulgaria and Mongolia, the systemic nature of the banking system problems became evident through breakdowns in the payments system. In Bulgaria at the beginning of 1996 substantial and unprecedented arrears emerged in the interbank clearing, reflecting burgeoning liquidity weaknesses in a number of banks and passing them on across the system. The public's understandable "flight to quality," with withdrawals from banks already suffering liquidity pressures, reinforced the liquidity problem. Although some of the withdrawn deposits were placed into the stronger banks, much went into the foreign exchange market, worsening the liquidity situation for the system as a whole. Banks without immediate liquidity problems sought to build up their own liquidity to protect themselves in anticipation of a further spreading of the crisis. In addition, the interbank market quickly segmented, with sound banks willing to trade only among themselves and the other banks dependent on the central bank to provide them with their liquidity needs.

Problems emerged in both the private and the public banks, although observers frequently attributed the weaknesses to one or other of the sectors.[72] Governments paid more attention to addressing and reviving the state banks, since they were the owners, and these banks were systemically the most important. The banking crisis led—at least temporarily—to a resurgence in the share of the banking sector owned by the state.

Implementation of banking crisis resolution

The countries considered here all made initial attempts to deal with the weakness in their banking sectors. However, these initial attempts, and especially the first attempts to close the weakest institutions, generally ended in failure and confusion. The authorities were hindered by the absence of a recognized legal framework, the lack of precedent, their own inexperience, the fear of losses among the banks' customers, and the political strength of owners or managers. In Mongolia, after one major bank was initially closed, the central bank governor reopened the bank and apologized to owners and staff. In Bulgaria, advance notice of the closures was given to banks' owners, and the banks' vaults were found to be empty once the authorities finally entered the premises. Also, the initial closures clearly did not address all the weak banks in the system, leading to pressures for—and expectations of—further bank closures in the near future.

The later and more successful attempts at dealing with systematic banking crises in these countries were characterized by their comprehensiveness and decisiveness. The authorities proved ready to close even very large institutions, to incur considerable costs, and to change the institutional framework supporting the banking sector.[73]

In most cases the weak surviving institutions were put under a much tighter oversight from the authorities, often involving memoranda of understanding and management changes—in part to mitigate the moral hazard effect of providing public support to insolvent institutions. The surviving banks' activities were curtailed, and reporting requirements enhanced, with the expectation of a turnaround of financial prospect and an ending of flow losses. In the event of insolvency, banks were recapitalized with government bonds, or their bad loans were bought by the government and placed into a newly formed AMC.[74]

The authorities also committed themselves to requiring strong efforts from the banks and the newly-established agencies to intensify loan collection, in part to recoup some of the government's outlays on the restructuring, and in part to avoid the moral hazard that debtors might think that the bankruptcy, or restructuring, of their creditor might relieve them of their obligation to service their debts. In Lithuania and Mongolia centralized asset management agencies were introduced; in Bulgaria the authorities maintained a decentralized approach. In all cases the pressure on debtors was intensified.

The process was made possible by the passage of supporting legislation, either immediately before the interventions (as in Mongolia) or rapidly thereafter (as in Bulgaria) to enhance the authority of the central bank, and to facilitate the process of liquidating insolvent institutions. In Mongolia the clear specification in the new legislation of the respective priorities of the claims of the various creditors of the banks formed the basis of the authorities' full protection of household deposits in the winding up of the major insolvent bank and the establishment of a successor institution. Prudential and accounting regulations were revised, so that the authorities could obtain a true picture of the state of the banks and provide appropriate remedies, and so that public confidence in the surviving institutions would be restored.

Meanwhile, in belated recognition of the costs of a weak banking system, tighter prudential requirements were placed on the surviving banks—for instance, capital adequacy requirements were brought to international levels—and central banks' supervision departments were enhanced. In Bulgaria the supervisors were given autonomy from the rest of the central bank, to minimize the risk of political interference. More staff were recruited to supervision departments, and enforcement of prudential requirements was taken much more seriously. There was also some recognition of the problems of conflict of interest. Restrictions on insider lending and large exposures were introduced and enforced. Politicians were disbarred from bank ownership— and a strong emphasis was placed on privatization to get the state out of the banks altogether.[75] In addition, licensing requirements were tightened, and minimum capital requirements increased, to avoid further weak new banks entering the market—and also to provide those interested in entering the market to purchase an existing institution.

The authorities also recognized the need to create a commercial banking culture. Collateral laws were passed; efforts were made to develop financial markets, including treasury bills, in part to create a supply of collateral that could support lending activity.

While there were broad similarities in how the countries handled their banking systems, there were also differences. Bulgaria had the highest level of banking sector intermediation of any transition economy, at the same time as it already had a huge fiscal burden. In the depth of the crisis, it would have been almost impossible for the authorities to issue any further government debt at any price. This severely constrained the authorities' ability to take a large share of the burden in addressing the banking sector losses, and thus led to a higher burden being borne by households and enterprises, in large part through the erosion of the bulk of banks' domestic currency liabilities through inflation. In Mongolia, by contrast, with bank intermediation only a small part of the economy, the magnitude of insolvency was much smaller relative to GDP, and the fiscal situation not in quite such dire straits; hence, it was possible to protect a much larger section of the public (i.e., all households and small enterprises) and to rely more on the issue of government securities.

In all cases the restoration of confidence after the crisis involved also macroeconomic stabilization. Indeed, the longer-term success of Bulgaria and Lithuania in recovering from their banking crises may be considered to derive in large part from their adherence to their macroeconomic stabilization programs over the ensuing years. In all three cases the banking crisis led to changes in the government. In both Bulgaria and Lithuania they unfolded in the context of far-reaching institutional changes, with the central banks transformed into currency boards. In the case of Bulgaria in particular the ability of the authorities to intervene in the banking sector through providing liquidity support was drastically curtailed, with support severely limited quantitatively by the amount of resources available in the banking department of the central bank, and institutionally by requiring that the head of supervision certificate that he considered that the liquidity support being provided was needed to combat a systemic threat.

VI. Some lessons from the resolution of the banking crises

The characteristics of the three economies at the start of their transition from central planning, plus their initial approaches to developing a banking sector, made inevitable the emergence of serious banking sector distress at some stage. The authorities in these countries recognized the risks and the emerging crisis, but often first postponed addressing the issues or undertook only half-hearted measures.

The long delays in initiating the restructurings made the process much more costly and difficult. One reason for the delays was the absence of adequate legislation and the lack of decent accounting figures. Perhaps more important was the lack of political willingness in that environment to confront the various interests that were defending the status quo, to allocate the inevitable costs between the affected parties, including the government, and to assume the risk that the intervention would go wrong.

Even when more forceful action was initiated, it often proved necessary to undertake several rounds of bank intervention. Such partial solutions can complicate and worsen the problem, by undermining the public's confidence in the banking system and creating perverse incentives for banks to take excessive risks or to strip assets. By contrast, the bank resolution in Mongolia in 1996 was thorough-going, even though not fully comprehensive; it served to stop the huge flow of losses at the worst banks and restore liquidity to the deposits of households and enterprises. To some extent, undertaking partial solutions, where the authorities take into account that more may need to be done later and work to prepare for the subsequent stages, may be the best available option where information (for instance about the state of the banks) and implementation capacity is limited.

Merely intervening in the most troubled institutions and curtailing their operations is not enough, nor will such an approach command political support, because it does not contribute to the maintenance of a functioning financial system. The nongovernment sector relies on the banking system to provide transaction services, extend loans, and offer savings instruments. The government also relies on the banks to conduct its business. In this sense, the continued functioning of a banking system represents a kind of "public good" that had to be maintained. In the countries covered in this study, the large costs incurred in maintaining this public good had to be borne at a time of great fiscal stringency, as the government faced myriad spending demands, diminished revenue, and limited financing.

Efforts at banking crisis resolution were successful only when it was carried out on a comprehensive basis, that is, when the authorities decided to deal with the entire banking sector as a whole and as part of a scheme that would preserve essential banking services. Restructuring is expensive, and will cause resentment, especially where fiscal constraints are very tight, as in these transitional economies. However, once one is in a crisis, these costs are largely unavoidable. Successful resolution requires a political consensus, which in turn requires that major interest groups see the need for action and the unavoidability of bearing some of the costs, yet the burden must be shared in a manner that is seen to be equitable. These efforts also had to be integrated with a program of macroeconomic stabilization.

Restructuring is primarily the responsibility of the government. The costs of restructuring, as well as the range of skills required, are well beyond the capacity of the central bank. Furthermore, the government must take the political decision as to how the costs of bank resolution are to be distributed. The government needs to coordinate closely with the central bank, for instance in the drafting of the relevant legislation, but with so much public money at stake it is clearly in the lead. Both Bulgaria and Lithuania established high-level coordinating committees, involving both the government and the central bank, that had overall responsibility for the restructuring.[76] Such coordination can frequently be critical.

Certain traditional approaches to banking sector weaknesses showed themselves to be largely useless. Bulgaria and Lithuania in particular had tried mergers, but merging two weak banks only served to create one large weak bank. There are few instances of successful mergers of weak banks without very drastic concomitant measures. Similarly, although privatization can be a useful component of an overall restructuring strategy, it is unlikely to be achievable during the early stage of a restructuring. Indeed, during the restructuring the size of the state sector is likely to increase. Privatization is not sufficient to improve the condition of a bank; any privatization has to be accompanied by a range of measures to ensure appropriate bank behavior post-privatization, including strict application of fit-and-proper criteria and limits on connected lending, as private banks are far from immune from governance problems. Strong disclosure requirements are an important way to address these concerns.

Poor functioning of the court system can be a serious hindrance. The required expertise on issues that can be immensely technical was generally lacking. In addition, the judges may have political or business links or may not respect the authority of the central bank, thus undermining the central bank's ability to supervise the banking system more generally. In virtually all countries where there was systemic bank restructuring the courts effectively served to subvert the restructuring process. Addressing this problem takes time and may require a variety of approaches. One possibility is the training of expert judges to handle these types of case; another is greater clarity in the law to balance the administrative needs of the regulatory authority with the legitimate rights of those who stand to lose by this administration; another is expediting the—often very lengthy—appeals procedures, including possibly through granting direct access to the courts by a dedicated restructuring agency.[77]

Banking sector problems have led to a serious loss of confidence in the banking system even in those cases where depositors did not in principle lose anything. In all countries there was a significant decline in the banking sector as a share of GDP with no rapid reversal of this trend. Revival requires that the authorities accompany their bank restructuring measures with macroeconomic stabilization, and possibly even the development of a new institutional framework. In this context one can note the success in the years since the crisis of the CBAs in Bulgaria and Lithuania.

The success of a centralized debt recovery strategy is as yet unclear. If a centralized agency is established, it needs to be constructed carefully—with a limited lifetime committed and professional management, direct access to the courts, and clear delineation of its functions and responsibilities.

There was a lack of understanding as to what deposit insurance could and could not achieve. Whatever one's priorities one cannot establish deposit insurance when a system is unsound, let alone when it is in crisis. Deposit insurance is therefore an important element in seeking to ward off a crisis. None of the three countries studied had a functioning system-wide deposit insurance scheme at the outset of their crises.[78] Protecting depositors during a banking crisis is a fiscal issue, depending on other priorities and on moral hazard concerns.

Lax licensing, and minimal initial capital requirements, may well have been a significant contribution to the banking crises. Ensuring fit-and-proper standards for successor owners is likely to be an integral element of recovery.

The upfront initiation of restructuring can be undertaken very quickly, as shown most clearly in the case of Mongolia. However, to complete the process takes energy and perseverance. Nonetheless, once a comprehensive restructuring has been successfully completed, prospects for avoiding a recurrence can be good, as long as bankers and their customers have been weaned away from the notion that the government will stand behind them, and will pay for everything, and if the authorities maintain sound policies both in handling the banks and the macroeconomy more generally. These lessons are not unique to transition economies, but they are most vivid where the economies were subject to exceptionally dramatic disturbances. The same lessons have been learned and relearned in the resolution of banking crises in developing and industrialized countries.

Appendix 11.I. Bulgaria—a banking crisis resolution facility

While the introduction of the CBA ultimately provided a framework for the resolution of the banking crisis, as well as of the macroeconomic disequilibria, a number of alternative innovations were considered during the period of the crisis. Among these, some attention was paid to the possibility of establishing a banking crisis resolution facility. Some elements of such a facility are discussed in this appendix.

Experience in banking crisis had already shown that a comprehensive banking sector restructuring is likely to be impeded by the absence of adequate financing. While there are a number of channels, including the World Bank, for providing finance in banking sector restructuring, the time dimension of such work is frequently not commensurate with the needs of a country in banking crisis.

A banking crisis resolution facility, on the other hand, could be designed to provide contingency funds to underpin a bank restructuring package agreed in the framework of a Fund-supported program. This could help cut through the credibility gridlock and enable the stabilization of a financial system. Such a facility could be used to restore reserves in the event of withdrawal of foreign currency deposits from a banking system, to backstop depositor protection to assist bank closures, or to provide recapitalization funds to banks under certain conditions. Funding could be derived from international financial institutions and bilateral donors. Security for the fund might be enhanced by the country pledging collateral, including gold or other assets such as future privatization receipts. Similar funds were established in several Latin American countries in recent years; for instance, the program approved for Venezuela in 1995 included a facility that involved contributions from the World Bank and regional banks.

A contingency facility can have a role in a situation where the financial requirements of a policy package are uncertain, but where substantial amounts may need to be potentially available (albeit sometimes with a low probability that they will be needed), in order to prevent serious economic losses that may arise because of market action against the contingency that the required funds are not available. A parallel example is the use of foreign exchange reserves by many countries. In that regard, the currency stabilization fund put together for Poland at the start of its reform program in 1989–90 may be viewed as a precedent. One would expect that the larger the fund, and the more explicit its availability for its specified purpose, the more likely that it would not be needed. The Polish fund was not drawn upon at all during its lifetime and contributions were returned to donors—or used according to the donors' requirements—at the end of this period.

A banking stabilization fund in some ways would have been analogous to a currency stabilization fund. In Bulgaria, deposit withdrawals persisted, at least in part, because of a perception that the authorities had insufficient foreign exchange reserves to meet all their payment obligations; the demonstration of the availability of such resources might have curtailed the withdrawals. The authorities' Fund-supported program was seen as underfinanced against a worst-case scenario. Establishing a contingency fund, hence, could reduce the risks to the Fund program.

A fund could be designed to cover various purposes—reserve replenishment in the event that reserves fall below a certain level; depositor protection (perhaps for foreign currency deposits) in the event of further bank closures; or possibly banking sector rehabilitation. The purposes need not be mutually exclusive and need not be simultaneous: for instance, one might envisage a two-year fund designed for reserves protection, at the end of which remaining amounts that contributors did not want returned could be used as "seed capital" for a properly funded depositor insurance fund, or could be used to recapitalize some banks. In any case, however, the purposes of the funds, and conditions for disbursements would need to be very closely specified in advance.

The question arises as to whether any collateral would be required for such a fund. The fund established for Venezuela under World Bank auspices (and those established earlier for Argentina and Bolivia) contained no provision for collateral. However, the provision of collateral could well entice additional donors. In the case of Bulgaria, for instance, collateral could have been provided by a gold pledge, or the earmarking of future privatization receipts. In this connection, the "big-ticket" item, under consideration at the time, would have been the telephone company. The authorities had already announced their intention to sell 25 percent of it during 1997. Receipts from such a project could be used to replenish a contingency fund or to compensate contributors, if necessary, when the fund was dissolved.

There are also questions of governance of such a fund. In some Latin American cases the resources of the fund were given directly to the local banking authority and were exclusively under its control. In the case of Poland, however, the fund was kept outside the country and any disbursements had to be approved by a committee comprising the IMF Executive Directors of the contributing countries. One might imagine that contributors would feel greater confidence in a fund with the latter form of arrangements. Funds might be kept in an international financial institution or, say, the New York Federal Reserve, and payments would have to be authorized by a board of officials representing contributors, with weights probably proportional to the size of the contributions.

In the event, such a fund did not materialize and has not been proposed in subsequent banking crises, although generalized "second lines of defense" were central elements in the first phase of addressing the Asian crises the following year. Among the factors against the establishment of a Bulgarian banking facility were that such a facility might reduce incentives for the Bulgarian authorities to undertake the needed banking sector restructuring, the difficulties of separating banking sector issues from macroeconomic problems more generally, and the probable lack of interest by those who might finance such a facility in light of the lack of credibility in the authorities' commitment to reform, given their poor track record in previous years.

Appendix 11.II. Lithuania—role of major banking institutions during and after the banking Crisis

State Commercial Bank (state owned)

- Insolvent, but large institution with wide branch network. Traditionally most important source of credit (mostly directed) to state-owned enterprises.
- Weakest among the state-owned banks.
- Government issued recapitalization bonds in summer of 1996; government provided liquidity support. In March 1997 by special law exempted from penalties arising from noncompliance with reserve requirements.
- Privatization plan drawn up but after several failed attempts bank was finally closed in March 1998, liabilities and viable assets transferred to the SSB, nonperforming loans to the AMC.

State Savings Bank (SSB) (state owned)

- Insolvent, major holder of household deposits.
- Recapitalization bonds issued in the summer of 1996.
- Continues to operate. Financially weak, but meets prudential regulations. Was slated for privatization in 1999 but privatization was delayed.

Agricultural Bank (state owned)

- Insolvent, major lending institution.
- In March 1997 exempted from penalties arising from noncompliance with reserve requirements.
- Continues to operate, financially weak but presently meets prudential requirements. Was slated for privatization in late 1998, but privatization was delayed to 2001.

Aura Bank

- Insolvent, placed by BOL under moratorium.
- License withdrawn. The "shell" of the bank became the AMC (Turto Bank) in June 1996.

Vakru Bank

- Insolvent, placed by BOL under moratorium.
- Under resolution.

Innovation Bank

- Insolvent, placed by BOL under moratorium.
- Declared bankrupt. In April 1997 special law provides phased and limited deposit insurance.[79]

Litimpex Bank

- Insolvent, initially placed by BOL under moratorium. Was allowed to restart operations in June 1996, albeit under special BOL supervision.
- Operating after capital infusion from Scandinavian investors.

Taurobank

- Small private bank. Failed in July 1997.
- Rapid bankruptcy procedures. Depositors compensated according to the deposit insurance law.

Small private banks

- Fourteen banks entered bankruptcy procedures before the outset of the acute crisis; the remaining eight institutions included institutions with widely differing economic standing.

- At least two private banks are of reasonable size and benefited from the return of confidence.

Appendix 11.III. Lithuania—role and functioning of the asset management company

A key element in the bank restructuring plan was the setting-up of an AMC, which was formally created in November 1996. This appendix summarizes the initial discussion, principles of the design chosen and operating principles of the Lithuanian AMC. It concludes with a brief summary of the implementation record to date.

Key arguments for an AMC

In deciding for an AMC the Lithuanian authorities weighed the following arguments in favor of such an arrangement:

- The bank employees who originally granted a loan should not be involved in the loan recovery, as there could be attempts to cover up mistakes made in granting the loan. Because connected lending was a problem in Lithuania, there was also fear of personal connections between the borrower and the bank.
- Equally important, banks being restructured should be forward-looking; a large proportion of the staff should not be engaged in correcting earlier mistakes.
- Some of the loans could be complicated, but as the AMC was to be staffed with a broad range of expertise, there was an expectation that there were better possibilities for the maximization of loan recoveries.
- Some borrowers might have loans with several banks being restructured. The possibilities to maximize loan recoveries should be greater if they are centralized.

Principles of design

The AMC was designed to have a finite life span of ten years. During this period it would use public funds to acquire nonperforming loans from banks that were being restructured. The principal goal of the AMC was to seek to maximize loan recoveries.

The AMC was given a number of options for dealing with bad loans. For example, a loan could be partially written-off or the interest rate lowered, if the borrower was likely to be able to service a smaller or less expensive loan. The AMC could restructure companies and sell them to potential investors, or it could merge good parts from different companies, thus making a viable company that could be sold to investors. The AMC could force bankruptcy and liquidations, or it could simply write-off unrecoverable loans completely.

Implementation: the "hospital bank" approach

Having decided upon the principle of an AMC, the authorities were contemplating the most efficient and cost effective venue. Upon weighing the options, it was decided to use the shell (personnel, infrastructure and expertise) of an existing bank for the purpose, an approach sometimes called "hospital bank."

The bank chosen to become the AMC, Aura Bank, was put under administratorship in the summer of 1995 when it faced liquidity problems. It was later taken over by the government, its management was replaced, and previous shareholders lost all their rights as well as the full value of their shares. Although the financial position of the bank was very weak—almost the whole loan portfolio, amounting to LTL 86 million, was nonperforming—it was chosen as the future AMC mainly because it was believed to have a fairly advanced information system, a limited number of staff, and a suitable office building.

The conversion process went as follows. Aura Bank had its bank license withdrawn and a new company, Turto Bank (Property Bank), was established. The new company was given a limited bank license, which specifically excluded collection of deposits or performance of any banking services other than those related to the collection of the transferred assets. Turto Bank was, however, allowed to borrow on market conditions from other banks in order to be able to extend credits to its customers under reconstruction. Turto Bank was given a 47 million LTL loan from the World Bank out of which it used LTL 44 million to satisfy the creditors of Aura Bank.

Turto Bank had a staff consisting of the former employees from Aura Bank (72) and 25 newly recruited staff, but plans existed to expand its operations to three cities and the number of employees to 200. It was receiving technical assistance from Swedish experts with experience in setting up and operating an AMC and from EC Phare.

Operating principles

Discussions with the government and the BOL were initiated regarding which loans to take over from banks being restructured. The three main criteria agreed were:

- First, the gross amount of each loan should exceed LTL 500,000 (US$125,000) and only loans classified as substandard, doubtful or a loss (categories 3, 4, and 5 in the loan classification system) should be transferred. However, if a borrower had loans classified as both performing (categories 1 and 2) and nonperforming, also the performing loans were to be transferred.
- Second, the value at which loans were to be transferred should be the gross value less required provisioning, implying that all losses were to be

taken by the bank before the transfer (i.e. loans were to be transferred at the estimated market value). After a loan had been transferred, the AMC would have 120 days to assess whether it agreed with the valuation of a loan and, if not, enter into negotiations on the price of the loan with the selling bank.

- Third, no loan that was believed to be fraudulent or criminal would be accepted.

As one of its initial tasks, the AMC drafted a manual specifying exactly the kind of documentation and information that was to be supplied by the "selling" bank to the AMC.

Implementation experience

The record of Turto Bank to date falls short of what was intended at the outset of the process. According to initial plans, the first transfer of loans was to take place in late December 1996 and all transfers were to be completed before the end of March 1997. In total, loans amounting to a gross value LTL 800 million were expected to be transferred.

In spite of earlier understandings there were delays in transfers of bad loans from the state-owned banks to Turto Bank. The first transfers only took place in early 1998. Furthermore, the loan recovery rate fell far short of the margin of 10 to 40 percent that was hoped for initially. With this low recovery rate, Turto Bank to date has had only a limited impact in offsetting the overall costs of the bank restructuring.

Appendix 11.IV. Mongolia: Action plan for implementation of bank restructuring

Day One (i.e., day of agreement on the restructuring, around 40 days before implementation)

1. Formation of high-level committee, and working group to service committee. Determination of schedule for meetings of the committee.
2. Agree for planning purposes on target bank restructuring day (BR day).
3. Consider technical assistance needs. Request technical assistance.
4. Commission contingency plan in case BR day needs to be accelerated.
5. Confirm legal basis for the various steps of the proposed strategy.
6. Decide nature and timing of inspections of banks to be placed into receivership; if appropriate, commission program of inspections.
7. Commission drafting of documents for establishment of the Savings Bank (SB), the MARA, and the RB.
8. Commission work on details of responsibilities of, and restrictions on, the MARA in order to maximize loan recoveries.

9. Consider and agree draft memorandum of understanding between the ministry of finance and Mongolbank.
10. Commission preparations for publicity campaign on restructuring program.
11. Prepare identification of management and staff, and buildings and equipment, of successor institutions.
12. Commission detailed planning of modalities of BR day.
13. Prepare initial estimate of cost and timing of operation, broken down by cash requirement and size of bond issue; confirm availability of resources.
14. Prepare arrangements for eventuality of liquidity pressures before and after BR day.
15. Commission preparation of measures to enable the SB to open as soon as possible after BR day.

BR day minus 7

1. Confirm BR day.
2. Arrival of technical assistance experts.
3. Review and approve work in categories 4, 5, 6, 7, 8, 9, 10, 11, 12, 13, 14, and 15 above. Commission any final preparatory work needed.
4. Finalize cash and bond costs to government in light of updated estimate of size of insolvency; prepare bond issue.

BR day

1. Implement receiverships.
2. Coordinated announcement by prime minister, minister of finance, the Governor of Mongolbank, and the Chairman of the Economic Committee of Parliament of the objectives and modalities of the restructuring exercise.
3. Implement contingency arrangements in case of liquidity pressures on surviving banks.
4. Establishment of the SB and the MARA. Issuance of bonds to the MARA.
5. Entry into largest bank in receivership to identify assets of value sufficient to cover household deposits.

BR day plus 2

1. Issue bonds to the MARA. The MARA to buy assets of largest bank in receivership from receiver in exchange for bonds. Receiver to transfer bonds and household deposits to the SB.
2. The SB to purchase from the receiver those assets it is eligible to hold.

BR day plus 3

1. Opening of SB. The SB sells banks to Mongolbank to meet required reserves.
2. The MARA to begin examining loan portfolios.
3. High-level committee to meet to review progress so far, and to prioritize further steps.

Notes

1. The authors are grateful to Craig Beaumont, Claudia Dziobek, Olivier Frécaut, Dong He, and Vitali Kramarenko for helpful comments. All errors of course remain the authors' own.
2. See Lindgren, Garcia, and Saal (1996).
3. See, for instance, Drees and Pazarbasioglu (1998).
4. See Lindgren and others (1999).
5. Hardy and Lahiri (1992) discuss some of the theoretical aspects of bank vulnerability during the transition.
6. Most banks had a capital asset ratio below the minimum requirement of 4 percent enacted in April 1990. Their minimum paid-in capital (leva 7–10 million, about US$350,000 at the 1992 exchange rate) was very low by international standards.
7. The first post-socialist government in Bulgaria, which had undertaken the initial reforms, had recently lost the subsequent election to a party descended from the former socialist regime.
8. About 60 percent of the loan portfolio of Economic Bank, one of the weakest banks, was to public enterprises.
9. State ownership in the ten banks ranged from 98 percent of Bulbank, the largest state-owned bank, to 69 percent in Yambol, and 12 percent in Postbank.
10. These were in general likely to show a less negative position than international accounting standards. All Bulgarian banks had by law to present amounts according to Bulgarian standards. A few banks, including Bulbank, prepared two sets of accounts so that they could show their position in a form understandable by the international markets.
11. A notable exception was Bulbank's holding of a large part of the household foreign exchange accounts.
12. In most industrial countries, banks with arrears in excess of 10 percent of portfolio are considered to be in serious financial difficulty.
13. Again, these data rely on Bulgarian banking and accounting standards and are likely to underestimate the problem. Moreover, earlier valuation gains from exchange rate depreciation, for example, had served to disguise banks' weak underlying performance, which became apparent as the exchange rate stabilized.
14. The authorities seem generally at this time to have regarded emerging banking sector difficulties as part of the legacy of the former system, rather than that the solvency of the sector was deteriorating rapidly under the new system. This attitude served to lessen the feeling of urgency with which the situation needed to be addressed.
15. The earlier rescue operations replaced nonperforming assets with government bonds, which in some cases did not pay market interest rates or did not fully cover the nonperforming portfolio. The experience of these recapitalizations shows that,

while replacing bad debts with government paper may make a bank technically solvent again, the lack of proper valuation of the government paper and the absence of concomitant measures to change the way in which the bank operates, means that the bank is likely soon to fall into difficulties again.

16. Similarly, the extent of government indebtedness, and hence the extreme difficulty that the government had in borrowing by this time, rendered impractical all measures that would have had a substantial fiscal impact, such as a government-financed recapitalization of the banking sector.

17. There was awareness of the banking sector difficulties at the BCC and BNB since late 1995. As noted above, the authorities had established a high-level inter-agency committee to address the situation at that time, but although this committee developed extensive plans for action little had actually been put into place by the time the crisis emerged into the open.

18. Immediate payment was possible but only in leva.

19. Even by 2001 only around half of the banks in question have been declared legally bankrupt.

20. In the process, in some cases, the BNB also lost its influence over the conservators working in the banks, who instead actively worked toward seeing them reopened.

21. After the negative reaction to plans in December 1995 to introduce explicit limited deposit insurance, the authorities during the crisis declared their intention to protect depositors in full. Shortages of foreign currency resources, in particular, as well as broader fiscal pressures, induced the authorities, however, to seek not to delay payment or to transform the obligations with less liquid forms.

22. The situation was greatly aggravated by the fact that reform efforts in the enterprise sector were stalled and many of the banks' major borrowers became illiquid during the period. While some banks had improved their loan collection efforts, the situation of the enterprise sector severely limited the degree to which banks could improve their loan portfolios.

23. The focus at this time was largely on liquidity rather than solvency criteria, since liquidity figures were considered more reliable, and illiquidity was having the most immediate effect in undermining monetary control.

24. The authorities cited technical reasons for the failure to close all "B-list" banks. In particular, the BNB felt that it had no legal mandate to close banks that had marginally positive capital and that had agreed after the May crisis with the BNB on an MOU until end-1996.

25. It was hoped that this would lead to popular pressure for an acceleration of the court processes. At the point when this decision was taken none of the banks closed in May 1996 had actually been declared bankrupt by the courts.

26. Given that the runs were predominantly on foreign currency deposits, the banks in question appear to have temporarily resorted to informal rescheduling. However, withdrawals could be accommodated through purchases of foreign exchange in the interbank market, where the BNB was a seller for almost all of the month of October.

27. It is arguable that the rapidly reemerging problems in the banking sector derived at least in part from failures in policies elsewhere, in particular the lack of progress in the enterprise restructuring to which the authorities had also committed themselves.

28. Discussions over the possibility of introducing a CBA developed at the same time as the banking crisis, in large part reflecting disillusion with the BNB's operation

of the existing systems of supervision and monetary control. By end-1996 all political parties had endorsed the objective of adopting a CBA.

29. The long positions (usually in excess of permissible prudential limits) originated largely from foreign exchange denominated ZUNK bonds.

30. Examples of countries where such arrangements had been put in place include Argentina, Estonia, Hong Kong, and Lithuania.

31. In the event the preparation of this ordinance postdated the establishment of the CBA by several months.

32. The scheme included government purchases of ZUNK bonds from Bulbank and the transfer of these bonds to the bank in question. A second round of the exercise, initially also planned prior to the move to the CBA, was postponed, once it was seen that the bank had ample liquidity and no crisis seemed imminent.

33. In the event, the introduction of private sector involvement into the state banks at the outset of the CBA fell short of what had initially been intended. Most notably, a management contract for the weakest state bank with a major international bank fell through shortly before completion. The authorities considered that the situation of the bank in question was sufficiently serious as to justify a delay in the implementation of the CBA.

34. Bulgaria already had a relatively advanced prudential framework, even before the most recent redesign of the regulations. As noted above, earlier problems derived in large part from the fact that compliance with these regulations was low because the BNB was not in a position to exert pressure on delinquent banks.

35. The election of a new government, which took office in April 1997, also served to increase market confidence.

36. The minimum price by law had earlier been set at 90 cents to the dollar. At a time when Bulgarian Brady Bonds (the closest comparator instrument) were trading around 50 cents to the dollar, this restriction meant that there was no trading in ZUNK bonds, which were therefore totally illiquid and deemed by observers to have minimal value.

37. Lithuania declared independence in 1990 and gained international recognition in 1991, after the failed coup attempt in Moscow.

38. In February 2002 Lithuania will repeg its currency from the U.S. dollar to the euro to facilitate EU accession.

39. The Russian crisis of 1998 provoked an economic recession, but the downturn has since been overcome.

40. The bank had initially been founded in 1922, but later became a part of Gosbank.

41. The talons replaced the ruble in October 1992. In a second currency reform in June 1993 the litas (plural litai, LTL.) replaced the talons. Prior to the currency reform, the BOL had no role in currency issuance, but was limited to collection of bills and physical distribution of currency among branches.

42. The banks taken over were the Social and Development Bank and the Industry and Construction Bank.

43. In October 1990 the Savings Bank became legally a state-owned Lithuania institution. However, as the vast majority of its assets were held in Moscow and could not be withdrawn, it remained dependent on the Russian State Savings Bank.

44. The figures for Lithuania are in line with other successor states of the former Soviet Union. However, other formerly centrally planned economies had deeper financial markets. For example, the ratio of quasi-money to GDP in 1993 for Bulgaria was

about 61 percent, nearly 50 percent for the Slovak Republic, and about 25 percent for Poland.

45. The regulations also foresaw stepwise adjustments in prudential ratios toward EU requirements.

46. Inflation, nevertheless, initially remained far above the rate in the United States despite the pegging of the LTL to the U.S. dollar.

47. Most banks had problems in complying with capital adequacy requirements, given initially low capital requirements at the time the banks were founded and erosion of the capital base due to high inflation (the minimum capital requirement was not adjusted from its 1991 level, in spite of high inflation and currency depreciation). In addition, the nonavailability of tax deduction for loan-loss provisions reduced the incentive to make adequate provisions.

48. In December 1995 about 40 percent of total deposits and nearly 70 percent of time deposits were denominated in foreign currency.

49. This episode illustrates why it is generally recommended that banking sector matters should be given urgent attention prior to the introduction of a CBA (Enoch and Gulde, 1997).

50. To appreciate the very limited extent of this intervention, it is worth considering that during the Swedish banking crisis from 1991 to 1992, the Swedish Central Bank increased its credit to commercial banks by Swedish kronor 37.5 billion, equivalent to more than 40 percent of reserve money outstanding at the beginning of the period.

51. The presumption was that a bank's managers were responsible for the difficulties of the bank and should not be given a chance to repeat these mistakes using taxpayers' money. Removal of management was also meant to send a strong, discipline-enhancing message to other bank managers.

52. For a summary of the role of individual banks in the banking crisis, see Appendix 11.II.

53. This decision was made without an inspection or independent verification.

54. The Agricultural Bank was already in the process of being restructured and was therefore not included in the bank restructuring plan.

55. For details see Appendix 11. III.

56. These were provisions of the deposit insurance law of December 1995. The law initially only covered deposits in domestic currency, but an amendment passed in February 1996 extended coverage to deposits in foreign currency.

57. In early 1998, state banks held more than 50 percent of all deposits, but less than 3 percent of the capital of the banking system.

58. Under the rules, domestic currency deposits are protected up to a maximum of LTL 25,000; including 100 percent coverage up to LTL 5,000; 90 percent between LTL 5,000 and LTL 10,000; 60 percent between LTL 10,000 and LTL 25,000.

59. Another small private bank closed because it failed to meet the increased minimum capital requirement.

60. The government held deposits at commercial banks in order to facilitate the disbursement of expenditures. The illiquidity of government deposits was exacerbated because an enterprise with an account at an illiquid bank could satisfy its tax obligations by transferring funds to the government's account at the same bank.

61. The movements were not monotonic, in part due to strong seasonal influences.

62. During 1997 the depositors successfully lobbied parliament to grant them full compensation.

63. The position of TDB was in some regards analogous to that of Bulbank in Bulgaria (see above).

64. Table 11.9 below presents estimates of the magnitude of losses at the two most insolvent banks once these had been validated. Ex ante estimates made before the closures in 1996 were of similar magnitude.

65. In most jurisdictions the victims of inappropriate official action may claim damages but the action is not undone. Mongolian law and precedent in this area was evolving.

66. The Banking Law gave equal priority to the repayment of claims on all juridical persons. The government waived its possible right to be considered a juridical person on a par with enterprises.

67. It was initially planned to make the bonds negotiable and of longer maturity in order to facilitate the further restructuring of the banking system, but the restrictions remained through 2001.

68. In the months before closure, the failed banks had run up large short foreign exchange positions in an effort to remain liquid, and the RB would have had to buy foreign exchange for restructuring bonds had the currency begun to depreciate sharply following the closure operation in order to avoid incurring large losses.

69. This factor facilitated the development of unregulated institutions outside the formal banking system. Of the countries in this study, Bulgaria was the most affected. Elsewhere, Albania and Romania experienced systemic and political crises following the exposure of pyramid schemes among nonregulated institutions.

70. Bulbank, the largest bank in Bulgaria, and TDB in Mongolia are examples.

71. This does not imply that, had there been no move to international standards of accounting and prudential norms, there would have been no crisis. Banking problems were growing and would have emerged sooner or later anyway. Continued opaqueness in the financial system might have delayed the crises for a while, but would have made them correspondingly larger and harder to deal with once they had finally emerged.

72. In Bulgaria, the state banks' financial position was dominated by assessments of the value of the government bonds that had been placed in them following earlier recapitalization exercise. As the crisis intensified, these bonds became totally untradable, devastating the assets side of the banks' balance sheets.

73. "Open bank resolution" (where a bank stays open for business while it is being intervened), such as practiced in some developed countries to deal with banking problems, was only a limited feasible option in these countries, given the scarcity of high-quality replacement management to run many banks under restructuring, and the absence of much good business within these banks to provide the core for the banks' revival.

74. In Lithuania the process was not completed for several years. Although an AMC was established as part of the crisis resolution in 1994, the authorities subsequently did not allocate the funds for transferring the assets out of the weak banks, so the AMC remained an empty shell, with the staff seeking therefore instead to obtain contracts to manage institutions' assets on a fee basis.

75. This has proved to be a protracted process, in part because of the time taken to reestablish sufficient confidence in the surviving banks in the aftermath of the crisis.

76. In Mongolia there was intensive coordination through a less formalized mechanism under the auspices of the Prime Minister's office.

77. This may be one area in which technical assistance from international sources may be particularly useful, in that legal precedent from elsewhere can provide useful guidance, although the specifics of each country's legal framework means that there will never be a "one size fits all" approach to such legislation.
78. In Bulgaria, the SSB benefited from an explicit government guarantee. There are important broader issues about the role of a savings bank in a transition economy, which are beyond the scope of this chapter.
79. Private depositors were to receive LTL 4,000 in 1997, LTL 4,000 in 1998, with any balance being paid in nontradable, noninterest bearing government bonds. Legal entities to receive only noninterest bearing government bonds, to be reimbursed later than the bonds issued to private depositors.

Bibliography

De Castello Branco, Marta, Alfred Kammer, and Effie Psalida, 1996, "Financial Sector Reform and Banking Crisis in the Baltic Countries," IMF Working Paper 96/134 (Washington: International Monetary Fund).

Drees, Burkhard, and Ceyla Pazarbasioglu, 1998, *The Nordic Banking Crises: Pitfalls in Financial Liberalization*, IMF Occasional Paper 161 (Washington: International Monetary Fund).

Enoch Charles, and Anne-Marie Gulde-Wolf, 1997, "How to Establish a Currency Board," IMF Paper on Policy Analysis and Assessment 97/7.

Frécaut, Olivier, and Eric Sidgewick, 1998, "Systematic Banking Distress: the need for an enhanced monetary survey," IMF Paper on Policy Analysis and Assessment 98/9.

Hardy, Daniel C., and Ashok Kumar Lahiri, 1992, "Bank Insolvency and Stabilization in Eastern Europe," *IMF Staff Papers*, Vol. 39, No. 4.

Lindgren, Carl-Johan, Gillian Garcia, and Matthew I. Saal, 1996, *Bank Soundness and Macroeconomic Policy* (Washington: International Monetary Fund).

Lindgren, Carl-Johan, Tomás J.T. Baliño, Charles Enoch, Anne-Marie Gulde, Marc Quintyn, and Leslie Teo, 1999, *Financial Sector Crisis and Restructuring: Lessons from Asia*, IMF Occasional Paper 188 (Washington: International Monetary Fund).

12
Interventions in Banks During Banking Crises: The Experience of Indonesia

Charles Enoch[1]

I. Introduction

This chapter takes the recent experience of Indonesia in closing, and otherwise taking over, banks as an example for drawing conclusions about bank closures. The experience is highly relevant; there were four major sets of bank closures between November 1997 and March 1999, and several sets of open bank resolution through bank takeovers; the authorities have also sought to address bank insolvency in some cases through recapitalization. To some extent these approaches are complementary, but to some extent also substitutes. The process in Indonesia has been very controversial, with the initial closures in particular subject to much criticism. The more recent closures, on the other hand, have been viewed much more positively by observers.

Interventions in banks are often an integral element of a government's program for addressing a systemic banking crisis. Interventions may be warranted because the banks concerned are deeply insolvent or riddled with fraud; they may be requiring substantial liquidity support from the central bank, thus putting strains on the operation of monetary policy. Interventions may be through "closures" or "open bank resolution," i.e. where a bank remains open for business, but under new rules for the conduct of business (such as new owners) or maybe as part of another institution. In either case, the cost of the intervention arises not only at the time of intervention, but as the assets and liabilities of the banks are dealt with.

Closures may be more cost effective than seeking some form of open bank resolution, such as recapitalization or purchase of problem assets. A closure strategy mitigates the moral hazard problems that would arise with any "bail out" of the bank; it may bring about a necessary reduction in banking sector capacity, thus improving the viability of the remaining banks; it may enable the government to share the costs to the public deriving from banks' insolvency, even in a situation where depositors are protected, by inflicting losses on the banks' shareholders and subordinated debt holders; and it may demonstrate that the government is serious about addressing the banking system's problems.

On the other hand, bank closures may be risky. Most significantly, where the extent of a crisis may not have been fully recognized by the public, the impact of the closures may lead to concerns about the remaining banks, and thus provoke bank runs; closures may disrupt credit or payment flows; and may inflict losses on vulnerable or, conversely, on powerful members of the community. Bank closures may be difficult to organize without provoking asset stripping by owners, managers, or workers. Closure will only be one element of the handling of a failed bank: loan collections may fall after a bank closure, thus increasing the ultimate cost of resolving the insolvency of the institution.

The focus on bank closures, and other forms of bank intervention, in this chapter does not mean to suggest that they are the only element in a bank restructuring process; indeed, they may not even be the main element. Governments need to introduce a comprehensive program, and closures may be part of this program.[2] Indeed, in Indonesia's case, the start of the closure process coincided with agreement on a comprehensive adjustment program—including a range of measures to address weaknesses in the banking system and more widely—to be supported by the IMF; subsequent measures too have been embedded in programs supported by the IMF, the World Bank, and the Asian Development Bank.

This chapter looks at the five principal examples of interventions into the banks in Indonesia (most of which included bank closures) during the banking crisis: in November 1997, February 1998, April 1998, August 1998, and March 1999. The main instruments employed were closure; "soft" open bank intervention by the Indonesian Bank Restructuring Agency (IBRA); full takeover by IBRA; and recapitalization. Lessons from the individual experiences are presented in each sector, and overall. Conclusions are drawn at the end.

II. November 1997

Bank closures and their aftermath

In late 1997 Indonesia began negotiations with the IMF on a comprehensive adjustment program. Since the unpegging of the Thai baht in July 1997, the rupiah had been under severe downward pressure. The authorities had abandoned the peg for the rupiah, and by October 1997 the currency had depreciated by almost 40 percent. At the same time, runs had been building up on some of the private banks, reflecting a "flight to quality" as depositors sought to move their funds out of the private banks that were believed to be in trouble into the state banks, which were widely thought to be more secure.

Data on the individual banks at this time were poor. Lack of adherence to international accounting standards, prudential regulations that were not commensurate with international best practices, and lack of monitoring and enforcement of data standards by Bank Indonesia (BI) concealed the extent of the banking system's problems. Nevertheless, intensive work by Bank Indonesia during this period, assisted by experts from the international financial institutions, resulted in a view that although the bulk of the banking system seemed still to be solvent, there were a significant number of banks that clearly were not. Many of these also showed evidence of illegal practices; many were already subject to runs.

After prolonged discussions, as part of a comprehensive adjustment program with the IMF, the government adopted a bank resolution package covering 59 banks (66 percent of the assets of the banking sector) with graduated resolution measures. As part of the package, it was announced on November 1, that 16 banks, comprising around 2.5 percent of the assets of the banking sector would immediately be closed. All depositors would be fully protected up to 20 million rupiah, equivalent to $6,000 at the then current exchange rate; this would cover 92.5 percent of depositors fully.

The immediate response to the announcement of the program was positive. The exchange rate rebounded slightly from its earlier steep falls. After a few days, the runs on the banks declined. Eligible deposits were transferred efficiently by BI from the closed banks to designated recipient banks.

Within a few weeks, however, the positive sentiment was entirely reversed. Runs—which earlier had been largely a flight to perceived quality, that is, transfers of deposits from weak private to state banks—became pervasive across the system as concerns over banks' safety merged into broader concerns over the currency and indeed the stance of economic policy overall. Between end-November 1997 and mid-January 1998 the rupiah lost 80 percent of its value. With depositors withdrawing dollar deposits from the banks, and banks seeking rupiah liquidity which they changed in the market to meet the demands from their customers for dollar liquidity, BI provided liquidity to the banking system amounting to 46 trillion rupiah (4.5 percent of GDP). As liquidity support and currency depreciation intensified, imminent financial "meltdown"—i.e., withdrawal of deposits from the banking system to such an extent that virtually all institutions would have to close their doors or rely on the central bank for constant support—seemed in prospect. Eventually, on January 26, 1998, as the liquidity support approached 60 trillion rupiah, the government announced a blanket guarantee for all depositors and creditors of all domestic banks, as well as the establishment of the IBRA, to take a coordinating role in handling the banking crisis.

Observations and lessons

Some commentators[3] have blamed many of the economic problems that occurred after November 1997 on the closure of the 16 banks. Such a conclusion seems too strong, and it is not clear what counterfactual policy prescription at the time would have led to fewer problems. The 16 banks were selected from an initial list of around 30 banks that aimed to resolve all banks that were clearly insolvent on the basis of data provided by the banks to BI; political pressures, however, ensured the removal of some well-connected banks from this list, although the condition of some of these banks was already well-known to the public. In addition, the closure of the 16 banks was one element of an overall bank resolution and macroeconomic program, and it was the failure to implement that program that is likely to have led to a loss of confidence in the banks, and in the economic management of the country more generally. A blanket guarantee had been introduced in Thailand a few months earlier, but because of the large moral hazard effect, it was considered preferable not to introduce such a guarantee at this time in Indonesia, particularly since the 16 banks being closed were all very small. Nevertheless, there are aspects of these closures that do provide lessons:

(i)   The actual process of closure was carried out efficiently. Despite having no significant earlier experience of bank closure, the central bank was able to carry out the logistics of bank closures effectively. Eligible deposits were transferred quickly.

(ii)   However, given the lack of experience with bank closures, no institutional arrangements were in existence for effective follow up. Remaining assets of these banks were therefore not secured. Moreover, deficiencies with regard to these closures were not corrected later,[4] and there has been no orderly process of liquidation. It is estimated that there are now very few assets remaining in the banks, so ultimate recoveries are likely to be minimal.

(iii)   Absence of reliable information, and natural tendencies for denial, may well have led to underestimation of the extent of the crisis at this point.

(iv)   On depositor protection, although 92.5 percent of depositors' accounts were fully protected, this only accounted for 20 percent of all deposits. Depositors who were not fully protected included some very powerful elements in Indonesia who were not prepared to accept their losses. There was serious intimidation of BI staff from these groups, leading to discouragement in actually inflicting the losses.

(v)   The criteria for banks to be closed was not sufficiently explained. Whilst the banks that were closed were all insolvent, the market was aware that some banks known to be also insolvent were kept open; this indeed was apparent from the announcements at the time.

(vi)   The authorities' commitment to carry through a banking reform program was cast into severe doubt when a well-connected owner of a closed bank was permitted by BI in mid-November to take over a small bank, which was granted a foreign exchange license by BI, and to use it as a platform to resume the closed bank's activities, thus effectively by-passing the closure process.

(vii) The failure of the Indonesian authorities to carry out key elements of their adjustment program led to public disillusion with the economic management of the country. Dollar withdrawals from the banks led to concerns about the ability of the banks to continue to meet the demands for liquidity, prompting further withdrawals. At this point the crisis had become fully systemic, in the sense that depositors were fleeing from the currency and from the banking system as a whole rather than (as earlier) from particular banks perceived to be weak.

III. February 1998

In order to try to stop the bank runs, restore monetary control, and address the banking sector's problems with the exchange rate appearing to head into free fall, the government announced in late January 1998 a blanket guarantee for all depositors and creditors of Indonesian banks, as well as the establishment of IBRA. Thereafter, the authorities moved quickly to make the agency effective. A highly-regarded senior ministry of finance (MOF) official was appointed its head; additional MOF staff, and several hundred BI supervision staff were seconded to IBRA in order to provide immediate staffing. By mid-February 1998, IBRA was ready to take action. It was proposed that all banks that had borrowed from BI at least twice their capital and had a capital adequacy ratio (CAR) below 5 percent should be brought under the auspices of IBRA, with IBRA officials on-site at all head offices and principal branches, and all owners of "IBRA banks" working under memoranda of understanding agreed with IBRA restricting their activities.

On Saturday 14 February owners of 54 banks[5] were summoned to BI, were warned about their parlous financial condition, and were invited to apply to come under the auspices of IBRA. All the bankers agreed. They were informed that IBRA officials had already entered their banks that morning.

While the interventions were determined on a transparent and uniform basis, and were carried out smoothly, the government introduced a last-minute change to the plans that severely undermined the operation. While on this occasion there was no interference in the selection of institutions for intervention, there was some concern that the interventions could provoke renewed runs; it was therefore determined that no publicity should accompany the operation.

Thus, instead of being able to demonstrate that they had started to take hold of the situation, IBRA officials had to work over the following weeks against a public perception that IBRA was still nonoperational. Also, with the lack of publicity accorded to the operation, IBRA officials in the banks appear to have carried little standing. It was not possible for officials to assert full control over the staff of the institutions, and to make clear to the staff the new direction in which the banks were now intended to be going. In any case, there seems to have been little change in the behavior of many of the banks. BI liquidity support continued at its earlier levels for several more weeks.[6]

Observations and lessons

(i)   Once again the logistics of the interventions were handled effectively, with several hundred IBRA officials securing banks representing 40 percent of the banking system over the weekend.

(ii)   The emphasis on uniformity of treatment was a marked advance over the experience of November 1997. The authorities were concerned to classify banks on the basis of simple transparent criteria. With information on banks' solvency position limited, categorization was by necessity on the basis of liquidity indicators,[7] in particular the size of borrowings from BI.[8]

(iii) February 1998 provided an example of "soft" open bank resolution, as opposed to the "hard" open bank resolution (involving full exclusion of former owners and managers) that took place in April 1998. There may well be a role for such interventions. Effectiveness, however, depends upon the elaboration of new rules under which the management and staff of the banks will operate the banks, and upon management and staff of the banks understanding that these new rules will be enforced. In the case of Indonesia at this time, where there was great uncertainty as to what the new rules were, and how far they would be enforced, the absence of any publicity for the operation was a major impediment.

(iv)   The establishment of the new restructuring agency was an important step forward. Contrary to some earlier plans, however, IBRA was established as an agency of the MOF, rather than in an autonomous role. This meant that over the following months its effectiveness was compromised by needing to obtain political authority even for its technical operations. Whilst such political oversight may well have been inevitable, some political interventions seemed to indicate a lack of commitment to IBRA's objectives. The refusal of the authorities to allow IBRA to publicize its February interventions was an early example.

(v)   While in theory an IBRA presence in the banks was expected to bring the banks under government control, this objective was seriously impaired by the nonremoval of shareholders and managers.

(vi)   The February 1998 interventions were logistically effective because of very close cooperation between IBRA and BI. However, the creation of IBRA was seen by many in BI as an indictment of their record, and relations were not always cooperative. As noted above, BI staff were subsequently progressively withdrawn from IBRA. There were reportedly also ongoing problems with the transfer of documents on the individual banks between BI and IBRA. While such inter-agency rivalry may be inevitable, it is necessary to have a clear conflict resolution mechanism.

IV. April 1998

By April 1998 it was apparent that forceful intervention into the banks was necessary in order to establish the credibility of the restructuring strategy and of IBRA, and to halt the continuing liquidity emissions from BI. A new IBRA team, appointed in March 1998, recognized the need for (a) transparency and uniformity of treatment of the banks; and (b) publicity for their actions. Considerable efforts were made first to ensure that, once criteria were established, they were applied entirely and consistently, and second, to prepare the public relations aspect of the exercise; a professional public relations firm was employed, and fully involved in all stages of the process.

With reliable information on the solvency of the banks still not available, and with an urgent need to curtail the liquidity emissions from BI, focus was again on liquidity support from BI. At this point, over 75 percent of total liquidity support to the banking system (comprising 222 banks) was accounted for by only seven banks, representing 16 percent of the liabilities of the banking system. Each of these banks had borrowed at least 2 trillion rupiah (US$240 million); four of the banks had borrowed 5 trillion rupiah (US$600 million). IBRA determined "hard" open bank intervention into these banks, i.e., the suspension of the shareholders' rights, and the assumption of ownership control by IBRA; and the replacement of the managers by management teams from designated state banks.[9] In addition, seven small banks, comprising 0.4 percent of total banking sector assets, which had each borrowed more than the equivalent of 500 percent of their capital, and more than 75 percent of their assets, from BI were closed. The action was to be validated through the conversion of past BI liquidity support into an IBRA stake in each bank, with the government recognizing its responsibility for the financing of bank restructuring by committing to issue bonds to BI to compensate it for the liquidity support.

Once again the operation was carried out smoothly, with IBRA staff intervening in the banks on the weekend of Friday, April 3. Frequent television press conferences took place over the weekend in which the minister of finance and the head and deputy head of the IBRA repeatedly explained what was happening, and that all depositors were totally protected. Given that these were the first bank closures since the runs following the closure of the 16 banks in November 1997, there was some nervousness among the authorities. In the event the closures were handled successfully and all depositors were able to have immediate access to the deposits from the designated state bank at the opening on Monday morning.[10]

While the closures were handled successfully, there was at this stage also some uncertainty among the public about the implications of the bank takeovers. This was a new concept in Indonesia, and some depositors were uneasy at banking at a bank that had been taken over and was being operated by IBRA (these became known as the BTO banks). There were some runs on one of the BTO banks which had been subject to protracted runs before. However, the safe transfer of deposits from the closed banks and the continuation of all banking services at the BTO banks ended the runs within about three weeks. Deposit withdrawals were also held in check by premium interest rates offered by most of the BTO banks.[11]

While the closed banks' liabilities were transferred efficiently, there were problems handling the banks' assets. Although IBRA was able to secure the premises of these banks, inordinate delays in the passage of the necessary legislation and subsequent implementing regulations and in the resolution of complex negotiations with BI over the valuation of the liquidity support, which was the basis for IBRA's equity claims on the banks,[12] meant that IBRA was unable to take control of the banks' assets until February 1999. This undoubtedly delayed the start of asset recoveries and led to severe erosion of the asset values.

Banks whose owners were politically connected were not protected from these interventions. One bank taken over by IBRA was part-owned by one of the president's closest associates, who at the time of the closure was in the cabinet. This nondiscrimination added significantly to public perceptions that the authorities were finally getting a firm grip on the banking sector.

Like the November 1997 experience, the announcement of the bank closures was followed rapidly by the announcement of agreement on an IMF-supported program. Unlike in November 1997, however, the authorities demonstrated commitment in the following weeks to carry out the other elements of the program.[13]

In the BTO banks, new managements were brought in from "twinned" state banks. Over the coming months, however, these managements were unable to undertake significant operational restructuring of these banks. Subsequently, in all cases, the managements were again replaced or the banks were closed.

Observations and lessons

(i)   Bank closures, if carried out effectively and on uniform principles, and provided that the cut-off point is explained and accepted by the public, and if this is set within a broader plan that is announced and credible, can have a positive impact on sentiment in assuring the public that the government has a coherent strategy for tackling the banking crisis.

(ii)   Investment in public relations is likely to be particularly rewarding. This is likely to involve both external consultants and a heavy involvement of time by the principal policymakers themselves.
(iii)   In the immediate term, efficient transfers of deposits to recipient banks will be the major operational exercise.
(iv)   The authorities need to have resources and legal powers to minimize the deterioration of the assets that have come under their control.
(v)   The costs resulting from the closures will be higher if the required legal powers for the supervisory agency are not fully in place. These include powers for the agency rapidly to take full control of the assets of the closed banks.
(vi)   Open bank resolution is not necessarily simpler to carry out, or cheaper, than bank closures. Keeping a bank open while under the control of the restructuring agency requires pre-identification of competent management to safeguard the agency's interest, and to provide confidence to the public that it is still desirable to do business with that bank. The managements brought in by IBRA necessarily had to be recruited at very short notice, and by and large did not prove successful in turning the banks around. Most of the BTOs offered very high deposit rates subsequently to try to regain lost deposits. The resultant negative interest margins added to the ultimate costs of resolving the banks.
(vii)   It is critical for the process that there is at least one "good" bank in which the public has confidence and which can be used as the recipient of the liabilities (and in some cases the assets) of the closed banks. In Indonesia, with limited time, capacity, and sound banks, options were very limited. All deposits from banks closed at this time were transferred to a single bank, state-owned BNI, widely regarded as the strongest bank in the country, although at the time still unrestructured.

V. August 1998

Over the course of the spring and summer of 1998 international accounting firms conducted portfolio reviews on the banks taken over by IBRA in April 1998,[14] as well as on 16 of the larger of the remaining private banks,[15] and on the state banks. Similar reviews were conducted for the remaining banks over the following months.

The first results for the banks taken over in April 1998 were devastating, showing levels of nonperforming loans ranging from 55 percent to over 90 percent of the banks' portfolios. Although there was some question as to whether the accountants had been excessively diligent in marking down the portfolios, there could be no dispute of their finding that the examined banks were deeply insolvent.

In June 1998, very soon after their completion, the results of the audits on the IBRA banks were leaked to the press. There was an immediate shock that the state of the banks was so bad; beyond that, however, the leaks prevented any further denial of the seriousness of the crisis, and forced the authorities to recognize that drastic further action was urgently needed.

The two largest banks taken over in April (PT Bank Dagang Nasional Indonesia (BDNI) and Danamon) were listed on the Jakarta stock exchange. Under stock exchange rules, shareholders' stakes could only be written down after a declaration of insolvency of a bank; this in turn required the calling of an extraordinary shareholders' meeting. In July 1998, IBRA obtained a declaration of insolvency for Danamon; the shareholders of BDNI, however, used technical procedures to prevent such a declaration for that bank.

By this time the authorities had begun to develop an overall plan for the eight banks they had taken over but not closed in April and May 1998. The one bank taken over in May (Bank Central Asia) was considered inherently sound, and IBRA began discussions as to its disposal. The one state bank (Exim) was essentially moved out of IBRA, pending merger with other state banks. Three of the remaining banks had been found to have almost no performing loans, and were therefore to be closed. The authorities' strategy was to use the largest remaining bank (Bank Danamon) as a sort of "bridge bank"—i.e., a repository for assets and liabilities of other banks, and possibly a source for specified banking services—and therefore to keep it open under IBRA control. The other two banks (PDFCI and Tiara Asia) were in marginally better condition, and—unlike the others—not riddled with prudential violations, in particular connected lending. These were to be merged into the bridge bank in the event that IBRA could not sell them within a specified period of time.

On the weekend of August 20, IBRA therefore closed three banks, representing 5 percent of the liabilities of the banking sector. Resource capacity was severely stretched, in part because the earlier mass secondments of staff from BI to IBRA had already been severely cut back. Deposits of the closed banks were transferred over the weekend to BNI. IBRA also intensified its control over its banks that remained open.

In the period thereafter, the IBRA management team at Danamon (and to a lesser extent in the other IBRA banks) made considerable efforts to restore their earlier deposit base. Deposit interest rates were among the highest of major banks in the country. While this may have looked good from the point of short-term stabilization of the banking sector, the large number of additional deposits generated on the basis of a substantial negative interest margin added considerably to the ultimate cost of recapitalizing the bank.

Observations and lessons

(i)   Open bank resolution procedures may be a prelude to bank closures later. The initial open bank resolution may provide time for the authorities to obtain a full picture of the bank, so as to decide what to do with it. In such cases the authorities are literally "buying time," since if a bank ends up being closed it is likely to be more expensive to do it later than if the bank had been closed at the outset, since losses are likely to continue to accumulate during the interim. Also, if the public realizes that open bank resolution may be a prelude to closure, confidence that there will be full and prompt protection of all depositors becomes even more critical.

(ii) Even large amounts of banking capacity can be taken out of the system without significant impact on loss of banking services, if properly handled. Depositor services were immediately made available in other banks. Few performing loans still remained in the closed banks. Where they did, IBRA subsequently sought to provide services to these borrowers, either directly or through the banks it had taken over.

(iii) A resolution strategy may involve a mixture of closures and open bank resolutions, so that the authorities maintain some core banking services and can use some institutions(s) for "bridge bank" purposes. Fraudulent banks and those with few performing loans are likely to be easiest, and cheapest, to resolve through closure. Where franchise value remains, and significant banking services are still provided, there may be grounds for seeking open bank resolution. The exact distribution between the two approaches will require careful consideration.

VI. March 1999

On September 26, 1998 the governor of the BI, on behalf of the government, announced a plan for the restructuring of the private banks. The objective was the retention of a residual private banking sector in an environment where the state sector had already increased its share substantially over previous months, and where there was evidence that most of the remaining significant private banks were also insolvent.

Under this plan, banks were to be subject to a threefold categorization. Those with estimated capital asset ratios greater than 4 percent (the minimum requirement for all Indonesian banks at end-1998) were deemed sufficiently strong not to warrant government support (the "A" banks). Those banks with capital asset ratios worse than –25 percent (the "C" banks) were too weak to warrant government support. Those with ratios between –25 percent and 4 percent (the "B" banks) were invited to submit business plans which would be assessed by independent advisors. If the plans were passed, and if the owners and managers passed a "fit and proper" test applied by BI, they would be eligible for joint recapitalization with the government. If the owners supplied unborrowed resources equivalent to 20 percent of the shortfall from the 4 percent capital asset ratio requirement, the government would supply the remaining 80 percent of the shortfall. The government would obtain a commensurate shareholding in the bank, but would leave the owners in day-to-day control of the bank, and provide the owners with the first option to buy back their shareholdings at the end of three years.

Implementation of the plan—which depended on the conclusions of a series of four interdepartmental committees—was to have been finalized by December 1998, but the need to achieve political consensus prevented the process from beginning until that month, and expected implementation was pushed back to February 1999. By early February, government ministers—wishing to avoid the risks of a sudden shock in expectations—were hinting strongly to the public that there would be a number of bank closures before the end of the month. By the last week of February, it was common knowledge that there were to be bank closings on the weekend of February 26. Two days before that date, however, the government announced a postponement. Political consensus had not been established on the treatment of a few of the banks. Public reaction was extremely negative, with a widespread perception—acknowledged by some officials—that there had been outside influence on the closure decisions.

Over the following two weeks, the various technical committees refined their estimates of the condition of the banks, and political consensus was established on the implementation of the restructuring plan according to the agreed principles. Also, owners of "C" banks were given a final opportunity to provide additional capital to raise themselves to "A" status; "B" banks without acceptable business plans were invited to resubmit plans.

On March 13 it was announced that 73 banks (representing 5.7 percent of the assets of the banking sector) had capital asset ratios above 4 percent ("A" category)[16] and could continue to function without government support. Nineteen banks (representing 3 percent of the assets of the banking sector) had CARs below –25 percent ("C" category) and were to be closed immediately. Of the remaining ("B" category) banks, nine (representing 10 percent of the banking sector) had passed the various tests and were eligible for recapitalization; seven banks (with 2.5 percent of the assets of the banking sector) had failed one or more of the other tests mentioned above, but were to be taken over by IBRA on the basis that they had at least 80,000 depositors; and 19 smaller banks (with 2 percent of the banking sector) would be closed with the "C" banks.

The announcement was well-prepared, and included major public relations efforts both from specialist consultants and the principal participants themselves. Market reaction was generally positive, with recognition that this was a careful and comprehensive resolution of the problems of the banking sector. Unfortunately, the closures and transfers of deposits did not occur as smoothly as in the previous closure operations. Although the total number of depositors in the closed banks was less than in the August 1998 operation, the sheer number of banks, their dispersion across the country, and the lack of prior IBRA access into them, made this operation more complicated than the earlier one. Even worse, the protracted period during which the closures had been expected provided the opportunity for workers facing redundancy to organize themselves, and to maximize their leverage in forthcoming redundancy negotiations by denying IBRA staff access to banks' premises. Thus, while the majority of deposits were successfully transferred by the middle of the following week to five designated recipient banks, in around 20 branches workers prevented IBRA from obtaining access to depositors' records and transfers could not be made.[17] For several weeks IBRA became involved in redundancy negotiations with these workers; senior management were therefore distracted from their core functions. IBRA gradually overcame the problem, obtaining alternative sources for the needed documentation, and obtaining settlements with the workers.

While the public basically maintained confidence in the banks taken over by IBRA, there was—perhaps surprisingly—a loss of confidence in some of the banks deemed eligible for recapitalization. Apparent confusion by the authorities in the remaining steps necessary for the recapitalization to take place, together with punitive comments by some officials about the requirements that would be put on these banks, distorted the story that these "B-pass" banks were to be the core of the private banking sector of the future. Significant runs on some of these banks led to liquidity squeezes. Confusion as to the distinction between the "B-pass" banks and the BTO banks was heightened by public statements from the well-connected owner of one of the BTO banks saying that he was only temporarily out of his bank and that he expected that the government would be helping him with his bank's recapitalization.

An additional issue arose from the operation of the interbank guarantee. While the depositor guarantee had been honored meticulously, the authorities had so far failed to make payments under the interbank guarantee, in part to try to contain fiscal costs.[18] Several of the prospective "B-pass" banks had substantial claims under this guarantee. Their uncertain status seemed to jeopardize the banks' eligibility for recapitalization.

By end-April most of these concerns had been largely resolved. IBRA had excluded the former owners from all the BTO banks, and changed all the managements.[19] IBRA officials had progressively taken control of the assets of the banks. The owners of seven of the nine banks declared eligible for joint recapitalization with the government had provided their share of the capital. One of the other banks was provisionally sold to a major international bank;[20] the other bank was taken over by IBRA. The government committed itself to honor claims under the interbank guarantee for all "B-pass" banks. In June 1999, the Head of IBRA announced that all the taken over banks (except the bank taken over in April) would be merged into Bank Danamon (the "bridge bank") over the coming months.

The interventions of March 13, and the subsequent implementation of the measures announced then, were well-received by the markets, and by outside commentators, even those who had been critical of earlier interventions. The general feeling was that finally the authorities had a full grip on the banking situation.

Observations and lessons

(i)   The absence of surprise by the time the interventions occurred gave those affected—staff, owners, and managers—the opportunity to seek to protect themselves from the consequences of the interventions. The occupation of bank premises by the staff added to the costs of the closures by delaying IBRA's achievement of full control of the banks' assets. Owners and managers are likely to have transferred assets from the banks in anticipation of the interventions.

(ii)   The comprehensive nature of the action, involving a resolution decision based on uniform and transparent criteria for each of the private banks, added to the credibility of the action, and to its favorable reception.

(iii)   The "too-big-to-fail" argument of the authorities, used to justify the takeover rather than closure of the banks with at least 80,000 depositors, was subject to criticism. Such an argument is frequently made by authorities handling systemic banking issues, but it is hard to spell out, and seems to contradict the principle of uniformity of treatment. In Indonesia the authorities made it at an early stage regarding the seven state banks, which together comprise 50 percent of the banking sector: all these banks were to be recapitalized, even though on the basis of the criteria applied to the private banks all would have fallen into category "C" and have been closed.

(iv)   The March 13 interventions, comprising the 38 bank closures, the takeover of seven banks, and the announcement of eligibility of the nine banks for joint recapitalization had a major positive impact on the credibility of the restructuring program, and hence on the government's economic management overall. At least partly as a result, with bank restructuring seen to be at the core of economic revival, market interest rates began falling rapidly from their crisis levels. With this fall in interest rates, prospects for the economy and for the banking system in particular, were dramatically improved.

VII. The closure process

The Indonesian experience since late 1997 has provided a number of lessons as regards the role of bank closures in a bank restructuring program.

(i)   In a case of massive insolvency and restructuring, such as Indonesia over this period, no single strategy with regard to closures could be put in place which would have worked successfully throughout the period. In practice, there had to be several phases as the true magnitude of the problem became apparent and the authorities over time moved to address it.

(ii)   The initial stages of a bank restructuring program are bound to be particularly difficult and messy. The authorities will always be acting on limited information. They are likely to have to operate with an inadequate institutional infrastructure and legal framework. They may well be working in a difficult political environment in which there are strong forces resisting change. While it will be critical to start to establish the infrastructure and legal framework immediately, it is likely that the authorities will not be able to wait until these reforms are completed before they have to intervene in the banking system.

(iii)   While every banking crisis is likely to be different, there may be a strong case for closures of some banks at the outset of a crisis. Some banks will be clearly deeply insolvent and racked with fraud. An open bank solution when there may be limited capacity to control further losses, and where the bank itself has lost credibility, may not be cost effective, either as regards the direct losses from the bank or in terms of demonstrating the government's commitment to serious adjustment. In bank closures gross costs are realized upfront, and can be more easily identifiable (most immediately the transfers of deposits), while in open bank resolutions the costs are realized over time, and increase dramatically if the intervened bank is not properly managed.

(iv)   One of the most tricky issues for the authorities to determine is whether they will introduce a blanket guarantee at this stage. Partial protection when further closures are in prospect is unlikely to be effective. On the other hand, providing a blanket guarantee to depositors and creditors may be costly, and—unless handled carefully—raise well-known moral hazard concerns (for instance, banks may be able to offer unviable interest rates to attract depositors). Nevertheless, once a banking crisis has become systemic, such a guarantee often becomes an integral part of the resolution strategy, notwithstanding its cost. The guarantee may not be immediately credible; credibility may be achieved only once the authorities have demonstrated the smooth working of the guarantee in practice.

(v)   Large and protracted liquidity support to a set of banks will quickly threaten monetary control. Bank closures may be an integral part of a package of measures to address this. With limited information on banks' solvency position, interventions at this stage are likely to be based on liquidity criteria. Evidence indicates that those banks requiring substantial liquidity support will also be deeply insolvent.

(vi)   Bank closures must be based on transparent, uniform, simple, and defensible criteria. There should be no exceptions to the specified rule, since the credibility of the entire operation will be only as strong as its weakest link—even one or two banks treated differently than indicated by the criteria can indicate political involvement, and thus discredit the criteria and the entire operation.

(vii)   In most cases, the authorities will have to identify one or more banks that will be in a position to immediately receive the deposits of the banks being closed. In the absence of a clear alternative, they are likely to select a state bank. While this may be appropriate in some cases (and in Indonesia there was probably little alternative), state banks may themselves also suffer from serious weaknesses, and there could be advantages in using a private, or possibly even a foreign, bank for this purpose if this does not serve to undermine further the public's confidence in the domestic banks.

(viii) The authorities will need to ascertain the true financial condition of the banks. Banks' reported figures are unlikely to give an accurate picture of the banks' health, so additional audits—by the banks' auditors, by international accountants, or by other professional experts—will be needed. The results of these audits are likely to show a much worse situation in the banks than hitherto believed. These results will serve to confront any tendency among the authorities to deny the depth of their banking crisis.

(ix)   Upon receipt of the results, the authorities will need to conduct a "triage" of the banks. The best banks can be left alone; the middle tier of banks will be eligible for some form of assistance based on quantitative and qualitative selection criteria; the worst set will need resolution. This resolution may involve closures, open bank resolution, or a mixture of the two. The choice will depend upon the number and size of the banks in this category, the state of confidence in the economy, capacity to close the banks, or conversely to operate the banks economically in an open bank resolution strategy. Overall, the chosen strategy should be that which restores the system to soundness while minimizing public expenditures, but reliable estimates will be very difficult to make.

(x)   Bank closures at this stage should be based on estimates of insolvency, together with absence of any owners or outsiders willing to recapitalize the bank, or of a business plan showing how the bank can restore itself to viability. The critical solvency level may vary depending on the circumstances in the country and could be anywhere substantially below the minimum capital ratio required in the country at the time. Thus, in some cases it could be above zero. In other cases, for instance where the entire banking system is deeply insolvent and there is a desire to keep at least a residual element of the sector in operation, it may be below zero. In the case of Indonesia, capital asset ratio no worse than –25 percent was established as a criterion for possible eligibility for joint recapitalization with the government. This is likely to have been an extreme case. It reflected the depth of the banks' insolvency, the recognition that some part of the insolvency was due to the unprecedented macroeconomic shock that had occurred, the desire to maintain at least some private banks in the system, and the belief (confirmed in the event) that a number of the owners had significant resources elsewhere which they would be prepared to use to share the recapitalization costs with the government.

(xi)   The closure process will, naturally, lead to a reduction in the number of banks, hence boosting the potential for profitability among those remaining. Given that most, or all, of the bank closures will occur in the private sector—and that open bank resolution will likely involve a takeover of private banks by the government—the share of state-owned institutions will rise during a bank restructuring. In Indonesia the domestic private banking sector shrank from 45 percent of the total in late 1997 to 15 percent in mid-1999. An important corollary—to which the Indonesian government has committed itself—is a program for the privatization of a large part of the private banking sector.

(xii) "Too big to fail" may be a valid criterion—if not over-used—for open bank resolution rather than closing banks that play a significant role in the payments system, or in providing services to parts of the market. Again, the authorities should specify transparent criteria. Preserving the banks should not generally mean retaining the owners or managers. Except in the content of an overall recapitalization plan such as the one described above, loss minimization for the public sector must mean the elimination of the rights of shareholders for banks formerly in the private sector. For banks in the public sector, careful attention must be paid to avoid increased capitalization costs—following negative interest margins or weakened loan recovery efforts—if management feel relieved of the discipline of profit maximization objectives.

Notes

1. I am grateful for comments from Philippe Beaugrand, Thanos Catsambas, Eric Clifton, Olivier Frécaut, Lorenzo Giorgianni, Luc Jacolin, Michael Keen, Carl-Johan Lindgren, Hassanali Mehran, Elizabeth Milne, Anoop Singh, and Timo Välilä.
2. The Indonesian bank restructuring program as a whole, together with related issues, is to be discussed in "Indonesia: Anatomy of a Banking Crisis" by Charles Enoch, Barbara Baldwin, Olivier Frécaut, and Arto Kovanen (IMF Working Paper 01/52).
3. See, for instance, "The East Asian Financial Crisis: Diagnosis, Remedies, Prospects," Steven Radelet, Jeffrey D. Sachs, *Brookings Papers on Economic Activity*, Vol. 01, pp. 1–74, 1998, Harvard Institute for International Development.
4. Legislation passed subsequently enhanced the powers of IBRA in closing banks (see below). Since the 1997 closures predated the establishment of IBRA and the follow-up work continued to be handled outside IBRA, it continues under the pre-existing legislation.
5. These were all private banks. A state bank, Bank Exim, also had borrowings from BI of more than twice its capital—due to trading losses—and was the 55th bank to be brought under IBRA. Together these banks comprised 40 percent of the banking sector.

6. Liquidity support tapered off during the following month when the liquidity facility was redesigned to provide for nonfinancial sanctions—including takeover of the bank by IBRA —in the event of prolonged use of the facility.

7. It has been generally found that major liquidity problems arise after a bank has become insolvent. Thus, while reliance on liquidity criteria probably means that some insolvent banks will escape intervention, it is unlikely that those banks in which the authorities have intervened will, in the event, be found to have been solvent.

8. Reliance on this particular indicator was warranted also by the urgency of restoring monetary control.

9. Except for the one state bank among the seven banks, Bank Exim, where the treasury department managers (who had been responsible for the bulk of the bank's losses) were replaced, but the remainder of the bank's management were left in place.

10. Newspaper adverts were run across double pages with IBRA on the left hand page announcing the closure of the seven banks, and the designated recipient bank, Bank Negara Indonesia (BNI), advertising on the right hand page welcoming its new customers to its branches and summarizing the services it could provide.

11. In order to mitigate the moral hazard effects of the blanket guarantee, the authorities placed a cap on the interest rates that banks could offer depositors. At this time the cap was set at 500 basis points above the deposit rates offered by the "JIBOR banks" (the group of banks whose interbank rates were used as the benchmark for calculating JIBOR). Several of the BTO banks used the maximum premium afforded by the cap in order to safeguard, and later recover, deposits.

12. Amendments to the banking law were needed to give IBRA powers to take control of assets from former shareholders. After considerable and unexplained delays, the law was passed and signed by the President in October 1998. To be effective, enabling regulations from the amendments were also needed. These eventually received presidential signature in February 1999.

13. In May 1998 implementation of the program was interrupted as a result of rioting and looting and the further collapse of the exchange rate; President Soeharto was replaced by Vice-President Habibie. There were concerted runs on the largest private bank, as part of widespread targeting of Chinese-owned businesses. Following massive BI liquidity support, the bank was taken over by IBRA on May 16. IBRA at this point had taken over banks with 23 percent of the deposits of the system.

14. The operational importance of the February 1998 takeover of 54 banks decreased markedly during this period, no doubt due in part to lobbying on the part of the owners of some of these banks. IBRA inspectors were progressively removed from these banks, and in July 1998 responsibility for supervising these banks—which had been transferred to IBRA—was passed back to BI.

15. These 16 banks were selected on the basis of initial assessment by the authorities that these might be the "core" of a revised banking sector, given their relative size and good reputation.

16. For one additional bank a full determination had yet to be made. It subsequently passed the tests to achieve "A" bank classification.

17. The closed banks had employed 15,600 workers. The banks taken over by IBRA at this time employed an additional 11,900 workers—a significant factor in the decision to take them over rather than close them.

18. Foreign banks consistently maintained that this failure to honor the interbank guarantee was a severe impediment to the restoration of confidence in Indonesia.
19. Except in one bank, which had been taken over by IBRA only because there were no shareholders able to put up their share of the bank's recapitalization requirement.
20. This takeover led to the discovery of side payments by the bank, Bank Bali, in order to obtain payments under the interbank guarantee in order to close the capital shortfall sufficiently that the bank would be able to participate in the joint recapitalization program. The "Bank Bali" scandal is beyond the scope of this chapter.

13
The Role of KAMCO in Resolving Nonperforming Loans in the Republic of Korea

Dong He[1]

I. Introduction

Nonperforming loans (NPLs) were at the heart of the financial crisis that engulfed the Korean economy during 1997–98. The recovery has also been characterized by a rapid and drastic reduction in the level of NPLs in the financial system.[2] The government played a leading role in financial and corporate restructuring, including strengthening the legal and regulatory framework, injecting public funds, and setting up new institutions for crisis management, such as the Korea Asset Management Corporation (KAMCO).

KAMCO played an important role in facilitating the restructuring process and helping to develop financial markets. First, KAMCO purchased distressed assets from banks and other financial institutions, which allowed lending to resume at a time when liquidity was scarce. This objective was complemented by increased supervision to ensure that banks were operating on sound commercial principles. Second, KAMCO's resolution of NPLs contributed to the good progress made in Korea in recovering public funds injected by the government for financial sector restructuring. In addition, KAMCO disposed of many of these distressed assets through a number of innovative methods, including by issuing asset-backed securities (ABS), which launched an important new market in Korea.

This chapter argues that the development of a market for distressed assets was critical to Korea's success in resolving NPLs. In many countries the asset management companies (AMCs) experience failed because the creation of AMCs did not lead to the development of a market for NPLs. Such a market is typically missing in less developed countries because information asymmetries and a lack of creditor coordination make it very difficult to price NPLs. KAMCO played a market-making role by overcoming such informational and coordination problems. Its active marketing activities brought together and intermediated between sellers and investors of NPLs. Most notably it successfully convinced major international players looking for distressed assets to become interested in the Korean market. Participation of foreign investors, in turn, encouraged participation of domestic investors. Initially KAMCO's catalytic role was monopolistic, but, as the market deepened, it became much less dominant.

This chapter also argues that KAMCO's incentive to dispose of NPLs rapidly was conditioned by a strong desire on the part of the Korean society for a quick recovery of public funds injected for financial sector restructuring (Box 13.1). Korea has an admirable tradition of fiscal conservatism and a deep rooted resistance to public debt (He, 2003). The political consensus on the need to reduce public debt helped KAMCO sharpen its focus on rapid disposal of acquired assets and recovery of public funds, rather than simply warehousing the assets, a problem that has plagued many publicly owned AMCs in other countries.

Box 13.1. Recovery of Public Funds for Financial Sector Restructuring

The Korean government has used public funds of W 157 trillion (32 percent of average GDP in 1998–2000) for financial sector restructuring. Of this total amount, about W 60 trillion was used to recapitalize financial institutions, W 39 trillion was used to purchase nonperforming assets, W 26 trillion was used to pay off depositors of closed institutions, and W 32 trillion was used to facilitate purchase and assumption transactions. The bulk of the funds were financed by the issuance of W 104 trillion of government-guaranteed bonds by Korea Deposit Insurance Corporation(KDIC) and KAMCO.

Good progress has been made in recovering public funds through sale of acquired government shareholdings, collection of NPLs, and sale of assets. The authorities had recovered 39 percent (W 63 trillion) of the total by the end of 2003, which compares well with the experience of other countries. The government estimates that it will recover a total of 56 percent (W 87 trillion), with W 24 trillion to be realized in the medium term.

For the unrecoverable residual of W 69 trillion, a burden sharing plan has been adopted: 70 percent of the unrecoverable amount will be explicitly recognized as government obligations, with the remaining 30 percent covered by a 0.1 percentage point surcharge in the deposit insurance premium, which went into effect in early 2003 and will be maintained for 25 years.

To implement the plan, W 49 trillion of the KDIC and KAMCO bonds maturing in the next four years will be converted into treasury bonds, and the remaining outstanding KDIC and KAMCO bonds of W 50 trillion will be serviced by increases in the deposit insurance premium and future recoveries of public funds. The budget will no longer provide subsidies to KDIC and KAMCO for interest payments on

▶

their bonds. The conversion of KDIC/KAMCO bonds into treasury bonds will raise explicit government debt by 8 percentage points of GDP.

Fiscal Costs of Selected Banking Crises

	Crisis Period	(In percent of GDP)		Recovery Rate (In Percent)
		Gross Outlay	Net Cost	
Chile	1981–83	52.7	33.5	36.4
Finland	1991–93	10.0	7.0	30.0
Indonesia[a]	1997–present	56.4	51.9	8.0
Japan	1997–2000	6.7	5.6	16.4
Korea	**1997–2001**	**32.2**	**21.9**	**32.0**
Malaysia[b]	1997–2001	7.2	4.0	44.4
Sweden	1991	4.4	0.0	100.0
Thailand	1997–present	43.8	34.8	20.5
United States[c]	1984–91	3.7	2.1	43.2
Venezuela[d]	1994–95	15.0	12.4	17.3

Source: Author's estimates.

[a]   Exludes a 40 trillion rupiah allocation to the deposit guarantee fund in September 2001.
[b]   Losses implied by the merger of two state-owned banks (Bank Bumiputra and Bank Sime) with private banks are excluded.
[c]   Refers only to the Savings and Loan crisis.
[d]   As of end-1998.

KAMCO's financial performance, however, has been mixed. Although KAMCO has strived to price its NPL purchases as close to approximate market values as possible, in hindsight, its record was overshadowed by its overly generous payment for Daewoo-related claims. In addition, profits earned from disposing of the NPLs were not sufficient to cover the high operating expenses. As a result, the Nonperforming Asset Management Fund (NPA Fund) is not able to break even. This observation does not negate KAMCO's overall contribution to the recovery of the Korean financial sector from the crisis. It only indicates that pricing of NPLs during financial crisis has been and will remain the most difficult challenge for publicly owned AMCs.

The remainder of this chapter is organized as follows. Section II provides an overview of KAMCO's role in the bank restructuring process. Section III describes KAMCO's governance structure. Section IV discusses operational issues involved in the purchase and disposal of NPLs. Section V analyzes financial performances of the NPA Fund. Section VI concludes.

II. Overview of KAMCO's role in the bank restructuring Process

High levels of NPLs in the Korean financial sector reflected a corporate culture that relished market share rather than profitability and a capital structure that relied heavily on external borrowing. The structural problems in the financial and corporate sectors became apparent in the second half of 1997, when the capital inflows were reversed as foreign investors—reeling from losses in other Southeast Asian economies—decided to reduce their exposure to Korea. Intensified withdrawal of credit lines quickly developed into a currency crisis (Baliño and Ubide, 1999).

Under an IMF-supported program, the authorities' strategy of crisis management and financial sector restructuring comprised four key elements (Chopra and others, 2002):

- Emergency measures to quickly restore stability to the financial system through liquidity support, a blanket deposit guarantee, and intervention in systematically important nonviable institutions.
- Restructuring measures to restore the solvency of the financial system by intervention in nonviable institutions, purchase of NPLs, and recapitalization.
- Regulatory measures to strengthen the existing framework by bringing prudential regulation and supervision in line with international best practices.
- Corporate restructuring measures to reduce corporate distress and the vulnerability of financial institutions exposed to the highly indebted corporate sector.

Swift resolution of NPLs was considered a critical component of this strategy. The government announced a program of NPL acquisition as a mechanism for delivering official support for bank restructuring in November 1997. A key component of the program was the establishment of a reorganized and expanded KAMCO, and the creation of the NPA Fund. KAMCO started purchasing NPLs with a face value of 4.4 trillion won (W) from Seoul Bank and Korea First Bank, the two insolvent and systematically important commercial banks, on November 26, 1997. This first transaction was followed two days later by a purchase of 2.7 trillion W of NPLs from 30 merchant banks.

The government released a progress report and future plans of the strategy to deal with the restructuring of the financial and corporate sectors in May 1998. The report estimated that, as of end-March 1998, the total NPLs of all financial institutions were W 118 trillion (27 percent of GDP), of which 50 trillion had been in arrears for three to six months and were classified as "precautionary," and the remaining W 68 trillion worth of loans had been in arrears longer and were considered more prone to default risks. Of the total W 118 trillion NPLs, the government decided to target W 100 trillion worth of NPLs for immediate disposal, including the core NPLs of W 68 trillion, a portion of the "precautionary" loans, and some allowance for potential increases in NPLs stemming from the corporate restructuring process. The government estimated that the total market value of these loans was about 50 percent of their book value, and planned to dispose of the loans through two channels: (i) half of the loans would be disposed of by financial institutions themselves by either selling off collateral or calling in loans; and (ii) KAMCO would purchase the remaining half.

Implementation of this strategy was effective (Tables 13.1 and 13.2; Figure 13.1). The decline in the level of NPLs was rapid, particularly in the banking sector. NPLs as a percentage of total loans in the banking sector declined from 17 percent as of March 1998 to 2.3 percent at end-2002 (Box 13.2). The decline was mainly due to continuing efforts of institutions to dispose of bad loans through sales to KAMCO, via issuance of ABS, extensive write-offs, and collections. KAMCO's purchase made a substantial contribution to this rapid progress, especially during the period March 1998 to December 1999. KAMCO's total purchase of NPLs amounted to W 44 trillion in this period, or 50 percent of the outstanding NPLs in the banking sector at the beginning of the period. In recent years, KAMCO's purchase has shifted toward the nonbank sector. Thanks to improved economic conditions and the development of a market for distressed assets, banks have been able to resolve and write off NPLs aggressively on their own since 2000.

Table 13.1.   Nonperforming Loans at Financial Institutions[a]

	Mar–98	Dec–99	Dec–00	Dec–01	Dec–02
NPL or substandard and below					
(in trillions of won)[b]	118.0	88.0	64.6	39.1	31.8
Banks	86.0	61.1	42.1	18.8	15.1
Nonbanks	32.0	26.9	22.5	20.3	16.7
As percent of total loans	17.7	14.9	10.4	5.6	3.9
Banks	16.8	12.9	8.0	3.4	2.3
Nonbanks	20.5	23.0	23.6	13.7	9.8
As percent of GDP	26.6	18.2	12.4	7.2	5.3
Banks	19.4	12.7	8.1	3.4	2.5
Nonbanks	7.2	5.6	4.3	3.7	2.8
Memorandum items (in trillions of won):					
Total loans	668.5	590.9	621.4	699.9	817.8
Banks	512.1	474.0	526.1	551.2	648.2
Nonbanks	156.4	116.9	95.3	148.7	169.6
GDP	444.4	482.7	522.0	545.0	596.4

Sources: Economic Bulletin May 1998; FSS Weekly Newsletters and Monthly Reviews; and author's estimates.

[a]   Including banks, nonbank lenders, insurance companies, securities companies, and investment trust management companies.
[b]   March 98 data refer to "nonperforming loans," and other data refer to loans classified as "substandard and below" using forward-looking criteria.

Table 13.2. KAMCO Purchase of Nonperforming Loans from Financial Institutions

	Nov 97– Mar 98	Apr 98– Dec 99	2000	2001	2002
KAMCO purchases (in trillions of won)	13.9	48.3	33.0	6.0	9.0
Banks	8.4	44.1	4.4	4.9	0.2
Nonbanks	5.5	4.2	28.6	1.1	8.8
As percent of NPL stock[a]	...	40.9	37.5	9.3	23.0
Banks	...	50.5	7.2	11.6	1.1
Nonbanks	...	13.7	106.3	4.9	43.3

Source: KAMCO.

[a] NPLs outstanding in financial institutions at the beginning of the period.

trillion won

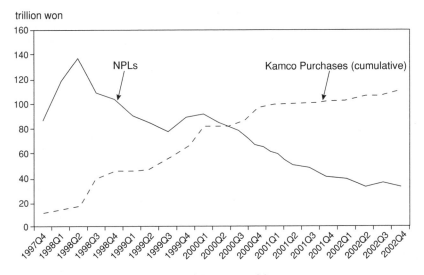

Figure 13.1. Nonperforming Loans of the Financial Sector

As of November 2002, the fifth anniversary of the creation of the NPA Fund, and by which time the mandate of the NPA Fund to purchase NPLs had expired, KAMCO had disposed of two-thirds of the NPLs it purchased (Table 13.3). The trade-off between speedy recovery and maximization of asset value shaped the evolution of the resolution methods chosen by KAMCO. At the height of the crisis, quick sale of assets was favored over management of impaired assets for future sale. Nevertheless, KAMCO managed to dispose of only a small fraction of its assets in 1998, mostly through monthly foreclosure auctions and collections. Since 1999, KAMCO diversified its resolution methods by adopting advanced techniques such as international bidding and ABS issuance. It also developed methods that would enable KAMCO to profit

Box 13.2.   Loan Classification and Estimating the Size of Nonperforming Loans

Historical data of NPLs have been subject to upward revisions as loan classification standards were gradually tightened. Prior to the crisis, only loans in arrears of six months or more had been classified as NPLs. When estimating the "true" magnitude of NPLs at the end of March 1998, however, the government followed internationally acceptable standards and included loans in arrears of three months or more. It arrived at the figure of W 118 trillion, or about 18 percent of total loans. Subsequently, banks in July 1998 were required to tighten asset classification standards by redefining NPLs as those loans in arrears of three months or more. Nonbank financial institutions followed suit in March 1999. In December 1999, financial institutions adopted a forward-looking approach in asset classification, taking into account the future performance of borrowers in addition to their track record in debt service. The forward-looking criteria (FLC) required creditors to make a more realistic assessment of loan risks based on borrowers' managerial competence, financial conditions, and future cash flow. Creditors classified loans as "substandard" when borrowers' ability to meet debt service obligations was deemed inadequate. NPLs would include substandard loans on which interest payments were not made. In March 2000, the asset classification standards were further strengthened with the introduction of the "enhanced" FLC, which would classify loans as "nonperforming" when future risks are significant— even if interest payments have been made up to that point. Based on the enhanced criteria, NPLs increased from W 66.7 trillion to W 88.0 trillion at end-1999.

Questions remain about whether the reported NPL numbers truly reflect the real magnitude of impaired assets that are still held by the financial sector. Some loans were classified as "precautionary" rather than "substandard" (for example, loans to Hynix) because of temporary exemption from the FLC of loan classification for restructured corporate debt. Commentators have also pointed out that debt issued by distressed companies, that is, companies with low interest ratios, exceeded by a large margin the reported NPLs of the financial sector. According to Lim (2002) using data provided by the National Information and Credit Evaluation, a credit rating agency, companies with interest coverage ratio consistently below 1.5 throughout the period 1999–2001 had interest-bearing debt of W82.2 trillion, which would be 11.7 percent of total loans of the financial sector. Evidence suggests that an interest coverage ratio below 1.5 for three consecutive years entails a significant risk of default. In contrast, the reported amount of loans classified as substandard and below on the balance sheet of the financial sector was only W 39.1 trillion, or 5.6 percent of total loans. However, these two sets of figures are not comparable, since those NPLs that remained on the balance sheet of the financial sector were only a part of the total outstanding debt of the distressed companies. Other possible holders of their debt include the KAMCO, ABS investors, joint-venture asset management companies and corporate restructuring companies, etc. In addition, the financial sector may have written off and removed from their balance sheets some part of the outstanding debt of the distressed companies.

from the upside potential of economic recovery, including sales of bad loan pools to joint-venture ASCs and large individual loan sales to joint-venture corporate restructuring companies.

Table 13.3. KAMCO Nonperforming Loans Portfolio
(As of end-April 2003, in trillions of won)

	Amount of NPL Purchased		Amount of NPL Resolved		Amount of NPL Remaining	
	Face Value	Amount Paid	Face Value	Amount Paid	Face Value	Amount Paid
Ordinary loans	30.7	9.4	25.5	11.1	5.1	0.5
Special loans	41.4	17.1	36.6	17.0	4.8	1.4
Daewoo loans	35.4	12.7	3.6	2.8	31.9	10.4
Workout loans	2.6	0.6	0.2	0.2	2.4	0.5
Total	110.1	39.8	65.9	31.1	44.2	12.8

Source: KAMCO.

III. KAMCO's governance structure

KAMCO can be described as a centralized publicly-owned asset management company (Lindgren and others, 1999; Ingves and others, 2004). It was established in April 1962 as a subsidiary of the Korea Development Bank (KDB). The corporation's main mission initially was to liquidate KDB's nonperforming assets. In 1966, KAMCO's scope of operations was expanded to other financial institutions, and it gradually established itself as a specialized real estate management company. In the 1980s and 1990s, KAMCO was commissioned by the government to manage and sell properties confiscated by the state in the context of tax investigations and other state-owned properties.

In November 1997, with the eruption of the financial crisis, KAMCO was reorganized pursuant to the newly enacted "Act on Efficient Management of Nonperforming Assets of Financial Institutions and Establishment of Korea Asset Management Corporation" (the KAMCO Act). Under the Act, KAMCO was empowered: first, to support financial institutions by normalizing their asset quality through cleaning up operations; second, to perform the role of a "bad bank" that supports corporate restructuring by extending loans, debt-equity swaps, and payment guarantees; and third, to recover public funds through efficient management and disposal of its assets. However, the KAMCO Act does not provide any special legal powers to KAMCO that the lenders from which it purchases NPLs do not have, since the Korean legal framework provides for clean transfer of titles and priority in the transaction of assets.[3]

KAMCO has the status of a public nonbank financial corporation, and is under the supervision of the Financial Supervisory Commission (FSC). Its major shareholders are the government and KDB, with the ministry of finance and eonomy (MOFE) owning 42.8 percent, KDB 28.6 percent, and other financial institutions 28.6 percent, of its paid-in capital. Under the KAMCO Act, KAMCO's main mandate of purchasing and resolving NPLs is to be exercised through the NPA Fund, which is distinct from KAMCO's own accounts. Thus KAMCO is the fiscal agent of the NPA Fund, which has a separate legal identity and different funding sources from KAMCO itself. The size of the NPA Fund amounted to W 21.6 trillion, of which 20.5 trillion came from issuance of government-guaranteed bonds, 573 billion were assessments on financial institutions in proportion to their holdings of NPLs, and 500 billion were loans from the KDB.[4] The Act also stipulates that the mandate of the NPA Fund to raise funding and purchase NPLs would terminate in five years. In other words, the NPA Fund could no longer acquire new NPLs after November 2002.

KAMCO is governed by a Management Supervisory Committee, which is composed of 11 members, including the Managing Director of KAMCO; representatives from the MOFE, the ministry of planning and budget (MPB), the FSC, and the Korea Deposit Insurance Corporation (KDIC); the Deputy Governor of the KDB; two representatives from the banking industry nominated by the Chairman of the Korea Federation of Banks; and three professionals recommended by the managing director, including an attorney-at-law, a certified public accountant or a certified tax accountant, and a university professor or a doctorate holder who belongs to a research institute. During the five-year period of November 1997 to November 2002, the Management Supervisory Committee met on average 1.5 times per month, and passed on average 2.6 resolutions in each meeting. Resolutions were passed if over half of the committee members were present at the meeting and if over half of the attending members agreed with the decision.

As a de facto public monopoly on the buy side of the market for distressed assets, at least in the first two years of its operation, KAMCO could have degenerated into a warehouse of NPLs and been used as a political tool to subsidize selected interest groups. Being a public agency, KAMCO does not offer performance-based bonuses to its staff, although merit increases of salaries do reflect relative performances. Thus financial motivation was not a primary driving force that shaped the behavior and performance of KAMCO's management and staff. Instead, KAMCO's relative effectiveness were in large part due to the particular environment of political economy in which it operated. Such an environment was characterized by a strong public interest in scrutinizing the use of public funds, and a close watch by international lenders including the IMF and the World Bank.[5]

Nevertheless, KAMCO's public agency nature occasionally compromised its operational autonomy from the government. On such occasions, commercial principles had to give way to other policy considerations. An example is KAMCO's purchase on Daewoo bonds from the investment trust companies (ITCs) in the aftermath of Daewoo collapse. KAMCO's purchase was at the behest of the government as part of its strategy to stabilize the ITC sector in the face of heavy redemptions, and the prices paid proved to be far higher than the likely rate of recovery (see more discussion below).

IV. The development of a market for distressed assets

When KAMCO started its operations under the new KAMCO Act in November 1997, it had little experience in purchasing and disposing of NPLs. However, with determined leadership and international assistance, it climbed up the steep learning curve and established itself as a competent and effective operator in the market for distressed assets.

Purchase of nonperforming loans

KAMCO's purchase of NPLs was selective and based on certain eligibility criteria. Eligible for purchase were salable loans whose security rights and transfer were legally executable, from among loans classified as substandard and below. KAMCO also assigned priority to purchase of NPLs whose removal was considered critical to the rehabilitation of the institution concerned from a public policy point of view, and NPLs that had multiple creditors. If a financial institution requested KAMCO to purchase its NPLs, KAMCO would analyze whether the loans were eligible for purchase, request relevant data from the selling institution, and conduct due diligence of the loans. A decision of purchase would be made by the Management Supervisory Committee, after which KAMCO would enter into an "assignment and assumption agreement" with the seller. KAMCO would then make a payment, receive documents evidencing the origin of the loan, and have the registration of security rights transferred.

KAMCO purchases comprised of four categories of assets: (i) "ordinary" loans of companies currently operating; (ii) "special" loans, which correspond to restructured loans under court-supervised receivership; (iii) "Daewoo loans" acquired mostly in 2000 in the wake of the collapse of the Daewoo Group; and (iv) "workout loans" of companies in the out-of-court workout programs. Secured special loans and Daewoo loans were the two largest categories of purchases, each representing 32 percent of the total. Secured ordinary loans took up 18 percent of total purchases (Table 13.4). More than 60 percent of the loans were purchased from banks, and just over 20 percent of the loans were purchased from investment trust companies (Table 13.5).

KAMCO paid for its purchases with bonds issued by the NPA Fund, in the total amount of W 20.5 trillion, and by recycling recovered funds. In the former case, the selling institutions would replace their NPL portfolio with NPA Fund bonds. These bonds carry an explicit government guarantee, are tradable and listed on the Korea Stock Exchange.[6] Most of the bonds were denominated in won, issued with a five-year maturity and floating interest rates that were indexed to the average yield to maturity of Class 1 National Housing Bond in the secondary market. Interest was paid quarterly (Table 13.6).[7] Trading of NPA bonds was most active in 2000, with the trading volume reaching 100 percent of the outstanding amount. Trading volume declined to 65 percent and 30 percent of outstanding volume in 2001 and 2002 respectively.

Table 13.4.   Nonperforming Loan Acquisition by Type of Loans
(Nov. 1997–Nov. 2002; in trillions of won, unless otherwise specified)

	Face Value	Amount Paid	Price in Percent	Share of Total[a]
Ordinary loan (secured)	10.6	7.1	67.0	17.9
Ordinary loan (nonsecured)	20.1	2.3	11.4	5.8
Special loan (secured)	27.0	12.8	47.4	32.2
Special loan (nonsecured)	14.5	4.2	29.0	10.6
Daewoo loan	35.4	12.7	35.9	32.0
Workout loan	2.6	0.6	23.1	1.5
Total	**110.2**	**39.7**	**36.0**	**100.0**

Source: KAMCO.

[a] Amount paid as percent of total amount paid.

Table 13.5.   Nonperforming Loans Acquisition by Type of Seller
(Nov. 1997–Nov. 2002; in trillions of won, unless specified otherwise)

	Face Value	Amount Paid	Price in Percent	Share of Total[a]
Banks	61.8	24.7	40.0	62.1
Investment trust companies	22.3	8.4	37.6	21.1
Insurance companies	7.4	1.8	24.3	4.5
Institutions resolved by KDIC	6.8	0.8	12.4	2.1
Foreign institutions	5.0	2.1	41.9	5.3
Merchant banks	3.5	1.6	46.3	4.1
Mutual savings	0.5	0.2	37.7	0.5
Securities firms	0.1	0.1	52.6	0.2
Others	2.6	0.0	0.4	0.0
Total	**110.1**	**39.8**	**36.1**	**100.0**

Source: KAMCO.

[a] Amount paid as percent of total amount paid.

Pricing of nonperforming loans

KAMCO's policy of pricing NPL purchases evolved as it gained experience through time (Table 13.7). Prior to September 1998, KAMCO employed the method of "blanket purchase on the condition of an ex post facto settlement," under which the final settlement prices were subject to lengthy and contentious negotiations. The discount rates used by this method corresponded roughly to the loan loss provisioning rates required by prudential regulations. Since then, it offered to buy assets at a specific price calculated using a formula

Table 13.6. Bonds Issued by the Nonperforming Asset Management Fund
(In billions of won)

Date	Amount	Maturity	Coupon	Type of Interest Payment
11/28/1997	2,000.0	11/28/2004	5 percent	Balloon Payment
11/28/1997	968.0	11/28/2000	<15 percent	Floating–Quarterly
11/29/1997	2,298.1	11/29/2000	11.95 percent	Fixed–Quarterly
12/15/1997	1,732.0	12/15/2000	12.14 percent	Fixed–Quarterly
2/19/1998	406.7	2/19/2001	12.14 percent	Fixed–Quarterly
7/23/1998	498.9	7/23/2003	10–15 percent	Floating–Quarterly
7/31/1998	606.6	7/31/2003		Floating–Quarterly
9/29/1998	5,869.0	9/29/2003		Floating–Quarterly
9/30/1998	1,969.1	9/30/2003	<15 percent	Floating–Quarterly
11/6/1998	233.9	11/06/2003		Floating–Quarterly
12/21/1998	938.4	12/21/2003		Floating–Quarterly
12/23/1998[a]	628.7	12/23/1999		3-month LIBOR+1%
12/30/1998	1,076.7	12/30/2003	<15 percent	Floating–Quarterly
2/13/1999	40.9	2/13/2004		Floating–Quarterly
2/23/1999	102.6	2/23/2004		Floating–Quarterly
3/31/1999	2.5	3/31/2004		Floating–Quarterly
6/30/1999	918.4	6/30/2004		Floating–Quarterly
9/16/1999	115.2	11/28/2000	11.95 percent	Fixed–Quarterly
12/30/1999	94.3	12/30/2004	<15 percent	Floating–Quarterly
Total	**20,500.0**			

Source: KAMCO (2000).

[a] Denominated in U.S. dollar, in the amount of US$512.85 million.

that reflects the specific characteristics and terms and conditions of the loan, and it was up to the seller to decide whether to accept the price. The final settlement price could be adjusted through negotiation, but was not expected to differ by a large margin from the initial offer price.

On average KAMCO paid 36 percent of the face value of the NPLs it purchased; in other words, the average discount was 64 percent. However the actual discount varied greatly from transaction to transaction (Figure 13.2). The type of loans bought appeared to be the primary factor determining the price. The highest prices were paid for secured ordinary loans (67 percent) and the lowest prices were paid for nonsecured ordinary loans (11 percent) (see Table 13.4). The variation of prices paid for loans bought from different lenders did not appear to be significant, except that loans bought from institutions to be closed and resolved by the KDIC were priced much lower than loans bought from institutions that were going concerns.

KAMCO appeared to have paid more on average for its NPL purchases in the period prior to mid-1999. After that, the prices were lower and more realistic, and indeed turned out to be low enough to allow the private market to price itself in and compete with KAMCO, facilitating the development of

Table. 13.7. Pricing of Nonperforming Loan Purchases

| | Pricing Formula | | |
	Secured	Nonsecured	Price Determination
Ordinary loans			
Nov. 97–July 98	70–75 percent of valid collateral value[a]	Doubtful: 10–20 percent of face value Assumed loss: 1–3 percent of face value	Subject to ex post adjustment
Since Sept. 98	45 percent of collateral value[b]	3 percent of face value	Fixed at the beginning
Special loans			
Nov. 97–July 98	70–75 percent of face value	20–60 percent of face value	Subject to ex post adjustment
Sept. 98–June 99	45 percent of collateral value[b]		
Since July 99	Present value of projected cash flows[c]		Fixed at the beginning

Source: KAMCO (2000).

[a] Valid collateral value is the least of "appraisal value—senior liens," "face value," or "maximum collateral amount."
[b] Collateral value = appraisal value – senior liens.
[c] Discount rate = basic discount rate + credit risk spread + maturity risk spread.

the private market for distressed corporate debt. Nevertheless, the numbers were distorted by the Daewoo affair.

KAMCO was directed by the government to purchase Daewoo bonds held by foreign creditors and by the ITCs at inflated prices, as part of the government's strategy to stabilize the financial system in the wake of the collapse of the Daewoo group. Although their purchase price was on average only 32.6 percent of face value (for assets other than secured commercial paper), the expected recovery rate on these unresolved Daewoo claims was much lower, as discussed below.[8] The pricing strategy of Daewoo debt to a large extent reflected the deficiency of the corporate insolvency framework—in order to speed up debt restructuring of the Daewoo group, the government opted for out-of-court settlement and some premium above the "fair value" identified by a due diligence review was paid to the creditors. In hindsight, a more transparent intervention strategy (for example, a court-supervised insolvency proceeding) would have allowed Daewoo debt to be priced more realistically. Nevertheless, it was courageous for the government to let Daewoo group fail.

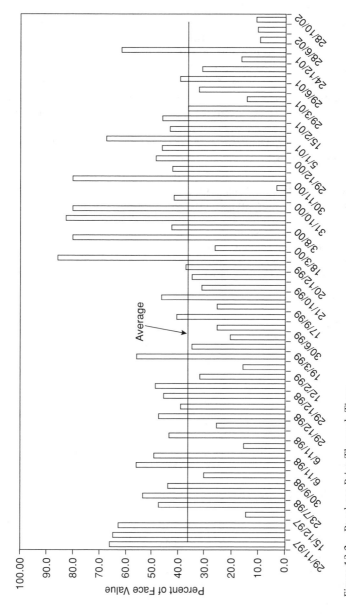

Figure 13.2. Purchase Price Through Time
Source: KAMCO.

Disposal of nonperforming loans

KAMCO adopted a number of techniques to dispose of the NPLs it acquired. In addition to traditional methods such as competitive auctions, collection of rescheduled repayments and recourse to the original seller, KAMCO also developed innovative techniques that broadly include bulk (pooled) sales, individual sales, and joint-venture partnerships (Table 13.8). The choice of a particular method depended on the nature and size of NPLs. Bulk sales typically include the issuance of ABS and international bidding, and aim for early resolution of NPLs and quick cash flows. The emphasis of bulk sales is usually paced on the price-fixing of each asset pool, and the value of each individual asset is accorded less importance. In contrast, individual sales focus on discovering the market value of each individual asset. Individual sales include public auction of collateral, foreclosure auction, and sales of individual loans. Joint venture partnerships are used as a vehicle to cooperate with foreign and domestic investment companies who have specialized technology and know-how in asset management and corporate restructuring.

Table 13.8.   Resolution of Nonperforming Loans by KAMCO
(Nov.1997–Dec.2002; in trillions of won; unless otherwise specified)

Resolution Method	Face Value	Purchase Price	Amount Retrieved	Recovery Rate[a]
International bidding	6.1	1.3	1.6	26.4
ABS issuance	8.0	4.2	4.2	52.0
Foreclosure and public auction	8.3	2.6	3.2	38.9
Collection	12.7	4.3	5.9	46.9
Individual loan sale	2.6	0.6	0.9	35.0
Sale to AMC	2.6	0.7	0.9	35.6
Sale to corporate restructuring company	1.8	0.4	0.7	36.5
Daewoo	3.3	2.2	2.7	81.3
Subtotal	45.4	16.3	20.1	44.3
Recourse and cancellation	19.3	10.2	10.2	52.8
Total	**64.6**	**26.5**	**30.3**	**46.8**

Source: KAMCO.

[a] The ratio of amount retrieved to face value, in percent.

At the height of the financial crisis and in the early stages of KAMCO's existence, KAMCO's operations focused on the purchase of NPLs, and disposal of NPLs was minimal. The pace of disposal gradually became brisk from late 1998, when the macroeconomic environment was improving, the sovereign rating was being upgraded, and KAMCO's active marketing activities such as road shows were beginning to bear fruit.

In KAMCO's first international auction in 1999, the sale of NPLs was accompanied by a simple profit-sharing agreement. The subsequent bids became increasingly more diversified, both in terms of assets pooled and the target investor base. In 1999, KAMCO broke new ground by international securitization of its NPL portfolio through issuance of ABS. With this transaction, KAMCO entered into its first joint venture with the Lone Star Fund to manage the disposal of assets. Its subsequent portfolio sales also attracted well-known names in the distressed-debt business, including Deutsche Bank, Morgan Stanley Dean Witter, Goldman Sachs, Cerberus Capital, and GE Capital. ABS issuance reached its peak in 2000. Also in 2000, the agency extended its resolution methods to direct sale of NPL pools and workout loans to joint ventures (JVs). These partnerships are charged with raising recovery values through efficient management of impaired assets and normalization of workout companies. By farming out the longer term management and normalization of impaired assets to specialized JVs, the agency has extended its role as a corporate restructuring vehicle. In 2001, KAMCO focused on resolution of Daewoo related loans by establishing JVs, and in 2002, it focused on individual loan sales (Figure 13.3).

In the process of adopting resolution methods to maximize recovery values, KAMCO has helped nurture a solid investor base in a new market for impaired assets by diversifying its products for various risk appetites. Several banks followed the path opened by KAMCO and have been selling their NPLs directly to foreign investors, including to KAMCO's partners. This new competition for NPLs is likely to have increased asset value and helped to speed up corporate and financial restructuring. The successful securitization of NPLs through ABS issuance has led to the development of an ABS market backed not only by impaired assets but also by healthy ones, further developing capital markets.[9] The issuance of ABS, which amounted to W 6.8 trillion in 1999, increased to 49 trillion in 2000, 51 trillion in 2001, and 40 trillion in 2002. ABS issued by nonfinancial firms amounted to W 29 trillion in 2002, making up one-third of total corporate bond offerings.[10]

V. Financial performances of the NPA Fund

The NPA Fund has earned a profit on the NPLs it has disposed of so far. By December 2002, it retrieved W 30.3 trillion from resolving NPLs with a face value of 64.6 trillion, for which it had paid 26.5 trillion when the NPLs were purchased from the financial institutions (see Table 13.8). However, this W 3.8 trillion profits was less than half of the operating expenses of the Fund (Table 13.9). The operating expenses of the NPA Fund have been high, amounting to on average 20 percent of the inventory of NPLs purchased, and close to 30 percent of the NPLs disposed of each year.[11]

Furthermore, the NPA Fund is likely to make a loss on the remaining NPLs yet to be resolved. As of April 2003, the NPA Fund still held W 44.2 trillion worth of NPL at face value that would need to be disposed of (see Table 13.4). All indications are that, in contrast to the 47 percent recovery rate it achieved

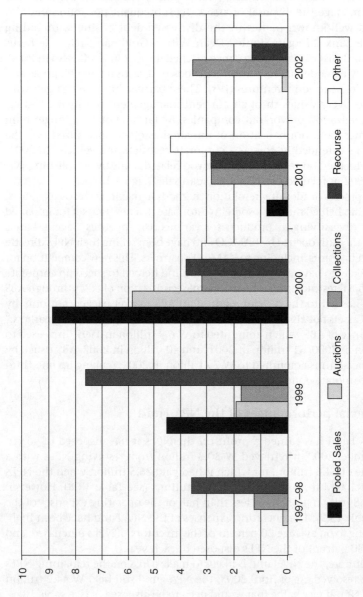

Figure 13.3. Nonperforming Loan Resolution Through Time

Source: KAMCO.

on the disposal of the first two-thirds of the NPLs, the recovery rate on the one-third remaining NPLs will be much lower, at around 15 percent.[12] A majority of these NPLs (70 percent) were Daewoo-related loans, for which KAMCO paid an average price of 36 percent. Thus a major source of the losses of the NPA Fund would be expected losses on Daewoo-related NPLs, which represented 32 percent of its total acquisitions.

Table 13.9. Operating Expenses of Nonperforming Asset Management Fund (In billions of won; unless otherwise specified)

	1999	2000	2001	2002
Net interest expense	762.4	957.4	710.6	350.5
Administrative expenses	61.0	65.1	62.1	52.1
Selling expenses	70.5	96.8	43.7	16.3
Other net operating expenses	881.8	2,306.1	767.1	666.2
Total	1,775.7	3,425.4	1,583.4	1,085.2
As percent of total assets	10.1	20.0	10.2	10.2
As percent of NPL inventory	15.9	25.2	16.5	27.0
As percent of amount of NPL disposed	18.4	38.3	29.8	27.2
As percent of profits from disposal	136.4	407.1	189.0	146.0
Memorandum items:				
Total assets[a]	17,598.0	17,162.4	15,533.2	10,668.0
Inventory of NPLs and real estate owned[a]	11,191.2	13,581.9	9,622.4	4,016.3
Proceeds from NPL disposal	9,654.7	8,934.0	5,321.5	3,987.4
Profits from NPL disposal[b]	1,301.6	841.5	837.9	743.2

Sources: KAMCO and author's estimates.

[a] At the end of period.
[b] Difference between amount retrieved and amount paid for purchase.

As a result of these expected losses and high operating costs, the NPA Fund has accumulated a large negative equity (Table 13.10). This negative equity is part of the net cost incurred for financial sector restructuring. It will have to be financed by a net increase in public debt and repaid by future tax revenues.

VI. Conclusions

This chapter has aimed to provide a balanced assessment of KAMCO's role in resolving the NPLs of the financial system in Korea. It has argued that a proper understanding of the incentive structure of KAMCO's governance and operations should start from an analysis of the political and economic environment. As Kang (2003) has argued, pressure for a speedy recovery of public funds injected for bank restructuring was a driving force behind the reprivatization of state-owned commercial banks. The same pressure was also driving KAMCO to resolve NPLs quickly and to experiment with innovative techniques of asset management and disposal. Such efforts led to

Table 13.10.   Balance Sheet of the Nonperforming Asset Management Fund
(As of end of period; in billions of won)

	1999	2000	2001	2002
Current assets	6,157	3,131	4,842	4,588
Inventories	11,191	13,582	9,622	4,015
NPL purchased	11,024	13,498	9,586	3,979
Ordinary loans	2,563	873	621	591
Restructured corporate loans	6,437	2,567	1,699	1,029
Workout corporate loans	...	11,495	10,332	7,080
Nonsettled NPL purchased	4,047	3,118	1,949	113
Total	13,048	18,052	14,600	8,812
(Allowance for bad debts)	(2,024)	(4,553)	(5,014)	(4,833)
Real estate owned	169	82	36	36
Long-term assets	247	450	1,068	2,065
Investment securities	247	450	1,068	2,065
Total assets	17,595	17,162	15,533	10,668
Current liabilities	3,384	1,707	3,889	13,315
Long-term liabilities	15,431	19,357	16,289	4,249
Total equity	–1,219	–3,901	–4,646	–6,896
Of which: net loss during the year	–518	–2,557	–669	–2,235
Total liabilities and equity	17,595	17,162	15,533	10,668

Source: KAMCO.

the development of a market for distressed assets in Korea and contributed
to the deepening of broader financial markets. On the other hand, KAMCO's
operations have been expensive. In addition, inflated transfer prices on
Daewoo-related claims, though possibly justified by the government strategy
of speedy out-of-court debt workout, overshadowed KAMCO's strive to follow
commercial principles in pricing loan purchases.

KAMCO's work is not yet finished—it still remains to dispose of all distressed
assets purchased by the NPA Fund. KAMCO's future has also been subject
to much public debate. It has been active in providing technical expertise
to AMCs around the world and is purchasing newly emerging NPLs, such
as nonperforming credit card debt, on its own account. Given KAMCO's
experience, there is a case to preserve its accumulated expertise and not simply
close shop. One promising strategy would be to sell the government-owned
shares of KAMCO to the private sector. This would ensure a commercial
orientation, thereby creating incentives to focus on core competencies,
economize on operating costs, and maximize profits and efficiency.

Notes

1. Comments by Cho Won-Dong, Paul Gruenwald, Peter Hayward, Meral Karasulu,
   and Steven Seelig are gratefully acknowledged. I would also like to express my
   gratitude to the management of KAMCO for their generous provision of data and
   kind cooperation

2. For an analysis of the Korean crisis experience, see Coe and Kim (2002).
3. A few special treatments were given to KAMCO in order to facilitate the resolution of NPLs, including exemption from financial transaction taxes.
4. The idea to establish a NPA Fund was initially floated in April 1997 with a size of W 1.5 trillion. The size of the Fund was increased a number of times as the financial condition of the financial sector continued to deteriorate in the second half of 1997, reaching W 10 trillion at the time of the establishment of the Fund in November 1997. Several further rounds of increase raised its size to W 33.6 trillion by July 1998, but it was reduced to 21.6 trillion in August 1999 as the government decided to transfer some of the resources to KDIC.
5. KAMCO indicated that it had an agreement with the World Bank and the IMF that it would dispose at least 50 percent of its acquired NPLs in three years.
6. Since these bonds were explicitly guaranteed by the government, they would be assigned zero weight in the calculation of the capital adequacy ratio of the selling institution, potentially improving the ratio, although the net impact on the ratio would also depend on the net capital loss or gain arising from the transaction. The original intention on the part of the government to provide a guarantee on the bonds was to allow them to be bought by the Bank of Korea (BOK), as required by the BOK Act.
7. The government made cash loans, annually from the budget, to the KAMCO in order for it to pay interest on the bonds. The government decided to waive the repayment of these loans from KAMCO as part of the burden-sharing plan described in Box 13.1.
8. It is noticeable from Figure 13.2 that in 2000, a number of purchases paid a price of more than 80 percent of face value, which appeared to be outliers from the norm. Those purchases were primarily secured commercial paper of the Daewoo group held by domestic banks. While the price paid for the Daewoo commercial paper was extraordinarily high, KAMCO seemed to have resolved these assets with a profit.
9. The enactment of the Asset Securitization Act in September 1998 was instrumental in facilitating the development of a market for distressed assets. Asset securitization allows the separation of assets from the originating institution and the use of these assets as backing for securities with different characteristics that appeal to investors of different risk appetite. The Asset Securitization Act ensures that the credibility of the ABS is separate from that of the originator, and the asset transfer from the originator to the Special Purpose Company takes the form of a "true sale" from a legal and accounting perspective. From the investor's point of view, the non-recourse credit risk is mitigated by a number of methods, including due diligence and credit enhancement by a third party.
10. FSS Weekly Newsletter, February 15, 2003.
11. In the United States the liquidation expenses (including legal fees) of the Resolution Trust Corporation and the FDIC amounted to less than 15 percent of collections on the NPLs.
12. KAMCO expects to recover W 7.3 trillion by 2018 through disposing of the remaining NPLs. It is not clear to what extent this estimate reflected recent improvements in the share prices of former Daewoo subsidiaries.

Bibliography

Baliño, Tomas Jose, and Angel Ubide, 1999, "The Korean Financial Crisis of 1997—A Strategy of Financial Sector Reform," IMF Working Paper No. 99/28 (Washington: International Monetary Fund).

Chopra, Ajai, Kenneth Kang, Meral Karasulu, Hong Liang, Henry Ma, and Anthony Richards, 2002, "From Crisis to Recovery in Korea: Strategy, Achievements, and Lessons," in *Korean Crisis and Recovery*, ed. by David T. Coe, and Se-jik Kim (Washington: International Monetary Fund and Korea Institute for International Economic Policy).

Coe, David T., and Se-jik Kim, eds., 2002, *Korean Crisis and Recovery* (Washington: International Monetary Fund and Korea Institute for International Economic Policy).

He, Dong, 2003, "Budget Formulation and Implementation in Korea: A Macroeconomic Perspective," in *Republic of Korea: Selected Issues*, IMF Country Report No. 03/80 (Washington: International Monetary Fund), pp. 22–35.

Ingves, Stefan, Steven Seelig, and Dong He, 2004, "Issues in the Establishment of Asset Management Companies," IMF Policy Discussion Paper No. 04/3 (Washington: International Monetary Fund).

KAMCO, 2000, "Nov. 1997–Aug. 2000 KAMCO Experience: Non-Performing Asset Management and Resolution."

Kang, Chungwon, 2003, "From the Front Lines at Seoul Bank: Restructuring and Reprivatization," IMF Working Paper No. 03/235 (Washington: International Monetary Fund).

Lim, Wonhyuk, 2002, "Korea: Corporate Vulnerabilities and Restructuring" (Seoul: Korea Development Institute).

Lindgren, Carl-Johan, Tomas Baliño, Charles Enoch, Anne-Marie Gulde, Marc Quintyn, and Leslie Teo, 1999, "Financial Sector Crisis and Restructuring: Lessons from Asia," IMF Occasional Paper No. 188 (Washington: International Monetary Fund).

14
The Public Sector Recapitalization Program in Turkey

Mats Josefsson

I. Background and summary of the Turkish banking crisis

The Turkish financial crisis emerged in two stages.[1] The first stage began with a collapse in investor confidence in November 2000 and the subsequent fall of a medium-sized bank. In the context of a Fund-supported disinflation program initiated at end-1999, the authorities responded with an interest rate defense of the exchange rate and a number of banking sector reforms. The second, more serious stage emerged in February 2001 with the floating of the Turkish lira following a major speculative attack on the currency.

The second, deeper crisis erupted in February 2001. Investor confidence had remained low, reflecting the continued deterioration in the economy. While the crisis was ignited by the public airing of tensions between the president and the prime minister, the credibility of the program had weakened. Fearing a reversal of macroeconomic policies, investors withdrew from the Turkish market. The Central Bank of Turkey (CBT) declared a bank holiday on February 20, 2001 to limit the loss of international reserves. When banks reopened, overnight rates, which had fallen to about 50 percent in mid-January, rose to over 2,000 percent, with peaks of 5,000 percent. This made it impossible to defend the peg and the exchange rate was floated on February 22, 2001.

In response to the first stage of the financial crisis, the authorities introduced a strengthened economic policy package in December 2000. The package included significant macroeconomic tightening, with the primary surplus for 2001 targeted to improve from 3 percent to 5 percent of gross national product, and a declining path envisaged for net domestic assets. This macroeconomic program was combined with a blanket guarantee of bank liabilities. The authorities also committed to sell all banks under Savings

Deposit Insurance Fund (SDIF) control by mid-2001, and to convert the stock of state banks' duty losses into securities bearing market interest rates.

The banking strategy focused on taking over and resolving insolvent banks awhile strengthening the private banking system. Between 1997 and 2004, the Banking Regulation and Supervision Agency (BRSA) took over 21 private banks, with a peak in 2001–02. These banks were relatively small but jointly represented about 20 percent of banking system assets. By 2004, all but one of the banks had been resolved through mergers, sales of individual and merged banks, and liquidations. The strategy to strengthening the private banking system focused initially on bank diagnosis and private sector recapitalization. Banks were required to assess their true financial condition based on new, stricter rules; raise capital by end-2001 as needed, or be intervened.

By June 2002, concerns that private banks would not be able to raise sufficient capital led the authorities to introduce a public support scheme. By the third quarter of 2001, adverse global economic and political developments (including the September 11 attacks) and persistently high real interest rates had made it difficult to raise capital. In addition, concerns existed about asset values in the banking system, reflecting slow implementation of loan classification, provisioning, and connected lending rules. In response, a public sector program was designed to give banks access to publicly funded capital (Tier 1 and Tier 2).

An important element of the public support program was to ensure that adequate design features were included to prevent misuse of public sector funds. Strict eligibility criteria were applied, including bank owners' participation in bank recapitalization. Participating banks would undergo an in-depth audit, thereby bringing full transparency about banks' financial conditions. This recapitalization program proved highly successful.

II. Design of the public sector recapitalization program

In January 2002, the BRSA announced a solvency support scheme. That scheme made public funds available to banks in their recapitalization efforts. The guiding principles for the solvency support scheme were (i) minimization of public sector costs; (ii) establishment of clear and objective rules; (iii) equal and fair treatment of all banks; (iv) transparency covering each step of the process; and (v) establishment of clear incentives ensuring the scheme is viewed as a last resort for bank shareholders.

Agency in charge

The BRSA and the SDIF, an agency within the BRSA, would jointly manage the support scheme. The BRSA would be responsible for managing the scheme, including the assessments about capital needs in banks, while the SDIF would provide the capital and thus become one of the owners in banks receiving Tier 1 capital support. The Treasury would provide the SDIF with government securities needed to finance the scheme. The authorities recognized that a conflict of interest exists when SDIF as owner of operating banks is supervised by the BRSA. However, as the authorities planned to make SDIF independent from BRSA, they felt this arrangement was acceptable, at least for a short period of time.

Eligibility

Strict eligibility requirements were established to participate in the recapitalization plan. Tier 1 and Tier 2 capital support was limited to private deposit taking banks incorporated in Turkey[2] with a market share of at least 1 percent of total banking system assets as of end-September 2001. Banks with a market share of less than 1 percent would only be eligible for Tier 2 support and would have to find merger partners such that the merged bank's assets exceeded 1 percent of total banking system assets in order to qualify for Tier 1 support. For mergers to qualify, irrevocable merger commitments had to be made by the parties involved.

   An initial estimate indicated the 27 privately owned banks were eligible to apply for the support. Further revisions reduced the number to 25 as two banks were intervened during the process. State banks had already been properly capitalized and thus not part of the exercise although one quasi publicly owned bank (Vakifbank) was included.

Assessments of the banks

All banks had to go through thorough targeted assessments to determine their capital needs and the level of losses to be borne by existing shareholders. A critical element of the scheme, therefore, was that all losses in the portfolios of banks had to be identified. Therefore, a number of assessments were carried out.

Assessments by external auditors

Banks were required to use acceptable accounting firms, typically the firms in charge of external auditing in the respective bank, to assess the bank's financial conditions. Issues addressed included, but were not limited to, the quality of loan portfolios, counter-party and related-party risks, and valuation of collateral. The assessments, which each bank had to pay for, also took into account planned changes in accounting and the regulatory framework, including the adoption of International Accounting Standards, made sure banks had adequately provisioned for potential losses for that accounting change, and that those losses were fully reflected in the respective bank's capital position. To ensure that the assessments would be done uniformly and according to best practice, BRSA issued regulations, instructions and guidelines, defining in detail the methodology for how the external auditors should carry out their assignments. The assessments should be completed within two months and no later than end-March, 2002 and the BRSA would closely monitors all banks during the assessment period and take necessary actions, if needed.

A concern existed about the objectivity of bank's external auditors. The BRSA recognized that the external auditors might be biased and unwilling to criticize their previous work, particularly if they had been the external auditors for several years. However, appointment of independent auditors would have substantially delayed the exercise and dramatically increase the cost. Thus, it was deemed acceptable to use the external auditors, particularly since BRSA had in detail defined the methodology to be used and also would ask for a third party review to confirm the assessments made by the external auditors (see below).

Areas covered in the assessments

The assessments focused on four areas: (i) capital adequacy; (ii) credit portfolio and counterpart risk; (iii) risk groups to which the bank belonged; and (iv) structured transactions and other income recognition issues. Detailed reporting schedules (roughly 100 tables) had been developed by the international investment firm assisting the authorities in developing the methodology to be used. Each bank was responsible for filling in the tables providing the data requested and the external auditors to verify that the data provided was consistent and accurate. The financial statements would be prepared using International Accounting Standards, including a framework for inflation accounting, and banks being the parent company for a financial group must prepare financial statements both on a solo and consolidated basis. The loan portfolio was of particular concern. The targeted assessments had to review whatever was highest of 75 percent of total loans or the 200 largest customer exposures. All group-related loans had to be included in the review. The valuation of collateral should be done either by using independent expert reports or real estate valuation company reports. The report to be prepared for each individual bank, as a result of the assessment, should include the bank's capital adequacy ratio (CAR), including capital charges for market risks, both on a solo and consolidated basis. In case either of these ratios was below 8 percent, the amount of capital needed to bring the ratio up to 8 percent had to be calculated and reported.

Third party review

To enhance the credibility of the exercise, BRSA designated independent auditing firms to carry out third party reviews of the work done by the external auditors. The objective of the reviews was to verify that the external auditors had carried out their assignments according to regulations, instructions and guidelines issued by the BRSA. Each bank would have to pay for those assessments, which should be completed no later than end-April 2002.

Final assessments made by the BRSA

The BRSA would make the final assessment about the capital need in individual banks, including the settling of eventual disputes between external auditors and a bank's management about the outcome of the assessments. The BRSA would use internal on-site examination reports prepared by the sworn bank auditors. To ensure that the process would be transparent and that banks with roughly the same capital deficiencies had been treated uniformly, BRSA made a commitment to later announce criteria and procedures used in determining the capital needs in banks.[3] BRSA informed in writing about the outcome of the exercise on June 12 and on June 16, 2002 the public was informed.

Procedures for raising capital

If the assessment showed that a bank had a CAR of at least 8 percent on a solo and consolidated basis, no further actions regarding capital would be needed. However, the BRSA might ask the bank to provide a business plan with detailed capital analysis on how the bank over time would make sure it would always be in compliance with the capital adequacy requirement.

If the CAR on a solo or consolidated basis was below 8 percent, the following procedures would apply:

- The outcome of the assessments would by respective bank be made available to shareholders, including the audited balance sheet, the profit and loss statement, the CAR and the amount of capital needed to restore the CAR to 8 percent on a solo and consolidated basis.
- The bank would be instructed in writing by the BRSA to call a shareholders General Assembly within 15 days after receiving the letter. At the General Assembly the shareholders would be asked to make a decision to write down the paid-in capital by the amount requested by the BRSA in order to absorb all the losses identified in the independent assessments. The shareholders would also be asked to make a decision to raise the capital needed to bring the CAR, on a solo and consolidated level, up to 8 percent within 15 days. Such equity capital should be paid in cash.
- The same shareholders General Assembly should approve minutes from the meeting, which should be passed on to the BRSA no later than the following day. The minutes should cover a number of issues such as (i) level of recapitalization; (ii) veto powers to board members appointed by the SDIF; (iii) retention of dividends; (iv) a pledge commitment contract; and (v) authorization to the board to apply for public support and to submit a recapitalization plan to the BRSA.
- If the required decisions were not made at the shareholders General Assembly, rules according to Article 14 in the banking law would apply,

which means that the bank would be intervened and taken over by the BRSA.

Criteria for Tier 1 capital support

Tier I capital support was available under special conditions. Criteria for getting such capital support were that (i) the bank or the planned merged bank had a positive CAR; (ii) the bank or the planned merged bank's balance sheet proforma had a market share of at least 1 percent; and (iii) the existing or new private investors could provide at least half of the Tier 1 capital needed to bring the CAR, on a solo or consolidated basis, up to at least 5 percent. If all these criteria were not met, the bank would be deemed unviable and rules according to Article 14 in banking law would apply, which means the bank would be intervened and taken over by the BRSA.

If a bank succeeded in raising the full amount of capital needed to bring the CAR, on a solo or consolidated level, above 8 percent, no further actions regarded capital would be needed. The BRSA might, however, require that the bank submit a business plan with detailed analysis showing how the bank would ensure that the CAR requirement would always be met. BRSA had also issued a guideline on how the business plan should be prepared, including what kind of detailed capital analysis would be needed.

The SDIF would match any injection of capital up to a Tier 1 CAR of 5 percent on a solo and consolidated basis. The SDIF would then provide convertible subordinated debt (Tier 2 capital) up to a CAR of 9 percent. The SDIF's capital injection could not exceed the private sector contribution, but could be less, if the bank so wished.

Status of shares and rights

Shares pledged as collateral

To qualify for public support, the majority shareholders in a bank would have to pledge, as collateral to the SDIF, shares held in the bank equal to SDIF's capital contribution. The shares would be used as collateral protecting SDIF for any losses that might occur when SDIF later sells its shares in the bank. If there were such losses, the majority shareholders would have the option to either compensate SDIF in cash or to allow SDIF to deduct the losses from the pledged shares, which then would be valued at no less than net book value. Remaining shares would be returned to the owners.

SDIF shares and special rights

The details of the required pledge would be spelled out in a contract between the majority shareholders and the SDIF. In the contract, the majority shareholders would have to (i) agree to cover the losses SDIF might face in selling its shares; (ii) give SDIF the voting rights associated with the shares; and (iii) not sell any of their shares held in the bank before SDIF had sold all its shares, unless approved by the BRSA. SDIF would determine the time for the sale of its shares but the majority shareholders would have the right of first refusal for 18 months. Moreover, the SDIF would have the right to appoint at least one board member, irrespective of its capital contribution. Such board member(s), which should have documented experience in banking, would exercise ownership rights and have veto powers on matters material to the ongoing soundness of the bank. In particular, it was expected such powers would be exercised on issues related to acquisition and disposal of assets and other matters, which could jeopardize the soundness of the bank. Unless approved by the BRSA, a bank would not pay any dividends and retained earnings would remain in the bank as long as the SDIF owned shares in it.

Price and payment for the shares

The SDIF would pay net book value for the shares. To pay for the shares purchased, the Treasury would provide the SDIF with tradable government securities issued on market terms.

Exit procedures

Existing majority shareholders would have the right of first refusal for the first 18 months to buy back the shares bought by the government. However, they would always have to pay whatever is highest of (i) SDIF's funding cost (principal and interest); (ii) net book value; or, (iii) market price, including third party offer. The existing shareholders would have to exercise their right of first refusal within 15 days after receiving the offer. If not, SDIF would have the right to sell its shares to third parties.

The majority shareholders would also have the right to buy back the government's shares in installments and in such cases other investors would not have the right to bid for the shares. The conditions for the buy back would be spelled out in a contract between the majority shareholders and the SDIF. The duration of the contract would be 18 months with four installments per year and with a price equal to SDIF's investment cost, including carrying cost plus a 5 percent spread. SDIF would remain in control of the shares until they were fully paid and if there was a default, only the principal would be repaid. Third party sales would be at the discretion of SDIF such as auction and by invitation.

Lending requirement

Banks receiving Tier 1 capital support had to make a commitment to extend credits equal to at least 60 percent of the government's Tier 1 capital contribution by end-June 2003. The credits, excluding credits to group companies, other related parties and financial institutions, should be granted based on sound banking principles and practices.

Tier 2 Capital support

Criteria

Any bank with a solo and consolidated Tier 1 CAR exceeding 5 percent would be eligible for Tier 2 capital support in the form of convertible subordinated debt up to CAR (solo or consolidated) of 9 percent.

Form of capital

The bank would issue convertible debt instruments to the SDIF with a maturity of seven years and carrying an interest rate 5 percentage points higher than the FRN rate. The instruments could be repaid ahead of schedule after approval by the BRSA.

Payment

The SDIF would pay for the debt instruments in floating rate notes (FRNs) with a maturity of seven years and issued on market terms. The bank would not be allowed to sell the FRNs to a third party, unless approved by the BRSA. The reason being to minimize SDIF's risk but also because the transaction then easily can be reversed once the instruments no longer are needed—the SDIF returns the debt instruments and the bank the FRNs.

Convertibility

Safeguards were included to ensure that bank capital remains above 5 percent of risk weighted assets. If a bank's CAR (solo or consolidated) drops below 5 percent and existing shareholders cannot bring it up to 5 percent again, subordinated debt instruments would be converted into Tier 1 capital. The conversion would be at a price of whatever is lowest of (i) net book value; (ii) price paid for any shares issued since SDIF became an owner; or, (iii) market price provided the bank is listed on the stock exchange.

III. Results of the program

In the event, there was low demand for public funds. The amount of capital to be raised in the system according to the three-stage audit was lower than expected, and concentrated in one large insolvent bank (Pamukbank). This bank was taken over after the BRSA rejected merger plans with another bank (Yapı Kredi) owned by the same group. Another private bank with capital shortfalls was able to raise the modest amount needed without government assistance. Only one bank (the state-owned Vakıf) asked for US$137 million in Tier 2 capital assistance from the SDIF.

  The private banking system strengthened as a result of all these efforts. Against a backdrop of favorable economic developments and growth in lending, financial soundness indicators improved. From 2001 to 2004, the capital adequacy ratio of private banks rose from 9 percent to 22 percent;

their ratio of nonperforming loans to total loans dropped from 27.6 percent to less than 5 percent; their level of provisions increased from 31 percent to 84 percent; and their return on assets increased from –7.5 percent to 2 percent.

Notes

1. A full chronology of the crisis is given in Appendix 14.I.
2. This meant that also foreign owned banks would be eligible for public support, although it was deemed highly unlikely that any foreign bank would apply for the support.
3. The BRSA has published on its website (www.bddk.org.tr) various reports and regulations, which in detail explain the recapitalization exercise.

Appendix 14.I. Chronology of Events, 2000–02

2000

January: IMF financial sector technical assistance report concludes that a substantial number of banks face financial difficulties, and urges improvements in the bank resolution framework.

March 31: Appointment of the BRSA's board.

May: MAE (Money and Exchange Systems Department) technical mission concludes that the cost for resolving the eight intervened banks increased by US$5 million a day, and that given the poor franchise value of seven institutions, the least-cost solution should be to liquidate those and recapitalize and sell the remaining bank. The authorities prefer to restructure all the banks.

June 1: 100 percent household deposit insurance lifted. Coverage reduced to TL 100 billion.

July 5: Amendment to the Principles and Procedures Related to the Preparation and Notification of Consolidated Financial Statements by Banks. Banks are required to report quarterly on a consolidated basis.

August 5: The CBT issues a circular on management of foreign exchange (FX) positions, effective on September 1, 2000. Liquid FX assets should be higher than 10 percent of liquid FX liabilities, and the ratio of FX assets to FX liabilities should lie between 80 percent and 110 percent, subject to weekly reporting. Penalty for noncompliance would be 1.5 times the CBT rediscount rate for short-term credits, on the excess position. The CBT could apply different rate to different banks or group of banks.

August 26: Regulation of SDIF defines the organizational structure, duties, and responsibilities of the Fund with conditions applicable to utilization of the Fund.

September 1: SDIF's Asset Management Unit (AMU) becomes operational.

September 9: Amendment to the Communiqué No. 6 related to Decree No. 88/12944 by Communiqué No. 27 on the Resource Utilization Support Fund. Fund deductions are differentiated by type of loan (consumer loans versus other types of loans). The ratio of fund deduction for consumer loans was increased to 8 percent from 3 percent.

September 28: Decision No. 59 of the BRSA. The license for accepting deposits and engaging in banking operations of Kibris Kredi Bankası revoked in accordance with paragraph 3 of the Article 14 of the Banking Law No. 4389.

October 27: Bank Kapital and Etibank taken over by the SDIF, increasing the total number of intervened banks to ten.

November:

- (1st week) Introduction of the "Proper and Fit criteria" for potential bidders interested in acquiring SDIF banks. Owners of failed intervened banks are not allowed to hold more than 10 percent shares in another bank.
- The functions of SDIF's AMU are taken over by a new Collection Department (COD). The BRSA prepares a legal amendment to give the SDIF extraordinary asset recovery powers and to establish new commercial courts.

November 15: Act No. 4603 establishes the legal framework concerning the restructuring of Ziraat, Halk, and Emlak Bank (state-owned banks), envisaging a restructuring and privatization period of three years and authorizing the council of ministers to prolong this period by up to one and a half years.

November 19: Regulation No. 24235 on Principles and Procedures for Applications to Establish or to Acquire or Transfer Shares of Banks.

November 20: Two of the largest banks (Ak and Garanti) refuse to roll-over their overnight lending to Demirbank, precipitating a liquidity crisis. After local credit is refused, the bank put a large amount of government securities for sale, triggering a sharp fall in price and therefore provoking the panic of international investors who decided not to roll-over overnight credit to Turkey.

November 22/23: The CBT injects US$2.4 billion into the system, US$2 billion of which into Demirbank at a 200 percent interest rate.

November 22/27: Regulation No. 24242, Laws on the Privatization of State Commercial Banks.

December 6: Demirbank is taken over by the SDIF, increasing the number of intervened banks to 11.

2001

January: The government issues a blanket guarantee for deposits, publicly clarifying its nature and scope.

January 25: BRSA's announcement of Demirbank's sale.

January 26: EGS Bank, Yurtbank, Yasarbank, and Bank Kapital merged into Sümerbank.

January 31: The Turkish authorities commit to reduce connected lending limits from 75 percent to 25 percent of bank capital, by 2006.

February 19: The public airing of tensions between the President and the Prime Minister of Turkey ignites another crisis. Investors and depositors lose confidence in the exchange rate regime and run on their banks.

February 22: Floating of the Turkish lira, which depreciates by 42 percent from February to March 2001.

February 28: Ulusal Bank taken over by SDIF.

March: Treasury starts injecting securities and cash to state banks in order to strengthen their capital base.

March 15: İktisat Bank taken over by the SDIF.

April 1:

- A decree allows for the merger of two state banks, Emlak and Ziraat.
- The administration and management of Ziraat and Halk is transferred to a joint board of directors, freeing them from political pressures, with the mission of restructuring and preparing them for privatization.

April 17: Ulusal is merged into Sumerbank.

May:

- The license of Emlak is revoked and its liabilities are transferred to Ziraat.
- The BRSA reissues the current loan provisioning rule, lifting the exemptions from loan classification and provisioning for Ziraat's agricultural reform loans.
- Parliament enacts an amendment of the banking law nominating all specific provisions to be made by banks as a tax deductible expense.
- SDIF banks' overnight liabilities, which amounted to US$5.2 billion in March 2001, are eliminated.
- Offers received on Demirbank and Bank Ekspres. Sümerbank is being prepared for bids (there was at least one qualified domestic buyer).

May 15: The Banking System Restructuring Program is launched.

June 15: Treasury conducts a successful voluntary debt swap, extending average maturity from 5.3 months to 37.2 months, and reducing private local banks' open currency positions.

June 15: Interbank, Esbank and Etibank merged into a second transition bank (Etibank).

June 27: Amendments to the Banks Act, including new powers granted to the SDIF. "The Regulation on Bank Mergers and Acquisitions" provides tax incentives for corporate mergers and acquisitions. A definition of consolidated own funds is issued, introducing limits for connected lending.

June 30: Bank Ekspres sold to Tefken Holding.

July:

- Introduction of new accounting rules consistent with international standards, bringing off-balance sheet repos onto banks' balance sheets.
- CBT introduces an interest rate monitoring system. Banks paying above normal interest would be scrutinized.

July 1: Türk Ticaret's banking and deposit taking license revoked. Objections for the liquidation accepted by the State Council. Its liquidation is on hold pending a court case.

July 9: Emlak Bank banking and deposit taking license revoked. Its assets and liabilities are transferred to Ziraat bank.

July 9: Kentbank, EGS Bank, Bayındırbank, Tarisbank, and Sitebank are taken over by the SDIF, having failed to comply with recapitalization plans, raising the total number of SDIF's banks to 18.

July 19: A derivatives exchange is established in Istanbul.

July 26: Announcement that taxes on capital gains on deposits with long maturity would be reduced while those on FX deposits would be increased. This measure is taken in order to make TL deposits more attractive and to lengthen their maturity.

July 31: SDIF starts the negotiation process of equity transfer of Sümerbank to Oyak Group.

August: COD is staffed and becomes fully operational. NPLs from Sümerbank, Bank Ekspres, and T.Ticaret are transferred to it.

August 6: IMF approves Ninth Review under Stand By Arrangement.

August 8: CBT starts remunerating required reserves.

August 9/10: One third of the balance sheet of Sümerbank is sold to Oyak group. The remainder is transferred to the SDIF for liquidation.

August 17: Confidentiality agreement signed between Iktisat and UniCredito Italiano S.A.

August 22: Confidentiality agreement signed between Etibank and the Koc Group.

August 31:

- Law on tax incentive for merger and acquisitions promotes consolidation of the banking system.
- A private bank, Körfezbank, is sold to Osmanlı Bank.

September 10/20: Demirbank is sold to HSBC.

October: In view of the government's difficulty in financing its domestic debt, the treasury carries out mandatory restructuring of sovereign debt obligations to Ziraat and Halk by capitalizing interest and principal.

October 26: Bank Ekspres merged with Tefken Holding, operating under Tefkenbank license.

October 30: Transfer of Demirbank to HSBC is completed.

November 23: Objections for the transfer of Tarisbank to the SDIF are accepted by the State Council. Legal process in progress.

November 30: Toprakbank is intervened by the SDIF.

December:

- Auctions of deposits of remaining SDIF's banks, backed by matching government securities.
- (Mid-December) Draft legislation of the Istanbul Approach for corporate debt restructuring.

December 7: İktisatbank's banking and deposit-taking licenses are revoked.

December 14: Osmanlı Bank is sold to Garanti Bankası.

December 20: Confidentiality agreement signed between Sitebank and NovaBank S.A

December 28: Etibank's and Kentbank's banking and deposit taking licenses are revoked.

2002

January:

- The parliament passes the Banking Issues Bill, the key element being the private banks' recapitalization scheme. In order to gain parliamentary support, the government makes some concessions, including a clause requiring state banks (not eligible for the scheme) to provide TL

1.5 quadrillion in loans to agriculture and small and medium-sized enterprises.

• Introduction of regulation on money laundering and financial crime.

January 11: Sitebank sold to Novabank S.A.

January 11: Merger of Sümerbank and Oyakbank approved, operating under Oyakbank license.

January 18: Amendment to the SDIF's Regulations to establish the Department of Human Resources and Budget, and the Department of Internal Auditing.

January 18: EGS Bank's banking and deposit taking license revoked and immediately merged into Bayındırbank.

January 16/25: Transfer of Sitebank to NovaBank complete, operating as Sitebank.

January 30/31: Sale process of Toprakbank initiated.

January 31:

• Act No. 4743 on "Restructuring of the Debts to the Financial Sector and Amendments to be Made to Some Laws."

• Provisional Article 4: privately-owned deposit taking banks shall go through a three-stage audit. Those satisfying certain conditions can receive a one-time support in the form of SDIF participation in Tier 1 capital or subordinated debt (Tier 2 capital), as necessary.

• Arrangements in the framework for voluntary corporate debt restructuring, authorizing the participation of SDIF banks.

• Regulation on Measurement and Assessment of Banks' Capital Adequacy, defining principles and procedures to calculate banks CAR on a consolidated and solo basis, incorporating market risk (replaces February 2001 law).

• Amendment to the Regulation on Loan-Loss Provisioning, revising procedures on the restructuring of NPLs and other claims.

• Amendment to the Regulation on Banks' Establishment and Operations, including a change in the definition of "own funds" and requiring a general loan-loss provision to Tier 2 capital without netting out.

• Tax incentives to encourage the establishment of asset management companies. SDIF participation limit of 20 percent.

• Additional regulation on state banks, limiting the employment of new personnel, providing incentives for early retirement, allowing for the restructuring of loans and requiring banks to extend new loans to the agricultural sector.

• Regulation on Principles and Procedures on the Implementation of FX net Position/Own Funds Standard Ratio for Banks on both Consolidated and Unconsolidated Basis.

February 1:

- Change in the "Uniform Accounting Plan and Standards to be Applied by Banks" requires the inclusion of repo transactions on bank balance sheets.
- Regulation on the Principles and Procedures of the Banking Sector Recapitalization Scheme.
- Regulation on the Principles and Procedures of Independent Auditing.

February 8: Regulation on "Banks Internal Audits and Risk Monitoring System" becomes effective.

March 29: CBT changed the implementation of reserve and liquidity requirements with a view to contribute to lowering financial intermediation costs and to provide liquidity management with a more flexible structure.

March 29: A private bank, Sinai Yatirim Bankası, is sold to T. Sinai Kalkinma Bankası.

April 4: The General Assembly Meeting revokes the liquidation decision on İktisatbank, Etibank and Kentbank. The three banks are merged under Bayındırbank.

May 29: Two independent audits to assess the capital needs of 27 private banks complete, in the context of the Public Support Scheme for the Recapitalization of Private Banks.

May 30: Tarisbank's intervention was approved and the bank is put up for sale.

June:

- Political uncertainty and a fall in financial markets. Besides the risk of a military attack on Iraq, there are concerns over the prime minister's health and disputes related to EU accession. Call for early elections in November.
- Istanbul Approach becomes operative. 24 banks and 13 nonbank financial institutions sign a Framework Agreement for debt workouts.

June 13: Letters are sent to each bank regarding the amount of capital they needed to raise.

June 19: Pamukbank is taken over by the SDIF, raising the total number of intervened banks to 20.

June 29: Pamukbank sale process is initiated.

August: Process of recapitalization of private commercial banks complete (the whole process took less than seven months).

August 9: The Extraordinary General Assembly Meeting decides on the dissolution and liquidation of T.Ticaret Bankası.

September 18: Principles for the Establishment and Operation of Asset Management Companies are published in the *Official Gazette*.

September 30: Toprakbank's banking license is revoked. The bank is merged into Bayındırbank.

October 25: Tarisbank transferred to Denizbank.

November 3: Early elections held. The Justice and Development Party or AK Party assumes the government.

November 22: The administrative court decides to reverse the BRSA intervention in Pamukbank.

December 27: Merger of Denizbank and Tarisbank complete.

Index

Compiled by Sue Carlton